PERSPECTIVES ON COGNITIVE PSYCHOLOGY

CONSCIOUSNESS

SOCIAL PERSPECTIVES, PSYCHOLOGICAL APPROACHES AND CURRENT RESEARCH

PERSPECTIVES ON COGNITIVE PSYCHOLOGY

Additional books in this series can be found on Nova's website
under the Series tab.

Additional e-books in this series can be found on Nova's website
under the eBooks tab.

PERSPECTIVES ON COGNITIVE PSYCHOLOGY

CONSCIOUSNESS

SOCIAL PERSPECTIVES, PSYCHOLOGICAL APPROACHES AND CURRENT RESEARCH

LLOYD ALVARADO
EDITOR

nova publishers
New York

Library of Congress Cataloging-in-Publication Data

Names: Alvarado, Lloyd, editor.
Title: Consciousness : social perspectives, psychological approaches and current research / editor, Lloyd Alvarado.
Description: Hauppauge, New York : Nova Science Publishers, Inc., 2016. | Series: Perspectives on cognitive psychology | Includes index.
Identifiers: LCCN 2016011283 (print) | LCCN 2016017231 (ebook) | ISBN 9781634850230 (hardcover) | ISBN 9781634850452 ()
Subjects: LCSH: Consciousness.
Classification: LCC BF311 .C6563 2016 (print) | LCC BF311 (ebook) | DDC 153--dc23
LC record available at https://lccn.loc.gov/2016011283

Published by Nova Science Publishers, Inc. † New York

CONTENTS

PREFACE

Consciousness is a phenomenon that puzzled many thinkers of the past in disparate fields, including theology, literature, art and philosophy, and continues to be a hot topic of debate at present. However, in the last few decades, the change of paradigm brought by cognitive psychology and the emergence of new techniques, which allowed the *in vivo* study of the human brain, have made the investigation of consciousness a respectable field of scientific research. This book discusses social perspectives of consciousness, as well as provides current research on psychological approaches.

Chapter 1 - The existence of spirit is described in terms of energy conservation in universe, where the being spirit is configured as the form of energy, where they are originally formed by five aggregates and four elements and spirit. The being forms are decayed and vanished after death, while the spirits are alive, the rebirth of spirits after death in the new holographic worlds is maintained, which is designated by the individual being activities(passions). The vanished spirit is i.e., no rebirth in any worlds, where the new form of energy is changed to be relics. The new worlds of rebirth depend on the individual past passion, where the middle passions will be rebirth within the Buddha worlds, while the lower and higher passions will be localized in the hell and heaven sides, respectively in the Hilbert space worlds.

Chapter 2 - In this paper, the scientific model and description of dependent origination law (DOL) is presented. The relationship between being spirit signals and DOL in terms of birth and death cycle generated by coupling activities is proposed. The scientific relationship between spirit signals and DOL generated by either before rebirth or after death related phenomenon is discussed. The related phenomenon such as stopping passion (light), Cerenkov radiation (aura), super power, Rabi oscillation which is introduced by meditation, which is discussed in detail related to the DOL principle. Such a proposed concept can be claimed as the instantaneous activities that will be interfered and merged into the spirit signals and being the being blueprint.

Chapter 3 - This paper discusses the general relationships between particular spheres of human knowledge – technology, science and philosophy – and draws attention to the fact that the latter alone constitutes the "leading edge" of intellectual progress. The paper describes three main mechanisms of concluding: induction, deduction, and abduction. Only the latter is capable of creating abstract representations of reality in the human mind, i.e., theories. Theories are the essence of science, where the main intellectual tools for theory building –

i.e., for connecting the already understandable with the not yet understandable – are the metaphor and the bluff.

Reality is composed of subjects, phenomena, and processes. Theories consist of words. In fact, every definition of a scientific term is a "miniature theory". It should precisely mirror the real thing it describes, but in fact it may merely correspond to it in some way. Language is therefore not merely a passive code for description, but an active tool with which to create an image of the world in the human mind. The quality of scientific terminology therefore directly determines the quality of science itself.

By definition, every theory (and every definition) is a simplification, which means its scope of applicability is always limited. In particular, mathematical descriptions are hardly applicable in psychology. Thus, in this discipline the systemic approach – born in the field of biology – seems promising. Especially useful is the theory of N.A. Bernstein, and the concept of the modalities' ladder (ML), derived from it. The latter forms the basis for description of structural aspects of the notion of "*consciousness*". Analysis of intentional operations enables the identification of functional aspects of this notion. Both structural and functional aspects enable the formulation of a definition of the term "*consciousness*" embedded in a system-theoretical approach. As consciousness is the foundational component of the larger complex system of human mind, the related terms "*self*" and "*soul*" are also defined. Moreover, consciousness activates knowledge, which is then processed by intellect. The latter may be regarded as a system (not a sum!) consisting of intelligence, instinct, and intuition.

In conclusion the author argues that, given the highly abstract nature of psychology's subject matter, empirical methodology – by definition tightly joined with observable reality – cannot be as effective as in, say, physics. Thus, in psychology, it is not empirical diligence that is needed, but brilliant fantasy. This may justify the assumption that psychology constitutes the greatest challenge for contemporary science.

Chapter 4 - Through consciousness, we human beings have been acquiring a great capability to master and autonomously act in our environment. In this chapter, the author put forward the hypothesis that attention plays an essential role in both the emergence of consciousness and the enhancement of our autonomy. In this regard, two main features of attention are of essence: its pulse-like nature and the possibility of being controlled top-down. These features allow for a constructive process composed of the segmentation of the continuous stream of undifferentiated information, and, with the support of working memory, the re-combination of isolated, attended pieces of information. This constructive process lies at the basis of every kind of language, and allowed for the creation of new "experiential dimensions", such as science, art, economy, and politics, which proved to be essential for the development and progress of the human species.

Chapter 5 - The use of computational models to simulate various behavioral, cognitive and neurobiological correlates of consciousness has become an increasingly accepted approach to the scientific study of consciousness. However, efforts to create a phenomenally conscious machine have been much less successful. The recent advocacy of cognitive phenomenology in philosophy has the potential to be a game changer in this regard. Cognitive phenomenology asserts that our subjective experiences are not restricted to just traditional qualia, but also encompass deliberative thought processes and high-level cognition. To the extent that this controversial idea is valid, it provides a new route to a deeper understanding of consciousness via computational studies. This route would focus on identifying possible computational correlates of consciousness based on neurocomputational implementations of high-level cognitive functions that are associated with subjective mental states. Identifying such correlates could lead to a better understanding of phenomenal consciousness in general, and perhaps even to a framework for creating an artificially conscious machine. Several potential computational correlates of consciousness are identified and discussed in this context.

Chapter 6 - CONSCIOUSNESS presents us with a challenging, disquieting, and somewhat contradictory mixture – parts of it are so simple they generally pass entirely without notice, while others are so far beyond our human capacity to understand, they seem permanently obscure. From the perspective of a working psychiatrist, it helps to separate these two aspects, so shedding light on this infinitely complex, yet vitally important topic.

This chapter therefore starts with its simplest characteristics – consciousness exists, but only when you are awake or unanaesthetised. It has a more straightforward relationship to 'mind' than is usually allowed – the two terms 'mind' and 'consciousness' overlap sufficiently for practical (psychiatric) purposes.

Next, comparing consciousness with the field of vision helps – the retina, after all, is neurologically speaking, an outgrowth of the very brain tissue itself. And the striking feature of eyesight is the focal point – a small area of high detail surrounded by blur, and the blurring increases the further you get from that point. Accordingly, it makes sense to acknowledge that the entrance channel to consciousness is also necessarily narrow – were it not, the authors would be overwhelmed too easily – "it all happened at once – so I lost track".

Thirdly, there is no future in elucidating consciousness without tackling the challenge of 'choice', or Free Will. Parts of this aspect are indeed wrapped in permanent obscurity – like Richard Feynman said of Quantum Mechanics – if you *think* you understand it, you don't. But as Samuel Johnson said in 1778, "All theory is against the Freedom of the Will; all experience for it" – time the authors paid more attention to the latter, it pays dividends to explore 'experience', here *clinical* experience, as fully as the authors can.

The chapter then examines how Newtonian physics fails to cope with the speed of light, or the nature of the photon. The Uncertainty Principle, without which modern electronics couldn't function, shows how essential it is to accept Uncertainty for some concepts, in order to proceed. Just as the electron doesn't have a pinpoint position, but is best thought of as being somewhere in a 'cloud', so too with descriptions of consciousness. As long as verbal labels are handled responsibly, then communication and therefore progress is possible.

The main thrust of the chapter is to highlight the similarity between software bugs in computing, and the anomalies of psychosis and violence – in both cases the authors have outcomes they don't want. Throughout the chapter, the psychiatric aspects are examined, especially problems which follow the unacceptable omission of consciousness from the DSM (the Diagnostic and Statistical Manual of Mental Disorders).

The chapter draws on the author's clinical experience 'de-programming' 60 murderers, including 6 serial killers, during 5 years working as a consultant psychiatrist in Parkhurst Prison, the UK's premier prison. Also the author's long-term work with infant trauma, and its impact on psychotic symptoms.

Consciousness is our species key adaptation for evolutionary survival. It is sobering to consider that Evolution invariably inflicts extinction on any and all species which fail to exploit their powers of adaptation, however apparently unique.

Chapter 7 - Consider the rehabilitation. Local functions of the brain can be complemented by other parts by training, even if they were lost by an accident such as external injury and internal bleeding. This is the dynamical redistribution of functions inside the brain. It can be regarded as a result of the Operating System (OS) function of the brain, on the analogy of computers. On the other hand, the passive consciousness hypothesis is known to be a powerful hypothesis in the sense that it figures out the difficult problems concerning consciousness such as the frame problem, binding problem, etc. Intrinsic problem of the hypothesis, however, lies in the dubious mechanism by which collective opinions are decided by "majority vote" in the unconscious system and are collected to the local conscious system in a bottom-up manner. No one has elucidated, so far, how the unconscious system and the conscious one are connected in the neural network. The Parasite Fermion Model is a physical model that solves those problems. The Model asserts that, only by assuming the multi-dimensional universe that is nowadays commonly discussed in the modern physics and two types of fermions (material particles), there exists the materialistic subject, called Parasite Fermion Object (PFO), in the extra-dimensional space. One can avoid above-mentioned difficulties, by assuming that the PFO plays a significant role in the OS function and decision process of the unconscious system. It is shown that the Model gives us an insight into the possibility of "life after death."

Chapter 8 - Neuromodulation consists in the alteration of neural activity through the delivery of electrical stimuli or chemical agents to targeted sites, as defined by the International Neuromodulation Society. It is possible to modify neurons' activity by shaping their synaptic plasticity properties through the application of electromagnetic stimuli, weak currents, or neurochemical agents. Electric currents may modify neurons' membrane polarity, thus affecting their synaptic and non-synaptic plasticity (which is the ability of synapses to strengthen or weaken over time in response to increases or decreases in their activity) according to, e.g., long-term potentiation or depression-like plasticity or spike-time dependent plasticity phenomena, depending in turn on possible several mechanisms, including depolarizing blockade, stochastic normalization of neural firing, axonal blockade, reduction of neural firing, and modulation of neural network oscillations. Electric current can be delivered by either electric stimulators, using constant or alternating currents (for transcranial electric stimulation), or magnetic stimulators (for transcranial magnetic stimulation), or implanted pulse generators wired to intra-cranial electrodes (for deep brain stimulation). In addition, technical advances have allowed other neuromodulation approaches, including auditory brainstem implant, functional electrical stimulation, peripheral nerve stimulation (vagus, hypoglossal, and occipital nerve), sacral neuromodulation, and spinal cord stimulation. Moreover, a newly emerging therapeutic approach, namely electroceutical, aims to find the electro-neural signature of disease at a cellular and neuronal network level, in order to restore the normal electro-signature patterns, potentially involving new neuromodulation therapy families, including optogenetics and nanotechnologies. Existing and emerging neuromodulation treatments have been employed in several diseases, including drug-resistant epilepsy, chronic pain conditions, Alzheimer's disease, stroke, spinal cord injury, sensory deficits, bladder or bowel or respiratory control, and chronic disorders of consciousness. Aim of this article is to review the current range of electric neuromodulation approaches in chronic disorders of consciousness, and their rationale of employment.

Chapter 9 - Consciousness is a phenomenon that puzzled many thinkers of the past in disparate fields, including theology, literature, art and philosophy, and continues to be a hot topic of debate at present. However, in the last few decades, the change of paradigm brought by cognitive psychology and the emergence of new techniques, which allowed the *in vivo* study of the human brain, have made the investigation of consciousness a respectable field of scientific research. In particular, the neuroscience of consciousness aims to find the biological roots of conscious states by identifying the brain mechanisms capable of supporting them. On the other hand, a complete different approach has been taken by the Eastern wisdom, which has always looked at the conscious mind as something essential for the human well-being, following the precept that having a healthy mind is necessary for having a healthy body. This tenet lies at the basis of all the different techniques aiming to train the mind, of which the most relevant is probably meditation. Although meditation has been practiced in the East for more than two millennia, Western scientific research and healthcare programs have only recently drawn their attention to it, especially to what is called "mindfulness meditation". To date there is increasing evidence that meditative practices can influence cognitive and emotional processes with benefit to physical and mental health. In this chapter the authors consider both consciousness and mindfulness meditation within a neuroscientific framework, reviewing some of the most interesting theoretical models as well as scientific findings about the brain areas that are thought to underlie conscious and meditative states. In particular, the anterior cingulate cortex, posterior cingulate cortex, prefrontal cortex, insula and thalamus are supposed to be crucially involved in both processes. This suggests that these brain areas may be part of two partially overlapping networks, which, notably, appear to play an important role in social cognition as well.

Chapter 10 - The search for possible neural correlates of consciousness is a particularly complex issue. Nonetheless, it appears ascertained that consciousness is the result of the simultaneous interaction between several brain areas. At a cognitive level, consciousness can be represented as an emergent structure typical of superior animal species that manages and coordinates different cognitive levels. However, the subjective characteristic of the conscious experience does not seem to be fully explained either by neural correlates or by a cognitive interpretation. The paper presents a formal solution of the so-called "hard problem" that takes as its starting point the important works of D. Hofstadter, G. Spencer-Brown and F. Varela.

Chapter 11 - Three main mental functions are global perception, memory imagery and abstract reflection, which are distinguished by the activity, passivity or neutrality of sense organs. Global perception is composed of elementary sensation and stimulated reminiscence. Elementary sensation is an uninterrupted physical chain of bottom-up information from extra-mental reality to active sense organs and specialized brain regions. Stimulated reminiscence and memory imagery without sense organ activity represent top-down information from different brain regions. Abstract reflection without sense organs allows abstraction by categorization, structuring and establishment of relations. Elementary sensation with direct physical interactions between the extra-mental environment, sense organs and specific brain regions reflects the present and is primary, self-evident, intense, unchangeable and incommunicable. Memory imagery retrieving anterior perceptions represents the past and is secondary, faint, modifiable, reproducible and communicable. Abstract reflection allows the abstraction of memory imagery to objective concepts allowing general consensus. Neurobiological investigations showed that elementary sensation with active sense organs activates the same brain regions as memory imagery without sense organ activity, whereas abstract reflection takes place in different prefrontal brain regions. The different brain locations may explain the hard problem. A first to third person gap does not allow an identical content of consciousness in two persons, since elementary sensation of the first person cannot be directly transmitted to a third person, but has to be recreated with the same environment and the sense organs of that person. Nevertheless, differences in sense organ constitution or information processing will not allow reconstitution of an identical content of consciousness. Especially experience from inside sense organs, like pain, cannot be transmitted to third persons. Elementary sensation is the starting point of a continuous process leading from sense organ transmitted bottom-up information to the two other mental functions, which build up human knowledge. By initiating the global perception function, elementary sensation acquires epistemic primacy, which induces complex subjective experiences representing the present and are encoded in the memory as fixed episodes of the past. They can be retrieved by the function of memory imagery. Finally the function of abstract reflection objectifies this information by abstraction into concepts. Epistemic primacy of elementary sensation has to be distinguished from ontological primacy of consciousness concerning the non-material existence of experienced consciousness different from the material world. However, epistemic primacy remains indecisive with respect to ontological primacy concerning the philosophical theories of materialism, dualism or panpsychism.

Chapter 12 - In this paper, the author argues against the conception of first-person thoughts defended by D. Rosenthal. According to this conception, the essentially indexical self-reference of a first-person thought only consists in one's being disposed to describe the individual that thought is about as the thinker of that thought. First, the author tries to show that such a disposition does not make a difference between an essential reference to oneself and an accidental reference to oneself. Second, the author establishes that in Rosenthal's approach there is no guarantee that one dispositionally takes the individual a first-person thought is about to be the thinker of that thought.

Chapter 13 - Etymologically the term anesthesia derives from the Greek ἀν-, an-, "without"; and αἴσθησις, aisthēsis, "sensation". Thus, general anesthesia is a temporary, medically induced condition that includes loss of consciousness, amnesia, analgesia, relaxation of skeletal muscles, and loss of control of reflexes in the autonomic nervous system.

How the anesthetics cause unconsciousness? Despite substantial advances in the authors' understanding on both neuroscientific and pharmacodynamic aspects of anesthetics, the authors do not have an overall picture of what happens to the brain during general anesthesia. Recently, several theoretical models have been proposed to describe the mechanisms of general anesthetics. These models, based on electroencephalographic data represent the need to simplify the intricate relationship between anesthesia and consciousness, which still seems particularly difficult to comprehend.

In 1994, Sigl and Chamoun described a novel measure of the level of consciousness during general anesthesia: the bispectral (BIS) analysis. It was the beginning of a revolution in anesthesia monitoring, as during the last 15-20 years a number of EEG-based technologies have become commercially available. Unfortunately, none of these technologies has definitively solved the problem of the anesthesia awareness, thus assessment of depth of anesthesia is still a serious problem.

This work focuses on molecular mechanisms and targets of general anesthetic drugs, as well as features, limits and new perspectives in depth of anesthesia monitoring.

In: Consciousness
Editor: Lloyd Alvarado
ISBN: 978-1-63485-023-0

Chapter 1

ORIGIN OF SPIRIT AND LIFE

Suphanchai Punthawanunt and Preecha P. Yupapin*
Kasem Bundit University, Bangkok, Thailand

ABSTRACT

The existence of spirit is described in terms of energy conservation in universe, where the being spirit is configured as the form of energy, where they are originally formed by five aggregates and four elements and spirit. The being forms are decayed and vanished after death, while the spirits are alive, the rebirth of spirits after death in the new holographic worlds is maintained, which is designated by the individual being activities(passions). The vanished spirit is i.e., no rebirth in any worlds, where the new form of energy is changed to be relics. The new worlds of rebirth depend on the individual past passion, where the middle passions will be rebirth within the Buddha worlds, while the lower and higher passions will be localized in the hell and heaven sides, respectively in the Hilbert space worlds.

Keywords: quantum life, origin of life, happiness, Buddhism and Modern Science, cognitive science, neuroscience

1. INTRODUCTION

Spirit is recognized as a form of energy, which is existed in the universe, where the combination of all energies must be satisfied the law of energy conservation. However, there is no evidence of the exact spirit existence time. To understand this concept, we begin with the great phenomenon called "big bang" in the astronomy, where the other galaxies are moving away from our own with very high speed, in all directions. They had all been propelled by an ancient explosive force. Before the big bang, we believed that the entire vastness of the observable universe, including all of its matter and radiation, was compressed into a hot, dense mass just a few millimeters across [1]. During the big bang, all forms of

* E-mail: preecha.yu@kmitl.ac.th.

energies were distributed throughout the galaxies, where the materials and non-materials including beings were formed and existed within some certain times.

Principally, there are many forms of energies taking place on Earth, where spirit is the basic element of being, which is a wave of energy and [2], while string is the basic element of materials (particles) [3]. The vanished spirit is claimed to be the real happiness [4], where the neutral mind situation is kept the spirit without vibration energy, where finally collapsed. Nirvana state is the vanished spirit situation, which more details can be found in the Tripitaka [5], which was established by Lord Buddha(Kodom Buddha). This is the truth that is existed in nature. In this article, we describe the existence of spirit existence based on the law of energy conservation. The worlds in Hilbert space (holographic worlds) are also discussed [6-8]. The change in rebirth worlds can be formed by changing the individual being spirit blueprint [3], in which the lower or higher world's bands depend on the activities in the birth and death cycle.

Passion reduction by meditation (mind-body consideration) has been the interesting method that can lead human beings to meet the real happiness without rebirth. The most popular methods of neutral mind situation are the meditation (single passion) and mind-body consideration [4, 5]. In my opinion, the technique that is suitable for the chaotic society is the mind-body consideration. This method the can be reached the neutral mind situation dynamically, which means that the mind-body consideration can be done in any situation in human life, for instance, walking, sitting, lying in bed and working. The main concept of this method is the mindfulness, where anybody with mindfulness can control any situation that has come across. Among people in the chaotic world, the method of meditation using the mind-body consideration is recommended rather than the other methods because the practice can be done any time and place.

The target of this method is the dead body consideration, where practically, the dead body consideration (own body) can reduce the passion, where finally, the mindfulness can be originated, where the final outcome is the concentration. This means that the non-passion state can be achieved, where the neutral mind without neither happiness or suffering is established, which is a real happiness. In Tripitaka, the Kodom Buddha life time is 5,000 years, where the being life time is not more than 120 years, which is more than 2,400 years left, then the new Buddha named "Sri Araya Metri" will be turned up, where the Dharma will have been mostly forgotten on Earth [9]. This Buddha range has the longer life in both being and Buddha range life times.

2. HOLOGRAPHIC WORLDS

In Figure 1, the different world bands are formed by hell, Buddha, heaven and others, where the being worlds are existed in the bands between hell and heaven in the Hilbert space [10, 11]. Regarding to the law of energy conservation, beings are localized in the worlds with different ranges(period of years), for instance, Kodom and Sri Araya Metri Buddha, where the life times of them are 120 and 40,000 years, respectively.

Being spirits are localized in Hilbert space, where originally, spirits are localized in all bands and Hilbert space in the holographic system. Spirits can be changed and transferred into all bands by changing the activities within the birth and death cycle.

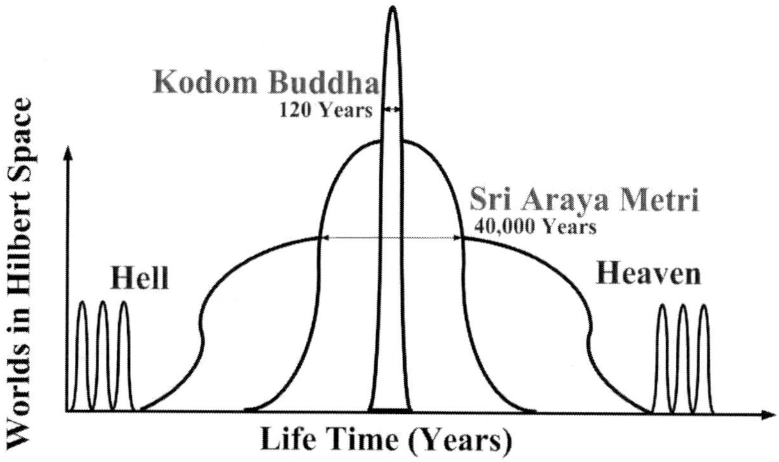

Figure 1. World bands and spiritual existence in the holographic worlds (Hilbert space).

Figure 2. The neutral mind situation between suffering and happiness [12].

In Figure 2, the neutral mind situation is existed between suffering and happiness, which is under the stopping light (passion) condition [12-16]. The stopping condition can be obtained by meditation, where the single passion situation is the target, which means that whenever the single passion is reached, then the non-passion state is not difficult to obtain.

CONCLUSION

In this paper, the existence of spirit is described using the conservation of energy in universe, where the being spirits are included within the total energy. The change in rebirth worlds within the holographic bands can be occurred by changing (improving) the birth and death cycle activities. The vanished spirits can also be established by the practical way called "meditation', where the neutral mind situation can lead to have the nirvana state, where the body becomes the cold body and eventually the relics, which is satisfied the law of energy conservation.

The end of Kodom Buddha range will be appeared by the turned up of chaotic society, where beings will have forgotten Dharma on Earth, where the rebirth of Dharma beings and angels will be in the new Buddha named "Sri Araya Metri".

ACKNOWLEDGMENT

The author would like to give the acknowledgment to King Mongkut's Institute of Technology Ladkrabang (KMITL), Bangkok 10520, Thailand for the research laboratory facilities.

REFERENCES

[1] E. J. Wollack, Cosmology: The study of the universe, Universe 101: Big Bang Theory: NASA, Retrieved November 10, 2014.

[2] T. Martin, Origin: The spirit of the past, Anime News Network, Retrieved by 10 November, 2014.

[3] P. P. Yupapin, S. Pantien and J. Ali, Novel Design Rabi Oscillation System for Human Quantum Life Detection Probe, *Life Science Journal,* 11(2), 235-243, 2014.

[4] F. Varela, What a relief! I don't exist: Buddhism and the Brain (Wes Nisker), *Inquiring Mind*, 16(1), 7-9, 1999.

[5] P. P. Yupapin, Dependent Origination Law: The Spirit Blueprint and Beyond, Journal of Life Science Research, 1(4), 1-5, 2014.

[6] P. P. Yupapin, Two Zero States: The Real Happiness, *International Journal of Buddhism,* 1(1), 1-3, 2014.

[7] S. Phunthawanunt and P. P. Yupapin, Birth and Death Cycle: The Scientific Approach, *Journal of Life Science Research*, 1(4), 77-79, 2014.

[8] S. Phunthawanunt and P. P. Yupapin, Science of Meditation and Therapy, *Journal of Hamonized Researches in Applied Science*, 2(3), 2014, 174-177.

[9] N. Bourbaki, Topological Vector Spaces, Elements of Mathematics, Berlin, Springer-Verlag, 1987.

[10] P. P. Yupapin and J. Ali, Čerenkov Radiation: The Space-Time Paradox. *Nat. Sci.,* 11(12):116-119, 2013.

[11] P. P. Yupapin and N. Pornsuwancharoen, Proposed Nonlinear Resonator Arrangement for Stopping and Storing light, *IEEE Photonics Technology Letters*, 22, 404-406, 2009.

[12] S. Suwandee, S. Phunthawanunt and P. P. Yupapin, New Concept of Mindfulness and Happiness: The Empirical Foundation, *IJSPK,* 1-5, 2014.

[13] S. Pantien and P. P. Yupapin, Wave-particle Duality Probe Model using Micro-optical Device for Neuro-quantum Investigations, *Science Jet,* 3, 2014, 61-64.

[14] P. P. Yupapin and N. Thammawongsa, Consciousness and Sub-consciousness Detection Model Under Čerenkov Radiation, *Microwave and Optical Technology Letters,* 56(7), 1584-1587, 2014.

[15] R. Jomtarak and P. P. Yupapin, Transmission Characteristics of Optical Pulse in Nested Nonlinear Microring Resonators and Gratings, *Journal of Optical Society of America B,* 31(3), 474-477, 2014.

[16] R. Gombrich, Thervada Buddhism: A social history from Ancient Benares to Modern Colombo Routledge and Kegan Paul, 85-85, 1988.

In: Consciousness
Editor: Lloyd Alvarado
ISBN: 978-1-63485-023-0

Chapter 2

SPIRIT BLUEPRINT AND BEYOND

Suphanchai Punthawanunt and Preecha P. Yupapin*
Kasem Bundit University, Bangkok, Thailand

ABSTRACT

In this paper, the scientific model and description of dependent origination law (DOL) is presented. The relationship between being spirit signals and DOL in terms of birth and death cycle generated by coupling activities is proposed. The scientific relationship between spirit signals and DOL generated by either before rebirth or after death related phenomenon is discussed. The related phenomenon such as stopping passion (light), Cerenkov radiation (aura), super power, Rabi oscillation which is introduced by meditation, which is discussed in detail related to the DOL principle. Such a proposed concept can be claimed as the instantaneous activities that will be interfered and merged into the spirit signals and being the being blueprint.

Keywords: original life, spirit blueprint, quantum life, life and behaviors, cognitive science, knowledge management

String is recognized as the basic element of things in universe [1], where similarly, spirit is proposed to be the basic element of beings in the worlds [2]. For mankind, the seeking of happiness and well-being has become the common ground for everyone, where the evidence of such a requirement was established based on the religions. One of the most importance evidences was the famous method called "meditation" [2, 3], in which the basic requirement is the reaching outcome which is named as none passion state. Such a state was established by Lord Buddha more than 2,500 years ago. To start this concept, we are going to make the understanding of the key situation called "stopping light". The stopping light (spirit or mind projection) concept was established by Lord Buddha long time ago, where he said to Aong-kulee-mal, where he was the bandit and converted by the Buddha that used the words "I have completely stopped but you do not", thus, the stopping in this statement is the stopping

* E-mail: preecha.yu@kmitl.ac.th.

passions, which was obtained by the use of Mindfulness Foundation [4], where there is no projection in all dimensions, especially, five aggregates (Fag). In fact, the stopping light concept in a certain medium has been established and used since the Lord Buddha enlightenment [5], which is satisfied well with stopping light concept in the scientific interpretation [6]. Lord Buddha has established that the stopping light, where nothing is moved, even time, which can be obtained when the gap between past and passions come closely together, which means that the smallest gap of these passions can be very small gap, e.g., zero. The concept of the stopping passion (light) can be described by using diagram in Figure 1, which is the none activity situation. This means that there is no projection in the stopping condition. The Fag projections are not found, especially, the mind projection. Thus, there are many behaviors occurred in this situation such as enlightenment, cold body, Rabi oscillation aura, super power and nirvana [7]. There is no passion (mind) projection, where the mind concentration to be single passion (coherent light, photon), which will move with speed greater than the speed of light in the brain medium (brain and whole body), where the Cerenkov radiation is taken place. There are four major behaviors established, where they are (i) no projection of Fags, (ii) stopping light condition, (iii) the nirvana element (cold body or Dhamma body) and (iv) the collapsed spirit. In this proposal, spirit (mind) is formed by coherent light (signal), which is oscillated by a certain Rabi oscillation frequency [8, 9]. Spirit is formed by the 3D brain signal superposition, which can be projected in three dimensions. Mind in mind is occurred within the stopping state, which can project to the worlds in all dimensions. The paradox states remain its functions while mind in mind is in active. The stopping spirit can be obtained by the stopping passion states, which can be observed by the aura situation in Cerenkov radiation of the brain signals (or spirit). However, one of the basic concepts that use to describe the two orthogonal states, i.e., the paradox states (pair) [7, 10], for instance, in the dream we are familiar with consciousness and sub-consciousness states, where they are the paradox states each other. After death, spirit will seek the suitable worlds and forms. Otherwise they will be brought to the given worlds by their own activities within the limit of time. They have to secure themselves by occupying the other worlds and forms, however, they can just temporary, which means that they will not last for long.

In this paper, we propose the use of the pattern known as a spirit blueprint for being life activities, which was establish by Lord Buddha called "Dependent Origination Law (DOL)" [11]. The dependent origination law (DOL) is one of the most important teachings of the Buddha, and it is also very profound. The Buddha has often expressed his experience of enlightenment in one of two ways, either in terms of having understood the four noble truths (FNT) [3], or in terms of having understood the nature of the dependent origination. However, more people have heard about the FNT and can discuss it than the ODL, which is just as important. Although the actual insight into dependent origination arises with spiritual maturity, it is still possible for us to understand the principle involved. The basis of dependent origination is that life or the world is built on a set of relations, in which the arising and cessation of factors depend on some other factors which condition them. This principle can be given in a short formula of four lines: When this is, that is. This arising, that arises. When this is not, that is not. This ceasing, that ceases. DOL emphasizes an important principle that all phenomena in this universe are relative, conditioned states and do not arise independently of supportive conditions. A phenomenon arises because of a combination of conditions which are present to support its arising. And the phenomenon will cease when the conditions and components supporting its arising change and no longer sustain it. The presence of these supportive conditions depends on other factors for their arising, sustenance and disappearance. ODL is being active in either good or evil activities after birth, which is known as a spirit blueprint, where there are (i) ignorance, (ii) perception information (iii) consciousness, (iv) mentality-materiality, (v) six fold, (vi) contact, (vii) feeling, (viii) crave, (ix) clinging, (x) becoming, (xi) birth. Causes and effects are introduced in the current spirit signals due to the ODL, which becomes the being blueprints. Good and evil activities are presented (embedded) in the blueprint with different patterns. Such patterns are formed by the being spirit signals, which they are signals formed by the Rabi oscillation, i.e., Rabi frequency, which they are localized in the suitable worlds after death (before birth), which is spread out through the embryos and become the individual spirit blueprint. The blueprint can be changed due to the instantaneous coupling activities, which they are related to the instantaneous coupling activities, relatively to the being life. In applications, the past and future activities are read from individual human being palm lines.

In Figure 1, regarding to the stopping condition, the elimination of past and future passions will be reached the same line within the certain time, which will be very short in time duration. This can be claimed as the stopping passion (time) situation. However, the last passion will become a single passion before it can be eventually obtained the none passion situation, in which the mankind will be hold at the states such as stopping, Cerenkov radiation, aura, cold body (Dhamma body), Rabi oscillation, super power and relics. In Figure 2, the spirit signal is connected to the Fag and Fe in the being embryos, where the origin of life begun. A, B, C and so on are the instantaneous coupling activities and introduced (embedded) in to the spirit signals (dynamic spirit signals). The instantaneous spirit oscillation is formed by Rabi oscillation, which is the spirit signal in human brain and oscillated with the Rabi oscillation frequency. The superposition of spirit signals due to the incoming interference activities can introduce the four-wave mixing (FWM) behaviors [12], in which the harmonic frequencies can be formed and localized in the different worlds. The final spirit signal of the cycle end will be the spirit blueprint of the being rebirths in the suitable worlds. In Figure 3, it begins with the stopping situation, when the cod body state is taken place, which is called a live nirvana (Dhamma body), where the remaining of energy will be turned (changed) to be aura (light). Alternatively, the nirvana is realized after the broken Fag, where in this case the remaining of energy will turn the form (body) to be nirvana elements, which is known as relics, which is ever lasting in nature (universe). Generally, the causes and effects will be interfered with the current spirit signals. The concentration of spirit signals are obtained by the meditation, which is operated under consciousness processor, while the paradox state is operated by the sub-consciousness, which is the paradox state that can be localized in the suitable worlds.

After the original spirit is embedded and spreading throughout the embryo, it will be patterned to the whole embryo (Fag and Fe), where one of the evidences is the palm lines [13]. DOL can be used to read and describe by mankind life line, where the life lines represent being vitality and the length of life. For mankind, this is the most important line on hands and will always be presented. The life line is the easiest to recognize and helps to determine where the other lines are represented, which is the line close to the thumb. The second most important line, the head line deals with the beliefs, which is the line located from middle of the hand to the life line, This line will inform the philosophy, the attitude on and how mankind approaching life.

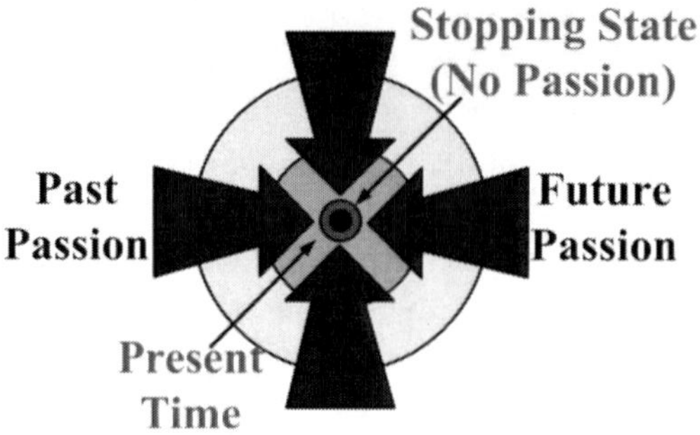

Figure 1. Schematic diagram of none passion (stopping mind projection) state.

It is a representation of the mentality and intelligence. Because it is so important, the head line must be present on the palm.

The head line begins just above the life line, on the side of the palm between the thumb and the index finger, and spans horizontally across the palm.

Regarding to the conservation of energy law, spirits are the parts of things in universe, the separation of the basic spirit (single spirit) can distribute throughout the worlds and universe. Originally, spirit is entered into the embryo (Fag and Fe) via a paradox channel (state) known as sub-consciousness, which will be coupled into the normal consciousness state later on. The superposition of spirit signals is occurred, in which the good and evil actions can be transferred to be positive and negative spirit amplitudes instantaneously in time (phase) from good and bad feelings.

The resultant activities can be presented in these four forms, where they are (i) instantaneous/sudden impact, (ii) personality, (iii) society, spirit blueprint. Generally, we should expect to die out of the birth and death cycle, which means that there are no more rebirths, i.e., nirvana, for instance, the thin body (suffering body) with smart mind is the good target. Good and evil actions can be embedded into the spirit blueprint, in which the causes and effects will be established by the reflected activities, where the interference of signals can be obtained.

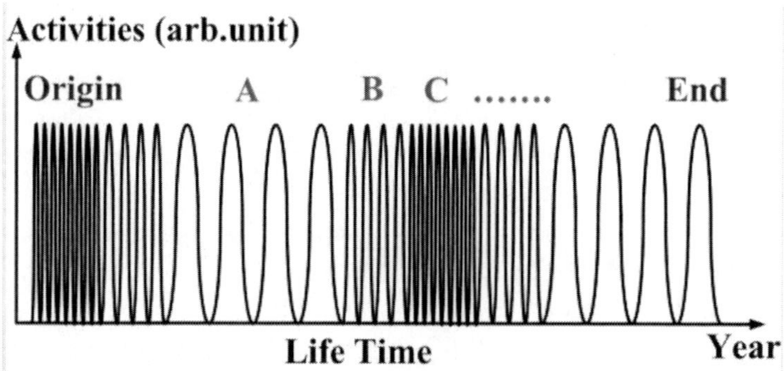

Figure 2. The spirit blueprint after death (before birth).

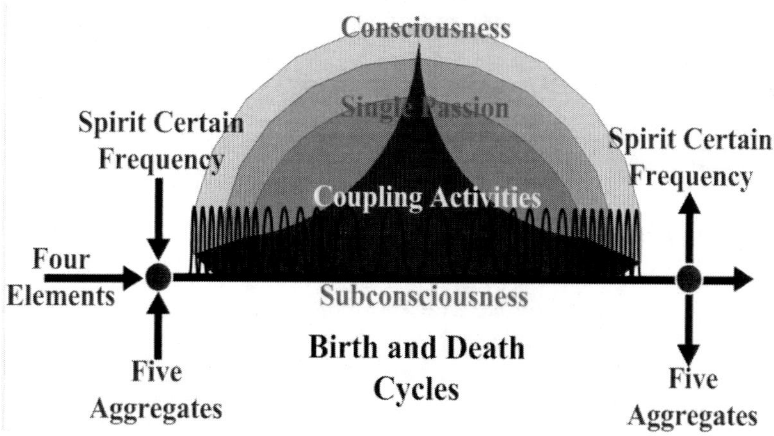

Figure 3. DOL and current activities.

In conclusion, the stopping condition of spirit is called a live nirvana, which is vibrated by spirit harmonic oscillator. Thus, the being life and activities are described by the spirit blueprint, which can be embedded into the spiritual signals in birth and death cycle. The change in activities in either good or evil ones will be embedded within the current spirit patterns. The past activities are already formed the spirit before birth, which can be changed due to the future activities in either good or evil activities. The single passion state can be obtained by spirit concentration, i.e., meditation. Being life is already laid out by the spirit blueprint, which is formed after death (before birth), however, it is not include the being nirvana, where the spirit is collapsed (no oscillation), where the Dhamma body will be turned to be relics. The collapsed energy is changed and merged with the Dhamma body and turned to be relics, where the law of energy conservation remains. Apparently, the spirit blueprint is seen by the human palm lines, which can be effects to their life, in which the causes and effects are introduced regarding to the DOL pattern, where they are the instantaneous embedded to the spirit pattern signals. Mind in mind is the spirit function under the stopping condition, where the consciousness is still working with the minimum Rabi oscillation frequency (energy), in which the paradox state, i.e., sub-consciousness is travelling freely in time under the cold body state, which is called the mind releasing, i.e., out-of-body experience (OBE), while the consciousness is operated with harmonic oscillator energy [12, 14, 15]. OBE body is undergone the cold body situation, which is the minimum energy with the harmonic oscillator, where the Dhamma body is called a live nirvana.

The author would like to give the acknowledgment to King Mongkut's Institute of Technology Ladkrabang (KMITL), Bangkok 10520, Thailand for the research laboratory facilities.

REFERENCES

[1] H. J. Schnitzer, String theory: a theory in search of an experiment, 2013: arXiv:physics/0311047.

[2] S. Phunthawanunt and P. P. Yupapin, Science of meditation and therapy, *Journal of Hamonized Researches in Applied Science*, 2(3), 2014, 174-177.

[3] E. William et al. (2009), Buddhist Philosophy: Essential Readings, Oxford University Press; ISBN: 978-0-19-532817-2.

[4] S. Phunthawanunt and P. P. Yupapin, Birth and death cycle: The scientific approach, Life Sciences, 2014(in press).

[5] Tripitaka, 2014, Wikipedia, 31 September, 2014.

[6] P. P. Yupapin and N. Pornsuwancharoen, Proposed Nonlinear microring resonator arrangement for stopping and storing light, *IEEE Photonics Technology Lletters,* 22(6), 404-406, 2009.

[7] P. P. Yupapin S. Pantian and and J. Ali, Čerenkov Radiation: The space-time paradox, *Nature and Science*, 11(12), 116-119, 2013.

[8] P. P. Yupapin, S. Pantien and J. Ali, Novel design Rabi oscillation system for human quantum life detection probe, *Life Science Journal*, 11(2), 235-243, 2014.

[9] A. F. A. Noorden, K. Chaudhary, M. Bahadoran, M. S. Aziz, M. A. Jalil, C. T. Ong, J. Ali and P. P. Yupapin, Computational Rabi oscillation within a microring resonator system, *Journal of Laser and Technology,* 2014 (Submission).

[10] A. Einstein, B. Podolsky, and N. Rosen, Can Quantum-mechanical Description of Physical Reality be Complete?, *Phys. Rev.*, 47, 777-780, 1935.

[11] O. Blanke and S. Aezy, The out-of-body experience: disturbed self-processing at the temporo-parietal junction, *Neuroscientist,* 2005 Feb.; 11 (1):16-24.

[12] Harmonic oscillator, Wikipedia, searched by 31 August, 2014.

[13] Palm lines, Google, searched by 31 August, 2014.

[14] J. H. Davis and E. Thompson, From the five aggregates to phenomenal consciousness: Toward a cross-cultural cognitive science, in A companion to Buddhist philosophy, edited by S. Emmanuel, Wiley-Blackwell, 2013.

[15] P. P. Yupapin and N. Thammawongsa, Consciousness and Sub-consciousness Detection Model Under Čerenkov Radiation, *Microwave and Optical Technology Letters,* 56(7), 1584-1587, 2014.

In: Consciousness
Editor: Lloyd Alvarado
ISBN: 978-1-63485-023-0

Chapter 3

CONSCIOUSNESS FROM AN EVOLUTIONARY AND SYSTEMIC PERSPECTIVE

Wacław Petryński*
Katowice School of Economics,
Katowice, Poland

If you would understand anything,
observe its beginning and its development.
Aristotle

ABSTRACT

This paper discusses the general relationships between particular spheres of human knowledge – technology, science and philosophy – and draws attention to the fact that the latter alone constitutes the "leading edge" of intellectual progress. The paper describes three main mechanisms of concluding: induction, deduction, and abduction. Only the latter is capable of creating abstract representations of reality in the human mind, i.e., theories. Theories are the essence of science, where the main intellectual tools for theory building – i.e., for connecting the already understandable with the not yet understandable – are the metaphor and the bluff.

Reality is composed of subjects, phenomena, and processes. Theories consist of words. In fact, every definition of a scientific term is a "miniature theory". It should precisely mirror the real thing it describes, but in fact it may merely correspond to it in some way. Language is therefore not merely a passive code for description, but an active tool with which to create an image of the world in the human mind. The quality of scientific terminology therefore directly determines the quality of science itself.

By definition, every theory (and every definition) is a simplification, which means its scope of applicability is always limited. In particular, mathematical descriptions are hardly applicable in psychology. Thus, in this discipline the systemic approach – born in the field of biology – seems promising. Especially useful is the theory of N.A. Bernstein, and the concept of the modalities' ladder (ML), derived from it. The latter forms the basis

* Corresponding author: waclaw.petrynski@interia.pl.

for description of structural aspects of the notion of "*consciousness*". Analysis of intentional operations enables the identification of functional aspects of this notion. Both structural and functional aspects enable the formulation of a definition of the term "*consciousness*" embedded in a system-theoretical approach. As consciousness is the foundational component of the larger complex system of human mind, the related terms "*self*" and "*soul*" are also defined. Moreover, consciousness activates knowledge, which is then processed by intellect. The latter may be regarded as a system (not a sum!) consisting of intelligence, instinct, and intuition.

In conclusion the author argues that, given the highly abstract nature of psychology's subject matter, empirical methodology – by definition tightly joined with observable reality – cannot be as effective as in, say, physics. Thus, in psychology, it is not empirical diligence that is needed, but brilliant fantasy. This may justify the assumption that psychology constitutes the greatest challenge for contemporary science.

INTRODUCTION

The claim that the main goal of science is building abstract representations of our world – theories – which produce understanding and result in the most reliable possible degree of predictability, is obviously an oversimplification. Moreover, as A. Einstein stated, "*the whole of science is nothing more than a refinement of everyday thinking*" (Einstein 1936). However, in order to describe the mechanisms of such a process, it seems instructive to use the following, slightly paraphrased metaphor by psychophysiologist I.M. Feigenberg (Feigenberg 2006).

Let us compare the world around us to a great, dark, icy space with a bonfire in the middle. The area around the fire is bright, cozy and warm. This area may be termed the Home of the Known, where obvious and smart **technology** makes the human being's life comfortable. The term "technology" should be understood metaphorically here, as a process of the creation of any product – material or mental – useful in daily life.

The next sphere is much colder and not so bright. This is the Forest of the Assumed, which human beings try to "tame" and bring into the fold of the Home of the Known. Here the main intellectual mechanism is **science**. Its "armed forces" are the matured, verified theories, which are acknowledged as being correct. They are abstract representations of reality, but possibly true, with their "feet on the ground", since they should be re-forged absolutely reliably into technology. According to physicist C. Rovelli:

> *I think science is not about data; it's not about the empirical content, about our vision of the world. It's about overcoming our own ideas, and about going beyond common sense continuously. Science is a continuous challenge of common sense, and the core of science is not certainty, it's continuous uncertainty* (Rovelli 2012).

Still further out stretches the dark and icy Ocean of the Unknown. In this region, the human disposes only of **philosophy** (Figure 1). It uses hypotheses, infrequently completely free from the constraints of reality, without striving for applicability.

According to mathematician and philosopher B. Russell, "*science is what you know; philosophy is what you don't know.*" As far as science is concerned, this is a slight overstatement, but in respect of philosophy it seems to be exactly right. Instructive here are the words of M. Planck, that "*scientific discovery and scientific knowledge have been achieved only by those who have gone in pursuit of it without any practical purpose whatsoever in view*". The same idea was more concisely (and wittily) expressed by another Nobel laureate, R.P. Feynman, who said: "*Physics is like sex: sure, it may give some practical results, but that's not why we do it.*" Hence, though often disregarded by "*genuine scientists*" (read: empiricists, who – sticking to Feynman's metaphor – use sex only to gain the most practical results possible), philosophy alone constitutes the "leading edge" of human cognition.

All this shows that the process of building certain, and, as far as possible, reliable science begins with "daydreaming", and with intellectually risky philosophy. As engineer and polymath M. Nadin remarked, "*philosophy remains a science of sciences*" (Nadin 1997, 525).

The main mechanism that enables expansion of all the fields listed above is anticipation, driven by curiosity and striving to reach beyond that which is already known. For those with their "feet firmly on the ground" in the Home of the Known, anticipation opens up the perspective on Science. For scientists with their "head in the clouds", who inhabit the wild Forest of the Assumed, anticipation enables entry into the still more mysterious Ocean of the Unknown.

Thanks to anticipation, human genius has enabled the mental creation of abstract representations of reality, more or less true, or completely virtual images, and, "*as Sir Karl Popper once elegantly put it, this design enhancement permits our hypotheses to die in our stead*" (Dennett 1995, 375). Parenthetically, in this statement one might trace a mechanism of intellectual evolution and a germ of immortality…

To sum up, according to physicist and philosopher M. Paty, philosophy should not exist separately from science, but it must reside inside active science – boiling, hungry for a new, more efficient image of the world – and as the main "working engine" driving its development (Heller 2014, 93). Hence, no matter how unwavering the belief of "genuine scientists" – with their noses in computers – in modern technology, the "leading edge" of human genius is undoubtedly free, joyful, aimless, even frivolous, philosophy. Thus, in even the most advanced science, commonly accepted methodology cannot replace original, independent thinking – however painful it may be.

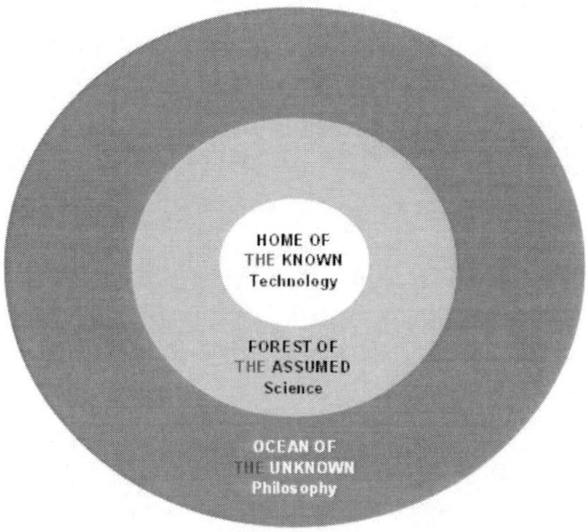

Figure 1. The world where we live: Home of the Known (Technology), Forest of the Assumed (Science), and Ocean of the Unknown (Philosophy).

The Epistemological Obstacle and Graspability Barrier in Science

Only properly ordered knowledge deserves the noble title of "Science" (with a capital "S"). Reality consists of facts, phenomena and processes, science of the mental representations thereof, expressed as accurately as possible through appropriate language. The specificity of language – or more precisely, the code of description – determines the manner and depth of knowledge ordering, and, as a result, the shape of science. In this respect, highly illustrative are verses by P.B. Shelley from "*Prometheus Unbound*":

> *He gave man speech, and speech created thought,*
> *Which is the measure of the universe* (Shelley 1906, 66).

The idea that language shapes human thought had already been formulated in the 18th and 19th century by the philosophers J.G. Herder and W. von Humboldt. In the 20th century the linguistic relativity hypothesis was developed by E. Sapir and B.L. Whorf (Hussein 2012). Hence, the collection of data – by observation or experiment – constitutes merely the first step in the creation of science. It is also, moreover, the least intellectually-demanding step. The crucial stage is abstract interpretation, with a specific language. Hence, mathematician, physicist and philosopher H. Poincaré stated that "*an accumulation of facts is no more science than a pile of bricks is a house*".

The phenomena and processes that psychology aims to study cannot be effectively ordered simply through elegant and user-friendly mathematics. Consequently, the use of other methods becomes necessary. Here, the heuristic seems highly promising. It does not include strict formalism, which in biological and psychological issues does more to constrain than to clarify, bringing order, certainly, but at the same time strangling the knowledge being ordered. The heuristic method, by contrast, leaves space for free interpretation, absolutely necessary in disciplines such as psychology. It is worth noting that even in physics and mathematics there are "free spaces" for unpredictable phenomena. Such spaces are filled with the theory of probability. This may, to some extent, mathematically "harness" **chance** (Heller 2014) – indifferent to human plans, embedded in the essence of the physical world – but not **intentionality**, being molded solely by the minds of human beings and resulting from what is perhaps the greatest attribute of the human being: free will.

Unfortunately, the heuristic does not "automatically" lead to reliable conclusions. Physicists and philosophers G.V. Coyne and M. Heller claimed:

> *In some cases, the equations turned out to be* wiser *than Einstein himself. (...). How could the equations know something that would be discovered fifty years after they had been written down? And this is exactly what often happens* (Coyne and Heller 2008, 122).

So, mathematics leads precisely, but "stiffly" towards the solution of the issue under consideration. Mathematical formalism determines both the path leading to the solution and its final shape. The same role is played by any other theory, which, while perhaps unable to attain the same precision as a mathematical one, may have more flexibility. Thus, a trade-off is necessary: if a high degree of flexibility is needed, one has to abandon exact mathematics and accept a lower level of precision. Another way of putting it might be to say: the less mathematics (certain and comfortable), the more original thinking (risky, arduous, sometimes even painful).

This latter discipline is necessary in every science. In contemporary psychology it must be achieved without mathematics. Fundamentally, the necessary precision depends on the accuracy of the code of description. In an ideal case, the language of science should precisely mirror the reality to which it refers. Unfortunately, according to the Löwenheim-Skolem theorem, even in mathematical logic this is impossible. Philosopher and mathematician J. Życiński wrote:

> (…) *this theorem* (by Löwenheim-Skolem – WP) *is comparable to the uncertainty principle by W. Heisenberg, because it shows the impassable limits of description. In the physics of the micro world there is a limit to the precision of description, and the conjugate parameters are necessarily fuzzy. Similarly, in formalized linguistic characteristics there is a limit of pinpointing notions, and the language properties, discovered by Skolem, manifest themselves in partly unexpected blurring the sense which one tried to describe precisely* (Życiński 2013, 126).

G. Bachelard described a similar phenomenon in linguistics as the **epistemological obstacle** (Bachelard 2002, 24). A natural language, then, cannot be absolutely precise. Hence, the ‘counterpart’ of the accuracy of measuring devices in the laboratory is the epistemological obstacle in the mind. On the other hand, an “intellectual fuzziness” resulting from this obstacle provides space for intuition and free interpretation, and, as a consequence, for mental progress – in science as in any other discipline.

The other important hindrance is what we might call the “**graspability barrier**”. This may be well illustrated with the words of the fictional character Woland, the devil’s prince, who, talking to the philosopher I. Kant, stated: “*It’s clever, maybe, but mighty unclear. You’ll be laughed at”* (Bulgakov 2008, 25). Or, in the words of another outstanding novelist, K. Vonnegut, “*any scientist who couldn’t explain to an eight-year-old what he was doing was a charlatan*” (Vonnegut 2010, 34).

Incidentally, the freedom of interpretation specific to the heuristic method enables the use not only of “orthodox scientific” and “deadly serious” papers, but also of other sources of valuable human thoughts and ideas, such as literary masterpieces, which, needless to say, would be frowned upon in “genuine science”.

In science then, as in daily life, there exists what might be termed the “graspability barrier”. It seems natural that specialists in humanities may not understand, say, mathematical differential and integral calculus. Unjustified application of terms incomprehensible even to authors of scientific (or, more precisely, scientifical) works was illuminated by mathematician and physicist A. Sokal in his famous “Sokal hoax” (Sokal 1994; Sokal and Bricmont 1999). According to the Urban Dictionary, the word “*scientifical*” – unlike the near-identical sounding term “*scientific*” – means “*a way to make yourself sound intelligent when you have no idea what you are talking about*” (Urban Dictionary 2015). Sokal showed, in a spectacular manner, that the postmodernist philosophers do not understand the mathematical notions they use in their papers. However, scientifical charlatanry aside, science can be useful and efficient only when it is not just reliable, but also comprehensible.

The production of intelligible representations of reality is the main task of science. However, reality is too complex to be grasped as a whole, and this makes the creation of understandable representations of it – theories – absolutely necessary. These constitute the *crème de la crème* of science.

Every theory creates a simplified representation of reality. Biologist J. Cohen and mathematician I.N. Stewart wrote: "*A theory is a kind of code that transforms complicated* messages *from nature into much simpler ones*" (Cohen and Stewart 2000, 363). Biologist P. Medawar stated succinctly that "*theories destroy facts*" (Stewart 2002, 377). One might add: "*And vice versa: theory may be built only on the dead bodies of facts, and not with direct, actual connection with them being alive*" (Figure 2). In short, theory is built not of facts, but of pure relations linking facts together; one might compare it to a "*body-less soul of reality*". Its advantage lies in its versatility: the same theory may yield reliable solutions for various tasks, depending on input data. In this respect it might be compared to a computer application program.

Incidentally, as a popular adage has it, "*philosophy is a game with objectives and no rules; mathematics is a game with rules and no objectives*". It is for this reason that mathematician R. Penrose stated:

> *There are two other words I do not understand* – awareness *and* intelligence. *Well, why am I talking about things when I do not know what they really mean? It is probably because I am a mathematician and mathematicians do not mind so much about that sort of thing. They do not need precise definitions of the things they are talking about, provided they can say something about the connections between them* (Penrose 1997, 100).

Speaking about what is not precisely defined is absolutely unacceptable in technology, and treated with a high degree of suspicion in physics. However, in the case of highly abstract subject matter, such as that of psychology, such a "mathematician-like" way of thinking, not closely and directly related to reality, seems indispensable. Nonetheless, even in theoretical analyses in highly utilitarian technology abstract thinking is absolutely necessary. As M. Heller has argued, "*science sees the world through theories*" (Heller 2011, 44). In the same book, he stated:

> *It seems that the possibility of idealization is not only a technical facilitation, but a trait profoundly connected with the existence of science* (Heller 2011, 58).

To sum up, we could say that the epistemological obstacle "resides" in the very nature of language (or, more precisely, codes of description), whereas the graspability barrier resides in the mind of the individual. However, they both determine the accuracy of science as a whole. The following statement by M. Heller may be regarded as a specific illustration of the epistemological obstacle in mathematics:

> *One may assume that the mathematical structures we use for modeling the world so much diverge with their simplicity from the richness of the real structure of the world that instead of similarity, we should rather speak of a specific resonance between the structure of the world and the structure of the mathematical models thereof invented by us. The structures we have designed somehow fall into resonance with the structure of the world so that, despite drastic simplification, they inform us about specific features of the world* (Heller 2011, 58).

In a more detailed way, J. Życiński argued:

> *It cannot be excluded that those fields* (emotions, esthetic, ethics – WP) *that determine the specificity of human soul, will turn out to be inaccessible to attempts of mathematization and thus one might speak about the relative transcendence of human spirituality as related to a mathematical matrix of the world* (Życiński 2013, 223).

However, in the same book, Życiński opened up a more optimistic perspective, writing:

> *Only thanks the works of Alfred Tarski has it become clear that to assume a given sentence, expressed in a specific language of logic, as being true, it is necessary to go beyond this language and to take into account the objective state of affairs using a metalanguage* (Życiński 2013, 143).

In this statement one might trace the spirit of the incompleteness theorem by logician and mathematician K. Gödel, probably most concisely described by cognitive scientist and polymath D.R. Hofstadter: "*In short, Gödel showed that provability is a weaker notion than truth, no matter what axiomatic system is involved*" (Hofstadter 1999, 19). Similarly, educationalist and psychologist Z. Chlewiński said: "*From Gödel's theorems it results that the creative intuition cannot be fully substituted by a sheer formalism*" (Chlewiński 1999, 21). So, when a system encounters an issue which is not resolvable within that system's limits, a new element has to be added, and thus a new system created, which in the future will also inevitably meet its applicability limit. This is why science creation is a never-ending story.

THE SPECIFICITY OF THE SYSTEMS APPROACH

Accepting the premise that mathematics is not appropriate for description of psychological issues, some other ordering mechanism has to be applied. In this respect, the systems approach, "born" as a scientific structure in the field of biology, seems highly promising.

According to J.M. Morawski, a **system** is a layered structure of information and energy transformations, built in keeping with the following axioms:

1. **The layers hierarchy axiom**. In each system there is a main control layer (*master*), and the other, background layers (*slaves*) support it.
2. **The layers autonomy axiom**. Each layer performs its specific tasks independently, without any additional information.
3. **The scales' conformity axiom**. Each layer has its own thinking specificity, time-space dimensionality and energy exchange range, which determine that layer's "identity" and, as a result, its potentialities (Morawski 1986; 1989; 2000; 2005, 162; Morawski and Zawalski 1986).

The latter was formulated by J.M. Morawski (1991; 1994; 1995a; 1995b). Essentially, it is the fundamental systemic rule, and may be termed **the layers identity axiom**. In fact, only the scales' conformity axiom underlies the discrete, layered structure and functionality of a system. The other "pillar" of the system's construction is the nonlinear relation between particular layers, which is "responsible" for emergent **system effect**.

The latter constitutes probably the most productive yet mysterious ability of a system. System effect may be explained by the attributes of its components, but cannot be fully derived from them. In short, in mathematics 2 + 2 = 4, whereas in systems theory 2 + 2 = 4 + unpredictable system effect. One might assume that a system consists of its individual parts and specific relations joining them together. Thus, the final product of the system depends partly on the specificity of its components, and partly on elusive relations between them. It should be emphasized that a system has a multilayered structure, and each layer has its own information processing modality (including specific logic). Moreover, the relations – especially between particular layers – are of a non-linear nature. This means that some dependencies between connected items from various layers are stronger than those between other connected items. As a result, a system may be so complicated in character that it cannot be described with elegant, obvious, and user-friendly mathematics. On the other hand, the system yields a much higher level of flexibility than mathematics, which is necessary in building the abstract, scientific representations of biological and – especially – psychological phenomena and processes.

Concluding in Science: Metaphor and Bluff

In building abstract representations of reality, the process of conclusion takes the form of sensory observation or empirical researches. In this respect, the words of philosopher C.S. Peirce seem useful:

> *Abduction is the process of forming an explanatory hypothesis.* ***It is the only logical operation which introduces any new idea*** (my emphasis – WP)*; for induction does nothing but determine a value, and deduction merely evolves the necessary consequences of a pure hypothesis.*
>
> *Deduction proves that something* ***must be****; Induction shows that something* ***actually is*** *operative; Abduction merely suggests that something* ***may be*** (Peirce 1958, 106; Desclés 2000, 92).

The three methods of reasoning listed by Peirce in this statement might be illustrated with the Induction-Abduction-Deduction (IAD) triangle, with the additional inclusion of the vertical abstraction axis (Figure 2).

The processes on the "abduction slope" of the IAD triangle may be aptly described in the words of physiologist P.K. Anokhin, who stated that "*(...) Einstein's approach consists in striving to present the empirically discovered regularities as logical necessities*" (Anokhin 1973, 20). The difference between abduction and deduction "slopes" of the IAD triangle may be illustrated by Einstein's statement that "*[a] theory can be tested by experience, but there is no way from experience to the construction of a theory*" (Einstein 1996, 85). The first part of this sentence concerns deduction, the second abduction.

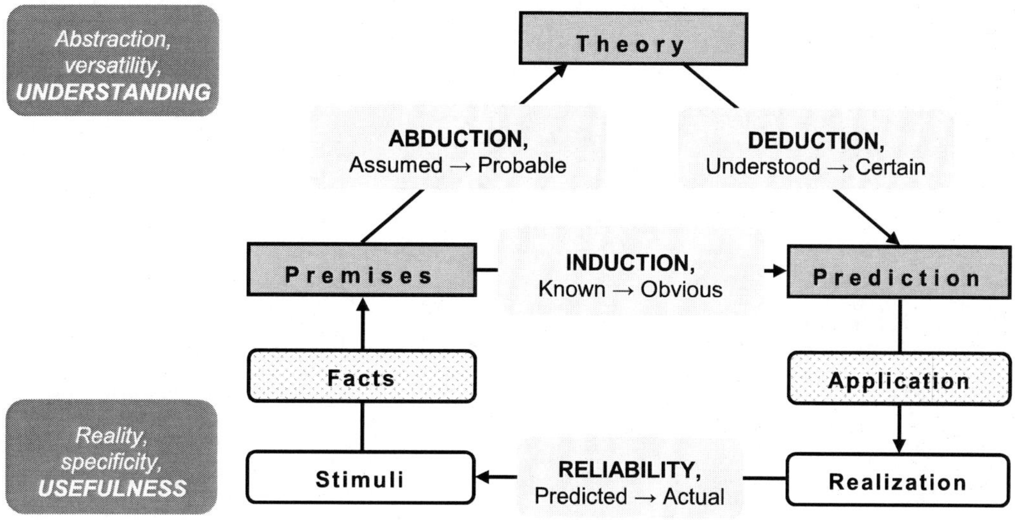

Figure 2. Concluding in science. The induction-abduction-deduction (IAD) triangle.

In Figure 2 the stimuli may be joined with reality, the facts with commonly accepted obviousness, the premises with assumptions, and the theory with the accurate abstract representation of reality. We may refer here to the view of evolutionary biologist R. Dawkins that "*careful inference can be more reliable than actual* observation, *however strongly our intuition protests at admitting it*" (Dawkins 2009, 15). This seems to be rather timid, since "*careful inference*" in fact constitutes **the only** method for the formulation of theory, and, as a consequence, science. The possible protests of our intuition, if any, would therefore be completely irrelevant.

It is worth noting that Figure 2 clearly shows the difference between **certainty** and **reliability**. The former is the product of theory and deduction; hence it "resides" in the **abstract** mind. The latter results from physical **realization** of what is mentally certain and makes a measure of coherence between what is mentally predicted and what is physically actual in the environment.

Examining Figure 2 in more detail, one may learn that at a low level of abstraction the main task of the scientist is to collect the facts. This is the essence of so-called **"empirical sciences"**. However, ascending higher and higher up the abduction slope – and the scale of abstraction as well – theoretical considerations become more and more important. As a result, the epistemological obstacle and graspability barrier, should they appear, become a more and more serious hindrance. Nevertheless, only so-called **"theoretical sciences"** – being in fact the only genuine sciences – may produce Science itself (with a capital "S").

We might also note that the ascent of the abduction slope is arduous and risky. With increasing distance from the safe ground of "hard facts", the intellectual terrain becomes more and more unstable. However, when the theory – mathematically described or otherwise – is already created, it becomes a safe refuge and a basis for travel either down the deduction slope (Figure 2) toward certainty and reliable applications, or up toward uncertainty and new, more abstract theories.

The journey down the deduction slope is relatively light, easy and certain. To put it bluntly, theory exempts us from… thinking! While thinking is absolutely necessary on the abduction slope, on the deduction slant it is sufficient merely to apply – sometimes even in a mechanical fashion – the appropriate theory.

Climbing up the abduction slope, a scientist disposes of two main instruments for re-forging the Unknown into the Known: the "polite" **metaphor** and the "barbarian" **bluff**.

The former consists in applying already known relationships discovered in one region of reality to another region. Thus, in doing so, one is familiar with the knowledge one is using; one knows what relations may be used to explain the hitherto unknown through the use of what is already known. This enables the arduous, methodical production of science of the already known modality, i.e., the primarily **quantitative development** of science.

The "barbarian" **bluff**, on the other hand, consists in the application of assumed, independently invented relations connecting the regions of the Known and the Unknown. To be optimally effective, it has to be freed from real constraints. As a result, scientists using it expose themselves to the charge of being "non-scientific daydreamers", charlatans even, especially if their ideas are not immediately understandable to other scientists, i.e., if they reach beyond the horizons of their comprehension. The bluff is therefore much riskier than the metaphor, but if it turns out to be accurate it enables a sudden leap in our understanding of the world: i.e., **qualitative progress**. This requires not just knowledge, but also sheer luck. Paradoxically, this knowledge should not be too profound, lest it block what psychologist R. Cattell terms "*fluid intelligence*" (Gerrig 2013, 248). The latter means looking for new solutions to tasks rather than merely using already known "rails of thought", which may be identified with what Cattell termed "*crystallized intelligence*". The most reliable, "hardest" rails of thought in contemporary science are those produced by mathematics. However, when traveling by rail, it is not the engineer that determines the direction of travel, but the rails alone.

The elusive nature of the bluff unfortunately makes it highly susceptible to unfair application, and one might well sense an atmosphere of charlatanry around it. On the other hand, it is only the brilliant bluffs – in the field of physics we might think of individuals such as M. Planck, A. Einstein, N. Bohr, or more recently P. Higgs – that have driven progress forward. It should be emphasized that the bluff, and only the bluff, is what leads to qualitative transformations.

There seems to be a general principle (we might call it "*The Principle of Sensitive Nobility*") that the more "noble" the product – be it technological or intellectual – the more susceptible that product is to improper use. On this view, the bluff is probably the most "noble" instrument for scientific reasoning.

Fittingly, all of the abovementioned scientists were physicists. The methodology of physics is not appropriate for application to psychological considerations. However, the subject matter dealt with by physics is much simpler than that of psychology; hence, some versatile regularities may be more readily visible in physics than in psychology.

To sum up, in broad terms we might say that the main intellectual mechanism in the Home of the Known is induction; in the Forest of the Assumed, deduction; and in the Ocean of the Unknown, abduction. While the former is certainly reliable and mentally non-taxing, its fruitfulness is limited. The latter requires a great deal of reasoning and is intellectually risky, but nonetheless may yield valuable results, qualitatively distinct from already-possessed knowledge.

The Nature of Theory and Definition

The multidimensional nature of reality makes it impossible for us ever to comprehend it as a whole – as illustrated as far back as Plato, in his Allegory of Cave. The slaves confined in the cave can see only the shadows of what is going outside, cast upon the wall, and their understanding of the world is thus based merely on what they infer from these shadows (Plato 2003, 240). A given scientific discipline may likewise be understood as a specific, two-dimensional shadow of actual, three-dimensional reality. This can be illustrated using the shadows model, inspired by D.R Hofstadter (Hofstadter 1999, 28), shown in Figure 3.

It is worth noting that each of the two-dimensional shadows comes from the same three-dimensional body; none is more or less true than the others but each, nevertheless, is different to the others. Therefore, every theory, but also every *discipline* of science casts a specific "*low-dimensional shadow*": in other words, a considerable simplification. It emphasizes only those attributes of reality which are crucial to a given discipline. As a result, every theory – being inevitably a simplification – has only a limited range of applicability. Moreover, as K.R. Popper put it, "*the more a theory forbids, the more it tell us*" (Popper 2002a, 42; 2002b, 48).

The most basic "chunk" of information necessary to build a theory is the 'notion'. To produce its verbal equivalent as precisely as possible, the notion has to be defined as precisely as possible: every definition is therefore a sort of 'mini-theory', with all its advantages and shortcomings. In short, it has to be as precise, as exhaustive, as graspable, and as concise as possible. Precision and exhaustiveness may run into the epistemological obstacle, and graspability and conciseness the graspability barrier. Unfortunately, achieving all of these goals at once is a case of squaring the circle in a particular way, and in this respect, specific compromises, determined by the particular goal of a given definition, are unavoidable.

Hence, as with the notion of consciousness, one must first choose the appropriate perspective, and only then create the definition based on selected premises. Inevitably, already at this stage one somehow demarcates the sphere and limits of applicability of the definition. Here, the words of statisticians G.E.P. Box and N.R. Draper seem instructive: "*(...) all models are wrong; the practical question is how wrong do they have to be to not be useful*" (Box and Draper 1987, 74). No definition can be absolutely precise and exhaustive then, but any scientist seeking to formulate a definition should keep in mind the following aphorism by A. Einstein: "*Everything should be made as simple as possible, but not simpler*". Accordingly, we may propose a specific hierarchy of the goals that a good definition should meet:

1. Graspability.
2. Accuracy.
3. Versatility.
4. Conciseness.

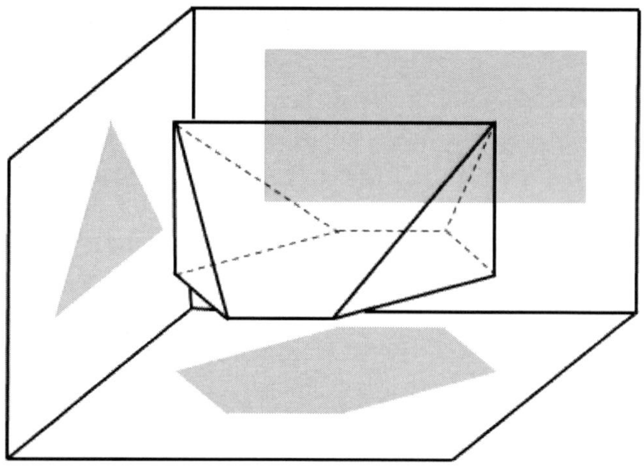

Figure 3. The shadows model showing different shadows of the same shape, cast on different planes: an allegory for reality and particular disciplines of science.

It is worth noting that if the graspability barrier is being violated, then the definition loses its functionality and *raison d'être*.

The very essence (perhaps even "soul") of the theory in general, and of the definition in particular, may be well illustrated with the drawing by engineer and biomechanist J.M. Morawski. Reality may be symbolized by the image on the left hand side of Figure 4, and theory with the drawing on the right.

A musical equivalent might be, for example, the pairing of Bach's "*Brandenburg Concertos*" and "*Popcorn*" by G. Kingsley. The former includes full, continuous melody (analogous to the image), and the latter merely discrete sounds played by a single instrument (analogous to the drawing).

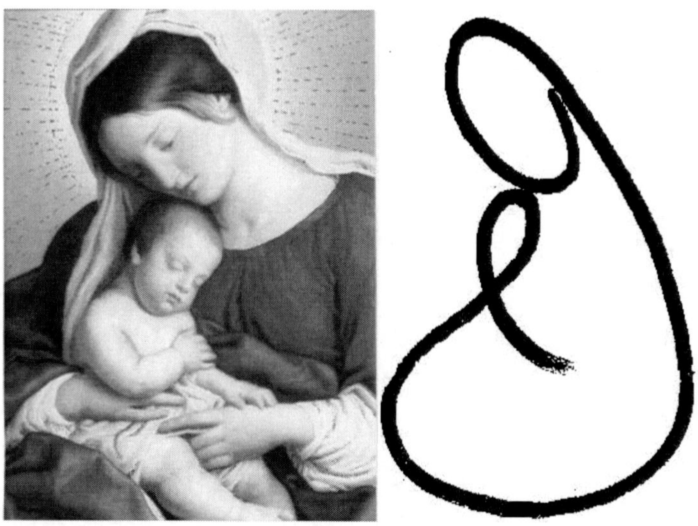

Figure 4. Graphical allegory of reality (left) and theory or definition (right). By permission of J.M. Morawski.

The drawing might well be enough to pray to, but if somebody were to examine, say, the shape of the child's nose, then the more detailed image becomes necessary. Similarly, in science, the scholar who discovers the "irrelevance" of a theory often triumphantly declares that s/he has "debunked the theory" because it turned out to be inadequate in solving the task at hand. In fact this testifies merely to that scholar's limited understanding of, say, the role of theory in science, or its advantages and limitations. In short, science is not a "Guinness Book of Records", but a continuous, never-ending story. It doesn't need "heroes", trampling over the corpses of representatives of "false" theories, but sages, who can learn even from those less clever than themselves. On the other hand, M. Heller, analyzing the profound nature of theory, remarked:

> *It is almost a regularity in the history of physics that the mathematical structure of a given theory becomes known in full only when this theory has already been replaced with a new one* (Heller 2011, 48).

However, following the old Roman principle *audiatur et altera pars*, it also seems worth quoting the following statement by cybernetician M. Mazur concerning the "functional face" of theory:

> *A systemic method, being of a theoretical nature, enables the discovery of each possibility according to uniform criteria. It thus has an advantage over empirical methodology, which – firstly – requires the arduous collection of details and – secondly – never gives certainty that all the relevant details have been taken into account* (Mazur 1987).

Even if the latter may be regarded as a slight overstatement, it nonetheless conveys fairly accurately the essence of the (desired) relationship between experiment and theory.

PHYSICS, BIOLOGY AND PSYCHOLOGY

Physicist and kinesiologist M.L. Latash wrote:

> *We live in very interesting times. A few previous centuries were those of physics. (...) If human beings want to survive as a species, the twenty-first century has to be the century of biology* (Latash 2008, v).

This formulation is in fact an elaboration of a statement by mathematician I.M. Gelfand (Latash, 2008, 56) expressing essentially the same idea. It thus seems rather seductive to think of physics as an "icebreaker" clearing the way for biology and psychology. Unfortunately, it will probably be unable to fulfil such a function. As physicist N. Bohr put it:

> *It is wrong to think that the task of physics is to find out how Nature is; physics concerns what we say about Nature.*

This idea points to the epistemological aspect of science. Accordingly, the language with which one "*says something about Nature*" is not a **passive** instrument for description, but the

active mechanism for shaping the image of the Nature in human mind. And the language of physics differs essentially from that of biology.

Appropriately, Bohr was physicist. For him, physics alone was (and is) the "main engine" of the whole of contemporary science. It is because it deals with relatively uncomplicated subject matter. J. Cohen and I.N. Stewart argued:

> *Physics takes a pragmatic and severely critical stance. It concentrates on simple, highly controlled systems; in return it expects impeccable agreement between experiment and theory (...). Physics deals with an invented, simplified world. This is how it derives its strength; this is why it works so well. (...) Sciences like biology are less fortunate* (Cohen and Stewart 2000, 12).

We might add: "*And, even more so, psychology"*.

Let us analyze this statement in more detail. Physics deals with short cause-effect chains, consisting of **stimulus** and **reaction**. They are coupled rather "stiffly", and their link is easily describable mathematically, even if in statistical or probabilistic terms.

In psychology, the cause-effect chain is longer. It consists of **stimulus** – **information**, which has to be identified and processed – and only then a **response**; no longer a straightforward reaction. In physics, the stimulus-reaction coupling is indifferent both to causes and effects. In psychology, somewhere in the background of the presented cause-effect chain resides intentionality. Unlike physical relations, this is not something that can be described mathematically (Domaciuk 2008).

In this respect it is useful to refer to D.R. Hofstadter, who sought to establish "*how it is that animate beings can come out of inanimate matter"* (Hofstadter 1999, P-2), i.e., how the Newtonian reaction to a physical stimulus became a biological sensorimotor response. The difference is that the physical reaction has no goal, whereas the biological response is always goal-orientated.

By way of illustration, let us recall a highly instructive fragment from "*Alice's adventures in Wonderland*", namely the scene where Alice talks to the Cheshire Cat. During the course of the conversation, the cat gradually vanishes, starting from his tail, until all that remains is his grin (Carroll 1982, 62). The question is whether or not the cat's smile is still a physical part of the animal. In other words, at what point do quantitative changes become qualitative ones? We face similar situations all the time in everyday life. For instance, when does an increase in the velocity of a car become acceleration? At what point do increments in speed transform into its **tendency** to change?

It is worth noting that Lewis Carroll was a mathematician by training, and the situation he depicts in fairy-tale form is in fact the basis of differential calculus. The problem is, when do **quantitative changes** convert into **qualitative transformation**? From this perspective one might assume that even the most primitive creatures are endowed with some kind of intellect, even if resembling the grin of the Cheshire Cat. Biologist L. Cuénot held that even the single cell disposes of a specific sort of intelligence (Goldsmith 2000). In the ML we are concerned with intramodal coherency inside a given level, and intermodal transformations (generally non-linear in nature) between particular levels. Such structure determines both the dynamics and economy of the system as a whole.

However, in analyses in the tradition of Bernstein we are dealing with the opposite situation. At a lower level, usually barely discernible, exists the elusive grin of the Cheshire Cat, and only at a higher one resides the whole animal.

The classic example in physics is the phenomenon of black body radiation. According to W. Heisenberg, this "*did not belong to the central parts of atomic physics*" (Heisenberg 2000, 3). However, this apparently marginal phenomenon transpired to be the "grin" of quantum physics in a Newtonian world. In motor control one is similarly dealing with such a "grin" at each of the borders between particular "rungs" of the ML. Thus, in physics there exists only one such border, between the quantum and Newtonian world, joined with the zone that obeys N. Bohr's correspondence principle. This principle states that the same laws are in force in the region of high energies in quantum physics and low energies in classical physics. According to physicist and philosopher M. Jammer:

> *There was rarely in the history of physics a comprehensive theory which owed so much to one principle as quantum mechanics owed to Bohr's correspondence principle* (Jammer 1966, 118).

Viewed through the ML perspective, there are four such "zones of correspondence" in the human psyche: between A-B, B-C, C-D, and D-E levels. This makes the subject matter of psychology much more complex than that of physics.

The simple physical reaction may therefore be interpreted as the "grin" of a much more complex biological response endowed with purposefulness. Thus, on the border between physics and biology we see the transformation of reaction, indifferent to future results, into goal-orientated response. Initially, the purposefulness is "hardwired" and the mechanism of its modification is natural selection. On the border between biology and psychology we encounter the even more mysterious transformation of purposefulness into consciousness. The latter is actively shaped by a cognizant living being. Broadly speaking, in animals, such intentional shaping of purposefulness – its limits delineated by range of anticipation – is confined to the "world of sensory experiences", whereas in humans anticipation expands into the realm of high abstraction, and, thanks to language, potentially becomes spatially and temporally unlimited.

To sum up, the physical, mechanical reactivity could be seen as a "grin" of biologically "hardwired" purposefulness, and the biological purposefulness as a "grin" of psychological intentionality based on intellectually active consciousness.

The Structural Aspect of Consciousness: Bernstein's Perspective

Before embarking on a detailed analysis of this issue, let us emphasize first of all that each and every conscious activity of any living creature may manifest itself in observable reality only through movement. As the philosopher A. Wohl argued: "*All that we dispose of, all that constitutes the resource of our culture, all the pieces of art, science and technology – all that results from motor activities*" (Wohl 1965, 5). In this respect, the physiology of activity – part of which is motor control – developed by the evolutionary neurophysiologist N.A. Bernstein, seems to be especially appropriate. Regarding consciousness, he wrote:

> *(...) for each human movement, whether complex or simple, full of deep meaning or feasible for any frog, consciousness obtains only information relevant to what is being managed by the leading level. This is how our consciousness is built. Its spotlight, as a rule, cannot illuminate more than one level at a time, although it is able to illuminate them successively* (Bernstein 1991, 220; 1996, 188).

In this formulation the following aspects should be emphasized:

1. "*Information*", i.e., an element of the knowledge already possessed by an individual.
2. "*Illumination*": it may be metaphorically associated with attention.
3. *"At a time"*: i.e., consciousness happens "*here and now*".
4. "*Leading level*": the systemic, multilevel structure of the management of movements in animals and humans; the leading level ("*chief*") needs focused attention, whereas the other levels – which make up the "*background*" – do not.

The sum of an individual's knowledge is vast. It may include, for example, ***information*** about the boiling of eggs, the solving of differential equations, the playing of Bach masterpieces etc. Thus, when applying one's existing knowledge to finding a solution to some or other particular task, in its entirety it would be completely inefficient. For it to become useful, it is necessary to reduce "active information" mentally to manageable dimensions. In Bernstein's theory this process is termed "*degrees of freedom reduction*" (Bernstein 1947, 17; 1991, 39; 1996, 29), akin in some ways to A. Clark's "*007 principle*" – i.e., "*to know only as much as you need to know to get the job done*" (Clark 1989, 64).

The necessary knowledge is ***illuminated*** through focused attention. This is a mechanism, shaped over the course of an individual's lifetime. Psychologist J.J. Gibson (1983, 51) termed this process the "*education of attention*". The attention enables the rapid "filtering" of new information and rejection of the knowledge useless at that particular moment.

"***At a time***" means that such filtering and illumination happen "here and now" to meet the immediate needs of the task at hand.

The term "***leading level***" pertains to Bernstein's theory, which he termed "***brain skyscraper***" (Bernstein 1991, 121; 1996, 99), and demands more detailed comment here. Analyzing the evolutionary development of sensory organs, the central nervous system, working organs, and consequently the motor potentialities of living creatures, Bernstein identified five levels of the "brain skyscraper" (BS):

A – rubro-spinal;
B – thalamo-pallidal;
C – half-cortical;
D – cortical;
E – cortical (Figure 5).

Bernstein assigned specific classes of motor operations to particular levels. For example, a motor habit is controlled by **leading** teleceptive C-level, and there the attention of the performer is focused, whereas the lower levels, engaged in the realization of the same motor operation – i.e., the contactceptive B-level and the proprioceptive A-level – work as a **background**, i.e., without concentration of precious attention.

In the West, Bernstein's name is most often associated with "Bernstein's problem", also known as the degrees of freedom problem. Bernstein himself, however, regarded the five-level structure of the construction of movements as the "central part" of his magnum opus "*O postroyenii dvizheniy*" ("*On construction of movements*") (Bernstein 1947, 5). Unfortunately, this concept did not feature in the first English publication of Bernstein's works (1967). It was presented in the book "*On dexterity and its development*", published in English only in 1996. Figure 5 depicts this five-level structure. (Bernstein himself never made such a diagram, despite being an excellent graphic designer).

The BS is in fact a neurophysiological structure based on evolutionary data. In itself, it is somewhat complicated, hence in everyday use one would come up against the graspability barrier. Detailed analysis of the neurophysiological phenomena and processes accompanying motor operations would be like a driver analyzing the combustion dynamics of an engine cylinder while driving a car – i.e., a substantial and completely useless endeavor. Thus, in order to make Bernstein's achievements more user-friendly and applicable, let us "distil" from the BS only the systemic structure of information-processing potentialities. In other words, let us leave aside the evolutionary and neurophysiological foundations and build the information processing "***modalities' ladder***" (ML), consistent with the systemic structure of its biological roots. The comparison of BS and ML has been presented in Table 1.

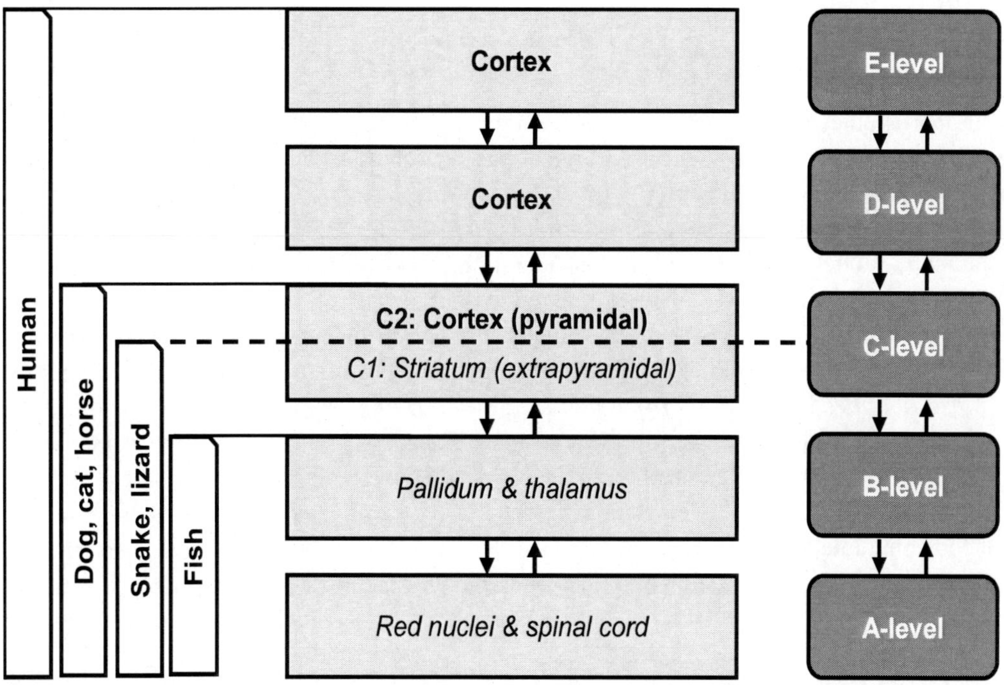

Figure 5. Evolutionary "brain skyscraper" by N.A. Bernstein (Petryński 2008, 166; Petryński 2014).

Table 1. The "brain skyscraper" and the "modalities' ladder"

<table>
<tr><th colspan="2">Brain skyscraper</th><th>Motor potentialities</th><th colspan="2">Modalities' ladder</th></tr>
<tr><td colspan="2">E
Topological motor representations</td><td>No motor operation, politics</td><td>E
Idea, symbols</td><td rowspan="6">A0 – Consciousness</td></tr>
<tr><td colspan="2">D
Geometrical motor representations</td><td>Performance, strategy</td><td>D
Program, words</td></tr>
<tr><td rowspan="4">A0 – Muscle tonus</td><td>C2
Net of muscle synergies, working organs, "fine motoricity"</td><td>Habit, tactics, dexterity</td><td rowspan="2">C
Scenario, teleception</td></tr>
<tr><td>C1
Net of muscle synergies, whole body, "gross motoricity"</td><td>Habit, tactics, agility</td></tr>
<tr><td>B
Two muscles' synergies</td><td>Automatism, technique</td><td>B
Template, contactception</td></tr>
<tr><td>A
Single muscle contraction</td><td>Reflex, strength control</td><td>A
Coupling, proprioception</td></tr>
</table>

Table 1 indicates that consciousness (A0) forms a basis for all the mental processes in the ML. It seems significant that sheer biological purposefulness should be positioned lower than A0 levels both in the BS and ML.

The ML inherits the general systemic order of the BS and the relations between phenomena and processes under consideration, but relieves those considerations of "neurophysiological ballast". This follows Einstein's way of thinking in physics. In his special theory of relativity Einstein eliminated the notion of ether (Einstein 1905; Hawking 1996, 30; Wróblewski 2006, 435). In the general theory of relativity, Einstein's *"giant step forward liberated gravitation from matter by describing it geometrically as space-time curvature"* (Wheeler and Tilson 1965, 11). Hence, he made physics more readily comprehensible and unveiled attributes of reality which were not visible from the perspective of classical physics. From Bernstein's perspective, we might say that Einstein's theories reduced some intellectual degrees of freedom. In a sense, Einstein changed the modalities of respective chunks of information and thus made the physical reasoning more "maneuverable". Here it is worth reiterating that the subject matter of physics is much less complex than that of psychology.

The specificity of the D and E level may be well illustrated with the following aphorism from Einstein: *"Time and space are modes by which we think and not conditions in which we live"*.

Analyzing both Figure 5 and Table 1 in more detail it becomes clear that the entire system of information processing levels may be divided into two parts: "sensory" (A, B and

C), and "mental" (D and E). Broadly speaking, the former are of reactive nature (stimuli-driven), and the latter of active nature (anticipation-driven). However, each of the levels has its own particular code of information processing, and consequently its own kind of consciousness.

The difference between B- and C-level processes was described by N.A. Bernstein as follows:

> *It is interesting to note that the reflex loop in primitive animals (...) works quite differently from how it functions in us. Consider a worm that crawls to an obstacle or a snail that reaches the tip of a grass blade. When there are complications of this kind, these animals start rather animated, aimless searching movements in all directions. In the more highly developed neokinetic animals, movements follow sensations; that is, movements are directed and controlled by sensations. In the lower animals the opposite is true; sensations are served and provided by movements* (Bernstein 1996, 75).

This fragment comes from an excellent English translation by M.L. Latash. However, it requires one small correction. In the original text, Bernstein used the formulation "*besporiadochnyje (...) ozhivlennyje oshchupyvaniya*" (Bernstein 1991, 94), which translates as "*orderless intensive groping*", not "*aimless searching movements*". From the system-theoretical perspective, the difference is significant. All biological actions, unlike physical reactions, are in some way or another goal-orientated, and not "*aimless*". This means that at each ML level there is an information processing with a specific code; this cannot be termed "*sub-consciousness*". However, the passage quoted above makes clear the difference between contactceptive and teleceptive modalities of information processing.

The multimodality of consciousness, as seen from the ML perspective, makes the notion of "sub consciousness" superfluous; in fact, one is dealing with the consciousness of various modalities, from the proprioceptive A, to the transcendental E.

Although the origin of the term "sub-consciousness" is often ascribed to S. Freud, he himself wrote:

> *I should also like to hear you admit that our designations* – unconscious, fore-conscious, *and* conscious *are much less likely to arouse prejudice, and are easier to justify than others that have been used or suggested – such as* sub-conscious, inter-conscious, between-conscious, etc. (Freud 1920, 257).

From a system-theoretical perspective (ML), the difference between the terms "sub-consciousness" and "fore-consciousness" is fundamental. The former concerns different modalities of consciousness, the latter the varying intensity of consciousness of the same modality.

We can illustrate the problem of multilevel (and multimodal) consciousness using R.A. Schmidt's gearshift analogy (Schmidt 1988, 477; Schmidt and Lee 2011, 451).

Shifting a gear, a novice performs seven separate operations:

1. Accelerator up.
2. Clutch down.

3. Shift lever forward.
4. Shift lever to the right.
5. Shift lever forward.
6. Clutch up.
7. Accelerator down.

With experience, the number of separate operations diminishes:

1. Accelerator up and clutch down.
2. Shift lever forward, to the right, and forward.
3. Clutch up and accelerator down.

Eventually, all of these movements "melt" into a single coherent, fluent operation.

From the ML perspective, all the operations listed by Schmidt should be placed at B-level. This relates to the change of control mode. At first, each of the component operations is performed separately and controlled in feedback mode, which requires attention engagement. However, with practice the particular sub-operations become "automated"; that is, their efficiency improves to a level such that it becomes possible to control them in the feedforward mode, which does not require attention focusing. They gain a level of reliability such that their conscious control becomes unnecessary. In this situation one may therefore interpret the whole process as a change in control mode rather than a shift from the field of consciousness to that of "sub-consciousness"; on this view, the term "sub-consciousness" becomes superfluous.

Similar process may also include several different ML levels. For example, the driver of a car knows (verbal D-level) that around the bend is a hill, so, s/he decides to change to a lower gear in advance. Approaching the curve, which is controlled visually (teleceptive C-level), s/he has to operate the accelerator and clutch pedals with his/her feet and the gearstick by hand (contactceptive B-level). The particular sub-operations have to have been mastered previously to such a degree that the D-level performance will "tow" the C-level habit, the B-level automatisms, and A-level reflexes belonging to it without the engagement of precious attention. So, sticking with Bernstein's metaphor, only the D-level (chief) is fully illuminated with a spotlight, whereas the lower levels (background) are enveloped in twilight, or even, ideally, complete darkness. Moreover, the higher levels – slower and more "intellectually expensive" – are not activated. Such organization determines both the effectiveness and economy of the motor operation being performed. It should be stressed that in this perspective our concern is with chief and background, not with consciousness and "sub-consciousness". In short, those operations that need attention focusing (controlled in feedback mode) are often termed "conscious", and those executed without attention engagement (controlled in feedforward mode) "sub-conscious". However, the ML perspective seems to have a greater level of "explanatory power" than dividing an individual's knowledge into "conscious" and "sub-conscious".

It is worth noting that the term "automated" appears above in inverted commas. The reason for this is that, while in technology the term "automation" means strict control in feedback mode with specific, sometimes highly sophisticated measuring devices, in psychology the same term means "loss" of control, i.e., transition from attention-consuming feedback to an attention-less feedforward mode of control.

The active "pushing" of undesirable knowledge toward the sphere of "twilight", or even complete "darkness", was described by Freud as "*repression*" (Freud 1920, 255; Gerrig 2013, 365).

Aside from consciousness, the lowest possible ML level capable of dealing successfully with a given task, the other way of achieving higher economy is by using the "cheapest" method of conclusion: induction. This may be exemplified in the following words by racing driver B. Collins (the mysterious Stig in the BBC program "Top Gear"):

> ***What defines a good driver? What attribute is necessary, and what merely useful?***
>
> *Anticipation. The racing driver is a person, who does not look for solutions to the problems that occur in a race. He/she knows those solutions, and when the situation comes, when the reaction becomes necessary, he/she simply performs the operations conducive to its successful resolution* (Jakóbczyk 2011).

Comparing this with Figure 2, one might imagine that, with increasing experience, the "abduction-deduction roof" in a given class of operations becomes flatter and flatter, with abduction and deduction gradually coming to an end and induction taking over. In general, this certainly makes the entire motor operation more efficient, but at the same time more resistant to any modifications (which require abduction) and susceptible to, for example, feints in sport.

CONSCIOUSNESS: FUNCTIONAL ASPECTS AND SEQUENCE OF CRUCIAL EVENTS IN HUMAN MOTOR BEHAVIOR

As already stated, the only observable manifestation of any mental process is **movement**. It seems useful therefore to follow the phenomena underlying the production of the "blueprint" of a motor response to extrinsic stimuli. Here the analogy with technology, much simpler than psychology, seems instructive.

"Naked" physical phenomena are not comprehensible to the CNS. Only those able to excite the sensory organs may be termed "stimuli" (Salomon 2005, 1). After reception of a stimulus the sensory organ produces the sensory input, i.e., a series of electrical neural impulses which are "understandable" to the CNS. This is the task for **sensitivity**, which may be likened to the **transducer** in technology.

The sensory input is then joined to information stored in memory. This constitutes the essence of **perception**, a technical "counterpart" of **detection**. The information is discrete in nature, i.e., it is made up of "chunks". The process of perception, especially in humans, may be activated either by an extrinsic stimulus, or by intrinsic memory trace (engram). The former underlies reactive behavior, and the latter active behavior, based on anticipation.

Perception may evoke extensive information of various modalities, which as a whole would be useless for an individual who has to construct a "blueprint" of the motor response. Hence, according to Bernstein's principle of freedom degrees' reduction, or Clark's "*007 principle*", the **attention** has to build a hierarchy of information. In technology, an analogous role is that of a **filter**. As a result, the most important information chunks will be transferred to the next stages of processing, and the unimportant ones eliminated.

In his seminal paper "The Magical Number Seven, Plus or Minus Two" (1956), G.A. Miller determined the maximum number of information chunks that the human mind is capable of processing simultaneously. The concrete number 7±2 he took from thin air, and, concluding his paper, he wrote: "*In fact, I feel that my story here must stop just as it begins to get really interesting*". It is worth noting that Bernstein, independently of Miller and nearly ten years earlier, had taken as a "starting point" for reasoning the assumption that the human mind may process only a limited number of information chunks. The reasoning of the two writers subsequently went in opposite directions however, with Miller concerned with how *many* information chunks human mind is able to process, and Bernstein with how *few* are necessary to solve a given task. The latter is consistent with Clark's "*007 principle*", and it seems correct, given that nature does not break records, but solves tasks as economically as possible.

Taking up Bernstein's spotlight analogy, if, at the stage of stimuli reception (sensitivity), one is in complete darkness, perception may be likened to the dawn. The next stage, attention, illuminates the most relevant information, shifts the less relevant into the shadows, and the irrelevant to complete darkness. Then, after passing through **motivation** (**input amplifier**), the **intellect** (**processor**) takes over and consciousness starts to work as a background.

The processor produces the blueprint of future motor operation, and **foresight** (**output filter**) assesses its quality. If it is judged to be good enough, the **decision** (**output discriminator and amplifier**) initiates the process of realization. At that stage, the **skills** (**controllers**) take over. Here again, romantic verses by P.B. Shelley appear illustrative:

> *The skill which wields the elements, the thought*
> *Which pierces this dim universe like light* (Shelley 1906, 65).

The final "internal link" in the sequence of critical events is the **efferent copies** creation (**recorder**). These enable one to discern the external effects of one's own operations and phenomena independent thereof, as well as creating "frames of reference" for possible improvements to similar motor operations in the future. The latter therefore constitutes a crucial sub-process of the process of learning.

Thereafter the appropriate sequences of motor commands are sent to particular **muscles** (**actuator**) and the final motor operation is realized (Figure 6).

Note that the diagram in Figure 6 concerns reactive behavior, i.e., receiving a reaction-producing stimulus from an environment – let's call it a "*releaser*" (Kurcz 1995, 103; Colman 2009, 864) – and only then reacting to that stimulus.

Over the course of evolution, speed has been one of the main factors determining the survival potentialities of living creatures. In an ideal case – impossible in reality due to the laws of physics – the reaction might be simultaneous with the releaser. However, in higher developed creatures there is a mechanism which enables the seemingly impossible process of reacting to a releaser even before its reception. As already stated, the process of response creation may be activated either by a real stimulus, or by its abstract representation, i.e., the memory trace (engram). Hence, in the process of anticipation the engram is activated prior to reception of a stimulus. This underlies the production of a prediction, which controls the behavior of an individual even without extrinsic stimulus.

The term "predictability", incidentally, may denote either the potential for reality to be reliably predicted (The Free Dictionary 2015), or the ability of an individual to produce reliable predictions (Cambridge Dictionary 2015).

Anticipation and predictability have turned out to be the most powerful "weapons" in the evolutionary struggle for life, and it is our possession of these abilities that has made the human being the most dangerous predator in the world.

Figure 6 shows the functional aspects of consciousness – the information processing mechanism – in the control of human behavior. It is worth noting that each element of the mechanism may include information regarding each modality from the ML. Moreover, returning to Lewis Carroll's metaphor of the Cheshire Cat we might say that each of the lower modalities is a specific "grin" of the higher one, deprived of important attributes of the latter. For example, the C-level modality includes "three-and-fraction" dimensionality (three Euclidean dimensions and short fragment of time axis, including only timing), whereas the D-level modality has full four-dimensional modality (three Euclidean dimensions and full time axis).

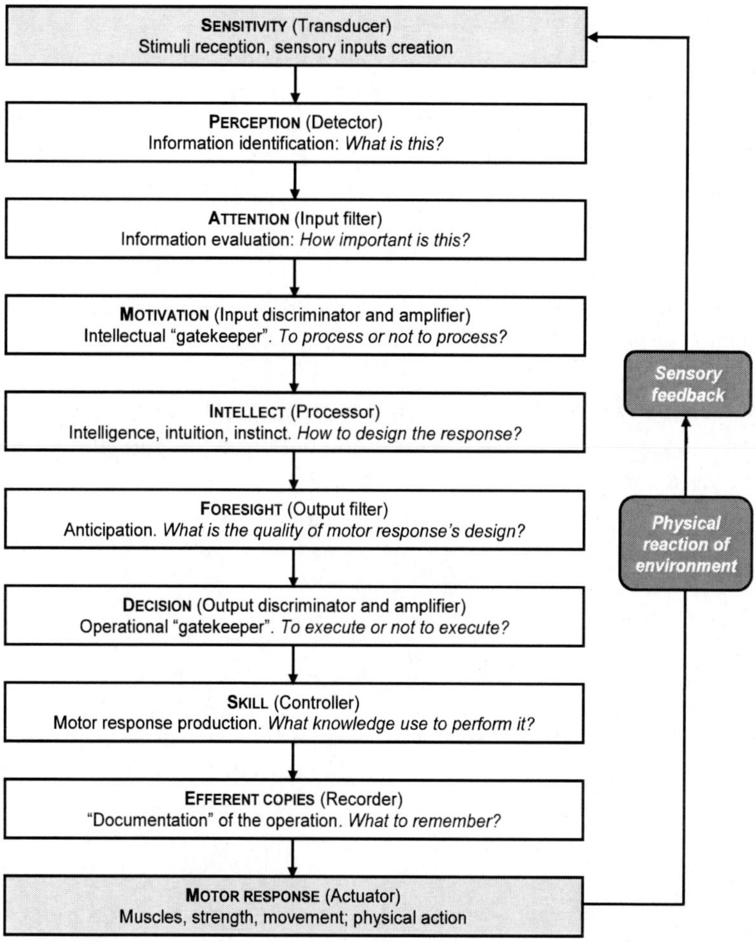

Figure 6. The critical events in a mental-motor operation in humans. White blocks symbolize the abstract mind (psychology), light gray blocks physiology (mind-environment interface), and dark gray ones the observable environment (physics).

The ML includes a specific trade-off: the lower level, the poorer information processing potentialities but at the same time more specific information, higher speed and resistivity to possible disturbances. This trade-off is necessary for self-preservation in the case of emergency.

For example, even while unconscious the human being breathes and his/her heart beats. Analyzed from the ML perspective, the phenomenon of the various levels of resistivity of the information processing system, based on consciousness (Table 1), at various levels of the modalities' ladder may be exemplified by the boxer's knock-out (Wasik 1991). When, after a severe knock-out – heavy concussion – the boxer has his "lights punched out", the referee counts. At "six" the boxer opens his eyes; at first comes A0-level basic consciousness (ML) and muscle tonus (BS); next comes A-level proprioception and capacity for strength production. Then come B-level contactception and harmony of movements, and thereafter C-level teleception, basic orientation in space and time, along with returning agility and dexterity. He is able, for example, to count how many fingers referee is holding up. Apparently able to fight again, the boxer takes up his fighting position, moves his hands and legs, and identifies his opponent, the referee, and the boundaries of the ring. However, an experienced coach is able to discern that things may not be quite right. D-level abilities – foresight and strategic planning – as well as E-level fantasy and invention are absent. The boxer primarily performs routine actions according to typical patterns learned in training. It is unlikely that in such a condition he would be able to solve a differential equation, or explain in detail the Kantian notion of transcendence.

To sum up, in analyzing the motor aspects of consciousness one might formulate the following take-home messages:

- According to Bernstein's theory, the whole information processing system – a basic component of which is consciousness – constitutes one coherent, yet not uniform (multimodal) system;
- There are only two "input gates" to the system from the environment (contactceptive B-level and teleceptive C-level "gate"), and only one "output gate", at A-level;
- Accordingly, movement is the only observable phenomenon which enables inference as to the inner workings of a human being's psyche, including the nature of consciousness, self and soul.

CONSCIOUSNESS, SELF AND SOUL

As physicists A. Sokal and J. Bricmont quite rightly point out, "*it's a good idea to know what one is talking about*" (Sokal and Bricmont 1998, 185). Essentially, this forms the basis of science as a whole. Hence, while considering the issue of consciousness, it seems to be instructive to keep in mind the following statement by philosopher W. James:

> *"Consciousness" is supposed necessary to explain the fact that things not only are, but get reported, are known* (James 1904).

In this statement the two elements should be emphasized:

- "*Things are*" – this may be connected to sensitivity, i.e., reception of extrinsic stimuli;
- "*Are known*" – this means that in the mind of observer arises an abstract representation of a given thing.

Neuroscientist A. Damasio described the notion of consciousness as follows:

> *In conclusion, in its standard form, consciousness is a state of mind that occurs when we are awake and in which there is private and personal knowledge of our own existence, situated relative to whatever its surround may be at a given moment. Of necessity, conscious states of mind handle knowledge based on different sensory material – bodily, visual, auditory, and so forth – and manifest varied qualitative properties for the different sensory streams. Conscious states of mind are* **felt** (Damasio 2010, 158).

In this statement the following formulations deserve special emphasis:

- *Consciousness is a* ***state*** *of mind,*
- *At a* ***given moment,***
- *Conscious states of mind handle* ***knowledge,***
- *Different* ***sensory material*** *– bodily, visual, auditory, and so forth,*
- *Conscious states of mind are* **felt.**

The last of these requires a comment. What does "*felt*" mean? Let us reformulate this question from the system-theoretical perspective: What information may be described with the term "*to feel*", and in what code? We might find the answer to this question in the same citation from Damasio, in the words "*different sensory material*". In the ML this sensory material evokes from memory specific information which may be assigned to particular rungs, and its processing in the intellect occurs analogously at all levels of the ladder. Of course, the characteristics of such processing depend on the modality specific to a given rung. The chunks of information which cannot be described verbally may be joined with the so called *qualia*, i.e., *"an unfamiliar term for something that could not be more familiar to each of us: the* ***ways things seem to us****"* (Dennett 1993, 381). For example, it is not possible to explain verbally (D-level) how to keep one's balance while cycling (B-level); the latter has to be "felt", i.e., in the case of cycling, built of B-level chunks of information.

Consciousness is not a "solitary island", but rather an important component of the system we might call the "human psyche". Accordingly, the presented concepts of consciousness open a specific perspective to two other important notions: **self** and **soul**. These are highly abstract notions – in systems theory terms, system effects – so it is not possible to base their definitions on any phenomena observable in reality. As a result, their definitions must be of a solely conceptual nature, not derivable from any experimental data. In the terms delineated in Figure 1, they reside in the Ocean of Philosophy rather than the Forest of Science – *however* *strongly the intuition of experimenters resists admitting it*, to paraphrase R. Dawkins (2009, 15).

Consciousness acts in the "here and now" and may be regarded as a current, active manifestation of the **self**: as Damasio writes: "*Consciousness is a state of mind with a self process added to it"* (Damasio 2010, 157). Here, there are two words which are of special significance: "*state*" in relation to "*consciousness*", and "*process*" in relation to "*self*".

The latter is virtually static when seen from the perspective of consciousness. It undergoes transformations, certainly, but these transformations occur somewhat slowly. This is why Damasio termed it "*process*". However, it is stable enough to create a "frame of reference" for consciousness, which occurs "here and now". Hence, in mathematical terms we might describe consciousness as a first time derivative of the self. The two things are related to each other, but at the same time they differ qualitatively.

The self is not determined in the here and now by an environment, hence a human, endowed with free will – residing in the Cartesian *res cogitans* – is able actively to shape it. The mechanism enabling it may be identified as the **soul**.

To sum up, from the system-theoretical perspective we might liken the process of **self**, as defined by Damasio, to a movie, being in state of continuous production, **consciousness** to the image projected onto the screen, and the **soul** to the director, actively molding the future shape of the movie, which in our metaphor symbolizes the self. The self and soul make the individual's inner world, while consciousness bridges the gap between the inner and outer worlds.

The descriptions presented above cannot be regarded as definitions, so let us formulate the following definitions:

> ***Consciousness*** – a dynamically changing component of a quasi-static whole; the multimodal knowledge of an individual, activated at given moment by perception directed by attention, aimed at dealing with a task at hand.
>
> ***Self*** – an individual's relatively stable awareness of their physical (geometrical and temporal) and social place, their role in surrounding world, and their will and potentials to influence it.
>
> ***Soul*** – an active mechanism for shaping one's own self.

These definitions are derived from Bernstein's theory, based on mechanisms originally "designed" by nature for the management of movements (Allott 1991). Hence, the ML makes one coherent, though not uniform, system.

It seems instructive here to point to the flexible nature of a system. This may be observed from various intellectual perspectives (Figure 3). The real function of consciousness, and therefore its abstract meaning and definition, depends on the situation at hand and the considerations it engenders. Accordingly, in addition to analysis of the "*consciousness-self-soul*" combination, it is possible to conceive of, say, "*consciousness-learning-new skill*", or "*consciousness-skill-motor operation*" systems.

Consciousness and Intellect from a System-Theoretical Perspective

The presented definition of consciousness may be an appropriate representation of its nature, but it creates only a basis for its functions.

From a system-theoretical perspective, the knowledge "illuminated" by attention and which creates consciousness corresponds roughly to the task at hand. This is consistent with what J.J. Gibson termed the "*education of attention*" (Gibson 1983, 51) and testifies to the fact that particular critical events in human mental-motor operations make up a system, with the elements of the cause-effect chain **mutually** connected to one another.

However, such "illuminated knowledge" is not sufficiently ordered as to enable the production of an effective internal "blueprint" for the motor operation, being merely a response to the current environmental challenge. Production of such a blueprint is the task of intellect. The system-theoretical reasoning strategy may be employed also for "illumination" of the mechanisms of the intellect.

A tacit assumption underlying the design of Table 1 is that consciousness is a basis for intellect. From the system-theoretical perspective, and including the idea of the Cheshire Cat's grin, we can conceive of the concept of **intellect** as comprising three instruments: **intelligence**, **instinct** and **intuition**. Let us formulate the following definition:

> ***Intellect*** *– an internal system of a living being that enables the processing of current information, shaped by attention, usually in order to work out the behavior pattern aimed at bringing about the desirable changes in an environment in the future.*

First of all let us remember that the only visible manifestation of any psychological processes in living beings is movement. Consequently, only while observing motor behavior is it possible to infer what is happening in the mind at a given moment. Unfortunately, the observable behavior is the system effect, hence it is impossible to distinguish which "part" of the behavior might be assigned to intelligence, which to instinct, and which to intuition. We might think of it like a situation where a researcher observes a moving car and attempts to ascertain the details of the action of the exhaust valve in the third cylinder. The notions of intelligence, instinct and intuition – much more complex than any technological issue – thus have to be defined arbitrarily.

The suggested reasoning begins from premises based not on "hard facts" (Figure 2), but on hypothetical assumptions. It seems that in the contemporary science as a whole the "explanatory power" of research based solely on cold empirical facts has been to large extent exhausted. While such research might ostensibly seem reasonable, in physics, it was M. Planck's *assumption*, and not observable *fact* – at that time undetectable – that resulted in the creation of quantum physics. On this view, in psychology "empirical facts" may turn out to be less a "source of life" than intellectual fetters. On the journey up the abduction slope, already-existing theories form the premises for a new abduction path, leading to more abstract theory. Ascending the abduction slope of the IAD triangle, science therefore enters more and more intellectually unstable ground, paved with theories increasingly distant from safe, obvious, reasonable "facts". However, it seems increasingly evident that psychology is more in need of intellectual daredevils and daydreamers, with their heads in the clouds, than sober, methodological researchers with their noses to the ground.

Of the three listed mechanisms of intellect, probably the most basic and simple is intelligence. At the same time, intelligence constitutes the "armed forces" of the intellect, as it ultimately creates the internal pattern re-forged thereafter into physical operations, observable in an environment. Both instinct and intuition are "hidden" more deeply in the individual's psyche.

Scientists as far back as C. Darwin (Darwin 1881, 97), H.S. Jennings (Jennings 1906, 334), and E. Heron-Allen (Heron-Allen 1915) reported intelligence in animals: worms (Darwin), *Protozoa* (Jennings), and *Foraminifera* (Heron-Allen). The physicist R.P. Feynman also observed – just for fun – the behavior of *Paramecium*, which might be termed "intelligent" (Feynman 1997, 91). As noted earlier, biologist L. Cuénot went further still, claiming that even a single cell in a multicellular organism disposes of a specific sort of intelligence (Goldsmith 2000). Accordingly, we may formulate the following definition:

> ***Intelligence** – the potentiality of a living being for building a reliable motor response with all necessary current information of the proper modality or modalities, and using logic appropriate to that information.*

In this definition, the term "logic" is used. This should not be confused with the term "intelligence". The former merely verifies the correctness of the connections between the links in particular cause-effect chain, whereas the latter is aimed at the creation of a useful solution to a current task. By way of illustration we might note the words of N. Bohr, who, in reference to A. Einstein, very aptly stated: "*You are not thinking. You are merely being logical".*

In a sense then, intelligence is an entirely internal mechanism. Instinct, on the other hand, may be regarded as a primeval instrument connecting intelligence to external reality. Hence, it controls the behavior of a living being in its environment using internal, "hardwired" patterns of behavior, of both species' and individuals' nature. The former is termed "*closed instinct*", the latter "*open instinct*" (Midgley 1973; Sadowski 2007, 383). It may be defined as follows:

> ***Instinct** – inborn (closed) or acquired (open) well established tendency to look for information necessary for solving a given task, in specific directions, where probability of its finding such information is greatest, or propensity for choosing by intelligence the definite methods of developing of response likely to produce desired results (Petryński 2007; Petryński 2011).*

Instinct, by definition, is relatively stable, rigid even, and may therefore be highly effective in everyday situations. However, it is unable to deal successfully with situations where flexible information processing is needed. In such situations, probably the most developed information processing tool is necessary, i.e., intuition. Intuition may be defined as follows:

> ***Intuition** – a potentiality of a living being for guessing the lacking information necessary for employment of intelligence* (Petryński 2007; Petryński 2011).

The significance of intuition, especially in scientific work, may be well illustrated with the following words by J.D. Norton:

> *(...) Einstein had quite particular strengths. They lay in an acute physical intuition that guided him to the fertile physical ideas and revealing experimental results. As long as Einstein used those particular skills to drive his work, he produced one great success after another. He was the right thinker, with the right abilities, in the right place and time.* ***Then Einstein changed his thinking. He was no longer guided so much by physical intuition as by mathematical simplicity. As that change set in, Einstein's work began to languish*** (my emphasis – WP) (Norton 2007).

Note that while intelligence works in the "here and now", instinct works in the temporal frames limited by earlier experience, and intuition in unlimited spatial-temporal space, in the region of fantasy even, completely free from real physical constraints. In lower organisms, intelligence and instinct may therefore be more or less clearly observed, whereas intuition resembles the grin of the Cheshire Cat. Nevertheless, only the system-theoretical philosophy that includes the mental structure of such a grin is conducive to the creation of a coherent, albeit not uniform, model of information processing in humans, from a simple patellar reflex (A-level) to the creation of general theory of relativity (E-level).

It is worth noting that has been described above as the philosophy of the Cheshire Cat's grin is equivalent to the mathematical reasoning of I. Newton and G.W. von Leibniz, with a quantity which approaches zero. It forms the basis of differential calculus.

CONCLUSION

Contemporary research technology makes empirical methodology productive, yet hardly fertile. As B.K. Forscher (Forscher 1963) argued, the mass production of "*new, original experimental data*", that which is light, easy and fashionable in contemporary science, has dominated the domain of scientific theory creation. Already in 1947 Bernstein argued:

> *The overflowing stream of new information in all the branches of natural science (...) teaches them* (scientists) *not to see the forest behind the trees even in their narrow area; emasculates creative thinking, impoverishes their work with respect to fresh ideas and wide perspectives* (Bernstein 1991, 13; 1996, 5).

In the terms of systems theory, this inability to see the wood for the trees leads to the elimination of the crucial phenomenon in science creation: the system effect.

Another threat to science lies in the application of methodology that has proven successful in other disciplines, but which may not be optimally suited to one's own. This practice may sometimes even be seen simply as vacuous mimicry, and may lead to deviation toward what R.P. Feynman termed "*cargo cult science*". Feynman described this as follows:

> *In the South Seas there is a cargo cult of people. During the war they saw airplanes land with lots of good materials, and they want the same thing to happen now. So they've arranged to make things like runways, to put fires along the sides of the runways, to make a wooden hut for a man to sit in, with two wooden pieces on his head like headphones and bars of bamboo*

sticking out like antennas – he's the controller – and they wait for the airplanes to land. They're doing everything right. The form is perfect. It looks exactly the way it looked before. But it doesn't work. No airplanes land. So I call these things cargo cult science, because they follow all the apparent precepts and forms of scientific investigation, but they're missing something essential, because the planes don't land (Feynman 1997, 340).

One aspect of such "*cargo cult science*" is the expectation of immediate usefulness of scientific discoveries and achievements. In this respect the following quotation from mathematician I. Stewart may be illustrative:

Mitchell Feigenbaum is a physicist. In the early 1970s he was working at the Los Alamos Laboratory. Some of his colleagues would have objected to that word – working – because nobody knew quite what it was that Feigenbaum was working on. Including Feigenbaum himself (Stewart 2002, 184).

Feigenbaum is one of the founders of contemporary chaos theory. So, science needs patience and very careful assessment of new ideas. In this respect it is worth remembering that Einstein presented his general theory of relativity in 1915, but only in 1919 did A. Eddington observe phenomena coherent with Einstein's theory (Wróblewski 2007, 562). In the 1960s P. Higgs invented a conceptual Higgs' boson (Wróblewski 2007, 528), which was only found nearly half a century later (O'Luanaigh 2013), resulting in his being awarded the Nobel Prize. Recently the gravitational waves have been detected which A. Einstein predicted a century earlier (Abbott et al. 2016). Let us emphasize, yet again, that the subject matter of psychology is much more complicated than that of physics. In psychology some ideas, crazy at first glance, may therefore require a much longer "incubation" period than those in physics. This is why there is room in psychology for daydreamers and visionaries to be allowed to elaborate their ideas without expecting results immediately applicable in practice. Even if only one in every thousand turns out to be right, the profits may be abundant.

The various shadows model shown in Figure 3 may be regarded as a consequence of the epistemological nature of science. This notion was expressed by psychokinesiologist R.A. Schmidt, who argued that "*since laws are the product of human creativity, different laws can be formulated by two different individuals who are examining the same observations. Laws do not automatically spring forth from the facts*" (Schmidt 1988, 29). The same idea is articulated in a more concise way by the fictional character Woland, the devil's prince, who stated that "*one theory is as good as another"* (Bulgakov 2008, 285).

The statement by cybernetician M. Mazur, that "*the mechanism of the psyche, as being inaccessible for observation, remains beyond the field of psychology"* (Mazur 1999, 43), seems very apt. The establishment of the first psychological laboratory in 1879 in Leipzig by psychologist W. Wundt (Gerrig 2013, 6) enabled carrying out observations, but in psychology their "explanatory power" – because of much higher "abduction roof" (Figure 2) – is by far smaller than that in physics. As a result, the elusive "*inference to the best explanation*" (Harman 1965), which might be identified with ascending up the abduction slope, is in psychology by far more significant than that in physics. Moreover, according to to mathematician R. Thom:

Since 17th century modern science has been possible only to the extent that theoretical progress overtakes the experiment. Great achievements we owe no more to discovery of new

> *facts, but they appear rather as new ways of thinking or interpretations of already known facts* (Sorman 1993, 61).

In psychology then, sticking too closely to "*new, original experimental data*" does not support genuine progress, but rather creates a barrier to it, sort of "cement shoes" for the key mechanism crucial for science production: interpretation. Moreover, the psychological response includes intentionality and the physical reaction does not (Domaciuk 2008); only the latter is describable mathematically. So, in physics mathematics makes useful and user-friendly language of description, whereas "*the sciences like biology are less fortunate*". They have to turn to "*careful inference*", believing that it "*can be more reliable than actual* observation". The mechanism termed by G.H. Harman "*inference to the best explanation*" (Harman 1965), using both metaphors and bluffs, is in fact the only method of science creation. Such inference, unimpeded by rigid mathematical formalism, is sometimes necessary even in physics. As the great physicist N. Bohr stated:

> *We must be clear that when it comes to atoms, language can be used only as in poetry. The poet, too, is not nearly so concerned with describing facts as with creating images and establishing mental connections* (Pranger 1972, 12).

Hence, even in physics there are direct and obvious relations neither between facts and theory, nor between theory and applications. Consequently, even physics experiments may make only a basis, and not the essence of the scientific image of reality; as already stated, the facts have to die to make room for theory. Even in physics certain phenomena and processes can be described not with the language of mathematics, but with the language of poetry, and this is the case to a perhaps even greater degree in psychology. Already in the 18th century Kant stated that "*general truths (...) must be independent of experience – clear and certain by themselves*" (Kant 1922, 1). More recently, the physicist A. Staruszkiewicz argued that the "*mathematical theorems are valid on the strength of proof, and not by observations*" (Staruszkiewicz 2001). M. Mazur argued:

> *In theory nothing may be justified with empirical knowledge. The theory in which even one evidential link is taken from empirical knowledge (e.g., because in all known cases it was observed) is no theory at all* (Mazur 1999, 43).

Experimental researches may unveil only a specific aspect of reality. Here, the words of writer and futurologist A. Toffler have an ominous resonance:

> *One of the most highly developed skills in contemporary Western civilization is dissection: the split-up of problems into their smallest possible components. We are good at it. So good, we often forget to put the pieces back together again* (Prigogine and Stengers 1984, xi).

Similarly, philosopher K.R. Popper stated:

> *...universities, completely foolishly, have fragmented knowledge into different, specialized branches; each of them, without any necessity, has been closed into its own ritual and terminology* (Sorman 1993, 343).

Psychologist J.T. Cacioppo argued:

> *Contemporary psychological scientists stand on the shoulders of those who went before. From this perch it is now possible to see that the bounded fields of the 20th century are related parts of the same landscape. This is a requisite step for bringing research on pieces of related problems together to address bigger questions and to develop more comprehensive scientific theories* (Cacioppo 2008).

From a system-theoretical perspective, such a fragmentation leads to the loss of the most elusive, yet most precious and fertile product of science, and of human genius as a whole: the intellectual **system effect**. This effect alone is what enables any progress in science, or even the very existence of science.

In psychology, intuition (theoretical and philosophical) and multidisciplinary approaches are thus much more important than empirical research. With the lack of direct connections between items being the point of interest of psychology, the equivalent of "hard and tangible" empirical data in physics, it is philosophy rather than mathematics that seems to be the most important "signpost" on the abduction slope to psychological theory. However, in psychology the IAD triangle is considerably higher than that in physics. In other words, psychological theories have to be much more abstract.

Nevertheless, though the methodology of physics is hardly applicable in psychology, the achievements of the former may be highly instructive for the latter. Nature has a systemic structure, and all of the various branches and disciplines of science are rooted in, and in one way or another inherit at least some characteristics of this structure. In the early years of the 20th century, physician, economist and philosopher A.A. Bogdanov had already founded the general science of organization, which he termed "*tektology*". Today this may be identified, broadly speaking, with systems theory. Bogdanov wrote:

> *Moreover, the quantitative relations I perceive as a specific kind of structural ones, and mathematics itself – as an earlier developed, because of other reasons, branch of general science on organization. This is why it has such gigantic power as a tool for life organization* (Bogdanov 1989, 9).

Hence, in physics, the common systemic nature of science is "mathematizable", because this discipline deals with relatively straightforward subject matter. It may therefore unveil such mechanisms, which are in force also in psychology, but considerably more difficult to uncover there. While the methodology of physics is hardly applicable in psychology, the achievements of physics may nevertheless be highly instructive for psychologists if they are applied rationally, and not simply aped.

In order that genuine progress be made, the abandonment of sober, safe "common knowledge" is necessary even in physics. Hence, N. Bohr said to W. Pauli (both were physicists, Nobel laureates):

> *We are all agreed that your theory is crazy. The question which divides us is whether it is crazy enough to have a chance of being correct. My own feeling is that it is not crazy enough* (Dyson 1958).

I cannot help the feeling that such a craziness is nowadays needed much more in psychology than in physics. Unfortunately, as mathematician R. Thom remarked:

> *Biologists are happy with simple recording of facts, because they are not able to grasp them. They collect information without understanding it and they cannot develop a coherent image of mechanisms they discover. Their knowledge has become a* cemetery of facts, *not liable to any synthesis. And this is because the biologists are fascinated like children with their observation devices. They neglect to think. Biology does not think, so it does not make any progress. Where there is no theoretical reflection, knowledge is merely a collection of archive records* (Sorman 1993, 60).

We might sense some maliciousness here on the part of the proud representative of the (alleged) "Queen of Sciences", but nevertheless, such an idea cannot be absolutely denied.

To sum up, experiments produce data, but not theories, which are the very essence of science. Psychology is therefore not a job for scientists with their noses in computers; there is a need more for thinkers than researchers. The issue of consciousness testifies very clearly to that. Sadly I have not heard of any new, inspiring papers by contemporary equivalents of the likes of W. James, C.S. Peirce, or N.A. Bernstein…

ACKNOWLEDGMENT

I would like to express my sincere thanks to the Authorities of my home university, Katowice School of Economics, Katowice, Poland, with Rector, Professor Krzysztof Szaflarski, for supporting me in my efforts to publish this work.

REFERENCES

Abbott, Benjamin P. et al. 2016. Observation of gravitational waves from a binary black hole merger. *Physical Review Letters* 116, 061102 (2016). doi: 10.1103/physRevLett. 116.061102.

Allott, Robin. 1991. The motor theory of language. In *Studies in language origins, 2*, edited by Walburga von Raffler-Engel, Jan Wind and Abraham Jonker, 12357. Amsterdam/Philadelphia: John Benjamins Publishing Company.

Anokhin, Piotr K. 1973. Principialnyje voprosy obscey teorii funkcionalnykh sistem (The basic problems of general theory of functional systems). In *Principy sistemnoy organizacii funkciy,* 561, Moscow: Nauka (in Russian).

Bachelard, Gaston. 2002. *The formation of the scientific mind.* Manchester: Clinamen.

Bernstein, Nikolai A. 1947. *O postroyenii dvizheniy* (*On the construction of movements*). Moscow: Medgiz (in Russian).

Bernstein, Nikolai A. 1967. *The co-ordination and regulation of movements*. Oxford: Pergamon Press.

Bernstein, Nikolai A. 1991. *O lovkosti i yeyo razvitii* (*On dexterity and its development*). Moscow: Fizkultura i sport (in Russian).

Bernstein, Nikolai A. 1996. On dexterity and its development. In *Dexterity and its development*, edited by Mark L. Latash and Michael T. Turvey, 1244, Mahwah, NJ: Lawrence Erlbaum Associates.

Bogdanov, Aleksandr A. 1989. *Tektologiya – vseobscaya organizacionnaya nauka* (*Tektology – the general science on organization*). Moscow: Ekonomika (in Russian).

Box, George E.P. and Norman R. Draper. 1987. *Empirical model-building and response surfaces*. Hoboken, NJ: John Wiley and Sons.

Bulgakov, Mikhail A. 2008. *The Master and Margarita*. Accessed November 11, 2015 http://www.paskvil.com/

Cacioppo, John T. 2008. A letter to young scientist. *Observer* 21(3): 3940.

Cambridge Dictionary. 2015. Accessed October 15, 2015. dictionary.cambridge.org.

Carroll, Lewis. 1982. *The complete illustrated works of Lewis Carroll*. London: Chancellor Press.

Chlewiński, Zdzisław. 1999. *Umysł. Dynamiczna organizacja pojęć* (*Mind. Dynamic organization of notions*). Warsaw: Wydawnictwo Naukowe PWN (in Polish).

Clark, Andy. 1989. *Microcognition: philosophy, cognitive science and parallel distributed processing*. Cambridge, MA: MIT Press.

Cohen Jack and Ian N. Stewart. 2000. *The collapse of chaos. Discovering simplicity in a complex world*. London: Penguin Books.

Colman, Andrew M. 2009. *Słownik psychologii* (*Dictionary of psychology*). Warsaw: Wydawnictwo Naukowe PWN (in Polish).

Coyne, George V. and Michał Heller. 2008. *A comprehensible universe. The interplay of science and theology*. New York, NY: Springer-Verlag.

Damasio, Antonio R. 2010. *Self comes to mind. Constructing the conscious brain*. New York, NY: Pantheon Books.

Darwin, Charles. 1881. *The formation of vegetable mould, through the action of worms, with observation on their habits*. London: John Murray, Albermale Street.

Dawkins, Richard. 2009. *The greatest show in the world. The evidence for evolution*. New York, NY: Free Press, Simon and Schuster.

Dennett, Daniel C. 1993. Quinning qualia. In *Readings in philosophy and cognitive science*, edited by Alvin I. Goldman, 381414. Cambridge, MA: MIT Press.

Desclés, Jean-Pierre. 2000. Abduction and non-observability. In *The reality of the unobservable: Observability and their impact on the issue of scientific realism,* edited by Evandro Agazzi, and Massimo Pauri, 87112. Dordrecht: Kluver Academic Publishers.

Domaciuk, Dominika. 2008. Zasady wariacyjne a ich teleologiczna interpretacja (Variational principles, teleological interpretation). *Zagadnienia filozoficzne w nauce*, 42: 5267 (in Polish).

Dyson, Freeman J. 1958. *Innovation in physics. Scientific American, September: 7482.*

Einstein, Albert. 1905. *Zur Elektrodynamik bewegter Körper (On the electrodynamics of moving bodies). Annalen der Physik*, 17: 891921 (in German).

Einstein, Albert. 1936. Physics and reality. *Journal of the Franklin Institute* 221(3): 34982.

Einstein, Albert. 1996. *Autobiographical notes*. Peru, IL: Open Court Publishing Company.

Feigenberg, Iosif M. 2006. Aktywność i wypełnianie luk informacyjnych (Human's own activity in fulfilling the information deficit). *Antropomotoryka* 35: 1725 (in Polish).

Feynman, Richard P. 1997. *Surely you are joking, Mr. Feynman*. New York, NY: W.W. Norton and Company, Inc.

Forscher, Bernard K. 1963. Chaos in the brickyard. *Science* October 18,142(3590): 339.

Freud, Sigmund. 1920. *A general introduction to psychoanalysis*. New York, NY: Boni and Liveright Publishers.

Gerrig, Richard J. 2013. *Psychology and life. Twentieth edition*. Harlow: Pearson Education Limited.

Gibson, James J. 1983. *The senses considered as perceptual system*. Westport, CT: Greenwood Press.

Goldsmith, Edward R.D. 2000. Intelligence is universal in life. *Rivista di Biologia* 93(3): 399411.

Harman, Gilbert H. 1965. The inference to the best explanation. *The Philosophical Review* 74(1): 8895.

Hawking, Stephen. 1996. *The illustrated a brief history of time*. New York, NY: Bantam Books.

Heisenberg, Werner. 2000. *Physics and philosophy*. London: Penguin Books.

Heller, Michał. 2011. *Filozofia nauki. Wprowadzenie* (*Philosophy of science. Introduction*). Krakow: Petrus (in Polish).

Heller, Michał. 2014. *Filozofia przypadku. Kosmiczna fuga z preludium i codą* (*Philosophy of chance. The cosmic fugue with prelude and coda*). Kraków: Copernicus Center Press (in Polish).

Heron-Allen, Edward. 1915. On beauty, design and purpose in the *Foraminifera, Proceedings of the Royal Institution of Great Britain*, 95: 6304.

Hofstadter, Douglas R. 1999. *Gödel, Escher, Bach. An eternal golden braid*. New York, NY: Basic Books, Inc.

Hussein, Basel Al-Sheikh. 2012. The Sapir-Whorf Hypothesis today. *Theory and Practice in Language Studies*, 2(3): 6426.

Jakóbczyk, Wojtek. 2011. Zawsze byłem sobą (I was always myself). *Cars. Magazyn o samochodach* 8(12): 2831 (in Polish).

James, William. 1904. Does „consciousness" exist? *Journal of Philosophy, Psychology, and Scientific Methods*, 1: 47791.

Jammer, Max. 1966. *The conceptual development of quantum theory*. New York, NY: McGraw Hill Book Co.

Jennings, Herbert S. *Behavior of the lower organisms*. New York, NY: The Columbia University Press.

Kant, Immanuel. 1922. *The critique of pure reason*. London: Macmillan and Co., Ltd.

Kurcz, Ida. 1995. *Pamięć, uczenie się, język* (*Memory, learning, language*). Warsaw: Wydawnictwo Naukowe PWN (in Polish).

Latash, Mark L. 2008. *Synergy*. New York, NY: Oxford University Press.

Mazur, Marian. 1987. Pojęcie systemu i rygory jego stosowania (The notion of system and the principles of its application). *Postępy Cybernetyki* 2: 219 (in Polish).

Mazur, Marian. 1999. *Cybernetyka i charakter* (*Cybernetics and character*), 3rd Edition. Warsaw: Wyższa Szkoła Zarządzania i Przedsiębiorczości im. B. Jańskiego (in Polish).

Midgley, Mary. 1973. The concept of beastliness: philosophy, ethics and animal behavior. *Philosophy* 48: 11135.

Miller, George A. 1956. The magical number seven, plus or minus two: Some limits on our capacity for processing information. *Journal of Experimental Psychology* 56: 48591.

Morawski, Janusz M. 1986. *Bezpieczeństwo a ekonomia w lotnictwie. U źródeł kontrowersji* (*Safety and economics in aviation. The origins of controversy*). Warsaw: Prace Instytutu Lotnictwa, 11: 1428.

Morawski, Janusz M. 1989. Myślenie systemowe (System thinking). In *Z warsztatów badawczych. Materiały VIII Szkoły Biomechaniki*, edited by Kazimierz Fidelus, 7090, Warsaw: AWF (in Polish).

Morawski, Janusz M. 1991. Safety vs. economy: System theoretic approach to the problem analysis. In *Proceedings of the sixth international symposium on aviation psychology*, edited by Richard S. Jensen, Vol 2, 67984. Columbus, OH.

Morawski, Janusz M. 1994. *Gospodarka informacją w układzie pilot-samolot* (*Information management in pilot-plane system*). Warsaw, Rzeszów: Wydawnictwa Politechniki Rzeszowskiej – Wydawnictwa Instytutu Lotnictwa (in Polish).

Morawski, Janusz M. 1995a. Human factors in avionics. Part I: Psychobehavioral backgrounds; Part II: Pilot-oriented and pilot-patterned avionic systems. I Krajowa Konferencja Awioniki, Bieszczady, 12-14 September. *Zeszyty Naukowe Politechniki Rzeszowskiej, Mechanika, z. 45 Awionika, cz. 1*: 5777.

Morawski, Janusz M. 1995b. Man-machine systems analysis and design: psychobehavioral approach (survey paper) In *Lecture notes of the ICB seminars biomechanics. Biocybernetical and biomechanical aspects of man-machine systems*, 23, edited by Adam Morecki and Krzysztof Kędzior, 10030. Warsaw: International Center of Biocybernetics.

Morawski, Janusz M. 2000. Dominanty ujęć systemowych (Dominants of systems approach). In *Wybrane problemy metodologii badań na potrzeby sportu*, edited by Janusz M. Morawski., 10427. Warsaw: Polskie Towarzystwo Naukowe Kultury Fizycznej (in Polish).

Morawski, Janusz M. 2005. *Człowiek i technologia. Sekrety wzajemnych uwarunkowań* (*Human and technology. The secrets of mutual relations*), Pultusk Academy of Humanities, Pułtusk (in Polish).

Morawski, Janusz M., and Krzysztof Zawalski. 1986. Technika, taktyka i strategia sportowa – systemowy punkt widzenia (Technique, tactics and strategy in sport – a systemic perspective). *Sport Wyczynowy*, 11: 311.

Nadin, Mihai. 1997. *The civilization of illiteracy*, Dresden University Press.

Norton, John D. 2007. *How did Einstein think?* Accessed November 11, 2015. http: //www.pitt.edu/~/jdnorton/Goodies.

O'Luanaigh C. (2013). *New results indicate that new particle is a Higgs boson*. CERN. http://home.cern, retrieved 2016-02-24.

Peirce, Charles S. 1958. *Collected papers of Charles Sanders Peirce*. Cambridge, MA: Harvard University Press.

Penrose, Roger. 1997. *The large, the small, and human mind*. Cambridge: Cambridge University Press.

Petryński, Wacław. 2007. Trzy sposoby przetwarzania informacji w sterowaniu ruchami – instynkt, inteligencja i intuicja (Three methods of information processing in motor control – instinct, intelligence, and intuition), *Antropomotoryka*, 39: 8193.

Petryński, Wacław. 2008. *Współczesne teorie uczenia się ruchów i sterowania nimi przez człowieka* (*Contemporary theories of movements learning and control in humans*). Katowice: Górnośląska Wyższa Szkoła Handlowa (in Polish).

Petryński, Wacław. 2011. System description of human motor performance: the movement construction matrix, *Selçuk University Journal of Physical Education and Sport Science* 13 (1): 16.

Petryński, Wacław. 2014. Consciousness – a system-theoretical approach, *Frontiers in Psychology*. Accessed November 11, 2015. doi: 10.3389/fpsyg.2014.00115.

Plato. 2003. *The Republic*. London: Penguin Books.

Popper, Karl R. 2002a. *Unended quest. An intellectual autobiography*. London and New York, NY: Routledge.

Popper, Karl R. 2002b. *Conjectures and refutations. The growth of scientific knowledge.* London: Routledge.

Pranger, Robert J. 1972. *Defense implications of international indeterminacy* (*Foreign affairs study*). Washington, D.C.: American Enterprise Institute for Public Policy Research.

Prigogine, Ilya and Isabelle Stengers. 1984. *Order out of chaos*. New York, NY: Bantam Books.

Rovelli, Carlo. 2012. *Science is not about certainty; A philosophy of physics*. Accessed October 10, 2015. http: //edge.org/conversation/a-philosophy-of-physics.

Sadowski, Bogdan._2007. *Biologiczne mechanizmy zachowania ludzi i zwierząt (Biological mechanisms of animals' and humans' behavior).* Warsaw: Wydawnictwo Naukowe PWN (in Polish).

Salomon, Ewa. 2005. Pobudliwość i powstawanie pobudzenia (Excitability and arising of excitation). In *Fizjologia człowieka*, edited by Ludmiła Borodulin-Nadzieja, 16. Wrocław: Górnicki Wydawnictwo Medyczne.

Schmidt, Richard A. 1988. *Motor control and learning. A behavioral emphasis. Second edition*. Champaign, IL: Human Kinetics Publishers, Inc.

Schmidt, Richard A. and Timothy D. Lee. 2011. *Motor control and learning. A behavioral emphasis. Fifth edition.* Champaign, IL: Human Kinetics.

Shelley, Percy B. 1906. *Prometheus unbound*. Boston, MA: D.C. Heath and Co.

Sokal, Alan and Jean Bricmont. 1998. *Fashionable nonsense. Postmodern intellectuals' abuse of science.* New York, NY: Picador.

Sokal, Alan. 1994. Transgressing the boundaries: Towards a transformative hermeneutics of quantum gravity. *Social Text* 46/47: 21752.

Sorman, Guy. 1993. *Prawdziwi myśliciele naszych czasów* (*Les vrais penseurs de notre temps*). Warsaw: Czytelnik (in Polish).

Staruszkiewicz, Andrzej. 2001. Filozofia fizyki teoretycznej Einsteina i Diraca (Einstein's and Dirac's philosophy of theoretical physics). *Foton* 73: 413 (in Polish).

Stewart, Ian N. 2002. *Does God play dice? The new mathematics of chaos. Second edition.* Malden, USA; Oxford, UK; Carlton, Australia: Blackwell Publishing.

The Free Dictionary. 2015. Accessed October 10. www.thefreedictionary.com.

Urban Dictionary. 2015. Accessed October 10. www.urbandictionary.com.

Vonnegut, Kurt. 2010. *Cat's cradle*. New York, NY: Dial Press Trade Paperbacks.

Wasik, Augustyn. 1991. Wczesne i późne następstwa urazów mózgu u bokserów (Immediate and delayed consequences of brain injuries in boxers). In *Rozprawy Naukowe Akademii Wychowania Fizycznego we Wrocławiu XXIV-B*. Wrocław: Akademia Wychowania Fizycznego (in Polish).

Wheeler, John A. and Seymour Tilson. 1965. The dynamics of space-time. In *Modern science and technology, edited by* Robert Colborn, 1120. Princeton, NJ: D. Van Nostrand Company, Inc.

Wohl, Andrzej. 1965. *Słowo a ruch. Z zagadnień teorii motoryczności ludzkiej* (*Word and movement: The selected issues of theory of human motoricity*). Warsaw: Akademia Wychowania Fizycznego (in Polish).

Wróblewski, Andrzej K. 2007. *Historia fizyki* (*History of physics*). Warszawa: Wydawnictwo Naukowe PWN (in Polish).

Życiński, Józef. 2013. *Świat matematyki i jej materialnych cieni* (*The world of mathematics and its material shadows*). Krakow: Copernicus Center Press (in Polish).

In: Consciousness
Editor: Lloyd Alvarado

ISBN: 978-1-63485-023-0

Chapter 4

Attention and Conscious Experience

Giorgio Marchetti[*]
www.mind-consciousness-language.com research center,
Pozzo d'Adda, Italy

Abstract

Through consciousness, we human beings have been acquiring a great capability to master and autonomously act in our environment. In this chapter, I put forward the hypothesis that attention plays an essential role in both the emergence of consciousness and the enhancement of our autonomy. In this regard, two main features of attention are of essence: its pulse-like nature and the possibility of being controlled top-down. These features allow for a constructive process composed of the segmentation of the continuous stream of undifferentiated information, and, with the support of working memory, the re-combination of isolated, attended pieces of information. This constructive process lies at the basis of every kind of language, and allowed for the creation of new "experiential dimensions", such as science, art, economy, and politics, which proved to be essential for the development and progress of the human species.

Keywords: conscious experience, attention, language

Introduction

The human species was able to develop what can be termed in a very general sense new "experiential dimensions", such as science, art, economy, and politics, which did not exist before and which have their own specific laws, procedures, techniques and features. The new experiential dimensions allowed human beings to produce new artifacts, develop new technologies, attitudes, expectations, ideas, and practices, create new realities and inhabit new "worlds", on top of the original one from which they originated and broke away. They proved

[*] Corresponding author: Giorgio Marchetti, www.mind research center, Pozzo d'Adda, Italy, Email: info@mind-consciousness-language.com.

to be useful for the development and progress of our species (just think of how the science of medicine helps the human species overcome diseases), and gave us new degrees of freedom (just think of how one can get in touch with anyone else at any time simply by using a cell phone), substantially enhancing our capacity to autonomously act in the environment.

There is no doubt that the capacity of our species to achieve such an advanced level of progress and autonomy, is largely due to the fact that it is endowed with a very sophisticated and evolved mind equipped with the fundamental faculties of consciousness, self-consciousness, and language.

Thanks to consciousness, not only can we perceive the environmental stimulus, but also and above all effectively and vividly simulate new situations and conditions, thus anticipating, at least to a certain point, the consequences of actions, imagining new scenarios, devising new solutions, etc. Language allows us to communicate what we think and imagine, and consequently to inter-subjectively verify the validity of our reasoning, anticipations, expectations, etc. Self-consciousness gives us the immediate notion that we can control our own actions, and can decide their course. Indisputably, all these faculties make our autonomy stronger and easier to achieve.

What is it that renders human consciousness such a powerful tool capable of simulating new situations, imagining future events, etc.? How can language transmit such impalpable things as thoughts? What are the mental processes that subserve these faculties?

In this chapter, I will put forward the hypothesis that what makes consciousness such a powerful tool is its capacity to abstract from present and proximal stimuli, and to process absent and distal stimuli. This capacity allows for the formation, among other things, of conscious contents such as simulations, imaginal and conceptual thought, and meanings. Once formed, these conscious contents can be transmitted by means of linguistic meaning, which is a socially codified form of meaning. The main mental process that subserves consciousness is attention. Attention plays an essential role in both the emergence of consciousness states, and the formation of conscious contents.

THE VIRTUAL NATURE OF CONSCIOUSNESS

In a very general sense, a system (whether organism, person, or artifact) can be said to be autonomous from the physical environment if it is not just "automatically" responding to environmental stimuli, that is, if its behavior is not determined and driven from the outside, but rather from its own self-generated goals and intentions. Likewise, a system is autonomous from its social environment, that is, from its cognitive-social agents, if it is able to act independently from their will to control or influence it. Finally, a system is autonomous if it is able to independently build its own knowledge, that is, resisting possible wrong information or suggestions, and on that basis to form justified, supported beliefs (Castelfranchi, 2012)[1].

Human consciousness proves to be a unique tool in helping us avoid on-line, automatic responding to environmental, actually given stimuli: people focus an average of 30%-40% of their thoughts on matters that are unrelated to what is happening here and now (Klinger and Cox, 1987). Even when conscious thoughts concern current behaviors, they are often used for

[1] Some other attributes (such as resource management) seem important to qualify a system as autonomous (see Thórisson and Helgasson, 2012), but these are subordinate to the system's goals and intentions.

the purpose of recalling similar behaviors from the past, anticipating the consequences of present behaviors, or pondering alternative courses of action (Baumeister and Masicampo, 2010).

As Hommel et al. (2001) show, the transition from a very primitive form of behavior in which the system only responds automatically to given stimulus condition, to a more sophisticated one in which the system plans its goal-directed actions, is marked by the development in its cognitive apparatus of a common representational domain for perceived events and planned action, on top of the old system for mapping and response selection. In fact, this common representational domain permits to bridge the two functional gaps introduced by the new sophisticated behavior: the gap between events going on at present and events forthcoming in the future, that is, between on-line generated perceptual representations and off-line generated conceptual constructions, and the gap between planned actions and intended future events. The common representational domain bridges the two gaps by creating a commensurate coding between events and actions, and between perceived present events and intended future events.

What is important here is that it is at the level of *distal*, rather than proximal, representation that event codes and action codes, as well as on-line perceptual representations and off-line conceptual constructions, can be generated and maintained in a common format. Distal coding refers to events in the world, where the body is in some sense part of the world, and as such irrespective of whether exteroceptive, interoceptive or proprioceptive senses inform it. In contrast, a code is proximal if it refers to the physiological correlates of the physical information reaching our sense organs (Hommel, 2009; Janczyk et al., 2009). Examples of distal coding are distance, size and location of stimulus or response; examples of proximal coding are the neural patterns in the receiving sense organs and closely related processing systems, such as retinal excitation patterns and the electrical activity in various parts of the visual cortex.

Why is this common representational domain dependent on distal representations and does not work with proximal representations? Hommel et al. (2001, pp. 877-878) offers two reasons. First, coordinating actions and events is much easier in terms of distal than proximal representations. Proximal representations are both incommensurate and incomplete, one class of representations referring to sensory features and the other to motor features. Any action planning on this basis would therefore require heavy interaction between these different domains of representation. Conversely, with distal representations, the coordination of actions and environmental events can be performed in a single and coherent domain. Second, the forecasting of events is much easier in terms of distal than proximal representations. Coordinating future actions with future environmental events requires representational resources capable of elaborating reliable scenarios for the future course of environmental events, as well as building one's own actions into this course in order to achieve certain goals. These two tasks are hard to solve with proximal representations. Forecasting future and environmental events in terms of their proximal (sensory) representations would imply an explosion of degrees of freedom, due to the virtually infinite number of the system's possible perspective on those events. The same would apply to the planning of future actions in terms of their proximal (motor) representations: there is always a virtually infinite number of bodily movement patterns through which a given action can be realized. Consequently, there is no reasonable way to plan the future in terms of proximal representations. Forecasting events and planning actions requires representational resources with distal reference.

Moreover, distal coding of stimulus objects and action plans offers some other computational advantages. Firstly, it greatly increases the inventory of the available codes: while proximal codes, such as feature detectors in the visual modality, are fixed and of a limited number, the resolution of distal coding is virtually unlimited, so much so that it can refer to complex and abstract dimensions as "sit-on-ableness". Secondly, it allows perception and action planning to abstract from domain- and modality-specific (visual, kinesthetic, etc.) coding characteristics, and refer instead to an event's informational content. As Snyder and Munakata (2010) observe, abstract representation allows for a general reduction of the computational effort: by encompassing groups of lower-level instances and generalizing over irrelevant within-category variance, abstract representations reduce competition from extra-category items, constrain the search space and reduce selection demands.

As Hommel et al. (2001) observe, the fact that the common representational domain only works with distal representations, explains one of the main phenomenal characteristics of human consciousness, namely why, when we look at a flower, we see a flower rather than for example the neural and chemical signal activity patterns in our brain elicited by the vision of the flower. That is, it accounts for the fact that conscious contents give the impression of being actual things "out there" in the world rather than being things "in here", in our brain.

This also explains, in my view, the "virtual" nature of human consciousness, that is, the fact that consciousness does not reach out into the external world, but is instead engaged in internal "world simulation" and "world presentation" - a fact well highlighted by Revonsuo (2006, p. 106): "The objects we experience around us, the objects directly present for us, are not the real physical objects out there in physical space, but purely experiential phenomena, located entirely within the sphere of the phenomenal level" (for a similar view, see Lehar [2003, p. 404]: "we cannot in principle have direct experience of objects in the world itself but only of the internal effigies of those objects generated by mental processes. The world we see round us can only be an elaborate, though very compelling, illusion, which must in reality correspond to perceptual data structures and processes occurring actually within our heads"). Indeed, once the system is deprived of a proximal, immediate contact with the environment, the only possibility for it to have a contact with the environment is in a *mediated* way. By cutting the direct links of the system with proximal environment, the transformation from a purely automatic, rigid stimulus-response processing style to an autonomous, flexible and constructive one driven by self-generated tasks, makes consciousness the only possible (virtual) reality or environment that the system can experience and in which it can live. The system does no longer passively process – like a thermostat - the pre-defined information of the environment, but actively contributes to construct and define it (and along with it, to construct the system's environment) according to its own needs, values and plans: a process which, as it seems, can only occur in a conscious medium, in the sense that in order for it to happen, it concurrently requires both the generation and the use of conscious experience.

Sometimes, the virtual and mediated nature of human consciousness has been described as a "fiction" or an on-going "movie" or "film" (Baumeister and Masicampo, 2010; Dennet, 1991), in which we are inescapably and continuously immersed, play the main character, and occupy the central stage. This metaphor could seem to be too strong, and some may not accept it. However, if we just consider how arbitrarily human consciousness constructs the reality, the metaphor will certainly become more comprehensible and acceptable. For example, because of the time taken by neural processing (Libet, 2004), our perceptual systems must draw conclusions based on data that are slightly outdated, so much so that we are bound to continuously live "in the past" (Eagleman and Sejnowski, 2000, 2007) and put together the best possible story about what's going on in the world. Visual illusions such as the colour-phi illusion[2], the Fröhlich effect, the tunnel effect, as well as many others analysed by Gestalt psychology, show that the way we perceive the world does not depend on a concern for faithfully representing and duplicating it. Rather, it depends on some other factors such as: the need for obtaining a representation of the world that is meaningful for us and the purposes and expectations we have (Gallagher and Zahavi, 2008; Vicario, 2001, 2005); the way our bodies are physically and biologically structured (Gibson, 1986; Maturana and Varela, 1992); and the specific neurobiological mechanisms responsible for producing consciousness-level perceptual awareness (Bachman, 2013). Finally, we see more than what is there (O'Regan and Noë, 2001). This has been shown for example by the phenomenon of the physiological blindspot or *punctum caecum* (that is, the place in the visual field that corresponds to the lack of light-detecting photoreceptor cells on the optic disc of the retina where the optic nerve passes through). Further evidence comes from McCloskey and Watkins'(1978) psychological experiments: when the full shape of a stimulus is moved back and forth behind a window cut in an opaque screen, more of the stimulus is seen at a given instant than is physically present. Change blindness experiments (Simons and Levin, 1997, 1998) and inattentional blindness experiments (Mack and Rock, 1998) also show that we see less than what is physically given. In this regard, Eagleman (2001, p. 920) ironically remarks that, in the cinema, we even "pay money to watch a succession of flat, still images that appear to be rich with motion and depth".

In brief, distal coding, allowing for a representation of events and objects that is abstracted from domain- and modality-specific characteristics, and not directly and causally linked to the "here and now", paved the way for the emergence of human consciousness as we know it today: a consciousness that "arbitrarily" depicts reality in a certain spatial and temporal (distal) way, lets us remember past events and imagine future events, and allows us to perceive, think about and conceive of the same physical object or event in several, different ways (a wood can be seen not only as such but also as "many trees" or "a beautiful place") and conversely perceive, think about and conceive of several, different physical objects or events in the same way (oaks, elms and pines can all be seen as "trees").

The Role of Attention in the Emergence of Consciousness

What are the main mechanisms allowing for the generation of distal, abstract codes and, consequently, phenomenal experience? Hommel et al. (2001) identify attention as one of the main mechanisms (even though not the only one) responsible for the formation of a common coding that represents the distal features of events and objects. In fact, attention is involved in both of the two main steps necessary to originate such coding, that is, the selection of the relevant features to be processed (Pashler, 1989), and the integration or "binding" of the selected features (Treisman and Gelade, 1980).

[2] Two differently coloured lights, with an angular separation of a few degrees at the eye, are flashed in succession. If the interval between the flashes is about 50ms, the first light that is flashed appears to move across to the position of the second light. Moreover, the light seems to change colour as it moves across the visual field.

Likewise, Barsalou (1999) assigns attention a central role in the formation of perceptual symbol systems, that is, the schematic memories that constitute the common representational system underlying perception and cognition. Attention is a key analytic mechanism in parsing experience into the schematic components that ultimately form concepts, whether of perceptual (such as "red" or "hot") or abstract nature (such as "true" and "false"). Through selective attention, individual perceptual components derived from modality-specific experience are extracted in schematic fashion - so that commonalities are abstracted across specific instances of perceptual states- and recorded, in bottom-up fashion, in long-term memory. Once formed, perceptual symbols can be reactivated or simulated in a top-down fashion, and used to support the range of symbolic and practical behaviors that subserve a fully functional conceptual system.

Hommel (2010) hypothesizes that attention is a by-product of action control in a distributed processing system: it "originally evolved to deal with control problems arising from distributed representation and processing and from the share of labor between offline, anticipatory action planning and online action adjustment in particular" (*ibid.*, p 134). He also hints at how attention could contribute to the formation of consciousness: as empirical research shows (Craighero et al., 1999; Müsseler and Hommel, 1997), a necessary condition for the emergence of consciousness is the attentional binding of the selected features (whereas the sole attentional selection of features would not be sufficient for consciousness to occur).

The idea that attention is linked to consciousness is not new (James, 1890; Posner, 1994; O'Regan and Noë, 2001). Currently, there is not yet a shared view on the nature of the relationship between attention and consciousness, and the debate is still open about whether attention is really necessary for consciousness (for a review, see Tsuchiya and van Boxtel, 2013). The positions range from those who maintain that attention and consciousness are distinct phenomena that need not occur together (Bachman, 2011; Koch and Tsuchiya, 2006, Lamme, 2003; van Boxtel et al., 2010) to those who maintain that the two are inextricably linked (De Brigard and Prinz, 2010; Mack and Rock, 1998; Posner, 1994). However, as I have tried to show (Marchetti, 2012; for a similar criticism, see De Brigard and Prinz, 2010; Koivisto et al., 2009; Kouider et al., 2010; Srinivasan, 2008), the view that there can be consciousness without some form of attention, originates primarily from the failure to notice the varieties of forms and levels of attention (Alvarez, 2011; Chun et al., 2011; Demeyere and Humphreys, 2007; La Berge, 1995; Lavie, 1995; Nakayama and Mackeben, 1989; Pashler, 1998; Treisman, 2006) and consciousness (Bartolomeo, 2008; Edelman, 1989; Iwasaki, 1993; Tulving, 1985; Vandekerckhove and Panksepp, 2009). Not all forms of attention produce the same kind of consciousness, and vice versa not all forms of consciousness are produced by the same kind of attention. There are cases of consciousness in the absence of a certain form of top-down attention, but in the presence of some other form of top-down attention. There are cases of consciousness in the absence of top-down attention but in the presence of some other form of attention, such as bottom-up attention. But there are never cases of consciousness in complete absence of some form of attention.

It should be noted that the fact that attention is necessary for consciousness does not imply that attention is the same thing as consciousness. In fact, not always does attention generate conscious phenomena: attention can also generate and modulate unconscious ones (Naccache et al., 2002; Montaser-Kousari and Rajimehr, 2005; Sumner et al., 2006; Bahrami et al., 2008). Moreover, as various authors have observed, some additional components other than attention are necessary for consciousness to occur, such as sense-organs, somatosensory organs, working memory, expectations and capacity of anticipation (see for example Baars, 1988; Edelman, 1989; Haikonen, 2003; Marchetti, 2010; Srinivasan, 2008). Finally, there are models of attention that explicitly add the functions performed by some of these components to the ones classically associated with attention (for example Knudsen [2007] proposes that attention reflects the combined contributions of four distinct processes: working memory, competitive selection, top-down sensitivity control, and automatic filtering for salient stimuli), which is tantamount to admitting that such additional components are also necessary for consciousness.

On the basis of empirical evidence showing the tight link between attention and consciousness, as well as the specific nature and features of attention, I put forward a proposal (Marchetti, 2010) aiming at explicitly accounting for the phenomenal character of consciousness in terms of the working of attention. My hypothesis is that the phenomenal character of conscious experiences can be explained by considering the organ of attention as the source of the organism's nervous energy[3], and attention as the nervous energy that gives the organism the possibility of performing actions capable of directly affecting the organism's state of energy. The attentional activity performed by the organism involves a temporary variation or disequilibrium in the state of nervous energy: this variation or disequilibrium constitutes the phenomenal aspect of consciousness[4]. The most basic, elemental conscious forms that such a variation gives rise to, are either that of a constraint or a lack of constraint (to act in general). This aspect was conveyed very well by Piaget (1937), who – in describing how the idea, or concept, of an object is built up during the first stages of intellectual development - observed that the subject recognizes his own reaction before he recognizes the object as such. The constraints that a person experiences when acting attentionally are determined by the applied level of attention, the specific structure of his body and the relations resulting from the interaction between his body and other entities.

The Periodic Nature of Consciousness and Attentional Processing

No doubt, one of the main features of conscious experience is its seamless, continuous nature. This feature is very well described by (Gallagher and Zahavi, 2008, p. 77):

"If we look at a pedestrian who is crossing the street, our perception will not be restricted to capturing the durationless now-slice of his movement. Perceptually, it is not as if the pedestrian suddenly appeared as out of nowhere; and further, we do not have to engage in an explicit act of remembering in order to establish the temporal context of his current position. Nor, however, will it be the case that all the previous slices of his movement are perceptually present in the same way as his current position. If that were the case, the pedestrian would perceptually fill the entire space he has just traversed".

[3] The concept of nervous energy – for which alternative terms, such as "psychic energy", "limited capacity processor", "resource", "effort", "pool of limited capacity", have also been used – has been analysed in various ways in relation to attention by many researchers and authors, for example: Csikszentmihalyi (1992), Kahneman (1973), Mach (1890), Wickens (1984).

[4] For a similar suggestion that consciousness results from a variation of the organism's internal state, see Damasio (1999, p. 25): "we become conscious when the organism's representation devices exhibit a specific kind of wordless knowledge - the knowledge that the organism's own state has been changed by an object".

Intuitively, this feature, which was also captured by James' (1890) fortunate expression "stream of consciousness", seems to rest on a seamless neural processing that goes on continuously and uninterruptedly. However, an alternative account of the underlying neural mechanisms is also possible and seems even more plausible: perception and conscious experience more in general would rely on *discrete* processing epochs (VanRullen and Koch, 2003). After all, it is well known that there is a certain minimal interstimulus interval (variable across senses, and estimated to be around 20-50 ms) below which two successive events are perceived as simultaneous (Hirsh and Sherrick, 1961; Szymaszek et al., 2009), and that no one can attend continuously and uninterruptedly to an object that does not change (James, 1890). Moreover, basic temporal integration mechanisms uniting disparate events into perceptual segments have been identified on different time scales and also in more complex intersensory perceptual tasks (for a review, see Wittmann, 2011). Neuroscientific studies seem to reveal that they are linked to brain oscillations of a specific frequency range. Varela et al. (1981) found a close correlation between the perception of apparent simultaneity and the alpha phase at which stimuli are presented: two flashes of light with always the same SOA are judged as simultaneous when presented at one particular phase, but as sequential when presented at the opposite phase. Doesburg et al. (2009) showed that perceptual switching during binocular rivalry is time-locked to gamma-band synchronizations which recur at a theta rate, indicating that the onset of new conscious percepts coincides with the emergence of a new gamma-synchronous assembly that is locked to an ongoing theta rhythm. Doesburg et al. (*ibid.*, p. 2) infer that "only one truly discrete perceptual experience may exist within a single theta cycle, and that the emergence of new perceptual experiences may be time locked to a particular phase of ongoing cortical theta rhythms".

In this regard, attention also seems to operate in a discrete manner, which further supports the hypothesis that attention and consciousness are inextricably linked: by means of rapid shifts, we can redirect our focus of attention away from one fixation and toward a different focus of attention. Although such discrete operating can theoretically be realized by an uninterrupted, continuous flow of attention rapidly switching between the different targets, evidence seems to favor the hypothesis that attention operates in a periodic, pulse-like manner. VanRullen et al. (2007) found that attention, even when focused on a single target location, samples information periodically like a blinking spotlight. Moreover, by analyzing the correlation between detection performance for attended and unattended stimuli and the phase of ongoing EEG oscillations, Busch and VanRullen (2010) showed that detection performance for attended stimuli actually fluctuated over time along with the phase of spontaneous oscillations in the θ ($\approx$7 Hz) frequency band just before stimulus onset. This fluctuation was absent for unattended stimuli. This pattern of results suggests that attention in fact exerts its facilitative effect on perception in a periodic fashion. Doesburg et al.'s (2008) findings support the view that gamma-band synchronization is the mechanism that implements the selective properties of attention, its integrative properties, and the special relationship between attention and consciousness. Landau and Fries' study (2012) shows that selective attention samples stimuli in rhythmic way. Further evidence of the link between attention and periodic brain processes is provided by studies in which oscillatory brain responses are entrained by periodic stimulation (Jones et al., 2002). Finally, the periodic nature of attentional processing is also visible at wider temporal scales: spontaneous eyeblinks, which occur 15-20 times per minute on average, are tightly correlated to attentional processing in that they tend to occur at breakpoints of attention, such as the end of a sentence while reading, a pause by the speaker while listening to a speech, and implicit breakpoints while viewing videos. This tight correlation has led Nakano et al. (2013, p. 702) to hypothesize that "eyeblinks are actively involved in the process of attentional disengagement during a cognitive behavior by momentarily activating the default-mode network while deactivating the dorsal attention network".

The Advantages Offered by Attentional Discrete Processing

What advantages might attentional discrete processing offer? From a purely computational point of view, there are certainly various advantages. According to Buschman and Miller (2010), restricting computations to discrete windows of time would:

(a) ensure that informative spikes occur with the temporal precision that is both necessary for integration by downstream neurons and for spike-timing dependent plasticity;
(b) act to stabilize and organize the neural network and its computations: periods of inhibition may act to "reset" the network to a base state, effectively limiting the number of states that neurons could obtain;
(c) allow for easier coordination of processing within and between brain regions, by providing a specific moment at which information must be available for computation in a specific region, and at which the outcome of the computation is available.

VanRullen et al. (2007) observe that the active, overt periodic sampling of the environment is a ubiquitous property of sensory systems (saccades in vision, sniffs in olfaction, whisker movements in rat somatosensation, and even electrolocation in the electric fish) and that attention might have evolved from these periodic processes, as a more economical means of covertly sampling endogenous representations.

In my view, however, the greatest advantages of discrete processing can be appreciated from the more general point of view of knowledge acquisition and production. Essentially, once the system has acquired the capacity to endogenously control attention[5], that is, to pilot it on the basis of the knowledge acquired from previous experience rather than of immediate sensory stimulation (Corbetta and Shulman, 2002; Posner, 1980), the periodic nature of attentional processing gives it the possibility of stopping at any time the ongoing sequence of attentional operations and initiating a new one (Logan and Cowan, 1984). This allows the system to *disengage* from whatever flow of information is being processed and, subsequently, focus on a different piece or level of information. This is precisely the necessary precondition for cutting the direct links of the system with its proximal environment, and making common coding and distal processing possible (Hommel et al., 2001). Indeed, in order to be able to

[5] It has been hypothesized that the endogenous system is phylogenetically younger than the exogenous one, which allows for the automatic responding to environmental demands and reacting quickly to stimuli that are likely to provide behaviourally relevant information (Carrasco, 2011). Ontogenetically, the ability to endogenously control attention is not fully given at birth, but emerges and develops progressively in infancy (Colombo and Cheatham, 2006); more in general, the ability to endogenously control behaviour comes later than the ability to react on an exogenous basis (Snyder and Munakata, 2010).

autonomously build the information necessary to satisfy its self-generated plans, the system must first stop to process the proximal information in an automatic, rigid stimulus-response way: this gives it the possibility of endogenously filtering out, selecting, assembling and integrating whatever information best fits its needs. As Haikonen (2003, p. 72) observes (commenting on the fact that when we scan a rough surface by mean of a rigid stick we do not perceive the vibrations of the stick against our fingers but rather the groove patterns of the surface, even if there are no nerves on the tip of the stick), distal processing is not achieved by the hard-wired system of nerve fibers and cells "but by the omission of nerve end position information".

We already saw some of the advantages implied by common coding and distal processing with regard to the coordination between perception and action, and more in general the possibility for the generation and execution of self-generated plans and actions. But common coding and distal processing also offer some other advantages. By making us perceive the origination point of a sensation as being somewhere other than the real point of origination of the nerve signal (that is, the sensor or the tip of the nerve), common coding and distal processing make it possible for us to detect objects' directions and distances - thus allowing for adaptive locomotion (Higuchi, 2013) -, create mental maps of the surroundings, distinguish between internally and externally generated sensations, and ultimately enhance the sense of self (Haikonen, 2003).

Additionally, the periodic nature of attentional processing enables the segmentation of the continuous and undifferentiated stream of environmental information into elemental pieces of information. With the support of some supplementary organ such as working memory, procedural memory and comparators, these elemental pieces can be used as basic *mental (whether perceptual or purely abstract) atoms or building blocks* for a constructive process in which they are variously and recurrently assembled, combined and related[6]. Such a constructive process paves the way to very fundamental enhancements for the autonomy of the system. Let's consider some of these.

The constructive process allows for the possibility of creating new experiential dimensions on top of the one from which they originate. By focusing on, selecting and combining otherwise unrelated elements, attention makes us have conscious experience of events, objects and features that we would have never had if it had not been for its working. Therefore we can imagine and simulate new scenarios and conditions: as observed by as Baumeister and Masicampo (2010, p. 958), the full power of human consciousness consists in using the mental capacity for constructing sequential thoughts to conduct simulations during wakefulness, without relying on sensory input.

Typical examples of new experiential dimensions that did not exist in nature are art, ethics and economy: each is built on a specific and articulated way of relating and combing the selected mental building blocks (Amietta, 1991; Ceccato, 1972; Marchetti, 1997). However, even more basic experiential dimensions are produced thanks to attentional discrete

[6] As Fingelkurts et al. (2013) show, by means of electroencephalogram (EEG) measurement it is possible to identify both the single, simplest mental building-blocks and their combinations: "It has been proposed that EEG quasi-stationary segments (…) are equivalent to *simple mental operations* (phenomenal qualities, primary cognitive operations and emotions). (…) The quasi-stationary EEG segments (..) are *glued* to one another by means of the *rapid transitional processes/periods* (RTPs). RTP are observed within a short-time window, when EEG amplitude changes abruptly. Each RTP has very short duration in comparison to quasi-stationary segments length and can therefore be treated as a point or near-point. Thus, RTPs (or abrupt jumps in EEG amplitude) are, in fact, the markers of boundaries between concatenated quasi-stationary segments" (pp. 8-9).

processing: one of these is time. Even though time seems to be a ubiquitous, absolute reality given universally and independently of us, a careful examination testifies to the contrary: time is primarily a transitory mental product. Firstly, as evidenced by studies of developmental psychology (Droit-Volet, 2001), the notion of time is not innate, but progressively develops in children until the age of 8-10. Secondly, we do not always experience the passage of time, but only occasionally and mainly when we are led by the context to do so. Thirdly, even the very experience of the passage of time does not prove to be really independent of us: indeed, it can be modulated by so many and various subjective factors such as stress, expectations, age, habit, etc. that the same physical event can be experienced to last differently according to which of these factors comes into play (Flaherty, 1999). The same holds for the experience of the succession of events: when attending to a particular stimulus, we perceive it earlier in time than if we had directed attention elsewhere (Spence, 2010).

The temporal dimension is primarily a mental construct: as such, we experience it only when, and according to the way in which, we attentionally constitute it (whether voluntarily or induced). As I have tried to show (Marchetti, 2009), time-sensation is determined by the quantity of incremental labor performed by the portion of our attention (A_t) that is kept focused on the conscious product of the activity performed by means of another portion of one's attention (A_e). The activity performed by A_t represents the "temporal activity" (for instance, estimating duration); the activity performed by A_e represents the "non-temporal activity" (for instance, perceiving the shape of an object). The amount of nervous energy - supplied by the organ of attention - expended to support the activity of A_t constitutes the basis on which the conscious experience of duration and more in general time-sensation are based[7].

A further advantage offered by the constructive process is the creation of new and ordered sequences of elements. Such ordered sequences are the basis of scientific knowledge and all kinds of procedures. They allow us to anticipate what will follow after a certain step of the sequence; if correctly repeated, they allow us to re-obtain what they originally yielded. Typical examples of ordered sequences are spatial order and temporal order. How is temporal order obtained? If we consider that a given event X can be associated with a certain level of expenditure of A_t, an event Y that is associated with more expenditure of A_t appears to us to happen "after" X, whereas an event Z that is associated with less expenditure of A_t appears to happen "before" X. A "succession" or "sequence" of events, actions, etc. as well as their "duration", can then be built out of the levels of nervous energy (A_t) associated with them. Since the level of A_t can only increase, this makes it possible to arrange or order events, actions, etc. in a univocal and exact way: precisely, in a temporal way. In spatial order, the possibility of using working memory to keep track of the various conscious sensations produced by a moving sense-organ, is fundamental in my opinion. Let us suppose that you are perceiving a surface by moving your index finger on it. By keeping present in consciousness, in an incremental way, the single sensations produced by the index finger while it moves, you will shape a sequence or succession of sensations, which is the basis for the formation of two-dimensional constructs, such as "path", "line" and "distance". Once an ordered sequence is created, it is possible to build various kinds of relations on it: relations of comparisons ("X is nearer to us than Y" or "X is brighter than Y"), spatial relations ("X was in front of Y"),

[7] Eagleman (2008, p. 134) puts forward a similar explanation: "duration is a signature of the amount of energy expended by neurons", even though he (Eagleman and Pariyadath, 2009) does not seem to directly link the notion of neural energy expenditure to attention.

temporal relations ("A arrived before Y"), causal relations ("It is X that moves Y"), logical relations, physical relations, etc[8].

An alternative way to ordered sequences for combining the selected mental building-blocks is the use of *correlators* (Ceccato, 1972; Ceccato and Zonta, 1980). Correlators are those mental constructs that, having the specific function to tie together two elemental mental building blocks, forms correlations. A correlation is the basic unit of linguistic thought and is produced with the support of working memory and procedural memory (Benedetti, 2006). Linguistically, correlators are designated by prepositions, conjunctions, cases (genitive, dative, etc.) and the implicit correlator (Benedetti, 2011). Other examples of correlators are the mathematical and logical operators. Language represents perhaps the most evident instance of the constructive process that attentional discrete processing affords. Through language, we can combine the single words and thus convey vastly, literally infinite new meanings and conscious experiences: as Baumeister and Masicampo (2010, p. 956) observe "conscious thinking and speech involve a process of actively combining concepts to make something that may have additional, unforeseen, newly emergent properties". Additionally, language also allows us to create new kinds of thoughts specifically based on sequential steps, such as logical reasoning.

As Benedetti's (2009, 2011) extensive and in-deep analysis shows, correlators are themselves constituted by sequences of elemental mental operations (among which the ones of attention play a key role) that are assembled and chucked together by means of working memory and procedural memory. More in general, I think that the meanings of all words convey a set of condensed instructions on the attentional operations one has to perform if one wants to consciously experience - either as a pure meaning, an image, a real perception, a thought process, a concept, or something else - what is expressed through and by them (Marchetti, 2010).

It should be noted that while there are no limits in combining the selected building-blocks, not always is the outcome of the combination a viable one (Glasersfeld, 1998). That is, even though we are completely free to select, relate and combine elemental building-blocks, it is not said that our attentional and combinatorial activity always produces satisfactory results: nature unavoidably places constraints and, like a sieve, selects only what can overcome the pitfalls and obstacles it presents. In this regard, language and more in general social cooperation play an important role in that they allow us to correct, validate and approve the shortcomings of our imagination and thoughts: by sharing our conscious experiences (ideas, thoughts, perception, etc.) with others, we can constantly verify their validity and the possibility of their usage and application (Baumeister and Masicampo, 2010).

Self-Consciousness

A person acquires his upmost degree of autonomy once he becomes self-conscious. Self-consciousness allows a person to directly control and guide the course of his actions by means of his conscious activity, self-determine his goals, values and behavior, regulate and monitor himself, take decisions, and voluntarily modify and adapt his behavior. From the moment in

[8] See also Carstensen's (2007, 2011) and Scheider and Kuhn's (2011) proposals on how attention can generate spatial and temporal orders.

which a person becomes self-conscious, his actions are primarily and directly governed not so much by his innate instincts as by what happens in his consciousness, even though the latter can be occasioned by the former.

Additionally, self-consciousness provides a person with the sense of being a persistent, coherent entity, self or agent. Even if a person undergoes changes and various experiences, he continues to exist as a unified and coherent whole, on and from which all his actions and experiences center and evolve: what the person feels makes him experience to be a consistent, persistent, unique agent, an "invariant dimension" to which the multitude of changing experiences constantly refer (Gallagher and Zahavi, 2008, p. 204).

It should be noted that although phenomenally the self seems to be a unitary, homogeneous, monolithic entity, at a closer inspection it turns out to be composed of different modules operating on different levels of representational and functional complexity. It is possible to distinguish a sense of agency (I am the initiator of my movements and thoughts) from a sense of ownership (I am the owner of the limb that moves or of the thoughts I have) (Gallagher and Zahavi, 2008). This distinction becomes apparent when, for example, someone pushes us from behind: we sense that it is our body (not someone else's) that is moving, and therefore we experience ownership for the movement, but we do not experience agency for the movement (because the movement was not caused or initiated by us). Moreover, both the sense of ownership and the sense of agency are in turn based on complex mechanisms on several levels: a very basic level of sensorimotor integration, a non-conceptual level, a propositional level, and a meta-representational level (Synofzik et al., 2008).

Neither is self-consciousness something that a person possesses from his birth, despite the sense of a persistency and continuity that it provides to the person. Rather, it is an ability that emerges chronologically in development "like onions, layers after layers, in a cumulative consolidation" (Rochat, 2003, p. 730), and that the person must "learn" (Cleeremans, 2008). As Vosgerau and Newen (2007) observe, one of the fundamental conditions for self-consciousness to emerge is the person's ability to make a distinction between his self and the world. This self-world distinction is not just given, because every sensation carries information about both the sensing system and the world, and moreover, the information about our sensory system changes dramatically during development (just consider how the weight of the limbs changes with age). For example, when we lift an object, we can distinguish between the weight of the object and the weight of our limb only if the force needed to lift the limb alone is subtracted from the actual force needed for the lifting movement. Therefore, self-world distinction must be *learnt* and *achieved*.

According to Vosgerau and Newen, self-world distinction requires some kind of division of input sensation into self-related and world-related information: this division is achieved through the development of a common coding (or a "table" grouping the different codes containing the same content as the basis of a common coding) that groups the systematic co-variation of a certain afference (e.g., the proprioceptive information of my limb's movement) with certain efferences (the corresponding motor commands). Such systematic co-variations can be found for example between motor commands and tendon receptor responses. Tendon receptors fire only when the muscle is contracted; in contrast, in passive movement, when no contraction of the muscle is involved, the tendon receptors do not respond. Since muscle contraction always involves an efference of the system (action), there is a systematic co-variation between efferences and tendon receptor afferences. The efferences can then be grouped with their caused re-afferences. Sensation can hence be divided into two classes: the class that is caused by the system itself and the class that is caused by the world. Another example of systematic co-variation that allows for self-world distinction is represented by self-touch: when touching ourselves, there is a systematic covariance between two different haptic afferences (the sensation derived from touching and the sensation derived from being touched) which does not occur when we touch an object.

Vosgerau and Newen observe that, in order for the system to develop such self-world distinctions, all it needs is to start to move somehow (which, incidentally is facilitated in children by a-priori, inborn behaviors such as sucking and grasping reflexes [Piaget, 1936]), and it has the ability to detect and store systematic co-variation, thereby creating a table grouping the efferences with the appropriate re-afferences. Vosgerau and Newen (*ibid.*, p. 30) explain this last ability as a "system-inherent feature of neuronal networks that simply register systematic contingencies". However, I think that this explanation is untenable: given the incredibly vast amount of signals and frequencies present in our brain, there is a high probability for any signal to be associated with whatever else signal. In order to detect and store co-variations and consequently develop a common coding, a more specific and dedicated process is needed: as we have seen when considering how common coding develops in general (Hommel et al., 2001), the most plausible candidate is attention. Finally, it is important to note that whatever the mechanism leading to self-world distinction (whether the tendon receptors hypothesized by Vosgerau and Newen or some other, such as the predictive coding proposed by Hohwy, 2007), it cannot explain by itself how conscious experience generates in general. Such a mechanism can certainly explain the subject's capacity to assign the cause of a certain sensation to an external agent rather than to himself, or to judge whether a certain conscious experience reflects a real object of the world rather than a hallucination. However, in order to work, it presupposes the existence of conscious experience (whether in the form of a sensation elicited by a tendon receptor, or in some other form).

CONCLUSION

In this chapter, we have seen that consciousness as we presently experience it emerged as a necessary consequence of the transformation of processing information from a purely automatic and rigid stimulus-driven response way to a more flexible and autonomous way driven by self-generated tasks. This transformation entails that a system does no longer passively process (or better, react to) the pre-defined information of the environment, but actively determines what information is important for it. In order to occur, this transformation first requires that the system is deprived of its proximal, immediate links with the environment, because they strictly limit and specify its behaviour. Once these links are cut, the system can build new, distal and *mediated* relations with the environment on the basis of its own specific and contingent values, needs and plans. Consciousness is precisely this *mediated* way of continuously relating the system with the environment.

Attention plays a fundamental role in shaping both the phenomenal, qualitative aspect of consciousness and its contents. The phenomenal aspect of consciousness results from the temporary variation in the state of the nervous energy of the system induced by the attentional activity performed by the system. The contents of consciousness are determined by the attentional segmentation of the continuous and undifferentiated stream of environmental information into elemental mental building blocks, and the ensuing association, combination and assembly of such elemental building blocks. Both the attentional selection of the elemental mental building blocks and their combination are guided by the system's main needs, values and self-generated tasks.

The selective and combinatorial working of attention produces both new basic experiential dimensions such as time and space, and complex cultural experiential dimensions such as ethics, art, etc. These new dimensions allow us to imagine and simulate new scenarios and conditions without relying on a direct sensory input, thus enhancing our capacity to autonomously control the environment. The working of attention also allows for the creation of ordered sequences, such as series of elements, procedures, spatial and temporal order, etc., and correlation of elements. Language represents the main visible way of correlating and combining single elements into theoretically infinite sequences. More in general, language conveys - through the meaning of the combined words - the condensed instructions of the attentional operations one has to perform if one wants to consciously experience what these combinations of words express.

REFERENCES

Alvarez, G. A. (2011). Representing multiple objects as an ensemble enhances visual cognition. *Trends in Cognitive Sciences*, *15*, 122–131.

Amietta, P. L. (1991). *La creatività come necessità.* Milano: Etas.

Baars, B. J. (1988). *A Cognitive Theory of Consciousness*. Cambridge: Cambridge University Press.

Bachman, T. (2011). Attention as a process of selection, perception as a process of representation, and phenomenal experience as the resulting process of perception being modulated by a dedicated consciousness mechanism. *Frontiers in Psychology*, *2*, 1-7. doi: 10.3389/fpsyg. 2011.00387.

Bachmann, T. (2013). Neurobiological mechanisms behind the spatiotemporal illusions of awareness used for advocating prediction or postdiction. *Frontiers in Psychology*, *3* (593), 1-8.

Bahrami, B., Carmel, D., Walsh, V., Rees, G. and Lavie, N. (2008). Unconscious orientation processing depends on perceptual load. *Journal of Vision*, *8*, 12, 1–10.

Barsalou, L. W. (1999). Perceptual symbol systems. *Behavioral and Brain Sciences*, *22*, 577-660.

Bartolomeo, P. (2008). Varieties of attention and of consciousness: evidence from neuropsychology *Psyche*, *14*, 1-33.

Baumeister, R. F. and Masicampo, E. J. (2010). Conscious Thought Is for Facilitating Social and Cultural Interactions: How Mental Simulations Serve the Animal-Culture Interface. *Psychological Review*, *117* (3), 945-971.

Benedetti, G. (2006). Operational Noology as a new methodology for the study of thought and language: theoretical aspects and possible practical applications. *Cognitive Processing*, *7*, 217-243.

Benedetti, G. (2009). The Meaning of the Basic Elements of Language in Terms of Cognitive Operations: Operational Semantics. *Advanced Studies in Biology, Vol. 1*, (6), 255 – 305.

Benedetti, G. (2011). *An Enigma in Language. The Meaning of the Fundamental Linguistic Elements. A Possible Explanation in terms of Cognitive Functions: Operational Semantics.* New York: Nova Science Publishers.

Buschman, T. J. and Miller, E. K. (2010). Shifting the spotlight of attention: evidence for discrete computations in cognition. *Frontiers in Human Neuroscience, 4*, 194, 1-9, doi: 10.3389/fnhum.2010.00194.

Bush, N. A. and VanRullen, R. (2010). Spontaneous EEG oscillations reveal periodic sampling of visual attention. *Proceedings of the National Academy of Sciences of the United States of America, 107* (37), 16048-16053.

Carstensen, K. U. (2007). Spatio-temporal Ontologies and Attention. *Spatial Cognition and Computation 7* (1), 13-32.

Carstensen, K. U. (2011). Toward Cognitivist Ontologies. *Cognitive Processing, 12* (4), 379-393.

Castelfranchi, C. (2012). Autonomy for AGI. *Journal of Artificial General Intelligence, 3* (2), 31-33.

Carrasco, M. (2011). Visual attention: The past 25 years. *Vision Research, 51*, 1484-1525.

Ceccato, S. (1972). *La mente vista da un cibernetico*. Torino: Eri.

Ceccato, S. and Zonta, B. (1980). *Linguaggio consapevolezza pensiero*. Milano: Feltrinelli.

Chun, M. M., Golomb, J. D. and Turk-Browne, N. B. (2011). A Taxonomy of External and Internal Attention. *Annual Review of Psychology, 62*, 73-101.

Cleeremans, A. (2008). Consciousness: the radical plasticity thesis. *Progress in Brain Research, 168*, 19-33.

Colombo, J. and Cheatham, C. L. (2006). The emergence and basis of endogenous attention in infancy and early childhood. *Advances in child development and behavior, 34*, 283-322.

Corbetta, M. and Shulman, G. L. (2002). Control of goal-directed and stimulus-driven attention in the brain. *Nature reviews neuroscience, 3*(3), 201-215.

Craighero, L., Fadiga, L., Rizzolatti, G. and Umiltà, C. A. (1999). Action for perception: A motor–visual attentional effect. *Journal of Experimental Psychology: Human Perception and. Performance, 25*, 1673–1692.

Csikszentmihalyi, M. (1992). *Flow. The Classic Work on how to achieve happiness*. London: Random House Group.

Damasio, A. (1999). *The Feeling of What Happens. Body and Emotions in the Making of Consciousness*. New York: Harcourt Brace and Co.

De Brigard, F. and Prinz, J. (2010). Attention and consciousness. *Wiley Interdisciplinary Reviews: Cognitive Scecnce, 1*, 51–59.

Demeyere, N. and Humphreys, G. (2007). Distributed and focused attention: Neuropsychological evidence for separate attentional mechanisms when counting and estimating. *Journal of Experimental Psychology: Human Perception and Performance, 33*, 1076-1088.

Dennett, D. (1991). *Consciousness Explained.* Boston, NY: Little, Brown.

Doesburg, S. M., Roggeveen, A. B., Kitajo, K. and Ward, L. M. (2008). Large-scale gamma-band phase synchronization and selective attention. *Cerebral Cortex, 18* (2), 386–396.

Doesburg, S. M., Green, J. J., McDonald, J. J. and Ward, L. M. (2009). Rhythms of Consciousness: Binocular Rivalry Reveals Large-Scale Oscillatory Network Dynamics Mediating Visual Perception. *PLoS ONE*, *4* (7) e6142, 1-14, doi:10.1371/journal.pone.0006142.

Droit-Volet, S. (2001). Les différentes facettes du temps. *Enfances et Psy*, *1*, 26-40.

Eagleman, D. M. (2001). Visual illusions and neurobiology. *Nature reviews. Neuroscience*, *2*(12), 920-926.

Eagleman, D. M. (2008). Human time perception and its illusions. *Current Opinion in Neurobiology*, *18*, 131-136.

Eagleman, D. M. and Pariyadath, V. (2009). Is subjective duration a signature of coding efficiency? *Philosophical Transactions of the Royal Society B*, *364*, 1841-1851.

Eagleman, D. M. and Sejnowski, T. J. (2000). Motion integration and postdiction in visual awareness. *Science*, *287*, 2036-2038.

Eagleman, D. M. and Sejnowski, T. J. (2007). Motion signals bias localization judgments: A unified explanation for the flash-lag, flash-drag, flash-jump, and Fröhlich illusions. *Journal of Vision*, *7* (4), 3, 287, 1-12.

Edelman, G. M. (1989). *The Remembered Present: a Biological Theory of Consciousness*. New York: Basic Books.

Fingelkurts, A. A., Fingelkurts, A. A. and Neves, C. F. (2013). Consciousness as a phenomenon in the operational architectonics of brain organization: Criticality and self-organization considerations. *Chaos*, *Solitons* and *Fractals*. http://dx.doi.org/10.1016/j.chaos.2013.02.007.

Flaherty, M. (1999). *A watched pot: How we experience time*. New York: New York University Press.

Gallagher, S. and Zahavi, D. (2008). *The Phenomenological Mind. An Introduction to Philosophy of Mind and Cognitive science*. London: Routledge.

Gibson, J. J. (1986). *The Ecological Approach to Visual Perception*. Hillsdale, NJ: Lawrence Erlbaum Associates Inc.

Glasersfeld, E. Von. (1998). *Il costruttivismo radicale. Una via per conoscere ed apprendere*. Roma: Società Stampa Sportiva.

Haikonen, P. O. (2003). *The Cognitive Approach to Conscious Machines*. Exeter, UK Imprint Academic.

Higuchi, T. (2013). Visuomotor control of human adaptive locomotion: understanding the anticipatory nature. *Frontiers in Psychology*, *4*(27), 1-9.

Hirsh, I. J. and Sherrick, C. (1961). Perceived order in different sense modalities. *Journal of Experimental Psychology*, *62*, 423–432.

Hohwy, J. (2007). The Sense of self in the Phenomenology of Agency and Perception. *Psyche*, *13*, 1-20.

Hommel, B. (2009). Action control according to TEC (theory of event coding). *Psychological Reseacrh*, *73*, 512-526.

Hommel, B. (2010). "Grounding attention in action control: The intentional control of selection", in *Effortless attention: A new perspective in the cognitive science of attention and action*, ed. B.J. Bruya (Cambridge, MA: MIT Press), 121-140.

Hommel, B., Müsseler, J., Aschersleben, G. and Prinz, W. (2001). The Theory of Event Coding (TEC): A framework for perception and action planning. *Behavioral and Brain Sciences*, *24*, 849-937.

Iwasaki, S. (1993). Spatial attention and two modes of visual consciousness. *Cognition, 49*, 211-233.

James, W. (1890). *The Principles of Psychology*. New York: Holt.

Janczyk, M., Skirde, S., Weigelt, M. and Kunde, W. (2009). Visual and tactile action effects determine bimanual coordination performance. *Human Movement Science*, *28*(4), 437-449.

Jones, M. R., Moynihan, H., MacKenzie, N. and Puente, J. (2002). Temporal aspects of stimulus driven attending in dynamic arrays. *Psychological Science*, *13*, 313–319.

Kahneman, D. (1973). *Attention and effort*. Englewood Cliffs, NJ: Prentice Hall.

Klinger, E. and Cox, W. M. (1987). Dimensions of thought flow in everyday life. *Imagination, Cognition and Personality*, *7*, 105–128.

Knudsen, E. I. (2007). Fundamental Components of Attention. *Annual review of neuroscience*, *30*, 57-78.

Koch, C. and Tsuchiya, N. (2006). Attention and consciousness: two distinct brain processes. *Trends in Cognitive Sciences*, *11*, 16-22.

Koivisto, M., Kainulainen, P. and Revonsuo, A. (2009). The relationship between awareness and attention: evidence from ERP responses. *Neuropsychologia*, *47*, 2891–2899.

Kouider, S., de Gardelle, V., Sackur, J. and Dupoux, E. (2010). How rich is consciousness? The partial awareness hypothesis. *Trends in Cognitive Sciences*, *14* (7), 301-307.

La Berge, D. (1995). *Attentional Processing. The Brain's Art of Mindfulness*. Cambridge, Massachusetts: Harvard University Press.

Lamme, V. A. F. (2003). Why visual attention and awareness are different. *Trends in Cognitive Sciences*, *7*, 12-18.

Landau, A. N. and Fries, P. (2012). Attention Samples Stimuli Rhythmically. *Current Biology*, *22* (11), 1000-1004.

Lavie, N. (1995). Perceptual load as a necessary condition for selective attention. *Journal of Experimental Psychology: Human Perception and Performance*, *21*, 451-468.

Lehar, S. (2003). Gestalt isomorphism and the primacy of subjective conscious experience: A Gestalt Bubble model. *Behavioral and Brain Sciences*, *26*, 375-444.

Libet, B. (2004). *Mind Time. The Temporal Factor in Consciousness*. Cambridge, Massachusetts: Harvard University Press.

Logan, G. D. and Cowan, W. B. (1984). On the Ability to Inhibit Thought and Action: A Theory of an Act of Control. *Psychological Review*, *91* (3), 295-327.

Mach, E. (1890). *Contributions to the analysis of the sensations*. La Salle: The Open Court Publishing Company.

Mack, A. and Rock, I. (1998). *Inattentional Blindness*. Cambridge: MIT Press.

Marchetti, G. (1997). *La macchina estetica. Il percorso operativo nella costruzione dell'atteggiamento estetico*. Milano: Franco Angeli.

Marchetti, G. (2009). Studies on time: a proposal on how to get out of circularity. *Cognitive Processing*, *10* (1), 7-40.

Marchetti, G. (2010). *Consciousness, Attention and Meaning*. New York: Nova Science Publishers.

Marchetti, G. (2012). Against the view that consciousness and attention are fully dissociable. *Frontiers in Psychology*, *3*, 1-14. doi: 10.3389/fpsyg. 2012.00036.

Matura, H. R. and Varela, F. J. (1992). *The Tree of Knowledge. The Biological Roots of Human Understanding*. Shambhala: Boston.

McCloskey, M. and Watkins, M. J. (1978). The seeing-more-than-is-there phenomenon: implications for the locus of iconic storage. *Journal of Experimental Psychology: Human Perception and Performance*, *4* (4), 553-564.

Montaser-Kousari, L. and Rajimehr, R. (2005). Subliminal attentional modulation in crowding condition. *Vision Research*, *45*, 839–844.

Müsseler, J. and Hommel, B. (1997). Blindness to response-compatible stimuli. *Journal of Experimental Psychology: Human Perception and Performance*, *23*, 861–872.

Naccache, L., Blandin, E. and Dehaene, S. (2002). Unconscious masked priming depends on temporal attention. *Psychologycal Science*, *13*, 416–424.

Nakano, T., Kato, M., Morito, Y., Itoi, S. and Kitazawa, S. (2013). Blink-related momentary activation of the default mode network while viewing videos. *Proceedings of the National Academy of Sciences of the United States of America*, *110* (2), 702–706.

Nakayama, K. and Mackeben, M. (1989). Sustained and transient components of focal visual attention. *Vision Research*, *29*, 1631-1647.

O'Regan, J. K. and Noë, A. (2001). A sensorimotor account of vision and visual consciousness. *Behavioral and Brain Sciences*, *24* (5), 939-1031.

Pashler, H. E. (1998). *The psychology of attention*. Cambridge, Massachusetts: The MIT Press.

Piaget, J. (1936). *La naissance de l'intelligence chez l'enfant*. Paris et Neuchâtel: Delachaux et Niestlé.

Piaget, J. (1937). *La construction du réel chez l'enfant*. Paris et Neuchâtel: Delachaux et Niestlé.

Posner, M. I. (1980). Orienting of Attention. *Quarterly Journal of Experimental Psychology*, *32*, 3-25.

Posner, M. I. (1994). Attention: the mechanisms of consciousness. *Proceedings of the National Academy of Sciences of the United States of America*, *91*, 7398–7403.

Revonsuo, A. (2006). *Inner Presence. Consciousness as a Biological Phenomenon*. Cambridge, Massachusetts: The MIT Press.

Rochat, P. (2003). Five levels of self-awareness as they unfold early in life. *Consciousness and Cognition*, *12*, 717-731.

Scheider, S. and Kuhn, W. (2011). Finite relativist geometry grounded in perceptual operations. *Spatial Information Theory*, *6899*, 304-327.

Simons, D. J. and Levin, D. T. (1997). Change blindness. *Trends in Cognitive Sciences 1*, 261–267.

Simons, D. J. and Levin, D. T. (1998). Failure to detect changes to people during a real-world interaction. *Psychonomic Bulletin and Review*, *5*, 644–649.

Snyder, H. R. and Munakata, Y. (2010). Becoming self-directed: Abstract representations support endogenous flexibility in children. *Cognition*, *116*, 155-167.

Spence, C. (2010). "Prior entry: attention and temporal perception", in *Attention and Time*, eds. A. C. Nobre and J T. Coull (Oxford: Oxford University Press), 89-104.

Srinivasan, N. (2008). Interdependence of attention and consciousness. *Progress in Brain* Research, 168, 65-75.

Sumner, P., Tsai, P. C., Yu, K. and Nachev, P. (2006). Attentional modulation of sensorimotor processes in the absence of perceptual awareness. *Proceedings of the National Academy of Sciences of the United States of America*, *103*, 10520–10525.

Synofzik, M., Vosgerau, G. and Newen, A. (2008). I move, therefore I am: A new theoretical framework to investigate agency and ownership. *Consciousness and Cognition, 17*(2), 411-424.

Szymaszek, A., Sereda, M., Pöppel, E. and Szelag, E. (2009). Individual differences in the perception of temporal order: the effect of age and cognition. *Cognitive Neuropsychology, 26*, 135–147.

Thórisson, K. R. and Helgasson, H. P. (2012). Cognitive Architectures and Autonomy: A Comparative Review. *Journal of Artificial General Intelligence, 3* (2), 1-30.

Treisman, A. (2006). How the deployment of attention determines what we see. *Visual Cognition, 14*, 411–443.

Treisman, A. M. and Gelade, G. (1980). A feature-integration theory of attention. *Cognitive Psychology*, 12, 97–136.

Tsuchiya, N. and van Boxtel, J. J. (2013). Introduction to research topic: attention and consciousness in different senses. *Frontiers in Psychology, 4*, 249. doi: 10.3389/fpsyg.2013.00249.

Tulving, E. (1985). Memory and consciousness. *Canadian Psychology, 26*, 1–12.

van Boxtel, J. J., Tsuchiya, N. and Kock, C. (2010). Consciousness and attention: on sufficiency and necessity. *Frontiers in Psychology, 1*, 1–13. doi:10.3389/ fpsyg.2010.00217.

Vandekerckhove, M. and Panksepp, J. (2009). The flow of anoetic to noetic and autonoetic consciousness: A vision of unknowing (anoetic) and knowing (noetic) consciousness in the remembrance of things past and imagined futures. *Consciousness and Cognition, 18*, 1018-1028.

VanRullen, R., Carlson, T. and Cavanagh, P. (2007). The blinking spotlight of attention. *Proceedings of the National Academy of Sciences of the United States of America, 104*, 19204-19209.

VanRullen, R. and Koch, C. (2003). Is perception discrete or continuous? *Trends in Cognitive Sciences, 7* (5), 207–213.

Varela, F. J., Toro, A., John, E. R. and Schwartz, E. L. (1981). Perceptual framing and cortical alpha rhythm. *Neuropsychologia, 19*, 675–686.

Vicario, G. B. (2001). *Psicologia generale. I fondamenti*. Roma-Bari: Editori Laterza.

Vicario, G. B. (2005). *Il tempo. Saggio di psicologia sperimentale*. Bologna: Il Mulino.

Vosgerau, G. and Newen, A. (2007). Thoughts, Motor Actions, and the Self. *Mind and Language*, 22(1), 22-43.

Wickens, C. D. (1984). "Processing resources in attention", in *Varieties of attention*, eds. R. Parasuraman and D. R. Davis (New York: Academic Press), 63-102.

Wittmann, M. (2011). Moments in Time. *Frontiers in Psychology, 5* (66), 1-9. doi: 10.3389/fnint.2011.00066.

In: Consciousness
Editor: Lloyd Alvarado

ISBN: 978-1-63485-023-0

Chapter 5

COGNITIVE PHENOMENOLOGY AND THE COMPUTATIONAL CORRELATES OF CONSCIOUSNESS

James A. Reggia*
University of Maryland, Maryland,US

ABSTRACT

The use of computational models to simulate various behavioral, cognitive and neurobiological correlates of consciousness has become an increasingly accepted approach to the scientific study of consciousness. However, efforts to create a phenomenally conscious machine have been much less successful. The recent advocacy of cognitive phenomenology in philosophy has the potential to be a game changer in this regard. Cognitive phenomenology asserts that our subjective experiences are not restricted to just traditional qualia, but also encompass deliberative thought processes and high-level cognition. To the extent that this controversial idea is valid, it provides a new route to a deeper understanding of consciousness via computational studies. This route would focus on identifying possible computational correlates of consciousness based on neurocomputational implementations of high-level cognitive functions that are associated with subjective mental states. Identifying such correlates could lead to a better understanding of phenomenal consciousness in general, and perhaps even to a framework for creating an artificially conscious machine. Several potential computational correlates of consciousness are identified and discussed in this context.

Keywords: cognitive phenomenology, computational explanatory gap, phenomenal consciousness, computational correlates of consciousness, machine consciousness, artificial consciousness, computer models

---

* Correspondence: James Reggia. Dept. of Computer Science, A.V. Williams Bldg., University of Maryland, College Park, MD 20742, USA (reggia@cs.umd.edu).

1. INTRODUCTION

The central assertion of *cognitive phenomenology* is that our subjective, first-person experience is not restricted to just traditional qualia involving sensory perception, emotions and visual imagery, but also encompasses deliberative thought and high-level cognition. Such an assertion might seem straightforward to the non-philosopher, but it has proven to be highly controversial in philosophy. Introductory overviews that explain this controversy in a historical context can be found in (Bayne and Montague, 2011a; Siewert, 2011), and a very balanced collection of essays arguing for and against the basic ideas of cognitive phenomenology are given in (Bayne and Montague, 2011b). A recent detailed analysis of cognitive phenomenology is also available (Chudnoff, 2015).

Most of this past discussion in the philosophy literature has focused on reasons for accepting or rejecting cognitive phenomenology. Philosophical theoreticians generally appear to accept that that some aspects of cognition are accessible to consciousness, so the arguments in the literature have focused on the specific issue of whether there are phenomenal aspects of cognition that cannot be accounted for by traditional sensory qualia and mental imagery. For example, an advocate of cognitive phenomenology might argue that there is a different non-sensory subjective quality associated with hearing the sentence "I'm tired" spoken in a foreign language if one understands that language than if one does not, given that the sensory experience is effectively the same in both cases.

Here we take a perspective that differs from most of this past discussion that has focused on the validity of cognitive phenomenology. We start with the assumption that cognitive phenomenology is correct and ask what that might imply. In other words, we start by *assuming* that there exist distinct non-sensory subjective mental experiences associated with some aspects of cognition. What would follow from this assumption? Past discussions concerning the implications of cognitive phenomenology have been relatively limited, although it has been speculated that the occurrence of cognitive subjective states would inform our understanding of the trustworthiness of introspection, of the functional role of consciousness, and of the relationship between the phenomenal mind and the intentional mind (Bayne and Montague, 2011a). Here we consider another specific hypothesis about such implications: *Cognitive phenomenology will provide a route to both a deeper understanding of human consciousness and also to a phenomenally conscious machine*. This hypothesis seems plausible because cognitive phenomenology makes a large body of research in AI and cognitive science, work that is developing neurocomputational implementations of high-level cognition, relevant to the issue of phenomenal consciousness. This work, while recognized as being relevant to intentional aspects of consciousness, has not generally been considered of direct relevance to phenomenology. This implication is an aspect of cognitive phenomenology that has apparently not been significantly considered previously.

In this context, we will focus in the following on the possibility of creating a conscious machine. While this is not a particularly new issue (Butler, 1872), it is only over the last two decades that it has motivated sustained work on developing computational models of the conscious mind, either via software on computers or by using physical robots. Such studies concerning artificial consciousness have been intended to advance our understanding of human consciousness and its relationship to cognition, to contribute to increased functionality in future AI systems, and (at times) to design a phenomenally conscious machine.

At present, efforts to study artificial consciousness remain highly controversial. Researchers in mainstream AI (with a few exceptions) have largely ignored work in this area. In philosophy, while a variety of opinions have been expressed, a significant number of these would make pursuit of machine consciousness appear to be a rather fruitless task. For example, it has been argued that, in general, the objective methods of science cannot shed light on consciousness due to its subjective nature (McGinn, 2004), making computational investigations a moot point. Further, a broad range of more specific arguments have been presented in recent years that phenomenal machine consciousness is simply not possible (Bishop, 2009; Bringsjord, 2007; Manzotti, 2012; Schlagel, 1999). Individuals who advocate or study the possibilities of machine consciousness have so far not found such arguments persuasive (Aleksander, 2005; Koch and Tononi, 2008). Further concerns arise from an ethical perspective of what it would mean should one actually produce a phenomenally conscious machine, and whether doing so might be dangerous (e.g., the "singularity").

In a recent review of work in the area of artificial consciousness, it was found that, in contrast to what one might expect based on such negative viewpoints, very substantial progress has been made over the last twenty years in the field of artificial consciousness (Reggia, 2013). Here we will see that by distinguishing between simulated correlates of consciousness and instantiated consciousness, it is possible to clearly delineate where significant progress is being made, and where the jury is still out. We then ask, in the context of the hypothesis above concerning cognitive phenomenology, and from a purely computational/engineering viewpoint: What is the main practical barrier to further progress on creating phenomenal/instantiated machine consciousness? The answer suggested here is that it is a *computational explanatory gap*: our current lack of understanding concerning how high-level cognitive computations can be captured in low-level neural computations (Reggia, Monner and Sylvester, 2014). The significance of this gap is that bridging it may be a critical step not only in developing a future conscious machine, but also in addressing the original philosophical explanatory gap, in gaining a better understanding of the physical basis of consciousness, and in making advances on the mind-brain problem in general during coming years. Bridging this gap may potentially identify new *computational correlates of consciousness*, specifically neurobiologically-inspired computational processes that are exclusively associated with phenomenally conscious information processing (Cleeremans, 2005). A non-exhaustive summary is given of several potential computational correlates of consciousness that are currently recognized. While a number of candidate correlates have been identified, at present none of these can yet fully meet the criteria we will define for being computational correlates of consciousness. This limitation highlights the need for further work in this area, with the hope that this will fundamentally improving our understanding of phenomenal consciousness.

2. The Nature of Progress in Artificial Consciousness

To understand the sense in which recent work on artificial consciousness has made progress, it is useful to distinguish between two possible objectives for such work: simulation of consciousness versus instantiation of consciousness. Such a distinction parallels the distinction often made between information processing aspects of consciousness (relates to functionalism, access consciousness (Block, 1995)) and subjective experience (phenomenal consciousness).

With *simulated consciousness*, the goal is to capture some aspect of the neural/behavioral/cognitive aspects of consciousness in a computational model, much as is done in using computers to simulate other natural processes (e.g., models of weather/climate). There is nothing particularly mysterious about such work: Just as one would not expect that a computer used to simulate a nuclear reactor would become radioactive, one should not expect that a computer used to model some aspect of information processing associated with consciousness would become phenomenally conscious. There is no claim that phenomenal consciousness is actually present in a machine in this situation. The results of a simulation are often assessed based on the extent to which they correspond to experimentally verified aspects of consciousness such as neurophysiological measures, or on the extent to which they may contribute increased functionality to future artificial systems.

In contrast, with *instantiated consciousness*, the issue is the extent to which an artificial system actually has phenomenal consciousness. Does it experience qualia and does it have subjective experiences? This is a much more difficult and controversial question. This dichotomy between simulated and instantiated consciousness is reminiscent of the distinction between weak AI (behavioral criteria) and strong AI (artificial mind) (Seth, 2009).

Recognizing the difference between simulated and instantiated machine consciousness clarifies the nature of the progress that has been made in artificial consciousness research over the last two decades. From the perspective of simulated consciousness, neurocomputational modeling has successfully captured a number of neurobiological, cognitive and behavioral properties of conscious information processing as machine simulations. For example, there are neurocomputational models that increase activation of their global workspace when performing difficult tasks associated with conscious effort in people (Dehanene et al., 1998), thereby supporting global workspace theories of consciousness (Baars, 1988, 2002). Other neurocomputational methods have been used to demonstrate that expectation-driven robots can recognize themselves in a mirror (Takeno, 2013), essentially passing the well-known mirror test used to identify self-recognition in animals. Still other models have shown that second-order neural networks can match behavioral data from human blindsight subjects during post-decision wagering tasks (Pasquali et al., 2010), supporting some aspects of higher order thought (HOT) theories of consciousness (Carruthers, 2005). Clearly, these and other computational models involving simulation of consciousness have provided useful information for advancing consciousness studies. As a result, they are increasingly being viewed as an acceptable approach to furthering the scientific investigation of consciousness, and they may help constrain the large number of theories of consciousness that exist (Katz, 2013) by clarifying their implications via modeling. A more detailed discussion of these and many other related models is given in (Reggia, 2013).

The situation is quite different from the perspective of instantiated consciousness. Only a very few investigators have claimed to know how to create phenomenally conscious artifacts. Further, substantial arguments have also been presented that instantiated machine consciousness is simply not possible. A few examples are that machines cannot be conscious due to their non-organic nature (Schlagel, 1999), that phenomenal machine consciousness would imply panpsychism (Bishop, 2009), that the absence of a formal definition of consciousness precludes conscious machines (Bringsjord, 2007), and that computation is insufficient to underpin consciousness (Manzotti, 2012). The intent here is not to explore in depth these claims (or counter-claims), but only to demonstrate that the possibility of instantiated machine consciousness remains controversial.

At the present time, no existing computational approach to artificial consciousness has yet presented a compelling demonstration or design of instantiated consciousness in a machine, or even clear evidence that instantiated machine consciousness will eventually be possible. Yet at the same time, no compelling refutation of the possibility of a phenomenally conscious machine has been generally accepted. From a history-of-technology perspective, the current situation resembles discussions concerning the possibility of heavier-than-air machine flight during the late 1800s. During this period, as primitive efforts were underway to create such machines, very plausible arguments were being made about the impossibility of machine flight, and these arguments were only put to rest when the Wright brothers' took wing at Kitty Hawk[1]. It remains to be seen whether work on artificial consciousness will have an analogous outcome. In the mean time, the current situation raises the issue of what can be done to resolve whether or not instantiated machine consciousness is possible. Resolution of this issue depends on clearly identifying the main barriers to further progress that are tractable, or at least amenable to scientific/technical investigation, and then hopefully overcoming them.

3. THE COMPUTATIONAL EXPLANATORY GAP

What are the main practical barriers at present to creating instantiated machine consciousness? Clearly, there is no shortage of well-known candidates. These include the absence of a generally agreed-upon definition of consciousness, our limited understanding of its neurobiological correlates, and the "other minds problem" applied to artifacts (how could one possibly know whether or not a machine is conscious?). While each of these difficulties is substantial, from a computer science/engineering viewpoint none appear to be sufficient to account for the lack of progress that has occurred. Significant progress has been made in artificial intelligence and artificial life without having generally accepted definitions of either intelligence or life. Our current inadequate understanding of the neurobiological basis of consciousness does not prevent one from conducting non-biological experimentation via computer modeling of existing theories, and the other minds problem has not prevented studies of phenomenal consciousness and self-awareness in humans and animals.

The central argument being made here is that there is another less recognized barrier, the *computational explanatory gap*, which is also critically important (Reggia, Monner and Sylvester, 2014). We will define the computational explanatory gap to be a lack of understanding of how high-level cognitive information processing can be mapped onto low-level neural computations. By "high-level cognitive information processing" is meant aspects of cognition such as goal-directed problem solving, executive decision making, planning, language, and metacognition – cognitive processes that are widely accepted to at least in part be consciously accessible. By "low-level neural computations" is meant the kinds of

[1] This analogy with flight is limited in that consciousness involves the other-minds problem, unlike flight. The analogy also raises the question of whether consciousness is an all-or-nothing property or lies on a continuum in the same way that "flying" does (person jumping, flying squirrel, hang gliding, bird flight, sustained plane flight, orbiting satellite, etc.). The primary point here is just that prior to 1900, many informed people argued that heavier-than-air flight was impossible.

computations that can be achieved by networks of artificial neurons like those that are widely studied in contemporary computer science, engineering, psychology, and neuroscience.

The computational explanatory gap can be contrasted with the well-known *philosophical explanatory gap* between a successful functional/computational account of consciousness and accounting for the subjective experiences that accompany it (Levine, 1983). While the computational explanatory gap is ultimately relevant to the philosophical explanatory gap, the former is *not* a mind-brain issue per se. Rather, it is a gap in our general understanding of how computations (algorithms and dynamical states) supporting goal-directed reasoning and problem solving at a high level of cognitive information processing can be mapped into the kinds of computations/algorithms/states that can be supported at the low level of neural networks. In other words, as illustrated in Figure 1, *it is a purely computational issue*.

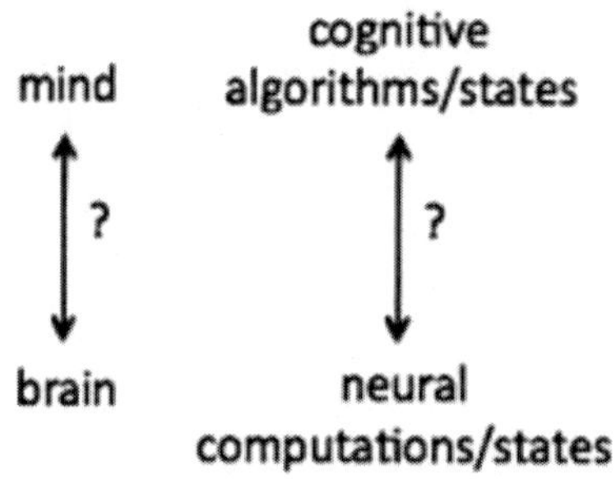

Figure 1. The well-known philosophical explanatory gap (on the left) and less recognized computational explanatory gap (on the right). The argument presented here is that the latter may ultimately prove to be the more fundamental problem, and that focusing on solving it rather than dismissing it may be the key to advancing future work on instantiated machine consciousness.

The computational explanatory gap is also not an issue specific to computers or even computer science. It is a generic issue concerning how one type of computations at a high level (serial goal-directed deliberative reasoning algorithms associated with conscious aspects of cognition) can be mapped into a fundamentally different type of computations at a low level (parallel distributed neural computations and representational states). It is an *abstraction* independent of the hardware involved, be it the electronic circuits of a computer or the neural circuits of the brain. If this abstraction is significant, then one would expect to find that it can be related to past consciousness studies occurring across a broad range of disciplines. Is this the case? It is suggested in the following paragraphs that not only is this true for disciplines such as philosophy, AI, cognitive psychology, and neuroscience, but also that the computational explanatory gap provides a prism through which to potentially unify past work relevant to conscious information processing across these different disciplines.

In philosophy, the computational explanatory gap relates to the long-standing discussion concerning the "easy problem" of accounting for cognitive information processing versus the "hard problem" of explaining subjective experience (Chalmers, 1996). This characterization is often qualified by comments that the easy problem is not really viewed as being truly easy to solve, but that it is easy to imagine that a solution can be obtained via functional/computational approaches, while this is not the case for the hard problem (e.g., Block, 1995). Nonetheless, the easy/hard contemporary philosophical distinction tends to largely dismiss solving the computational explanatory gap, as it is just part of the easy problem. Such a dismissal fails to explain why the computational explanatory gap has proven to be largely intractable during more than half a century of efforts (since McCulloch and Pitts (1943) first captured propositional-level logical inferences using neural networks). This intractability is somewhat mysterious, given that the brain somehow readily bridges this gap. While the brain's structure is of course quite complex, it appears unlikely that this complexity alone could be the whole explanation, given that mainstream top-down AI has been qualitatively more successful in modeling high-level cognition when compared to neurocomputational methods. It seems likely that something more fundamental is being missed here. Specifically, a reasonable conjecture is that, with high probability, the unfortunate terminology of the "easy" and "hard" problems that dominates contemporary philosophical thought will ultimately turn out to be precisely backwards. In other words, the computational explanatory gap is actually the more fundamental and difficult-to-resolve issue, and that once this gap is bridged, the philosophical explanatory gap may be found to be much more tractable and fade away. This issue is discussed further in the next section.

In AI the computational explanatory gap relates to the long-standing debate concerning the relative values of top-down (symbolic, etc.) vs. bottom-up (neural, swarm, etc.) approaches to creating machine intelligence (Franklin, 1995). This (in)famous and continuing debate has largely missed the point that these two approaches are not so much competing alternatives as complementary in what they have each captured so far concerning intelligence. Top-down symbolic methods have excelled at modeling high-level cognitive tasks such as goal-directed reasoning, metacognition, problem-solving, decision making, "understanding" natural language, and planning, but they have been much less successful at pattern recognition and low level motor control. In other words, they have been relatively successful in capturing aspects of high-level deliberative reasoning and sequential behavioral control that, in a person, are associated with conscious, reportable components of cognition. Top down methods have also generally been found to be brittle, for example, failing dramatically in the context of noise, minor unexpected events, or small changes to the contents of memory. In contrast, bottom-up neurocomputational methods have roughly the opposite strengths and weaknesses. They are remarkably effective and robust in learning low-level pattern classification ("input") and low-level control ("output") tasks, but are not nearly as effective for high-level cognitive tasks. For example, neurocomputational systems have proven to be very effective in learning procedural knowledge that, in a person, is largely carried out in an automatic unconscious manner. Examples include robotic arm movement neurocontrollers (Gentili et al., 2015) and steering of an autonomous automobile (Pomerleau, 1993). Compared to top-down symbolic AI methods, neurocomputational methods are less brittle in the context of external noise or substantial random changes to stored information (random weight changes, random loss of simulated neurons, etc.). In short, past work in mainstream symbolic AI has so far done relatively little to bridge the computational explanatory gap. The field of AI largely remains split into two opposing camps today, in part directly due to the computational explanatory gap.

In cognitive psychology too, the computational explanatory gap becomes evident when one considers past efforts to characterize explicitly the properties that distinguish human conscious versus unconscious cognitive information processing. For example, human conscious information processing has been characterized as being serial, relatively slow, and largely restricted to one task at a time (attempting to carry out multiple tasks requiring conscious direction simultaneously leads to interference and errors) (Baars, 1988, 2002;

Dehaene and Naccache, 2001). In contrast, unconscious information processing is parallel, relatively fast, and can readily involve more than one task simultaneously with limited interference between the tasks. Conscious information processing appears to involve widespread "global" brain activity and is internally consistent, while unconscious information processing appears to involve more localized activation of brain regions and varies in its internal consistency. Conscious information processing is often associated with inner speech and is operationally taken to be cognition that is reportable,[2] while unconscious information processing has neither of these properties. The key point here is that psychologists explicitly trying to characterize the differences between conscious and unconscious information processing have implicitly, and perhaps unintentionally, identified the computational explanatory gap. The properties they have identified as characterizing unconscious information processing – parallel processing, efficient, modular, non-reportable – often match reasonably well with those of neural computation (no explanatory gap here). For example, being "non-reportable" matches up well with the nature of neurocomputational models where, even once a neural network has learned to perform a task very successfully, what that network has learned remains largely opaque to outside observers and often requires a major effort to determine or express symbolically (Huynh and Reggia, 2012). In contrast, the properties associated with conscious information processing – serial processing, relatively slow, holistic, reportable – are a much better match to symbolic top-down algorithms, and a poor match to the characteristics of neural computations. In this context, the unexplained gap between conscious cognition and the underlying neural computations that support it is strikingly evident. This is particularly remarkable because identifying the contrasting properties of conscious and unconscious aspects of cognition was not an explicit effort to characterize the nature of the computational explanatory gap.

Finally, the computational explanatory gap is also evident in neuroscience, where substantial efforts have focused on identifying neural correlates of consciousness (Crick and Koch, 1990). Roughly, a neural correlate of consciousness is some minimal neurobiological state whose presence is sufficient for the occurrence of a corresponding state of consciousness (Chalmers, 2000). This approach to understanding consciousness has identified several candidate correlates, such as specific activity patterns in the brain's electrical activity (e.g., widespread synchronized 40 hz cortical oscillations), activation of specific neural structures (e.g., thalamic intralaminar nuclei), global brain activation, etc. (Metzinger, 2000b). However, in spite of such work and an enormous neuroscientific endeavor in general over more than a century, there remains a large difference between our understanding of unconscious versus conscious information processing in the brain, as follows.

Consider unconscious information processing, such as the automatic motor control mechanisms underlying leg movements during walking, or the mechanisms that store information in long-term memory. There is nothing really mysterious about these mechanisms today in the sense that we can identify neural circuits and computations that plausibly account for these functions: central pattern generators for oscillatory movements, Hebbian synaptic changes for associative memory, and so forth. In contrast, for high-level cognitive tasks that relate more closely to conscious cognition, such as goal-directed problem solving and

[2] Although such a criterion has substantial limitations, being verbally reportable has long been widely used in experimental psychology as a major objective criterion for accepting that a person is conscious of (subjectively aware of) an event (Baars, 1988; Dehaene and Naccache, 2001).

understanding the meaning of spoken natural language, we remain relatively lost in neurocomputational terms. This is in spite of the fact that we know a great deal about high-level cognition and the brain today. For example, a lot is currently known at the macroscopic level about associating high-level cognitive functions with brain regions (pre-frontal cortex "executive" regions, language cortex areas, etc.), and a lot is known about the microscopic functionality of neural circuitry in these regions, all the way down to the molecular and genetic levels. What remains largely unclear is how to put those two types of information together, or in other words, how the brain maps these high-level cognitive functions into computations over the low-level neural circuits that are present. Once again, we encounter the computational explanatory gap. It remains unclear why this mapping from cognitive processes to neural computations is so opaque today given the enormous resources that have been poured into understanding these issues. This widely-recognized situation has led to a recent call by prominent neuroscientists for a "brain activity map initiative" that would develop the technology for bridging this gap (Alivisatos et al., 2013). The key point here is that this large gap in our neuroscientific knowledge about how to relate the macroscopic and microscopic levels of information processing to one another is, at least in part, also a manifestation of the underlying computational explanatory gap.

4. Bridging the Gap

Why is bridging the computational explanatory gap of critical importance in addressing the possibility of instantiated machine consciousness? The reason is that bridging this gap would allow us to do something that is currently beyond our reach: It would allow us to directly and cleanly compare (i) neurocomputational mechanisms associated with conscious/reportable high-level cognitive activities, and (ii) neurocomputational mechanisms associated with lower-level unconscious information processing. In effect, this comparison would allow us to determine whether or not there are *computational correlates of consciousness* in the same sense that there are neurobiological correlates of consciousness (Cleeremans, 2005). The term "computational correlate of consciousness" as it is used here means minimal neurocomputational processing mechanisms that are specifically associated with conscious aspects of cognition but *not* with unconscious aspects. Importantly, in the context of the computational explanatory gap, we are specifically interested in *neuro*computational correlates of consciousness, i.e., computational correlates related to the representation, storage, processing, and modification of information that occurs in neural networks. Computational correlates of consciousness are a priori distinct from neural correlates (Cleeremans, 2005). As noted above, proposed neural correlates have in practice included, for example, electrical/metabolic activity patterns, neuroanatomical regions of the brain, and biochemical phenomena (Chalmers, 2000) - correlates within the realm of biology that are not computational. Neurocomputational correlates are abstractions that may well find implementation in the brain and thus can sometimes also be candidates for neural correlates of consciousness as well, but as abstractions they are intended to be independent of the physical substrate that implements them (brain, silicon, etc.).

If convincing computational correlates can be identified, many individuals concerned with the mind-brain problem would probably concede that this could at least provide insight into the nature of access consciousness. However, the suggestion here is that, should neurocomputational correlates of consciousness be discovered, they may also provide a direct route to investigating the possibility of instantiated machine consciousness, to identifying candidate properties that could serve as objective criteria for the presence/absence of phenomenal consciousness in machines and people, and perhaps even to a better understanding of the fundamental nature of consciousness. Pursuit of neurocomputational correlates of consciousness is a worthy endeavor regardless of the ultimate outcome of such work: Even if no differences between the neurocomputational implementation of conscious and unconscious cognitive functions can be found, that too would have tremendous implications for the modern functionalist viewpoint of the mind-brain problem, for example lending support to theories that incorporate some aspect of dualism (e.g., naturalistic dualism (Chalmers, 1996)).

In other words, what is being suggested here is that a complete characterization of high-level cognition in neurocomputational terms may, along the way, show us how subjective experience arises mechanistically. This claim is made in the context of the ongoing discussion in philosophy concerning cognitive phenomenology, as was described in the Introduction. Cognitive phenomenology emphasizes that our subjective first-person experience is not restricted to just traditional qualia involving perception and affect, but also encompasses deliberative thought and high-level cognition, precisely the subject at issue in the computational explanatory gap as we have defined it. While the cognitive phenomenology viewpoint is controversial (Bayne and Montague, 2011a), to the extent that this viewpoint holds it indicates that bridging the computational explanatory gap will provide evidence directly relevant to a deeper understanding of phenomenal consciousness.

Further, even if bridging the computational explanatory gap does not provide a full mechanistic account of subjective experiences, doing so could still provide more meaningful conditions for investigating phenomenal consciousness in an artifact. Importantly, bridging the computational explanatory gap could make the hard problem largely fade away. A familiar historical analogy with vitalism may help in understanding why this latter point is at least plausible.[3] The concept of life seemed just as mysterious to many scientists during the early 1800's as the concept of consciousness does to us today. As a result, many scientists at the time accepted the philosophical doctrine of *vitalism* (Garrett, 2006). Vitalists attributed some non-physical "vital spirit" or "life force" to living entities that was not possessed by inanimate objects. In other words, vitalists believed that the laws of physics and chemistry by themselves would never be able to account fully for living processes. In effect, there was an apparent philosophical explanatory gap between the property of being alive and what could be accounted for mechanistically (i.e., there existed a life-body version of the "hard problem"), similar to the philosophical mind-body explanatory gap concerning consciousness today. However, at present we believe that much of the mystery underling this philosophical explanatory gap concerning life was really due to a "biological explanatory gap," i.e., to the limited scientific understanding two hundred years ago of how processes associated with living entities (metabolism, reproduction, inheritance, etc.) could be implemented by

[3] While some philosophers support the analogy with vitalism that is used here (e.g., Dennett, 1996), others have argued that it is inadequate because consciousness involves the mysteries of subjective experience while life does not (e.g., Chalmers, 1996, 2007). However, this latter view simply reflects the demystification of the concept of life that has occurred for contemporary authors due to scientific advances in the biosciences. See (Garrett, 2006) for further recent arguments supporting the merit of this analogy.

biochemical and biophysical mechanisms. Today, even though much is still not understood about the physics and chemistry of living processes, and there is still not even a generally agreed upon definition of life (Regis, 2008; Wolfram, 2002), vitalism and much of the mysteriousness of life that gave rise to it has faded away. This has occurred due to scientific advances, including the ability to synthesize organic molecules from inorganic ones, a mechanistic understanding of cellular energy metabolism, our knowledge of molecular genetics and evolution governed by DNA, and the recognition that self-organization based on simple rules can generate high-level behaviors as emergent properties in complex systems (Wolfram, 2002). If one replaces "life" with "consciousness," and "biological explanatory gap" with "computational explanatory gap," the analogy is clear. The expectation, based on this historical analogy, is that even if bridging the computational explanatory gap does not fully account for the hard problem of explaining subjective experience or produce a crisp definition of phenomenal consciousness, it will at least greatly demystify it, and consequently the hard problem may fade away.

5. Identifying Computational Correlates of Consciousness

From a computational point of view, the recognition that high-level cognitive processes may have distinct subjective qualities associated with them (our assumption; see the *Introduction*) has striking implications for future research on consciousness. Cognitive phenomenology raises the possibility that ongoing research focused on developing neurocomputational models of higher cognitive functions is directly relevant to understanding the nature of consciousness. Unlike work explicitly studying artificial consciousness, much of this work on neurocognitive architectures attempts to map higher cognitive functions into neurocomputational mechanisms independently of any explicit relationship between these functions and consciousness. Such work may identify neurocomputational mechanisms associated with phenomenally conscious information processing that are not observed with unconscious information processing. This would potentially provide examples of computational correlates of consciousness, and ideally would provide a deeper understanding of the nature of consciousness in general, just as molecular biology contributed to demystifying the nature of life and deprecating the theory of vitalism.

Of course, such a concept may be quite controversial at present in some quarters. For example, influenced by the distinction made in AI and cognitive science between top-down symbolic computations and bottom-up neural computations, a number of past models that are explicitly intended to explain consciousness are based on the *distinction* between local symbolic representations and distributed neural representations (Chella, 2007; Kitamura et al., 2000; Sun, 1999, 2002; Wilson, Sun and Matthews, 2009). These hybrid models consist of a high-level symbolic module that interacts with one or more lower-level neurocomputational modules. Such models start with the *claim* that symbolic information processing per se in the high-level module is the basis of conscious information processing, and thus they essentially build in the computational explanatory gap. However, while such models may implicitly recognize the computational explanatory gap as described here, they do not attempt to provide a solution to it. The critical issue raised by the computational explanatory gap as defined here is how to *replace* the symbolic modules of such models with neurocomputational implementations. How such replacement could be done remains stubbornly difficult and mysterious today. It is the essence of the computational explanatory gap, and bridging this gap will require identifying at the "microscopic level" of neural computations how "macroscopic level" symbol processing can be supported.

If one allows the possibility that the "easy problem," represented in part by the computational explanatory gap, is important and a substantial barrier both to a deeper understanding of phenomenal consciousness and to instantiated machine consciousness, then the immediate research program becomes determining how one can bridge this gap and identify computational correlates of consciousness. Encouragingly, there has been a substantial and increasing effort over the last two decades by researchers who are examining issues that relate to such a program. What computational correlates of consciousness has this work proposed?

When one reviews past models in artificial consciousness (Reggia, 2013), it becomes evident that many of these models can be interpreted as being founded upon specific candidates for computational correlates of consciousness, and this observation suggests that such models are directly related to addressing the computational explanatory gap. More generally, work reported outside of the artificial consciousness literature on neurocognitive architectures implementing high-level cognitive functionality via neurocomputational mechanisms may also suggest computational correlates of consciousness. In the following we will consider some representative examples of such computational correlates, dividing them into five classes. These classes separate computational correlates into those based on representational properties, system properties, self-modeling, relational properties, and cognitive control.

Representational Properties

One class of computational correlates of consciousness is based on intrinsic properties of the neural representation of information used in cognitive states/processes. For example, a number of theoretical arguments and several early recurrent neural network models of consciousness have been based on hypothesizing that attractor states, certain specific neural activity patterns ("bubbles"), the stability/strength/distinctiveness of activity patterns, or even the explicit encoding of information in general, are associated with or characterize consciousness (Aleksander, 1996; Cleeremans, 2005; Mathis and Mozer, 1995; O'Brien and Opie, 1999; Taylor, 1997). For example, advocates of adaptive resonance theory have suggested that all conscious states are resonant states (Grossberg, 1999).

The difficulty with identifying computational correlates of consciousness based on their representational properties is that there are many physical systems that are generally not viewed as conscious that have properties such as attractor states or activity patterns, leading to past suggestions that just representing consciousness in such a fashion is not helpful: It may relate to the contents of consciousness, but it is arguably not useful because it involves no "internal experience" (Taylor, 2003) or because it implies panpsychism (Cleeremans, 2005). It has been suggested that some of this difficulty may be ameliorated by taking trajectories, rather than instantaneous patterns, in the state space of possible activation patterns as representational primitives for qualia and subjective experience (Fekete and Edelman, 2011).

System Properties

Another class of computational correlates of consciousness is based on system-level properties of a neurocomputational system. The term "system-level properties" is used here to mean those computational properties that characterize a neural system as a whole rather than, as with representational properties, depend on the specific nature of neural activity patterns that represent/encode cognitive states and processes. Two examples are given here: global information processing and information integration.

In computer science, one often makes a distinction between processing that is localized (e.g., local variables) versus global (global variables). Similar terms can be used classify information processing in neural nets, where the terms local and global refer to the spatial extent of a specific type of information processing. A number of empirical studies have suggested that information processing during conscious mental activities is widely distributed or "global" across cerebral cortex regions and also associated with increased inter-regional communication (Baars et al., 2003; Massimini et al., 2005). Such empirical results support the claims of global workspace theory (Baars, 1988, 2002) that consciousness is associated with distributed/global information processing throughout the neural networks of the brain.

Inspired by these experimental results, a number of neural network models have been studied in which conscious/effortful information processing can be associated with computational processes involving the recruitment of hidden layers and hence widespread network activation (Connor and Shanahan, 2010; Dehaene et al., 1998; Newman et al., 1997; Raffone and Pantani, 2010; Shanahan, 2008). An example neural architecture of this type is illustrated schematically in Figure 2. This specific example concerns a Stroop task where one must either read aloud each seen word or name the color of the ink used in the word, the latter being more difficult and effortful with incongruous words. Significant widespread activation that includes the "global workspace" occurs when the model is dealing with a difficult naming task that requires conscious effort by humans, and not with the easier, more automatic word reading task. While most past work on these models has focused on simulated rather than instantiated consciousness, it has at times been suggested that similar global information processing provides a plausible neurocomputational bases for phenomenal and access consciousness (Raffone and Pantani, 2010).

There is a lot to like about the basic hypothesis that global information processing is a computational correlate of conscious mind. It is consistent with the substantial scientific evidence summarized above that widespread cortical activation correlates with conscious brain states, and it provides a partial intuitive account for the unity of consciousness and a clear statement about what distinguishes conscious from unconscious brain activity. It has also received support from mathematical analysis based on information theory suggesting that machine consciousness based on a global workspace model will, after sufficient time, possibly lead to failure modes reminiscent of those seen in humans (Wallace, 2005, 2006). However, neural global workspace models of consciousness have not yet shed significant light on *why* global information processing should lead to phenomenal consciousness. Further, there are other multi-layer neural networks with architectures similar to global workspace models that include low-level information processing that is generally not viewed as conscious (van der Velde and de Kamp, 2006).

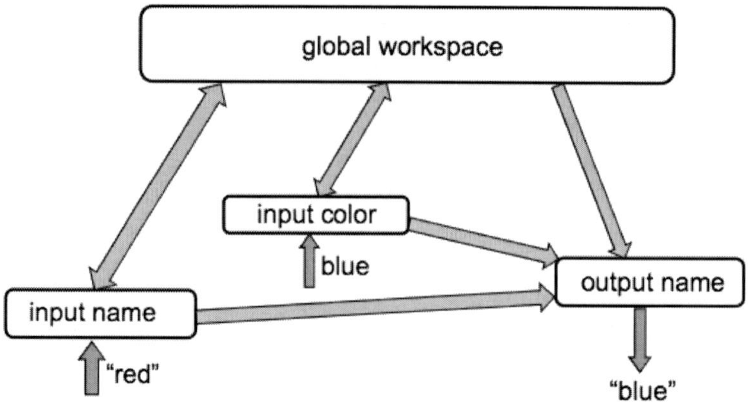

Figure 2. A schematic representation of the architecture of a neural global workspace model for a word-color Stroop task (Dehaene et al., 1998). Each rounded box represents a set/layer of neurons. Local processing occurs in the special purpose input and output layers, while with global processing, substantial activation also occurs throughout the workspace layer.

A second system property that has been postulated to be associated with phenomenal consciousness is the ability to integrate information. Information integration theory hypothesizes that consciousness is a graded concept, equivalent to the capacity of a system to integrate information into a unified experience and to differentiate among a large collection of different conscious states (Tononi and Sporns, 2003; Tononi, 2004, 2008; Balduzzi and Tononi, 2008). The theory provides a quantitative measure ϕ of a specific neural network's ability to integrate information based on the calculated mutual information of all possible bi-partitions of the network. The basic idea is that this mutual information among network components that is above and beyond their information content as individual components enables them to interact in a constructive fashion. The larger ϕ is, the more phenomenally conscious a network is. So, for example, it is possible to estimate ϕ values associated with different modules in a neural control system, and when one does that it suggests that modules that serve to gate other module's activity have the highest ϕ values and thus are more closely associated with phenomenal consciousness, according to this theory (Gamez, 2010). Information integration theory makes some strong claims, including that a system's subjective experience is equivalent to its capacity to integrate information, that the "informational relations" of a system's components define a space of qualia, and that a limited form of panpsychism holds (Tononi, 2004, 2008).

From a computational perspective, information integration theory is attractive in providing a specific, well-defined theoretical framework within which to study and quantitatively measure the extent to which a system, natural or artificial, is conscious. However, integrated information theory faces substantial philosophical and practical barriers. From a philosophical perspective, at the present time it remains an open question as to whether the measure ϕ has anything to do with the subjective experience that we associate with conscious mind rather than with the information processing properties of a system, conscious or not (Manzotti, 2012). In significant ways, the ϕ score seems more directly related to a system's potential to exhibit intelligent information processing rather than subjective experience. For example, it has been shown that, with a suitable selection of synaptic weights, one can construct simple, fully connected neural networks having arbitrarily high ϕ values (Seth et al., 2006). According to integrated information theory, at some (unspecified) ϕ value such networks would therefore exhibit instantiated/phenomenal consciousness, a conclusion that is difficult for some to accept. Even if one does accept this conclusion, it is unclear that it sheds any light on the nature of consciousness (Seth, 2009). It has also been argued that this theory does not have some basic properties that any functional theory of consciousness needs to satisfy in order to be well formed (Cerullo, 2011). On the practical side, a major limitation of information integration theory is that one cannot compute ϕ directly for neural networks of appreciable size, and it is extremely difficult to interpret what any given value of ϕ actually means (i.e., ϕ is just a relative measure, not an absolute measure).

Self-Modeling

Another class of computational correlates of consciousness involves *self-modeling*. Self-awareness has long been viewed as a central, if somewhat poorly understood, aspect of conscious mind (Samsonovich and Nadel, 2005; Searle, 2004). Metzinger's philosophical analysis of the first-person perspective provides a useful framework in which to consider work in this area (Metzinger, 2000a). The key idea is that our mind includes a *self-model* that is supported by neural activation patterns in the brain. This self-model is based on an internal representation of the spatial properties of the body that is referred to as a *body image*. The body image is a *virtual model* that, while in part innate, is highly adaptable. The body image's virtual nature is illustrated by astronauts in weightless situations who lose their subjective body axis (i.e., their spatial frame of reference), and by phantom limbs where a person who has lost an arm still subjectively experiences the presence of the arm. Metzinger's argument is that the subjective, conscious experience of a "self" arises because the body image is always there due to the proprioceptive, somatic and other sensory input that the brain constantly receives, and because of the inability of our cognitive processes to recognize that the body image is a virtual representation of the physical body. The argument is that, within this philosophical framework, self-modeling of the body as an agent that causes one's behavior leads to phenomenal subjectivity and conscious experience.

From a computational perspective, the key idea is that an intelligent agent has an internal model encompassing not just the external environment, but also including a model of itself, as illustrated in Figure 3. In recent years, AI and cognitive science researchers have made a number of proposals for how subjective conscious experience could emerge in *embodied agents* from such self-models. One suggested possibility is that self-models could lead to "strong self-reference" whereby an artificial agent that reasons about itself can reason about its own reasoning about itself, leading to a "strongly self-referring loop" (Perlis, 1997). Another possibility is that phenomenal consciousness could emerge from introspective reasoning mechanisms about perception (McDermott, 2007). It has alternatively been suggested that some key properties of a self-concept (existence, continuity over time, supervenience on a physical substrate, etc.) can form the basis for self-modeling in intelligent agents, regardless of whether or not they are embodied. Building on this latter idea, it has been proposed that introducing a self-concept during learning is the key event in creating "computational consciousness" in suitable cognitive architectures (Samsonovich, 2007).

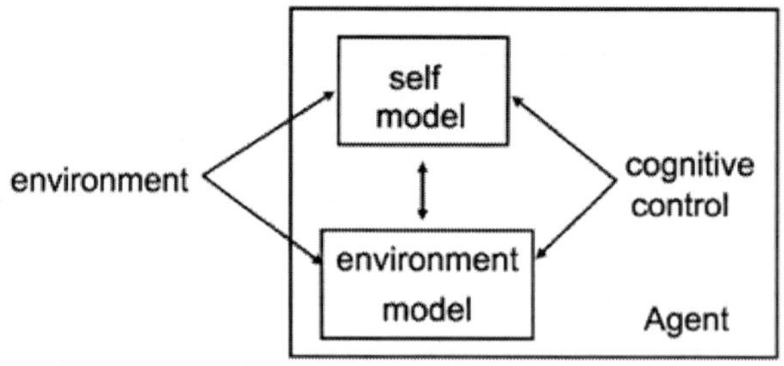

Figure 3. Architecture of an agent that has not only a model of the external environment, but also a self-model about which it can reason.

One specific type of internal model that is claimed to capture various features of consciousness is the *virtual machine architecture* (Sloman and Chrisley, 2003). In computer science, a virtual machine is a simulation of one machine, implemented in software, that runs on a different physical machine (hardware). This approach views a conscious human mind as a virtual machine (software) that is being executed by the brain (hardware), where, like the rest of the body, the brain is considered to be a machine. The "mental" states of the virtual machine are generally but not necessarily causally connected to one another, consistent with a functional view of consciousness. Self-modeling occurs in a suitable virtual machine when the machine develops concepts for categorizing and labeling its own states as sensed by internal monitors. In this context, qualia are defined to be what virtual machines "refer to when referring to the objects of internal self observation" (Sloman and Chrisley, 2003). In other words, qualia are viewed as being a side-effect of having an executive or meta-management component as part of the virtual machine that allows it to examine its own internal functioning and representations. These investigators recognize that many people would object to this characterization of qualia because it fails to address the hard problem of consciousness. Their response to this is "the fact that many people do think like this is part of what needs to be explained by any theory of consciousness" (Sloman and Chrisley, 2003).

Given the rich history of using internal models in robotics, it is perhaps not surprising that a number of studies concerning self-modeling as the basis for artificial consciousness have been done in the context of physical or simulated robots. For example, there is a robotics study that has focused explicitly on self-awareness (Takeno, 2013). This work, done over a period of several years, has studied "conscious robots" that are controlled by recurrent neural networks that undergo supervised learning. A central focus of this work is handling temporal sequences of stimuli, predicting the event that will occur at the next time step from past and current events. The predicted next state and the actual next state of the world are compared at each time step, and when these two states are the same a robot is declared to have instantiated consciousness ("consistency of cognition and behavior generates consciousness"). In support of this definition of consciousness, these expectation-driven robots have been shown to be capable of self-recognition in a mirror (Takeno, 2008). Such a demonstration was motivated by past studies involving a *mirror test* of self-awareness in which scientists examined whether animals recognize that the image they see in a mirror is themselves and not another animal of the same species (Gallup, 1970). In this case it was possible to have a small commercial robot (Khepera II) imitate the movements of its own image as reflected in a mirror. Because this was done more successfully than imitating the movements of other robots, the investigators claim that it represents self-recognition (Takeno, 2008).

As illustrated by this robotics study, a key aspect of a self-model is that it has predictive value, allowing an agent to set up expectations for what is about to occur. This is an ability that has previously been argued to be associated with consciousness (Ascoli, 2005). The concept that an internal self-model is a crucial aspect of consciousness is thus quite appealing. It is widely recognized in engineering that models of the external environment can be useful aspects of robotic control, such as in effectively navigating the environment or in recovering from unexpected changes. Work on self-models extends this recognition of the usefulness of models to include self-models. Self-modeling is also consistent with an earlier proposal by the evolutionary biologist Dawkins that evolution of the ability of the brain to simulate may have culminated in consciousness when such simulation of the world became sufficiently complex that it could incorporate a self-model (Dawkins, 1976, p. 63). However, a significant limitation of past work on self-modeling is that most of the neurocomputational self-models developed to date are quite simple and deal primarily with low level sensory and motor processing. Predictions have focused on what sensory input to anticipate next, or the outcome to be expected from taking a certain action. These types of predictions do not come close to capturing the richness of human meta-knowledge about other aspects of the self, such as one's own cognitive processes.

Relational Properties

A third class of potential computational correlates of consciousness is based on relationships between entities. Symbol grounding, higher-order thought theories, and network gating architectures all fall within this category.

The term *symbol grounding* is often used to indicate that the symbols (such as words) used in information processing systems must be grounded (associated with entities in the external world) in order for those symbols to have meaning. In other words, representations of symbols must have a relationship with external entities for meaning and understanding to occur. It has been suggested symbol grounding is a computational correlate of consciousness. Specifically, the claim is that any system that maintains a correspondence between high-level, symbolically represented concepts and low-level data stream entities, and that has a reasoning system which makes use of these grounded symbols, has true subjective experiences corresponding to qualia and a sense of self-awareness (Kuipers, 2005). In other words, symbol grounding that anchors symbolic representations to selected spatio-temporal segments of the sensory data stream, is taken to be responsible for consciousness. The plausibility of this idea has been evaluated by assessing its ability to meet the eleven criteria that Searle (2004) has argued any philosophical-scientific theory of consciousness should satisfy. The conclusion of this evaluation was that the essential features of consciousness may, in principle, be implemented in an embodied machine that has sufficient computational power (Kuipers, 2008). However, not all would agree with this viewpoint: It has recently been argued that the dimensionality reduction implied by symbol grounding is just the opposite of what is needed to create phenomenal machine consciousness (Chella and Gaglio, 2012).

The hypothesis that symbol grounding is a computational correlate of consciousness makes neurocomputational systems that learn to ground symbols in "sensory streams" consisting of auditory phoneme sequences potentially relevant to the issue of consciousness (Weems and Reggia, 2006). These systems ground symbols by associating them with aspects of simple visual images during learning. Such models, while quite limited at present, can learn to produce the meaning of sentences describing a very simple external world that is observed, including for novel objects and novel descriptive sentences (Monner and Reggia, 2011, 2012a). They can even correctly answer questions by observing question-answer pairs (Monner and Reggia, 2012b). Most importantly, these models sometimes learn/discover a *latent symbol system* – a system for symbol processing that was not built into the structure of the network but instead emerged as part of the learned distributed representation adopted by the network (Monner and Reggia, 2012c). While the network's internal symbols are latent from our perspective as outside observers, they are very real in the sense that they are accessed, manipulated and inspected by the neural architecture itself when interpreting sentences, including novel ones. Learned gating of neural circuitry is being used at a fine-grained level of individual simulated neurons gating the input, output, or activity persistence of other individual neurons.

A second potential computational correlate of consciousness involving relational properties is based on *higher-order thought theories* (HOT theories) of consciousness (Rosenthal, 1996). HOT theory views consciousness as a relational property: it depends on the relations between different mental states. Specifically, HOT theory postulates that a mental state *S* is conscious to the extent that there is some other mental state (a "higher-order thought") that directly refers to *S* or is about *S*. It has been suggested that artificial systems with higher-order representations consistent with HOT theory could be viewed as conscious, even to the extent of having qualia, if they use grounded symbols (Rolls, 1997, 2007).

HOT theory has served as a framework for developing *metacognitive networks* in which some components of a neural architecture, referred to as higher-order networks, are able to represent, access, and/or manipulate information about other parts (lower-order networks) (Cleeremans et al., 2007). Metacognitive nets have been applied to several tasks. In practice, this has involved architectures having a first-order network that performs a primary task such as pattern classification, and a second-order network that observes states of the first-order network as the basis for making decisions on a secondary task, as illustrated in Figure 4. It is the second-order network's learned reference to the first-order network's internal representations that makes the latter functionally conscious, according to HOT theory. The claim is that "conscious experience occurs if and only if an information processing system has learned about its own representation of the world" (Cleeremans et al., 2007). While individuals investigating metacognitive networks like this typically do not claim their models have instantiated consciousness, they may suggest that the higher-order representations formed in their metacognitive models do capture the core mechanisms of HOT theories of consciousness (Pasquali et al., 2010).

Models of conscious information processing based on HOT theory face some important challenges. For example, contemporary computers are generally believed by many people not to be conscious (Reggia, Huang and Katz, 2015), and yet modern computers have monitoring systems that keep track of their internal states, indicating that they are conscious according to HOT theory (Rey, 1983). Does HOT theory really solve the hard problem of consciousness, as is sometimes claimed (Rolls, 1997, 2007), being able to account for the existence of qualia? At present this remains controversial. A recent review of higher-order representation theories of consciousness has discussed several objections to such theories (Lycan, 2009).

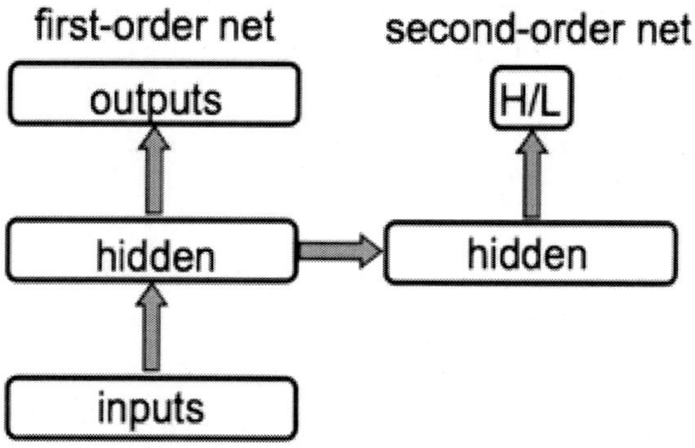

Figure 4. A caricature of a typical metacognitive neural architecture (Cleeremans et al., 2007). Boxes indicate network layers, and gray arrows indicate all-to-all adaptive connections between layers. The first-order network on the left is used to learn pattern classification tasks. The second-order network on the right has no causal influence on the first-order network's performance. It monitors the first-order network's hidden layer representation and outputs a high or low estimate as to the correctness of the first-order network's output for each input pattern that it receives. The correctness of this output over time reflects the extent to which the second-order network has learned a meta-representation of the first-order network's representation.

Cognitive Control

A fifth class of computational correlates of consciousness is based on *cognitive control*, the process of managing other cognitive processes (Schneider and Chein, 2003). Examples of cognitive control include directing attention, response selection, working memory maintenance, goal setting, and inhibition of irrelevant signals. The limited ability of current neurocomputational methods to support higher-level cognitive control functions is somewhat surprising in that the human brain handles such issues routinely, establishing that neural computations clearly have the capacity to do so. Here we consider two examples of how cognitive control can suggest computational correlates of consciousness: via attention control mechanisms and network gating architectures.

At each moment in time, a person is only consciously aware of a fraction of the ongoing stream of visual, auditory, touch and other sensory information being received. The *attention control mechanisms* that actively select what we attend to have the ability to focus on behaviorally important aspects of sensory information, selecting, for example, which specific seen object to attend to based on its location in space, what type of object it is, and/or its general properties. A very large amount of research in cognitive psychology has demonstrated that attention mechanisms are controlled by both bottom-up (exogenous) and top-down (endogenous) processes in the brain that operate over many levels, from subcortical nuclei through a network of inter-connected cortical regions. While attention and conscious awareness are not equivalent processes, normally they are closely linked and highly correlated (Koch and Tsuchiya, 2006; Lamme, 2003; Treisman, 2009). It is therefore not surprising that several studies related to artificial consciousness have viewed attention mechanisms as computational correlates of consciousness.

For example, Haikonen (2007) has proposed a conscious machine based on a number of properties, including inner speech and the machine's ability to report its inner states. The machine is composed of a collection of inter-communicating modules that are similar to the unconscious specialized processors in global workspace theory, but in this case there is no separate global workspace. Instead, the specialized modules communicate with one another, operating in the same fashion regardless of whether the overall system is considered to be conscious or unconscious. The distinction between a topic being conscious or not is based on whether the machine as a whole attends to that topic, as follows. At each moment of time, each specialized module of the machine can broadcast information about the topic/problem it is addressing to all of the other modules. Each broadcasting module competes to recruit other modules to attend to the same topic that it is processing. The subject of this unified collective focus of attention is claimed to enter consciousness. Specifically, "The machine becomes 'conscious' about a topic when the various modules cooperate in this way in unison and focus their attention on the percepts about this topic." It is the collective, cooperative attending to a single topic that represents a computational correlate of consciousness. Recently implemented in a robot (Haikonen, 2012), this design suggests that a machine can only be conscious of one topic at a time, and that it can be self-aware if its collective of modules are all working on a topic that involves the machine itself. Like global workspace theory, this model is consistent with neurobiological evidence that conscious brain states are associated with global communication between cerebral cortex regions (Massimini et al., 2005).

Other attention-based models suggest that the efference copy (or corollary discharge) associated with top-down attention control mechanisms can be viewed as a computational correlate of consciousness. An efference signal or corollary discharge is a copy of the output of a control system that is fed back to input regions of the control system. In one study like this, Cotterill (1995, 1996) theorized that efference copies, generated by premotor and supplementary motor cortex and sent to posterior sensory cortex, are a critical aspect of information being attended to and becoming conscious in the brain. This theory was a key feature of the design of CyberChild, a system intended for studying consciousness whose complex neural controller was strongly based upon neuroanatomical structures of the human brain (Cotterill, 2003). A subsequent related study, known as the Corollary Discharge of Attention Movement (CODAM) model, is intended to simulate control of changes in the focus of attention, or "attention movements" (Taylor, 2003, 2007, 2012). Figure 5 shows a slightly simplified version of the CODAM architecture. The executive system sends top-down control signals via an inverse model that selectively modulate posterior sensory cortex input, amplifying inputs deserving of attention and reducing other inputs that are to be filtered out of the sensory stream. Taylor hypothesized that, just as with physical movement control, the inverse model produces a corollary discharge that quickly tells a monitoring system the predicted changes in the focus of attention. The corollary discharge is postulated to redirect the focus of attention as needed, and to contribute to error correction. The basic argument here is that consciousness is specifically due to the corollary discharge signal, making the latter a computational correlate of consciousness (Taylor, 2007). The central claim is that this signal, buffered in the monitor, is directly responsible for the conscious experience of ownership of actions that control one's attention to various topics. Such ownership provides a sense of agency – a sense that the self is responsible for the actions being taken by one's own cognitive control mechanisms.

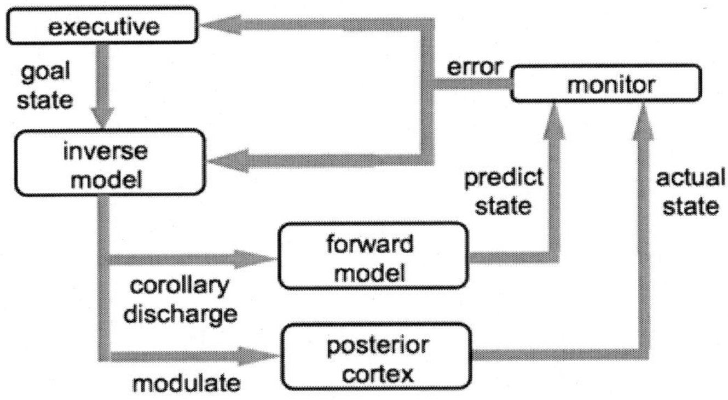

Figure 5. The CODAM model of attention control, slightly simplified. See text for details.

The second type of computational correlates of consciousness that relate to cognitive control involves *network gating architectures*. The term "gating" as used here has a specific meaning. In neural networks in general, modules exchange information via neural pathways. In neural networks that are gating architectures, the modules also gate the actions of one another: a module may turn on/off the activity of other modules, and may determine when they retain/discard their activity state, when they learn/unlearn information, and when they generate output. Unlike with HOT theory, which is concerned with relations between neural representations (activity patterns, for example), gating architectures are concerned with hard-wired neural connections and the control of neural processing.

Neurocomputational systems developed within the GALIS framework[4] provide examples of network gating architectures (Sylvester et al., 2013). Such systems are focused on general cognitive control, an umbrella term for goal-directed executive cognitive systems that manage other cognitive processes, including not only attention but also working memory, planning, and action selection, etc. Developing neural architectures capable of modeling cognitive control processes in a general sense has proven to be surprisingly challenging, consistent with the concept of a computational explanatory gap. Neural systems struggle to represent the goals and rules of various cognitive tasks (Marcus, 2001), in striking contrast to symbolic AI systems (Simen et al., 2010). GALIS architectures consist of a set of neural modules that learn to perform tasks involving temporal sequences A control module learns a temporal instruction sequence needed to perform a specific task. The key functional enhancement used to make this work effectively in GALIS is to allow control modules to gate the actions of other modules and itself. In other words, a control module learns to turn on/off the actions of other modules, thereby determining when input patterns are saved or discarded, when to learn/unlearn information in working memory, when to generate outputs, and even when to update its own states. An example of a control module designed to supervise the performance of n-back working memory tasks (a standard psychological task) simultaneously for different values of n, is shown in Figure 6. This specific architecture produced accuracy and timing results reminiscent of those seen in humans performing similar tasks, and made testable predictions (Sylvester et al., 2013). More recently, the GALIS framework has been adopted for more general problem-solving tasks involving "game playing."

[4] GALIS is short for Gated Attractors Learning Instruction Sequences.

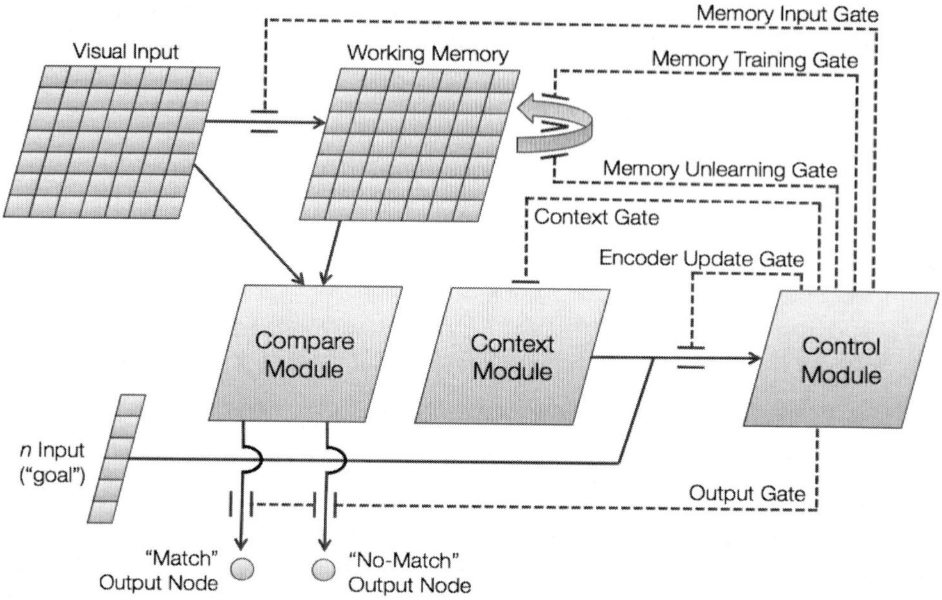

Figure 6. A neurocomputational model for the n-Back task developed within the GALIS framework. Thin, solid arrows are one-to-one connections. A working memory layer is recurrently connected (broad arrow). Dashed lines are the gating outputs of the control module shown on the right. This control module autonomously gates the flow of activity via pathways in the architecture, determines when output occurs, and decides when and where learning occurs.

The GALIS framework is only a small step towards bridging the computational explanatory gap: its ability to learn temporal sequences of discrete "instructions" in a "computer-like fashion" produces a level of executive functionality that is more typically associated with top-down symbolic AI systems. The two critical computational mechanisms in GALIS that might be viewed as candidate computational correlates of consciousness are the ability to learn temporal sequences of discrete instructions that are needed to perform a task, and the ability of a higher-level cortical control region to learn to gate other cortical regions performing the task (i.e., to turn other regions on/off). The idea of top-down gating like this is particularly intriguing as a potential correlate of consciousness, and may relate to the concept of top-down causation discussed in the free will literature. The fact that gating has been suggested to be important to consciousness independently in other contexts, such as in neurocontrollers (Gamez, 2010) and in latent symbol systems (Monner and Reggia, 2012c) as described earlier, only reinforces this possibility.

Discussion

Existing computational models have successfully captured a number of neurobiological, cognitive and behavioral aspects of conscious information processing as machine simulations. Put simply, it has been possible to develop limited forms of what we have called simulated consciousness. This achievement is extremely important: These computational studies are providing a way to test whether theories about key neural, cognitive and/or behavioral features of consciousness, when implemented as computer models, can produce results in agreement with experimental data. Computational modeling also represents important progress towards producing machines that can exhibit external behaviors that are associated with human consciousness, and thus may lead to future artificial agents that have increased functionality and are able to interact with people in more natural ways (Aleksander, 2013; Charkaoui, 2005; McCauley, 2007; Sanz et al., 2012). Put simply, work on *simulated* consciousness has become a recognized and increasingly accepted methodology for the scientific study of consciousness, especially within the framework of functionalism.

In contrast, at the present time our understanding of the phenomenology of consciousness remains incredibly limited. This is true both for human consciousness and for considerations about the possibility of machine consciousness. No existing approach to artificial consciousness has presented a compelling demonstration of instantiated (phenomenal) consciousness in a machine, or even clear evidence that instantiated machine consciousness will eventually be possible. While some investigators have made intriguing claims that the approach they are using is or could be the basis for a phenomenally conscious machine, none is currently generally accepted as having done so.

The central argument presented here is that this apparent lack of progress towards a deeper understanding of instantiated machine consciousness is largely due to the computational explanatory gap: our current lack of understanding of how higher-level cognitive algorithms can be mapped onto neurocomputational algorithms/states. While those versed in mind-brain philosophy may generally be inclined to dismiss this gap as just part of the "easy problem," such a view is at best misleading. This gap has proven surprisingly intractable to over half a century of research on neurocomputational methods, and existing philosophical works have (to my knowledge) provided no deep insight into *why* such an "easy problem" has proven to be so intractable. On the contrary, the view offered here is that the computational explanatory gap is a fundamental issue that needs a much larger collective effort to clarify and resolve.

It is in this context that the concepts of cognitive phenomenology are so significant. These concepts imply that substantial past computational work reported outside of the artificial consciousness literature is of potential relevance to consciousness studies. As described and illustrated above, a great deal of past work on neurocognitive architectures has attempted to map higher cognitive functions into neurocomputational processes, thereby directly addressing the computational explanatory gap, including work that does not explicitly consider its relevance to machine consciousness or consciousness studies in general. As can be seen from the examples above, the results from this past work, and from many other related studies, suggest that there now exist several potential computational correlates of consciousness, including some that are beyond those presented previously or identified by investigators working on artificial consciousness. These include the ability to learn sequential attractor states, the use of adaptive gating mechanisms to exert top-down influences, and the presence of a learned emergent symbol system.

Our current ability to identify several candidate computational correlates of consciousness is very encouraging. However, a fundamental difficulty remains: Many hypothesized computational mechanisms identified so far as correlates are either known to also occur in neurocomputational systems supporting non-conscious activities, or their occurrence has not yet been excluded in such settings. In other words, the main difficulty in identifying computational correlates of consciousness to date has been in establishing that proposed correlates are *not* also present with unconscious aspects of cognitive information processing. For example, the metacognitive neural networks that HOT theory has inspired suggest that information processing in such neural architectures can be taken to be a computational correlate, but there are analogous types of information processing in biological neural circuits at the level of the human brainstem and spinal cord that are associated with apparently unconscious processing. Thus, "second-order" information processing in neural architectures *alone* would not fully satisfy our criteria for being a computational correlate of consciousness. Similarly, global/widespread neural activity per se does not appear to fully satisfy our criteria because such processing also occurs in apparently unconscious neural systems (e.g., interacting central pattern generators in isolated lamprey eel spinal cord preparations produce coordinated movements involving widespread distributed neural interactions (Ijspeert, 2008), but it is improbable that an isolated eel spinal cord should be viewed as being conscious). Very similar points can be made about gating mechanisms, integrated information processing, and even self-modeling.

For this reason, it remains unclear at present whether any of the hypothesized candidates for computational correlates of consciousness will ultimately prove to be satisfactory without further qualifications and refinements. This is not because they fail to capture important aspects of conscious information processing, but primarily because similar computational mechanisms have not yet been proven to be absent in unconscious information processing situations. These neurocomputational mechanisms are thus not yet *specifically* identifiable only with conscious cognitive activities. In short, while a great deal of progress has been made by studies of machine consciousness and neurocognitive architectures over the last two decades, only limited progress has been made by this work that is relevant to resolving the computational explanatory gap and identifying computational correlates of consciousness.

As stated earlier in this paper, bridging the computational explanatory gap may well make bridging the philosophical explanatory gap more tractable, and it may ultimately lead to an operational test for the presence of phenomenal consciousness. In other words, the suggestion is that a complete characterization of high-level cognition in neurocomputational terms, even if it does not fully show us how subjective experience arises mechanistically, will substantially demystify the nature of phenomenal consciousness and perhaps even provide necessary and sufficient tests for phenomenal consciousness in an artifact. Such a view is compatible with and complementary to recent arguments made by others in the expanding literature of cognitive phenomenology (as described in the Introduction). Bridging the computational explanatory gap is possibly *the* most critical step we could take during the next few decades to advance prospects for a phenomenally conscious artifact and a deeper understanding of the mind-brain problem. Perhaps if progress can be made in this way, the insights provided will reveal that the "hard problem" is ultimately much easier, or at least more understandable, than it currently appears.

REFERENCES

Aleksander, I. (1996) *Impossible Minds*, Imperial College Press.
Aleksander, I. (2005) *The World in my Mind, My Mind in the World*, Imprint Academic.

Aleksander, I. (2013) Phenomenal Consciousness and Biologically Inspired Systems, *International Journal of Machine Consciousness*, 5, 3 – 9.

Alivisatos, A., et al. (2013) The Brain Activity Map. *Science*, 339, 1284-1285.

Ascoli, G. (2005) Brain and Mind at the Crossroads of Time, *Cortex*, 41, 619-620.

Baars, B. (1988) *A Cognitive Theory of Consciousness*, Cambridge University Press.

Baars, B. (2002) The Conscious Access Hypothesis, *Trends in Cognitive Sciences*, 6, 47-52.

Baars, B., Ramsey, T., Laureys, S. (2003) Brain, Conscious Experience, and the Observing Self, *Trends in Neuroscience*, 26, 671-675.

Balduzzi, D., Tononi, G. (2008) Integrated Information in Discrete Dynamical Systems, *PLoS Computational Biology*, 4, 1-18.

Bayne, T., Montague, M. (2011a), Cognitive Phenomenology: An Introduction, in Bayne, T., Montague, M. (eds.), *Cognitive Phenomenology*, Oxford University Press, 1-34.

Bayne, T., Montague, M.; eds. (2011b), *Cognitive Phenomenology*, Oxford University Press.

Bishop, M. (2009) Why Computers Can't Feel Pain, *Minds and Machines*, 19, 507-516.

Block, N. (1995) On a Confusion about a Function of Consciousness, *The Behavioral and Brain Sciences*, 18, 227-247.

Bringsjord, S. (2007) Offer: One Billion Dollars for a Conscious Robot; If You're Honest, You Must Decline, *Journal of Consciousness Studies*, 14, 28-43.

Butler, S. (1872) *Erewhon*, 1872.

Carruthers, P. (2005) *Consciousness – Essays from a Higher-Order Perspective*, Oxford University Press.

Cerullo, M. (2011) Integrated Information Theory, *Journal of Consciousness Studies*, 18, 45-58.

Charkaoui, N. (2005) A Computational Model of Minimal Consciousness Functions, *Proc. World Academy of Science, Engineering and Technology*, 9, 78-85.

Chalmers, D. (1996) *The Conscious Mind*, Oxford University Press.

Chalmers, D. (2000) What is a Neural Correlate of Consciousness? In: Metzinger, T. (ed.), *Neural Correlates of Consciousness*, MIT Press, 17—39.

Chalmers, D. (2007) The Hard Problem of Consciousness, in Velmans, M. and Schneider, S. (eds.), *The Blackwell Companion to Consciousness*, Blackwell, 225-235.

Chella, A. (2007) Towards Robot Conscious Perception, in A. Chella and R. Manzotti (eds.), *Artificial Consciousness*, Imprint Academic, 124-140.

Chella, A. and Gaglio, S. (2012) Synthetic Phenomenology and High-Dimensional Buffer Hypothesis, *International Journal of Machine Consciousness*, 4, 353-365.

Chudnoff, E. (2015) *Cognitive Phenomenology*, Routledge Press.

Cleeremans, A. (2005) Computational Correlates of Consciousness, in S. Laureys (ed.), *Progress in Brain Research*, 150, 81-98.

Cleeremans, A., Timmermans, B., Pasquali, A. (2007) Consciousness and Metarepresentation: A Computational Sketch, *Neural Networks*, 20, 1032-1039.

Connor, D., Shanahan, M. (2010), A Computational Model of a Global Neuronal Workspace with Stochastic Connections, *Neural Networks*, 23, 1139-1154.

Cotterill, R. (1995) On the Unity of Conscious Experience, *Journal of Consciousness Studies*, 2, 290-312.

Cotterill, R. (1996) Prediction and Internal Feedback in Conscious Perception, *Journal of Consciousness Studies*, 3, 245-266.

Cotterill, R. (2003) CyberChild – A Simulation Test-Bed for Consciousness Studies, *Journal of Consciousness Studies*, 10, 31-45.
Crick, F., Koch, C. (1990) Towards a Neurobiological Theory of Consciousness, *Seminars in the Neurosciences*, 2, 263-275.
Dawkins, R. (1976) *The Selfish Gene*, Oxford University Press.
Dehaene, S., Changeux, J.-P. (1997). A Hierarchical Neuronal Network for Planning Behavior, Proc. *National Academy of Sciences USA*, 94, 13293-8.
Dehaene, S., Kerszberg, M., Changeux, J. (1998) A Neuronal Model of a Global Workspace in Effortful Cognitive Tasks, *Proc. National Academy of Sciences*, 95, 14529-14534.
Dehaene, S., Naccache, L. (2001) Towards a Cognitive Neuroscience of Consciousness, *Cognition*, 79, 1-37.
Dennett, D. (1996) Facing Backwards on the Problem of Consciousness, *Journal of Consciousness Studies*, 3, 4-6.
Fekete, T., Edelman, S. (2011) Towards a Computational Theory of Experience, *Consciousness and Cognition*, 20, 807-827.
Franklin, S. (1995) *Artificial Minds*, MIT Press.
Gallup, G. (1970) Chimpanzees: Self-Recognition, *Science*, 167, 86-87.
Gamez, D. (2010) Information Integration Based Predictions about the Conscious States of a Spiking Neural Network, *Consciousness and Cognition*, 19, 294-310.
Garrett, B. (2006) What the History of Vitalism Teaches us about Consciousness and the "Hard Problem," *Philosophy and Phenomenological Research*, 72, 616-628.
Gentili, R., Oh, H., Miller, R., Huang, D., Katz, G., Reggia, J. (2015) A Neural Architecture for Performing Actual and Mentally Simulated Movements During Self-Intended and Observed Bimanual Arm Reaching Movements, *International Journal of Social Robotics*, 7 (3), 371-392.
Grossberg, S. (1999) The Link between Brain Learning, Attention, and Consciousness, *Consciousness and Cognition*, 8, 1-44.
Haikonen, P. (2007) Essential Issues of Conscious Machines, *Journal of Consciousness Studies*, 14, 72-84.
Haikonen, P. (2012) *Consciousness and Robot Sentience*, World Scientific.
Holland, O., Goodman, R. (2003) Robots with Internal Models, *Journal of Consciousness Studies*, 10, 77-109.
Huynh, T., Reggia, J. (2012) Symbolic Representation of Recurrent Neural Network Dynamics, *IEEE Transactions on Neural Networks and Learning Systems*, 23, 1649-1658.
Ijspeert, A. (2008) Central Pattern Generators for Locomotion Control in Animals and Robots, *Neural Networks*, 21, 642-653.
Katz, B. (2013) An Embarrassment of Theories, *Journal of Consciousness Studies*, 20, 43-69.
Kitamura, T., Tahara, T. and Asami, K. (2000) How Can a Robot Have Consciousness? *Advanced Robotics*, 14, 263-275.
Koch, C., Tononi, G. (2008) Can Machines be Conscious, *IEEE Spectrum*, June, 55-59.
Koch, C., Tsuchiya, N. (2006) Attention and Consciousness: Two Distinct Brain Processes, *Trends in Cognitive Sciences*, 11, 16-22.
Kuipers, B. (2005) Consciousness: Drinking from the Firehose of Experience, *Proc. 20th National Conference on Artificial Intelligence*, AI Press, 1298-1305.

Kuipers, B. (2008) Drinking from the Firehose of Experience, *Artificial Intelligence in Medicine*, 44, 155-170.

Lamme, V. (2003) Why Visual Attention and Awareness are Different, *Trends in Cognitive Sciences*, 7, 12-18.

Levine, J. (1983) Materialism and Qualia: The Explanatory Gap, *Pacific Philosophical Quarterly*, 64, 354-361.

Lycan, W. (2009) Higher-Order Representation Theories of Consciousness, in Bayne, T., Cleeremans, A. and Wilken, P., *The Oxford Companion to Consciousness*, Oxford University Press, 346-350.

Manzotti, R. (2012). The Computational Stance is Unfit for Consciousness, *International Journal of Machine Consciousness*, 4, 401-420.

Marcus, G. (2001) *The Algebraic Mind: Integrating Connectionism and Cognitive Science*, Cambridge, MA: MIT Press.

Massimini, M., Ferrarelli, F., Huber, R., et al. (2005) Breakdown of Cortical Effective Connectivity During Sleep, *Science*, 309, 2228-2232.

Mathis, D., Mozer, M. (1995) On the Computational Utility of Consciousness, in G. Tesauro, D. Touretzky, T. Leen (eds.), Advances in Neural Information Processing Systems, 7, 10-18.

McCauley, L. (2007) Demonstrating the Benefit of Computational Consciousness, *Proc. of the AAAI Fall 2007 Symposia*, 108-114.

McCulloch, W., Pitts, W. (1943) A Logical Calculus of the Ideas Immanent in Nervous Activity, *Bulletin of Mathematical Biophysics*, 5, 115-133.

McDermott, D. (2007) Artificial Intelligence and Consciousness, in P. Zelazo, M. Moscovitch, E. Thompson (eds.), *Cambridge Handbook of Consciousness*, Cambridge University Press, 117-150.

McGinn, C. (2004) *Consciousness and Its Origins*, Oxford University Press.

Metzinger, T. (2000a) The Subjectivity of Subjective Experience, in *Neural Correlates of Consciousness*, T. Metzinger (editor), MIT Press, 285-306.

Metzinger, T (2000b) *Neural Correlates of Consciousness*, MIT Press.

Monner D, Reggia J. (2011) Systematically Grounding Language Through Vision in a Deep Recurrent Neural Network, *Proc. Fourth Intl. Conf. on Artificial General Intelligence*, Schmidhuber J, Thorision K, Looks M (eds.), Springer, 112-121.

Monner D, Reggia J. (2012a) A Generalized LSTM-like Training Algorithm for Second Order Recurrent Neural Networks, *Neural Networks*, 25, 70-83.

Monner D, Reggia J. (2012b) Neural Architectures for Learning to Answer Questions, *Biologically Inspired Cognitive Architectures,* 2, 37-53.

Monner D, Reggia J. (2012c) Emergent Latent Symbol Systems in Recurrent Neural Networks, *Connection Science*, 24, 193-225.

Newman, J., Baars, B., Cho, S. (1997) A Neural Global Workspace Model for Conscious Attention, *Neural Networks*, 10, 1195-1206.

O'Brien, G., Opie, J. (1999) A Connectionist Theory of Phenomenal Experience, *Behavioral and Brain Sciences*, 22, 127-196.

Pasquali, A., Timmermans, B., Cleeremans, A. (2010) Know Thyself: Metacognitive Networks and Measures of Consciousness, *Cognition*, 117, 182-190.

Perlis, D. (1997) Consciousness as Self-Function, *Jour. of Consciousness Studies*, 4, 509-525.

Pomerleau, D. (1993) Knowledge-based Training of Artificial Neural Networks for Autonomous Robot Driving. In J. Connell, S. Mahadevan (Eds.), *Robot Learning*, Kluwer, 19-43.

Raffone, A., Pantani, M. (2010) A Global Workspace Model for Phenomenal and Access Consciousness, *Consciousness and Cognition*, 19, 580-596.

Reggia, J. (2013) The Rise of Machine Consciousness, *Neural Networks*, 44, 112-131.

Reggia, J., Huang, D., Katz, G. (2015) Beliefs Concerning the Nature of Consciousness, *Journal of Consciousness Studies*, 22, 146-171.

Reggia, J., Monner, D., Sylvester, J. (2014) The Computational Explanatory Gap, *Journal of Consciousness Studies*, 21 (9), 153-178.

Regis, E. (2008) *What is Life?,* Farber, Strauss and Giroux (New York).

Rey, G. (1983) A Reason for Doubting the Existence of Consciousness, in Davidson, R., Schwartz, G. and Shapiro, D., *Consciousness and Self-Regulation*, Vol. 3, Springer.

Rolls, E. (1997) Consciousness in Neural Networks? *Neural Networks*, 10, 1227-1240.

Rolls, E. (2007) A Computational Neuroscience Approach to Consciousness, *Neural Networks*, 20, 962-982.

Rosenthal, D. (1996) A Theory of Consciousness. In N. Block, O. Flanagan, and G. Guzeldere (eds.), *The Nature of Consciousness*, MIT Press, 729-753.

Samsonovich, A. (2007) Universal Learner as an Embryo of Computational Consciousness, in Chella, A. and Manzotti, R., editors, *AI and Consciousness: Theoretical Foundations and Current Approaches,* AAAI Fall Symposium, AAAI Technical Report FS-07-01, 129-134.

Samsonovich, A., Nadel, L. (2005) Fundamental Principles and Mechanisms of the Conscious Self, *Cortex*, 41, 669-689.

Sanz, R., Hernandez, C., Sanchez-Escribano, M. (2012) Consciousness, Action Selection, Meaning and Phenomenic Anticipation, *International Journal of Machine Consciousness*, 4, 383-399.

Schlagel R (1999) Why not Artificial Consciousness or Thought? *Minds and Machines*, 9, 3-28.

Schneider, W., Chein, J. M. (2003). Controlled and Automatic Processing: Behavior, Theory, and Biological Mechanisms, *Cognitive Science*, 27(3), 525-559.

Searle, J. (2004) *Mind*, Oxford University Press.

Seth, A. (2009) The Strength of Weak Artificial Consciousness, *International Journal of Machine Consciousness*, 1, 71-82.

Seth, A., Izhikevich, E., Reeke, G., and Edelman, G. (2006) Theories and Measures of Consciousness, *Proceedings of the National Academy of Sciences*, 103, 10799-10804.

Shanahan, M. (2008) A Spiking Neuron Model of Cortical Broadcast and Competition, *Consciousness and Cognition*, 17, 288-303.

Siewert, C. (2011), Phenomenal Thought, in Bayne, T., Montague, M. (eds.), *Cognitive Phenomenology*, Oxford University Press, 236-267.

Simen, P., Vugt, M., Balci, F., Freestone, D., Polk, T. (2010) Toward an Analog Neural Substrate for Production Systems, *Proceedings 10th International Conference on Cognitive Modeling*, 223-228.

Sloman, A., Chrisley, R. (2003) Virtual Machines and Consciousness, *Journal of Consciousness Studies*, 10, 133-172.

Sun, R. (1999) Accounting for the Computational Basis of Consciousness, *Consciousness and Cognition*, 8, 529-565.

Sun, R. (2002) *Duality of the Mind*, Erlbaum.

Sylvester J, Reggia J, Weems S, Bunting M (2013) Controlling Working Memory with Learned Instructions, *Neural Networks*, 41, 23-38.

Takeno, J. (2008) A Robot Succeeds in 100% Mirror Image Cognition, *International Journal on Smart Sensing and Intelligent Systems*, 1, 891-911.

Takeno, J. (2013) *Creation of a Conscious Robot*, Pan Stanford.

Taylor, J. (1997) Neural Networks for Consciousness, *Neural Networks*, 10, 1207-1225.

Taylor, J. (2003) Neural Models of Consciousness, in M. Arbib (editor), *Handbook of Brain Theory and Neural Networks*, MIT Press, 263-267.

Taylor, J. (2007) CODAM: A Neural Network Model of Consciousness, *Neural Networks*, 20, 983-992.

Taylor, J. (2012) Does the Corollary Discharge of Attention Exist? *Consciousness and Cognition*, 21, 325-339.

Tononi, G (2004) An Information Integration Theory of Consciousness, *BMC Neuroscience*, 5:42.

Tononi, G. (2008) Consciousness as Integrated Information, *Biological Bulletin*, 215, 216-242.

Tononi, G., Sporns, O. (2003) Measuring Information Integration, *BMC Neuroscience*, 4:31.

Treisman, A. (2009) Attention: Theoretical and Psychological Perspectives, in Gazzaniga, M. (editor), *The Cognitive Neurosciences*, MIT Press, 189-204.

van der Velde, F., de Kamps, M. (2006) Neural Blackboard Architectures of Combinatorial Structures in Cognition, *Behavioral and Brain Sciences*, 29, 37-108.

Wallace, R. (2005) *Consciousness: A Mathematical Treatment of the Global Neuronal Workspace Model*, Springer.

Wallace, R. (2006) Pitfalls in Biological Computing: Canonical and Idiosyncratic Dysfunction of Conscious Machines, *Mind and Matter*, 4, 91-113.

Weems, S., Reggia, J. (2006) Simulating Single Word Processing in the Classic Aphasia Syndromes, *Brain and Language*, 98, 291-309.

Wilson, N., Sun, R., Mathews, R. (2009) A Motivationally-Based Simulation of Performance Degradation Under Pressure, *Neural Networks*, 502-508.

Wolfram, S. (2002) *A New Kind of Science*, Wolfram Media.

In: Consciousness
Editor: Lloyd Alvarado
ISBN: 978-1-63485-023-0

Chapter 6

CONSCIOUSNESS: USING CLINICAL EVIDENCE TO LINK CONSCIOUSNESS WITH ITS TWIN PERILS OF PSYCHOSIS AND VIOLENCE

Bob Johnson**, *PhD
Consultant Psychiatrist, MRCPsych, MRCGP, PhD (med computing), MA (Psychol) Ventnor, Isle Of Wight, UK

ABSTRACT

CONSCIOUSNESS presents us with a challenging, disquieting, and somewhat contradictory mixture – parts of it are so simple they generally pass entirely without notice, while others are so far beyond our human capacity to understand, they seem permanently obscure. From the perspective of a working psychiatrist, it helps to separate these two aspects, so shedding light on this infinitely complex, yet vitally important topic.

This chapter therefore starts with its simplest characteristics – consciousness exists, but only when you are awake or unanaesthetised. It has a more straightforward relationship to 'mind' than is usually allowed – the two terms 'mind' and 'consciousness' overlap sufficiently for practical (psychiatric) purposes.

Next, comparing consciousness with the field of vision helps – the retina, after all, is neurologically speaking, an outgrowth of the very brain tissue itself. And the striking feature of eyesight is the focal point – a small area of high detail surrounded by blur, and the blurring increases the further you get from that point. Accordingly, it makes sense to acknowledge that the entrance channel to consciousness is also necessarily narrow – were it not, we would be overwhelmed too easily – "it all happened at once – so I lost track".

Thirdly, there is no future in elucidating consciousness without tackling the challenge of 'choice', or Free Will. Parts of this aspect are indeed wrapped in permanent obscurity – like Richard Feynman said of Quantum Mechanics – if you *think* you understand it, you don't. But as Samuel Johnson said in 1778, "All theory is against the Freedom of the Will; all experience for it" – time we paid more attention to the latter, it pays dividends to explore 'experience', here *clinical* experience, as fully as we can.

* Corresponding author: e-mail DrBob@TruthTrustConsent.com. GMC speciality register for psychiatry, www.DrBobJohnson.org, reg. num. 0400150.

The chapter then examines how Newtonian physics fails to cope with the speed of light, or the nature of the photon. The Uncertainty Principle, without which modern electronics couldn't function, shows how essential it is to accept Uncertainty for some concepts, in order to proceed. Just as the electron doesn't have a pinpoint position, but is best thought of as being somewhere in a 'cloud', so too with descriptions of consciousness. As long as verbal labels are handled responsibly, then communication and therefore progress is possible.

The main thrust of the chapter is to highlight the similarity between software bugs in computing, and the anomalies of psychosis and violence – in both cases we have outcomes we don't want. Throughout the chapter, the psychiatric aspects are examined, especially problems which follow the unacceptable omission of consciousness from the DSM (the Diagnostic and Statistical Manual of Mental Disorders).

The chapter draws on my clinical experience 'de-programming' 60 murderers, including 6 serial killers, during 5 years working as a consultant psychiatrist in Parkhurst Prison, the UK's premier prison. Also my long-term work with infant trauma, and its impact on psychotic symptoms.

Consciousness is our species key adaptation for evolutionary survival. It is sobering to consider that Evolution invariably inflicts extinction on any and all species which fail to exploit their powers of adaptation, however apparently unique.

Keywords: consciousness, psychosis, violence, evolution, epistemology, uncertainty principle, extinction, choice, free will, 'intent', computers

INTRODUCTION

Verbal booby-traps bedevil any and all discussions of consciousness – does this word mean the same as that one, or how much does their meaning overlap, if at all? Though words here represent our only channel of communication, consciousness is the very source from which all words originate, so a topic that is already elusive enough, risks disappearing into the mists of confusion altogether.

These basic points are covered as best I can in my position paper on consciousness, published separately, the bulk of which I include here in full, since it outlines the most reasonable pathway through I can muster. However, though the conclusions to both this chapter and the position paper remain identical, this chapter has the advantage that it allows the extra space needed, to include adequate amounts of *clinical* data. I regard this as highly significant, since evidence from the real world of symptoms, pains and remedies, bolsters the theoretical argument most directly, in a manner which is uncommon in such discussions. I am fortunate in having received an excellent grounding in philosophy, especially linguistics and epistemology, which I later consolidated in my subsequent clinical work. My PhD in medical computing serves to head off yet another loop hole.

Those looking for a scientific definition, indeed a scientific approach to consciousness should ponder the problems posed by such an approach to 'pain'. As a working doctor, I have had to abandon the notion of ever finding a scientific definition of 'pain', since none has been forthcoming, nor is likely to be, else medical practice risks being reduced to the level of veterinary surgeons. Consciousness is of course, vastly more important than 'pain', indeed the latter cannot exist without it – so a practical approach is vital, and all theories must conform to experience of what actually happens in practice – otherwise, if the theory is flawed, the outcome is guaranteed to be dire, as so often with contemporary versions of what consciousness 'really' is. Despite all these tribulations, the topic of consciousness is by far the most fascinating in our entire cosmos, and is therefore well worth the extra mental exertions it entails. The prize of improving our understanding of it, not only promises to be glorious, but also, as I argue here, vital.

SIMPLIFYING CONSCIOUSNESS

SIMPLICITY is the key to understanding. When a topic becomes too complex, the mind goes blank, "this is beyond me", it's as if someone has just turned off the light. This accounts for the glaring omission of consciousness from the most powerful (and misguided) psychiatric text book ever written, "The DSM" (see below). As a working psychiatrist, omitting consciousness from psychiatry is unacceptable – herewith my prescription for remedying this costly and perilous anomaly. What's needed is a robust framework to accommodate all references to consciousness, here divided into three Bins – the Known, the Knowable, and the Unknowable – Bins A, B and C, respectively.

Bin A, the Known, is self-evident. Consciousness exists, but only when you are awake, or at least alive. Bin B, the Knowable, is the interesting one, which features prominently in this chapter. It traces a thread which links the characteristics of consciousness to those of psychotic symptoms, and of violence, and their remedy. Many readers will promptly dump these, without a second thought, straight into Bin C, the Unknowable – which more properly contains such notions as where consciousness comes from, what it's 'made' of, or more prosaically – "will I wake up in the morning?" – 100% unknowable until it arrives.

Bin A, the Known, is the one to start with, building confidence in the obvious, so as to reduce the risk that the reader ceases to read, of his or her going 'blank' and reading no more. The first thing to do is address one or two bear-pits, which entrap the unwary (including the DSM) without fail. Thus the word 'mind' overlaps sufficiently with consciousness as to be equivalent. There is no need to fret over the distinction. Consciousness can only occur in the 'mind', which, by common consent, takes place in the brain. This is 'known', or at least accepted by those wishing to explore the most fascinating phenomenon in the entire cosmos. Unhappily a deeper bear-pit lurks beneath – too many confuse mind with brain – a costly illusion – as unwieldy as supposing that analysis of the leg will account for why so many insist on running the Marathon. A decade of the 'leg'?

So what else can we comfortably put in Bin A, the Known? The next important item is focus. We tend to think of one thing at a time, or at least a coherent string of things – one thing follows another, it's known as a 'line of thought', and vital it is too. The best illustration of this is to compare it with the field of vision. Fix your sight on a spot, and without moving the eye, note how everything else becomes increasingly blurred as you 'look' further from this focal point. This is a fact of life, so it lands securely in Bin A, the Known.

Neurologically speaking, the retina, which contains this focal point, is an actual outgrowth of brain tissue itself, so the link between eyesight and consciousness is reliable. It also impacts on how consciousness works – thinking of one thing at a time, overlaps with 'seeing' or scrutinising one thing at a time – the focus in both cases being indispensable to progress. If everything you saw was 'central' you'd be lost – "everything happened at once", so nothing made sense. The same applies to consciousness – if the mind is overwhelmed, and loses its thread, then it might as well go 'blank', it's no longer working as it should. It's called 'overload', and happens more often than you might think. It can be guarded against by taking small steps, cautiously, making sure of the first footfall before venturing the second. Also by repeatedly going back to where you were before being overwhelmed, reducing the load, and carrying on. Narrow though the focal point may be, it is astonishing how much can be achieved by diligent and repeated application in this way.

As if these first two bear-pits were not enough, there's a third that's even more calamitous. You might have thought that the Mind/Brain Controversy, plus the realisation that you can never see the whole picture (i.e., 'everything') at one given time, might suffice – but no, compared with these two, the next is little short of seismic. It's choice. And it alone can rescue us not only from these first two, but also from the two perils noted above – without choice, we are doomed – but use it prudently, and a pathway opens through those perils which otherwise threaten extermination.

Into which Bin will you put 'choice'? Bin A the Known, or Bin C the Unknowable? There's a delicious irony here, were the consequences less dire – can you choose whether you have 'choice' or not? For too many, the choice they make is 'no', they cannot – which makes no sense, an 'irrationality' from which the suffering is limitless and the outlook perilous.

Scientifically speaking, when there's doubt, decide it on the evidence. Here, I can't resist introducing an evidential point made 500 years ago, in the 1620s, expressed with admirable poetic brevity – *"A man that looks on glass, On it may stay his eye; Or if he pleaseth, through it pass, And then the heav'n espie."* [George Herbert]. Is this true? Can you choose to look through the glass? Or has it already been decided, somewhere else, that what you see is pre-ordained, and talk of 'espying heav'n' is illusory poppycock? 'Heaven' plays a bigger part in our consciousness than is generally recognised, and not always a benign one. Many, including Newton and Einstein felt compelled to stitch up voids in Bin C, the Unknowable, by resorting to the Supernatural – for myself, coming from a different perspective and time-frame, the Natural is quite awesome enough, happily.

As will already be clear, the DSM is utterly bear-pit bound – not only does it comprehensively omit what must surely be the pinnacle of humanity, consciousness, it then dithers over 'Mind/Brain'. Further, it omits the limitations of 'focus', while succumbing to them in full, and it has not one word to say about 'choice', which is the only reliable remedy we have, or are ever likely to have. There is even a mesmerising discussion in the preface to DSM-IV, 1994, as to how best to eliminate the concept of 'mind' from the full title of "Diagnostic And Statistical Manual Of Mental Disorders" (DSM), while deploying arguments guaranteed to fail any High School philosophy exam. If the DSM prefers 'brain' to 'mind', neurology to psychiatry, why does it pretend otherwise? What a travesty. Unhappily, since DSM-III, the myopic approach it empowers, has now commandeered the heights of my profession, monopolising research funds, clinical promotions, and all medico-political education and legal advice.

Before moving on to Bin C, the Unknowable, which is rather more extensive than we would wish, a brief outline of the practical remedy offered here, might help. If the reader can avoid going 'blank' at this point, the 'answer' to these three bear-pits contains all we require for their resolution. If you can once put 'choice' into Bin A, the Known, then you can use this to 'choose' which bit of the picture to focus on, and from there it's a simple decision to concentrate attention (and funds) on the 'mind' rather than the 'brain'. Neat eh?

DETHRONING NEWTON

'CONSCIOUSNESS' – the very word induces a mental blur, not only for me and you, but for everyone who thinks about it – it's like trying to define the shape of a pint (or litre) of water. It soon becomes too arduous, even painful, so it's much easier to stop thinking about it, to go 'blank'. Worse, you'll get people in this corner loudly maintaining that water is 'square-shaped', while over there, others declaim it's 'circular'. Science doesn't help. The atmosphere risks going from tense to violent – thereby strangling any chance of progress. It is to circumvent such tantrums that I enlisted the three Bins. This may sound like a bit of a hobby, but what it entails could not be more serious – there are two further words, equally resistant to scientific definition, which impact on us all, willy-nilly – they are 'pain' and 'extinction'.

To fill Bin A, the Known, it is essential to have a clearer grasp of what words can do, and what they cannot. We use words all the time. We all need to be understood, which entails meaning what we say. So use of these verbal tools is paramount. But this vital linguistic equipment wobbles, it can prove fickle and crumbly, especially in a crisis. There are many who hope that eventually Science will solve this problem for us, once and for all, by providing us with a definition which everyone must use, and cannot deviate from – it'll all be scientifically proven. Except it won't. Bin C, the Unknowable, which Science has recently been intended to empty, is, and will remain, prodigiously huge, and growing. Again, as with 'consciousness', minds tend to blur when such 'heresies' are voiced – so let's examine words more closely, and see what happens.

The first bear-pit above related to the words 'consciousness' and 'mind'. My advice is not to fret over the distinction between them – indeed, every time 'consciousness' comes up, it might be helpful to use the word 'mind' instead. This could limit the tendency to blur. Mind is an everyday item, we use it to choose our breakfast, what to put on, what needs to be done today – all without a second thought. So to pretend mind doesn't exist is for the birds.

This whole question of verbal stability thrusts us all forcibly and directly into Bin C, the Unknowable, to which we now turn. The central aim of all Scientific Laws was to remove the need for this Bin altogether, by simply extending the notion of Law and Order from politics and the school room, into the mind. We'll pass a Law prohibiting you from using a word that hasn't been scientifically proven. It's an interesting idea, and works better in the kindergarten than in the wider world, but worst of all it breeds the notion that there are Laws out there, in the universe, that will apply all over and to everyone. Well, at the risk of losing a whole swathe of passionate believers, there aren't, and there haven't been, at least not since David Hume in 1739. Carlo Rovelli (2011) puts the matter most succinctly.

> "**Facile** nineteenth-century **certainties** about science – in particular the glorification of science understood as definitive knowledge of the world – **have collapsed. One of the forces responsible for their dismissal has been the twentieth-century revolution in physics, which led to the discovery that NEWTONIAN PHYSICS, despite its immense effectiveness, IS ACTUALLY WRONG, in a precise sense.** Much of the subsequent philosophy of science can be read as an attempt to come to grips with this **disillusionment.** What is scientific knowledge if it can be **wrong** even when it is extremely effective?" *[emphases added]*

"Newtonian physics . . . is actually wrong" – can you read that without gasping? Take note of the rider "in a precise sense". There is irrefutable scientific evidence that the world out there does not behave as we might reasonably have expected, and then some. Newton's Laws of Motion and of Gravity are wonderful, as far as they go – but they do not go nearly far enough. They may help us sort out our car crashes, or launch our rockets, but they do nothing for our understanding of photons. And this is not a vague or woolly 'protest', nor is it in any way anti-scientific – "in a precise sense" means that when you focus right down on what actually happens on our curious planet, you find that however right Newton may have been elsewhere, photons, and their ilk, invariably disobey his Laws as if for sheer devilment. They do so with 100% impunity, and there's not a blind thing we can do about it.

The one I like is the Law of Gravity. Food and drink stays on the table, unless you break this Law, and defy it 100% by lifting both, past your lips. Try eating when your arm has gone 'dead'. If Newton's Law applied 100%, to real meal times, we'd all starve. Newtonian physics does not distinguish between inert food, and hungry consumers – this used to be part of its charm, but when carried too far, it's not.

There are other problems with Knowledge which can be stated simply enough, though however simplified, there's still no guarantee against blanking out. In reality, Bin C, the Unknowable, has rock solid foundations which no amount of scientific or other human endeavour can dislodge, indeed they can easily be exacerbated. Hume started it in 1739 (as Kant acknowledged, but failed to refute), by suggesting that because an event followed a cause today, it could not *certainly* be *known* to do so tomorrow. Well, everyday experience confirms this. I know the car will start because (by-the-cause) of my turning the key – but will it, will it with 100% certainty when I next try? Not in our real world it won't, nor, practically speaking, do we expect it to. But somehow, when we hear the magic, quasi-religious word 'scientific', we go all coy, and roll over. Time this stopped.

Nor is it only that the links in our chains of cause and effect are suspect, so is their origin – there is no First Cause to start them all off, and that's not for want of trying. Perhaps worst of all, we live in a multi-threaded universe, where no single event ever has a single cause – there are an infinite number of causes for any event you care to name, and there always will be. You may be able to limit this by enforcing "laboratory conditions", or, in medical terms by going *in vitro* – but to do us any good, you eventually have to return to the real world, with its infinite complexities, *in vivo*, where we all have to live out the rest of our lives. In reality, the whole shooting match was already in full swing before we even arrived, however fervently we might wish and suppose otherwise.

Intriguingly the three bear-pits which so hamstring the DSM, also highlight a feasible way round this 'scientific' quagmire. The one that gives so much grief to "Scientism" is the third bear-pit, 'choice'. Once you place this firmly, and irrevocably in Bin A, the Known, then you can exercise discretion about what does make sense out there, and what does not. So if once you choose to accept that minds exist, you can then decide which bit of the next 24 hours to focus on, and finally how persistently you intend to 'choose' and thereby ensure that the words you use, accurately tally with reality, and what you want to say about it. Choice confers **responsibility**, and the penalty for irresponsibility is not some Divine or Scientific Law, but merely that you will be mis-understood, your irresponsible actions will impair your **ability** to **respond** and adapt, which gives a sound biological underpinning to the more technical use of the word **'responsibility'**. For once living organism fail to adapt, they perilously soon perish. The Iron Law of Evolution applies with or without Newton, Hume,

Kant, Darwin, Einstein or either me, or you – adapt to physical reality, to your current surroundings – or you're extinct, or partially extinct. In this strict sense therefore, when DSM eliminates 'mind', this 'irresponsibility' carries a precisely perilous risk, not because I or anyone else says so, but because that's life.

ALL THE UNKNOWABLES

It is important, though painful, to cement Bin C, the Unknowable, firmly and irretrievably into place. This Unknowability is a permanent feature of our human mental landscape, and will always remain so. Many, as mentioned, are happy to fill the void with the Supernatural, of one sort or another. But for those of a more sanguine disposition, it's important to obliterate the Scientism escape route entirely. Science was hoped to release us from this troublesome Bin forever. In the 1890s, it almost looked likely. But even by then, the perfidious photon had already muttered betrayal, and with its close cousin, the electron, it continues to do so today. Sceptics are invited to ask any Theoretical Physicist within range, where the electron actually is. Even what it actually is. Ask them to define where you can reliably find one. Pin onto them the standards of scientific definition commonly pinned onto those who talk of emotions, of choice, even of mind. Probabilities, or improbabilities of electronic whereabouts may do wonders for our technology, but they leave our serenity in tatters.

More intriguing is the notion that if you do define where an electron is, the very act of doing so alters its nature even its position, radically. When similar allegations are aimed at those discussing emotions and 'intents', the mind of the interrogator goes blank, casting the pragmatic practitioner adrift. So if we can agree to grasp this nettle firmly by the throat, it helps to concede that words, for one thing, will never have pristine scientific definitions either. What words mean is what we intend them to mean, sometimes more, sometimes less – but 'choice' or 'intent' are indispensable to any language. So if you deny 'choice' then you risk talking parrot-fashion permanently, with a severely limited range of meanings, if any. Here too, the Principle of Responsibility applies in full – if you coin sentences knowing them to be false, you limit your ability, and of those who hear you, to respond to what is really going on in your and their surroundings, with commensurate risks of failure to adapt to reality. The Iron Law of Evolution, adapt, respond or perish, applies whether you believe you have 'choice', or not. Prime Ministers, and others, ignore this at our peril.

So, accepting that just as electrons and their ilk exist in a 'cloud', rather than in a pinpoint position, why not apply the same leeway to words? In practice, we all adjust our words to mean what best conveys our perception of reality at a given time, though never with 100% accuracy, repeatability or success. It is noteworthy that the concept of Evolution took some time to penetrate the ethos, since it actually seemed to subtract from the supremacy of (wo)man. A similar lapse of time was also needed before Relativity gained favour, and in both cases there are still robust pockets of resistance, where the argument is not about our realities, but about what we would really wish to be the case, what our preferred wishful thinking is.

One irrefutable impact of Relativity is the explicit emasculation of Absolutes – once the quality or characteristics of your observation depends on your speed, your time frame, the impact of gravity, and other entirely *relative* circumstances, then there will never be, in a strictly accurate scientific sense, any 'fact' or view which by its very Absolute Authority obliterates all others. We would like to think there is, we have Popes and Emperors, even Kaisers, whose word is Law, or used to be – but this can no longer be justified scientifically. And taking the points listed earlier, especially that of our existing in a multi-threaded universe, such Absolute Authorities exist only in the minds of those who aspire to have them, never in the real world, however much Science we deploy.

No, all is now *relative*, and will always be so. This places increasing and enduring **responsibility** on every observer of the scene, any scene, to reflect as truthfully as they can, what occurs there. Yet, while Absolute Scientific Knowledge passes us by, intriguingly, Evolution offers us a remedy, if we can once choose to grasp it, something that is ruled out of court if 'choice' is not yet securely in your Bin A, the Known.

The Iron Law of Evolution, respond, adapt or perish, actually provides solid scientific evidence that by virtue of being alive, we do have an element of choice. Only by possessing some ability to change, to choose, to initiate new chains of cause and effect, can Evolution logically and scientifically take place. Things happen which never happened before. Nothing flew before insects did, and they too, mischievously and Unknowably, defy the Law of Gravity, 24/7. How or why or where this possibility came from is lodged firmly in my Bin C, the Unknowable. This happy device allows more emphasis, more focus to fall on choice, 'intent' and other mysterious life-saving actions.

If you once accept that Evolution does occur, that new events, processes, organisms actually *evolve*, i.e., come into being, that were never there before – then you see before you in the entire biosphere something akin to choice, to 'intent' going on all the time. Well, all the time those organisms are alive. Because the one thing you can know Absolutely, is that death is terminal – no evolution follows those species that perish, whether because their earlier choices proved unfortunate, like the Dodo's disinclination to fly, or in our species, by the tools we have devised for our own thermonuclear self-extermination.

The upside is that once 'choice' is firmly placed in Bin A, the Known, then we can also acknowledge and therefore promote creativity, intention and a host of other wonders which occur in the mind, and enable consciousness to blossom. This adaptation, vouchsafed by the Iron Law, relates not to freewheeling ad lib, or whatever goes, but to increasing realism, better acclimatisation, closer awareness of the environment (both human and otherwise) of the reality around us, to which we need to respond in order to continue to survive in it. What a tragedy – to discard the one key to our survival, 'choice', on the insubstantial grounds that it is indefinable – such unwarranted verbal fastidiousness would promptly cripple our astonishing electronic wizardry.

How 'Simple' Are Computers?

SIMPLICITY is indispensable for understanding psychosis and violence, if we are ever to curtail them. What is less obvious, and becoming less so by the decade, is that *simplification* is also at the very heart of computers, without which all our quasi-miraculous delights of Information Technology (IT) would be stillborn. Circumstances largely outside my control allowed me a remarkably broad education, amongst which it was my privilege in

1967, aged 30, to attend one of the earliest computer seminars ever held. There I was taught that the unsung hero of computation, Alan Turing, had propounded 30 years before, in the 1930s, that any machine which could subtract and 'left shift' could solve any and all mathematical equations. That was 20 years before digital machines were even thought of. What is especially remarkable, is that he applied this simplicity to every single mathematical problem or challenge, ever. What universality, what insight, what creativity.

It's worth unpacking that phrase. First of all it applies to mathematical equations – thus anything that can be expressed mathematically can be computerised, conversely anything which cannot, cannot. Included in the latter, however fervent your mathematical leanings, are the two non-scientific terms mentioned earlier, 'pain' and 'extinction' – nothing numerical about them, nor ever will be. Secondly the only two mathematical processes Turing required to retain, were subtraction, which everyone knows, and 'left-shift', which means multiplying by 10 on the decimal scale, or by 2 on the binary. So a device of any type whatever that could multiply by 10 or by 2 or by 8, depending on its numerical 'base', which could also subtract, could cope with all mathematics in any of its vast and astonishing variety. Without this unprecedented insight, computers, and digital technology in its entirety, could not be.

At the heart of both the simplest and even the most complex computer is the singularly simple binary digit, zero or one. This will never change, it's what powers IT. Being so simple, means it can be fast, being fast it can cope with an astonishing, though not unlimited, range. By itself 'machine code' (i.e., strings of '0s' and '1s'), which is what the computer runs on, all computers do, is intensely boring, difficult for humans to handle, and perpetually liable to error. Watch how this works. Noughts and ones are simplicity itself, 'yes' or 'no', 'there' or 'not-there' – but, and here's the rub, this very simplicity opens a deep and hazardous pit. What if that particular binary digit doesn't exactly match what the programmer wanted? What if by striving to get real-world benefit from this astonishing process, the machine though doing entirely what it was told, or 'programmed' to do, came out with the 'wrong' answer. It could not be a mathematical error, but it could well be a reality error. Noughts and ones don't get you very far, just as a simple or blank 'yes' or 'no' doesn't, in the real world – so they have to have context, they have to have colour, they have to have some vestige of reality. But it's being so simple that gives the binary digit it's power, lose that simplicity (something which you have to do to be useful) and you inexorably open the door to software errors or 'bugs'.

If you spoke only binary, you too, would be clear, precise and certain, though perhaps not fast. You'd also be excommunicatively boring. Once you deviate from elemental machine code, so as to gain wider benefits, by adding human characteristics to inanimate overgrown calculating machines, you lose the certainty of computation, and introduce an element of, yes, uncertainty, another Uncertainty Principle to complement that of Quantum Mechanics. There's a deeper link here too, relating to the limits of knowledge, something touched on above. (It's coping with that 'cloud' again.)

But what has programming digital machines to do with psychosis and violence? Well, in both cases we have an outcome which is not the one we want. And it so happens, that the resolution for both is the application of many minds, sympathetic and cooperating minds at that. In computing terms the phrase "many eyeballs make for shallow bugs" means that the more people who examine a programme, and work out what it is really meant to do, then the fewer and briefer are the bugs or errors. Cooperation computer-style works in the real world of commerce, entertainment, knowledge, automation – and we haven't seen anything yet.

Why should it come as a surprise that the same applies to human behaviours in general, and especially to those twin perils of consciousness, violence and psychosis?

What is the overlap between digital computers and human beings, especially the latter's elusive consciousnesses? Well, for one thing humans have choice, computers are programmed what to choose. For another, programming a computer to do anything useful takes years, millions of lines of code are commonplace – but the longer they are, the more prone to flaws. Human beings are also slow to develop – it happens that the input channel, described above as the second bear-pit, focus, is remarkably narrow, a point so often almost deliberately minimised. You can only focus on one thing, or a small group of things at one time. This is a fact of life. So just as with computers, our tasks must first be divided up into small fragments or mouthfuls – a challenging task at the best of times – but when skilfully and *responsibly* done, the outcomes can be fabulous. When not, the results can be destructive, whence psychoses and violence.

So when is the programming done for all human behaviour? It happens in the long post-natal gestation, ages zero to 16, 18 or 21. What you do in adulthood is selected from the choices and examples offered to you in infancy. The language you speak, your 'mother tongue', your view of yourself and your fellows, your prospects and in some crucial ways, your future or expectations – all receive input over these 'formative' decades. Few would contest that children are impressionable – though true to form, the DSM never even mentions childhoods.

My privileged education also involved working for five years in a maximum security prison wing for especially violent, unstable lifers from the entire UK prison system. I explored the 'programming' of 60 murderers, including 6 serial killers, and my life was threatened on three occasions by men who used violence, especially lethal violence, to make their point. I would not have worked there, or for so long, had I not had an inkling as to where this violence came from, and how to remedy it. Being threatened with death by those who knew how to do it, had already done it, and who carefully planned how to do it again – this is not a threat to be tolerated lightly.

Why did I stay? It is probable that I would still be there, had the politicians of the day, not closed the Special Unit in Parkhurst Prison, on myopic, self-expedient grounds. I would have stayed because there is nothing more fascinating in this entire cosmos than untangling software bugs in human beings. Coercion doesn't work. Prisoners kill other prisoners, because they've learnt how to do it – any amount of coercion doesn't stop them. Unpacking their irrationality, the 'bugs' in their programming – that stops them. Even while there, the violence evaporated – alarm bells had been rung on average every two or three weeks – yet there were none in the last 3 years, objective and irrefutable evidence of success (though challengeable) in curbing violence, you might think – but that overlooks the narrowness of the human input channel. Powerful people tend to choose to focus only on what they think benefits them. I claim to have saved over a dozen lives among UK prisoners in the last two decades, a claim enthusiastically supported by a prominent ex-inspector of prisons – but then, as with all doctors' prescriptions, there is no Absolute necessity to implement what has been prescribed, however cheerfully – personal choice operates at all levels, individual, social and also political.

THE ROOTS NEED PRUNING

Where does psychosis and violence come from? What is it that actually goes wrong? Below, I include long dialogues and other clinical data, to show where the lines of thought deviate from the norm, that is from the reality or environment surrounding them at the time. It all relates to trauma, and how the human mind is peculiarly susceptible, in infancy. My explorations into the childhood origins of irrationality, and indeed of irresponsibility, were elucidated by spending two decades in general practice, something I had not planned nor expected to do. After 19 years as a family doctor, in September 1986, a 40 year old woman, let's call her Mary, disclosed how, aged 6, her father appeared to have threatened her life with an axe. This took ages to emerge. It would never have emerged at all, had I not been the family doctor, who had therefore known her father, medically, up to his death, 4 years earlier. What it showed both to me and her, was that the axe was still hanging over her head, not in reality, but in her mind. Her mental world, and therefore her consciousness, was beset with a lethal parental figment, which for her to challenge unaided would induce her instant death by decapitation. Or not.

Unless Mary had trusted me, she would never even have mentioned this lethal threat. What if I were in league with her late dad? Perhaps all men were like him, including me, with a hatchet hidden behind our backs, waiting to strike. Or perhaps not. This is the software bug. This is the learnt error that cripples today's consciousness. It is also brutally simple to remedy – persuade the sufferer that you are powerful enough, to defeat any childhood demon, yet safe enough to be their ally, to do so. Until that point – and how many threatened souls would freely invite a powerful person into their deepest, most shameful, and deadliest secret? – yet until they reverse the lessons of a lifetime, then the threat remains alive, and must be vigilantly countered. Until it is, your survival is at risk. Only by keeping it secret, well buried, well hidden, can you hope to survive another minute. Except that today, the threat and trauma, thus powerfully, carefully and deliberately obscured, no longer exists in the real world. If you think it's difficult persuading sceptics that we do have 'choice', you can see how much harder it is to persuade sufferers that they now have the power to 'choose' to say 'stop'. But when you can, they do.

Serendipity through family contacts with the prison pioneer, John Marriott, lead me to try out this nascent model among the most violent prisoners in the UK prison system, in Parkhurst Prison. Sadly this remarkable prison governor also later fell foul of the same uncaring, *irresponsible*, politician, with devastating results.

Lenny, a man in his mid-40s, was my first success among the prisoners, he saved my bacon. Without him, I might have agreed with the conventional wisdom that psychopaths are born not made. As it was, he changed within 8 weeks from being terrified of his mother 'battering' him again, as she did aged 8, to grasping her hand so as to stop her ever attempting that again. He stopped her both in real life, and in his mind – if only someone had talked to him like this aged 18, he said, he never would have murdered. The prison service didn't like to see this restoration, so he was routinely devastated too – "you must have made a lot of enemies", he told me. I never dreamt that challenging norms could prove so widely hazardous.

What Lenny and the other 59 murderers showed was that violence comes from obsolete survival strategies. In the kindergarten, the bigger thug wins. Frightening your bullies works, leading insecure infants to believe that deterrence is optimal. Which in badly organised (or governed) kindergartens, it undoubtedly is. Sadly, owing to the narrowness of our focal points, such deeply learnt strategies are mighty difficult to shift. There is a clear parallel between Mary's fixatives, and Lenny's. Every act of violence is kindergarten based. If you have time, resources, and 'intent' enough, you can weary out all violence, especially lethal violence, as I proved to my personal satisfaction, and survival, in Parkhurst Prison.

If you doubt that such crippling strategies can persist unchanged for decades, even centuries, consider the humble QWERTY keyboard. Note that though 'E' is the commonest letter in English, it has been quite deliberately allocated to the left middle finger, commonly among the weakest of all 10 digits. This was because, when first conceived, the linkage between key and typeface was problematic, and needed hobbling to limit mechanical tangles. How many typists have suffered because this initial strategy was never updated? How many more will suffer because kindergarten notions of violence and deterrence persist, because of a fundamental, and identical mismatch between today's reality and yesterday's.

The thrust of this chapter is that both psychosis and violence arise from software bugs, not hardware. This point turns on what consciousness is for. Here it is assumed that consciousness is the key adaptation by which our species, homo sapiens, adapts and so survives in evolutionary terms. Of course, those who doubt evolution will also fail to see just how vital a correctly functioning consciousness really is. For those that do, consciousness is not just an intriguing facet, but the very key to our survival – the incipient violence of our armaments testifies to how far we can deviate from this sociable norm. Alice Miller was surely right in claiming that no person brought up in a stable loving childhood could ever become a murderer – certainly the 60 murderers I got to know really well, had, universally, childhoods from hell. Indeed their adult behaviour testified to this, just as their relinquishing violence confirmed that they had not been born that way. How many readers will be persuaded to place this firmly in Bin A, the Known – I wonder.

The roots of violence that need cutting are simply stated. "Get your revenge in first" is the operating maxim. It's a close relative of Mutually Assured Destruction, our current military strategy for survival, better known as 'Deterrence'. It operates even in fiction – analysing Sherlock Holmes's 30 murderers shows that the key obsolete motivation, is 'Revenge'. It certainly drove all 60 of those I explored in Parkhurst Prison. "I'll hurt you (or myself) now, not for what you're doing, but for what you (or someone) did". The past so clearly drives the present. Wrong. The current enemy is never identical to the old one – generals are not the only ones who persist in fighting the last war. Somewhat to my surprise, and certainly to theirs, the murderers I explored, did not want to be violent, and 'turned' as soon as they saw a convincing alternative. This reflects Stephen Pinker's conclusion that violence is '*stupid*' – so is revenge. So too is every psychiatric symptom, including psychoses.

Just as childhood 'pain' is indispensible for adult violence, as "From Pain To Violence" [Zulueta, 2006] so clearly indicates, so too, psychoses arise inescapably from infant pains. Rather to my surprise, and certainly to my delight, all the psychiatric disorders I now meet, arise exclusively from the disjunction, this 'bug' in emotional and strategic development. It is 'unreal' to operate infant survival patterns in adult life – parenting keeps infants alive, and adults insane or 'unreal'. In the last few years, two people in particular have allowed me a glimpse into where their psychotic symptoms came from. One, Freda, eventually confided that she kept her mother alive in part of her mind, where she went whenever she felt stressed.

This despite us both being well aware that her mother had died 32 years earlier. The other, Sam, eventually conceded that he too kept his deceased mother alive, to protect himself from a variety of childhood abuses. I have known both Freda and Sam for 15 years, since 2000. It has taken that long for us to build sufficient trust for them to disclose these vital secrets.

Without trust, reality is far too terrifying to think about, let alone disclose. Conversely, by gently persuading these two, and others, to say (and indeed to *think*) what in infancy was unthinkable, then they blossom. What a privilege. "Grow up therapy", "Emotional Education", requires courtesy, consent and exceptionally careful handling – but it's a delight to watch 'choice', or 'intent', growing stronger, and thereby to evaporate all insanities, across the range. Symptoms of psychosis are the deepest, but the rest remit too, from anorexia, through panics, depressions, bi-polar, manic-depression, aversions, addictions, psychopathies, paedophilia, all the way up to violence against self and others. Unreality costs. Realism, if supportively and tactfully delivered, with express and fully informed consent, borders on the miraculous.

At this point, I include thee clinical cases, to put flesh on the bones of this argument. The first arises from a couple of pages I took entirely at random from my 150 prison and psychiatric reports, over the last 25 years. I renamed the prisoner 'Tommy', and anonymised place names and dates, as I have done both in the second, a spontaneous letter from a prisoner, and in the third clinical case, a tight verbal transcription of psychosis in action.

The First Clinical Case: Violence

I saw 'Tommy' on a prison hospital visit sometime in the mid-2000s. These two pages were written some 10 years before I saw him, when he would have been aged mid-20s. I only ever saw him the once, I had no input into these pages. The fact that no-one followed up any of the blistering clues showing where his aberrant behaviour came from, reflects badly on the state of forensic psychiatry at the time, and since. What is remarkable about these two pages is the clarity of the descriptions, which ring so true, and which are repeated ad nauseam throughout all my prison, forensic psychiatric work. The central reason they were not followed up to the obvious benefit of the patients, of their carers, to say nothing of society as a whole, is because of the bear-pits mentioned earlier in this chapter, the exclusion of those crucial elements of humanity from the DSM, and the current grossly mistaken view of violence and psychoses.

Firstly, I give the verbatim report in full, followed by a line by line commentary. See how the raw text strikes you, see if you can spot the points I raise in that later commentary. I have numbered the lines, so you can jot down your comments, and then compare same with mine.

1. **Pamela's report, a Social Worker, following referral for anger management.**

2. Pamela reported on the work she had been doing with Tommy. Pamela said that
3. Tommy was brought up in HomeTown and he had been abusing solvents from
4. the age of twelve. He describes "living day to day being anxious, frightened,
5. angry and high and in a deaf/blind state with strong feelings of anxiety".
6. He started to think that people were ignoring him and describes seeing people

but not hearing them. It was reported that he came from a family of offenders and who used drugs, that his father was dead and was an alcoholic. He would phone his mother a lot but she would unload on him. He can't go back to HomeTown because of the offence and being known there. He has had relationships in the Hospital with X1 and X2 and with males as well.

Regarding the offences, Pamela said that Tommy can picture the victim, see him (the victim) in front on him and then go into denial and shut down, feeling out of control. The victim was twelve years old and he was frightened and wanted to run. Pamela thought he saw a way out with glue sniffing. He is angry at himself and of rejection and saw himself and her as the victim. He couldn't describe the offence of rape itself. He had engaged in sodomy in 1988 and the case was dismissed and in 1990 he spoke about 'repeated' (unconfirmed) abuse on himself. He would steal from washing lines but Pamela did not know what he would steal. He reported feeling sexually attracted to adult females and had sex with a man in the Hospital, X3, with mutual masturbation. He claims fantasies about adult women. Tommy had gone on an outing with Pamela and seen Bloxville Castle, he had never seen it before and he wanted to go to the airport and Bloxville Zoo. They did go to the Zoo and there were young girls around and Tommy didn't react. Finally she thought there were lots of family secrets.

Second meeting with Pamela. Pamela spoke more about Tommy's offences. He said the first offence was when he was twelve years old, he went to HomeTown to sniff glue. He intended to steal the bike of a boy. He was teasing the boy who was smaller than him and said that he had got a knife. He said it was nice to have power over the victim and he felt excited and high. He said he demanded the shoes of the victim to humiliate him and that he thought he was doing to the victim what was done to him in the past. This made him not the victim. He enjoyed teasing the boy, the boy challenged him and Tommy got angry with this because he could be the victim again and therefore pushed the boy. He talked to the boy saying he was sorry. Tommy enjoyed the attack and Pamela said he thought that Tommy may see this as normal, this is what others do and he was achieving something and wanted respect.

He then anally buggered the boy. The case was dropped for unknown reasons. Pamela said that before, Tommy has always acknowledged the theft but had not discussed the rape before this. Pamela reported when he was talking about this his face was puce and sweating.

Pamela said that Tommy had said that he had been sexually assaulted before the index offences in past notes but that more recently he said he can't remember being abused before, only the one time. Pamela thought he was prostituting

47. himself from the ages of ten to sixteen.
48. Tommy's first alleged assault was in 1985 when he was thirteen and the girl was six
49. and he laid on top of her. In 1987 a child accused him again of lying on top of her.
50. He has talked about these before but the more recent discussion was the first time
51. Pamela said that he said he recognised himself as being in power.

52. He said he describes having temper tantrums as a child, she thought he would
53. exhaust himself with the offences and then the offence would stop. She reported
54. that a bus driver had been grooming Tommy, but Tommy had said that there
55. "must be something in me than makes me look homosexual".
56. She said that he worships his father but that she said the father failed to protect him
57. when his Uncle Bill assaulted him and she wonders whether the father abused him.
58. He said he liked to talk about the dreams when he was on the glue. He is also working
59. with Johnnie, Team Leader on Z, to discuss with the man what had happened to him
60. and see that a man won't be appalled. Pamela thought that he would benefit
61. from a life map and she had done a list of whom was good and bad people in his life.

62. **Hand over session with Pamela and Tommy**.

63. Pamela said initially that Tommy was handling feelings of problems of anger,
64. the offences, the abuse and doing a life story. Tommy said that he had been learning
65. how to talk more for example, talking after phone calls to his mother and
66. his mother would put problems on him and he would feel angry because he couldn't
67. do anything. He said they had also cut down phone calls to once a week and that
68. he would try and talk about the good bits and take more control. Tommy said
69. that his mum has hassles to do with the offences and Tommy feels that that's his fault.
70. He reported feeling good about schoolwork and having a positive view of the future.
71. Pamela said that he had been in the pantomime at Christmas and managed not to get
72. high and to handle it well.

73. Tommy said when he first came into care he couldn't care less about anybody
74. and now that he is not as high, he is able to stop the thoughts and before
75. he used to be bottle up being anxious and he doesn't now. He said that he feels
76. anxious and scared about moving out and what will happen, he feels he is
77. strong enough to stay away from drugs but is frightened about his anger.
78. Pamela indicated to Tommy that my main role would be understanding
89. his anger further and also his low self-esteem. Pamela also indicated that
80. I would be doing a life story book (which I have not planned).

Here is the same text again, this time with comments to illustrate the points about consciousness made earlier in the chapter.

Table 1.

The record	My comments
1. Pamela's report, a Social Worker, following referral for anger management.	The intervention of a social worker is good, it shows a certain promise, which sadly, is not fulfilled. Also beneficial, is the fact that Tommy has requested it, one way or another. In this case 'consent', or choice has been expressed, therefore Tommy has provided a 'handle' which could have been used to release his emotional turmoil, if only it had been expertly handled
2. Pamela reported on the work she had been doing with Tommy. Pamela said that	What is remarkable is how fruitful the 'work' proved to be – Tommy clearly confides in Pamela, which is not common between prisoner and staff – the fact that these painful biographical details flow freely onto the page is a compliment to both parties.
3. Tommy was brought up in HomeTown and he had been abusing solvents from	Abusing solvents is a stark symptom – it testifies to a mental 'pain' that needs to be muted, with whatever comes to hand, however disabling.
4. the age of twelve. He describes "living day to day being anxious, frightened,	Evidence of this 'pain' is clear from this comment – it's not intermittent, it never leaves him.
5. angry and high and in a deaf/blind state with strong feelings of anxiety".	Indeed, he prefers to render himself 'deaf/blind' than face the insoluble emotional challenge – which would seem to be a non-responding father.
6. He started to think that people were ignoring him and describes seeing people	Had I been treating this man, I would have pointed out that 'people' here stands in for 'dad'. I frequently do this in my prison work today, especially when, as here the father is deceased, but his 'figment' continues unabated, until I or someone trustworthy, can persuade the sufferer to 'choose' to throw him out.
7. but not hearing them. It was reported that he came from a family of offenders	This is clear social withdrawal – emotional freezing, with dreadful consequences for his self-esteem, his social skills, and indeed his future.
8. and who used drugs, that his father was dead and was an alcoholic.	He clings to memories, figments, of his father who seems to have been both an 'offender' and an alcoholic – neither of which promises Tommy a sound, secure social beginning in life
9. He would phone his mother a lot but she would unload on him.	Here again, we have standard infant emotional survival strategies – his mother couldn't protect him when young, and now 'unloads' on him today – both would benefit from emotional weaning.

The record	My comments
10. He can't go back to HomeTown because of the offence and being known there.	Again, a strike against him, that is unlikely to change, but which could be resolved differently.
11. He has had relationships in the Hospital with X1 and X2 and with males as well.	Sexual activity is implied here, which may or may not be significant – depending whether it was consensual or not.
12. Regarding the offences, Pamela said that Tommy can picture the victim,	These two lines are highly significant. At first, Tommy *can* see the victim, and then he can't.
13. see him (the victim) in front on him and then go into denial and shut down,	Here we have consciousness 'shutting down', which is where both psychosis and violence come from. Being shut down, it means Tommy cannot grow emotionally – so is hammering around with infant-emotions in an adult's world.
14. feeling out of control. The victim was twelve years old and he was frightened	No wonder he feels 'out of control'. He is still pulling infant levers, which didn't work then, and don't now, instead of self-confident adult social skills.
15. and wanted to run. Pamela thought he saw a way out with glue sniffing.	Confirmation here that glue-sniffing did offer some relief from his mental pains – I yearn to follow up this godsend, crying out for amelioration.
16. He is angry at himself and of rejection and saw himself and her as the victim.	Several 'victims' seem mixed up here, but the negative emotions are clear enough. Consciousness can sort these out, provided 'choice' or 'intent' or 'will power' is enlisted to show how.
17. He couldn't describe the offence of rape itself. He had engaged in sodomy in	Again, this is 'shut down' – it doesn't mean it didn't occur, or that he cannot recall it – just that he finds the whole area too painful to contemplate for long enough, to do so. Again, he needs support to sort this 'bug' in his mental and social software.
18. 1988 and the case was dismissed and in 1990 he spoke about 'repeated'	'Sodomy' here is again an aggressive act for his childhood revenge, arising from his inadequate parenting.
19. (unconfirmed) abuse on himself. He would steal from washing lines	Here is another tantalising hint of what really lurks in his consciousness – abuse which he couldn't stop, nor his parents – and which he has subsequently coped with by 'denial', 'shutting down', which sadly removes the one reliable means of dispatching the past, wholesale. His current symptoms confirm he was abused – the fear and anger arise from nowhere else, neither did his stealing.
20. but Pamela did not know what he would steal. He reported feeling	What he stole is less significant than that he did. He was, partly, trying to compensate for parental inadequacy,

Table 1. (Continued)

The record	My comments
21. sexually attracted to adult females and had sex with a man in the	Again, sexuality features in the report – it's full significance is probably overrated – it reflects more, how consensual his behaviours, i.e., how mature.
22. Hospital, X3, with mutual masturbation. He claims fantasies about adult women.	Pamela appears to doubt his claims. The remedy for aberrant sex is straightening out his infant emotions.
23. Tommy had gone on an outing with Pamela and seen Bloxville Castle, he had	This is excellent. A social event, without stigma, coaxing him into accepting that adulthood can blossom without the detriments of his particular infancy.
24. never seen it before and he wanted to go to the airport and Bloxville Zoo.	Clearly deprived in infancy, these are the first sprigs of an adult springtime.
25. They did go to the Zoo and there were young girls around and	More good news – though again, more emphasis placed on sex/gender than was perhaps needed.
26. Tommy didn't react. Finally she thought there were lots of family secrets.	Pamela again is spot on – family secrets, locked away in Tommy's mental furniture, because too toxic to ventilate. Persuade him to ventilate, as he begins to above, and their toxic nature evaporates. The bugs in consciousness hate the sunshine of today's truth.
27. Second meeting with Pamela. Pamela spoke more about Tommy's offences.	Again Pamela continues to make headway. Tommy is clearly beginning to trust her more, an essential ingredient for debugging anyone's consciousness.
28. He said the first offence was when he was twelve years old,	I'm not convinced he did not 'offend' before 12 – 'naughty' boys are speaking with body language – as do ADHDs.
29. he went to HomeTown to sniff glue. He intended to steal the bike of a boy.	By the age of 12, he is more mobile, and can, at last, seek some remedy for his mental pain.
30. He was teasing the boy who was smaller than him and said that he had got a knife.	Note his 'vengeance' here for earlier slights to himself.
31. He said it was nice to have power over the victim and he felt excited and high.	Power and choice were so clearly lacking in his earlier childhood – sadly lording it over smaller fry does nothing to sate his parental deficit.
32. He said he demanded the shoes of the victim to humiliate him and that	Again, this is trivial compared with what he would like to do to his 'carers' – at least their figments.
33. he thought he was doing to the victim what was done to him in the past.	Spot on.
34. This made him not the victim. He enjoyed teasing the boy,	Loss of logic here – that software bug again – when this is straightened out, then emotional maturity is assured.
35. the boy challenged him and Tommy got angry with this because	Anger that roles are reversed, and an earlier fear of adult abuse of him raises itself in his mind.

The record	My comments
36. he could be the victim again and therefore pushed the boy.	He asserts his superior size against his victim – he is not yet able to do this against his paternal figment.
37. He talked to the boy saying he was sorry. Tommy enjoyed the attack	Mixed emotions here – the real boy, and the figment parent swap places.
38. and Pamela said he thought that Tommy may see this as normal, this is	Wanting respect is germane. Normal people are seen through the perspective of his own childhood family – not healthy, but 100% remediable.
39. what others do and he was achieving something and wanted respect.	We all need respect, children especially – different sources for it in adulthood, once consciousness can be fully engaged.
40. He then anally buggered the boy. The case was dropped for unknown reasons.	Aggression more than sex here, and again powered by covert anger against parental figments.
41. Pamela said that before, Tommy has always acknowledged the theft	Talking theft is easier than talking sex.
42. but had not discussed the rape before this. Pamela reported when he was talking	Again Pamela shows how much she has earned his trust – excellent work, pity it wasn't carried through.
43. about this his face was puce and sweating.	Totally mixed emotions – today's and yesterday's
44. Pamela said that Tommy had said that he had been sexually assaulted before the	Further confirmation of the still rather murky abuse he received – it needs tightening, and evicting
45. index offences in past notes but that more recently he said he can't remember	It's intrinsically unlikely that his abusing others sexually comes out of the blue – far more likely to have been 'shown' how to do it – see Freud, April 1896 "pseudo-hereditary". [Freud, 1896]
46. being abused before, only the one time. Pamela thought he was prostituting	Again, when he has recalled it once, then it shows there is something still needs 'debugging'.
47. himself from the ages of ten to sixteen.	Low self-image, self-esteem.
48. Tommy's first alleged assault was in 1985 when he was thirteen and the girl was six	Again, more like a revenge on someone smaller, weaker, with a sexual colouration.
49. and he laid on top of her. In 1987 a child accused him again of lying on top of her.	Same.
50. He has talked about these before but the more recent discussion was the first time	Not clear – but at least this gateway is open to some degree.
51. Pamela said that he said he recognised himself as being in power.	Only with people smaller than him, not yet with people his own size or parent-sized – not yet. . . .
52. He said he describes having temper tantrums as a child, she thought he would	Anger in infancy, driven by fears, by insecurity, possibly by injustices as in abuses of various kinds.

Table 1. (Continued)

The record	My comments
53. exhaust himself with the offences and then the offence would stop. She reported	Not at all likely – the source of his 'vengeance' needs ventilating then evaporating, so ceasing.
54. that a bus driver had been grooming Tommy, but Tommy had said that there	Entirely possible, low self-esteem has this way of showing itself.
55. "must be something in me than makes me look homosexual".	The same.
56. She said that he worships his father but that she said the father failed to protect him	Note the present tense – yet his father, we note from above, is already dead. And offered no protection when alive.
57. when his Uncle Bill assaulted him and she wonders whether the father abused him.	Again, astonishing to have this so clearly verbalised – this is the precursor to letting the whole thing slip into the past where it belongs.
58. He said he liked to talk about the dreams when he was on the glue. He is also working	Glue-induced dreams pleasanter than painful reality – where earlier abuses live on and degrade consciousness.
59. with Johnnie, Team Leader on Z, to discuss with the man what had happened to him	Male authority figures might ease his father-figment.
60. and see that a man won't be appalled. Pamela thought that he would benefit	I'm not convinced.
61. from a life map and she had done a list of whom was good and bad people in his life.	A life map is already outlined in what he's said – all he needs is confidence to shout back at yesterday's abuser/s.
62. Hand over session with Pamela and Tommy.	It appears this is all reported speech written down by the person Pamela 'handed over to'.
63. Pamela said initially that Tommy was handling feelings of problems of anger,	The way to handle anger, is to uncover its roots, then he can see how it links to offences and abuse.
64. the offences, the abuse and doing a life story. Tommy said that he had been learning	Tommy clearly had been learning from an excellent supportive relationship – pity there aren't more like it.
65. how to talk more for example, talking after phone calls to his mother and	He is beginning to accept help for emotional problems imposed by his mother.
66. his mother would put problems on him and he would feel angry because he couldn't	Anger both at and for her.
67. do anything. He said they had also cut down phone calls to once a week and that	Cutting them down instead of sorting them out, as above is a poor solution.
68. he would try and talk about the good bits and take more control. Tommy said	Excellent thinking.
69. that his mum has hassles to do with the offences and Tommy feels that that's his fault.	His mother would weave in problems from her earlier married life too, also possible guilt at abuse she failed to prevent.
70. He reported feeling good about schoolwork and having a positive view of the future.	Consciousness is there to blossom – pity more hasn't been done to facilitate this, both for him and the staff.

The record	My comments
71. Pamela said that he had been in the pantomime at Christmas and managed not to get	Socialising better – excellent.
72. high and to handle it well.	
73. Tommy said when he first came into care he couldn't care less about anybody	Social isolation, he'd known nothing better beforehand, nothing genetic, merely 'training'.
74. and now that he is not as high, he is able to stop the thoughts and before	Adulthood offers so much more than a hectic, insecure childhood, which, as here, lingers.
75. he used to be bottle up being anxious and he doesn't now. He said that he feels	Bottled up with nowhere to go – release, by persuading that the childhood is now over.
76. anxious and scared about moving out and what will happen, he feels he is	He's not been given social confidence.
77. strong enough to stay away from drugs but is frightened about his anger.	The stronger he gets, the more his consciousness can blossom, the less the need to hide painful memories behind drugs, bullying, sex or anything else.
78. Pamela indicated to Tommy that my main role would be understanding	Pamela was right.
79. his anger further and also his low self-esteem. Pamela also indicated that	When his low self-esteem goes, as he grows up emotionally – then his anger will too.
80. I would be doing a life story book (which I have not planned).	The life-story is looking at you from the above details.

The Second Clinical Case: A Prisoner's Letter

The object of this chapter, is to provide the reader with clinical evidence that might not generally come his or her way. The closer that evidence comes to what really happened, the better. So here, I include a letter written to me by a prisoner who I examined for a court report, and at the same time, explored his childhood memories, hoping to unpack these for him in a way that can shed light on how consciousness can become unpickled.

He writes –

*'Freddy', prison number 12345 dated ** 20**, ** prison,*

*Dear Dr Bob How are you, I hope you are well and having, or have had a lovely Christmas. Have you managed to take some precious time off from your work to enjoy a break with your family and friends. I was sitting in my cell here at ** last night watching Channel 4. I had seen "Psychopath night" advertised during the week and I was keen to see it. Well Dr Bob as you know it is a very informative and interesting program. At a certain point the commentator begins introducing a Doctor who had done "fantastic" work at Parkhurst Prison. "Fantastic" is my choice of words, I will explain why later. Well blow me down who appeared on the screen "my own Dr Bob". The Americans as usual seemed to talk out of their ten gallon hats ! I felt so proud to see a man who in only about 1½ hours opened "Mental Gates" in my brain. Yes Dr Bob you did it, you opened them gates for me. Take a step forward and*

give yourself a good pat on the back, you deserve it. When we spoke I listened to you and learnt such a valuable (priceless) coping skill. I regularly look to my side and discuss with good manners the "Negative" feelings my father "bless him" is giving me.
At first I was sceptical of the technique, but with practice at critical times, it is one of the most beneficial things in my life. I thank you Dr Bob from the bottom of my heart. I think that explains my use of the word "fantastic".
. . . . . .
Also to return to my wonderful mother will be a gift beyond comprehension I know I may have to serve more time and even if things go wrong a life sentence but at least I will be a "whole" person of which you are a part. Dr Bob you have my love and respect and that will never change.
Yours sincerely
'Freddy'
Transcribed.

This gently describes how his view of his father has been updated. His father had already been dead a number of years, and this had led to increasingly serious suicidality on Freddy's part. The letter shows that there is a way through these ferocious emotions, provided you can establish a clear and trustworthy enough relationship. His suicidality vanished 100%.

THE THIRD CLINICAL CASE: PSYCHOSIS

It is fascinating to recast the challenge of consciousness into the legendary model of medical discoveries – examining closely what happens when a given organ goes wrong. Medical examples that come to mind are the realisation that the frontal lobes are tightly involved with forward planning after that unfortunate engineer survived a steel bolt dynamited through his temples; he survived, but with a dissolute life-style. Cutting the corpus callosum provides tantalising glimpses into brain cell interconnectivity. So it is with psychoses. The classic symptom of psychotic thinking, without which a diagnosis of psychosis is hardly justified, is 'thought disorder'. This means broken sentences, blocked phrases, starting one sentence but finishing another. Here the very process of thinking is broken. A phrase such as "shoes and ships and sealing wax" is acceptable in a comic verse about oyster-eating walruses, but pathological anywhere else. The mind progresses along 'rational' lines, it's how we sort out what we need to do immediately next, if we are to survive. So when it goes wrong, then we may conclude two things – 1) there must have been powerful forces at play to interrupt what is in reality a vital part of staying alive, and 2) if that 'force' can be identified, and then abated, normal cognition should also be fully restored, not to say cured.

Unhappily, since DSM-III in 1980, the psychiatric profession has been advised to be 'atheoretical', i.e., give no thought to causative factors, let alone 'choice' nor will power. This has the unfortunate effect of discouraging explorations into either of the above two points. Here we cheerfully dispense with such crippling medical handicaps, and launch into direct clinical data of what actually happens when psychosis interrupts thinking, and also what happens when it doesn't.

I have transcribed a 5 minute audio clip taken from some 3 hours of group therapy sessions. This reflects a decade and a half building up confidence and trust between myself, and two sufferers, 'Sam', now 45, and 'Freda' 40. Again, I have numbered the lines. Read through the unannotated version before checking the comments I make. Look in particular for those software 'bugs' which are obvious when 'seen' but which otherwise so cripple the most glorious entity in the entire cosmos, our consciousness.

Sam's remarks show that he was hit by his father aged 2. That was 43 years ago – so how is it that he is still "being hit" today? He didn't want to believe this, any more than you do. So listen carefully to how he stumbles over the word 'hit', how he argues against the idea that he is currently stronger than his dad, even though the latter is now 74, and that even thinking he is stronger is 'prohibited' to him, by him. Whether he was actually hit or not, I don't know, and I'm not interested – what matters is that he still thinks he is being hit today – and he isn't, that is something I ***do*** know. The key is that he begins to feel 'relief' once today's reality percolates through the cognitive mire. You don't have to believe me, but if you want solid clinical evidence, have a listen. Osler told you to listen to the patient, because s/he is telling you the diagnosis. Here I invite you to listen to the dialogue, because Sam and Freda are telling you the pathology.

Freda is now aged 40. Her mum died 32 years ago, but still paralyses her thinking, even in the supermarket – check it out below. Listen to her struggling to 'think what we're thinking about'. Everywhere else, she is coherent. Here she's 'blocked'.

You could dismiss these 5 minutes, as being just a bee in my bonnet trying to link thought blocks and childhoods. Or you could listen, say to line 35, where Freda says "I can't say it" – is this true, and if so why? If she wants her mum 'to go' ("*I want to think her gone,*" line 22), why can't she think clearly enough so that she does? Is her cognition really clogged? Is this what psychosis is all about – gummed up cognitive processes, because the sufferer 'thinks' the trauma is still 'alive' in her head? If you provide her with adequate trustworthy emotional support, could you persuade her that, since her mum is dead, it's over? If you did, would she be cured? We know childhood traumas ceased long ago – both these two don't – what would happen if they caught up with reality? They keep desperately pressing me for more, because think they'd be cured. Do you?

The model is simple, though far from easy. Infants learn to cope with erratic parenting. Dad shouts, mum dies, or vice versa – the actual event is not material, the context is all. Infants have no physical defence, so they devise a mental one – "this isn't happening to me". So here's a message to Sam's dad, and to all parents – no parent I have ever met wants to give their child a psychosis, and I'm sure Sam's didn't – but some infants are caught on the hop, and get stuck. They can be unstuck, but only when they can be persuaded that thinking is safe again – simple, but not easy. Infant survival strategies prolonged into adulthood, 'infantism' – it doesn't work, it can be shown not to work, and with enough emotional support, non-psychotic thinking can be restored. Or can it?

Like any 'thought-coach', I use whatever 'verbal spanners' I can that come to hand. You may find my responses brusque – but such is the trust between the three of us that they take it on the chin, and profess to be helped by it. Could this be clinical evidence of efficacy? They think it is, do you?

HEALTH WARNING – since the trauma is still going on in the head, though not in reality, expert care is needed in ALL SUCH CASES, not to make matters immeasurably worse – re-traumatisation is a constant, inevitable risk – so TAKE EXTRA CARE. What seems simple, and at one level is, defeats many, inflicting enormous mental pain – don't make it worse because you don't know what you're doing.

This audio clip is available for download at www.DrBobJohnson.org/audio – handle with care. I reproduce it here with permission.

5 MINUTE EXCERPT, sometime in 2015. B is Bob, me; F is Freda; S is Sam; ~ is 'blocking', where the speaker hesitates, or the thinking stream is broken or pauses. It takes something substantial to interrupt our key evolutionary survival mechanism, our thinking things through, and that something is fear – it's as if the person were walking cautiously, across a verbal minefield, and it is my task to persuade them they are all now duds, which they certainly weren't, long ago.

1. B: *[to Freda]* So how does your experience agree with Sam's?
2. F: um ~~ very much ~ the same
3. B: Go on – in what way?
4. F: I'm finding it SO difficult to think. . . and not just th~. . I find it ~ to think about what's being said, so difficult
5. B: *[softly]* Wow. That's interesting, isn't it. Why is it so difficult to think?
6. F: In this context . . .
7. B: yes
8. F: we're talking about thinking about what we're thinking about . .
9. B: yes
10. F: how to ~ stop our parents stop us thinking. What I'm doing ~. It happens ~ that I can't think about it. But I can't think ~ about the supermarket shopping when my mum's in my head either. It goes on everywhere. But here, I can't ~ I tried to get on the point of what Sam's saying, 'cos it's relevant. . .
11. B: It is relevant, yes.
12. F: . . . and I can't think [*sighs exasperatedly*]. I can't think properly [*sighs again*].
13. B: *[gently]* It's training, right. You've trained yourself not to think
14. F: mmm
15. B: say that
16. F: ~~ I've trained ~. I have ~ trained, I've trained myself not to think.
17. B: yes, 'and now I have to train myself TO think.'
18. F: *[smoothly]* and now I have to train myself to think.
19. B: what do you have to think?
20. F: I have to ~ think ~ what I want to think, individually
21. B: yes? And what with respect to your mum?
22. F: ummm. I want ~ if I want. I want her to go. I want to think her gone. I really have to believe that, that I want to think her gone, so that I can think. I get myself little rhythms, and tongue tied things that I . . .
23. B: you also have to look her in the eye, I'm afraid. And *beat* her. Not in a physical sense, but in a victorious sense. 'I'm stronger than you mum' – off you go.
24. S: *[coughs]*
25. F: er ~ I ~~~ I'm stronger than ~ you-mum. *[rapidly]*
26. B: well, that wasn't very convincing was it?
27. F: *[brightly]* I actually believe it.
28. B: what do you believe?

29. F: that I'm stronger than my mum
30. B: well say so then, not with b-b-g, it's called muttering. Come on. Off the top, come on . . .
31. F: I'm stronger than you mum.
32. B: it's a bit feeble still, isn't it? [2mins 18]. I mean you know, it wasn't, you know, 100%. Sit her down there *[loudly]* 'HELLO MUM' . . and tell her, go on.
33. F: umm. Hello mum, I'm stronger than you
34. B: do you believe that?
35. F: I~ um~~. I can't say it.
36. B: *[loudly, lots of emphasis]* WHY NOT?
37. F: *[giggles nervously]* ~ for thinking and speaking ~ for myself
38. B: a very good idea, try again
39. F:~~ I'm stronger than you mum
40. B: *[to Sam]* what do you think of that diction? It's not good, is it?
41. S: mmm
42. B: what do you think? What's your comment on that diction? [2:54]
43. S: . . . ummm. *[softly]* Doesn't quite believe it.
44. B: she doesn't, does she?
45. S: no
46. B: go on, tell her.
47. S: ugh.
48. B: *[brightly]* what about you? Are you stronger than your dad?
49. S: . . . . I don't, I don't think so, no.
50. B: well I want you to say 'HELLO DAD, I'M STRONGER THAN YOU, you're 70, heh, heh, heh'.
51. S: all right, OK. Hello dad, I'm stronger than you, you're 74. [3:28]
52. B: 74? It's gone up since I last asked. And what happens to you when you say that?
53. S: . . . a little tiny bit of relief
54. B: Ha! So if you said it and believed it you'd have lots of relief. Is that correct?
55. S: probably, yeah
56. B: what do you mean 'probably'. The whole object of the exercise is to get you some relief. 'Tiny bit of relief !' Do it again.
57. S: hello dad, I'm stronger than you, you're 74 *[chuckles briefly]*
58. B: Hey ! See the giggle. So what happened then?
59. S: . . . . ummm . . . . like he dies or something?
60. B: it's just real. If you're stronger than him, he's not going to hit you. Say that please.
61. S: if I'm stronger than you, you can't hit me *[hurried]*. . ~ can't hit me
62. B: what happened to that sentence? Say it again *[insistently]*.
63. S: if I'm stronger than you, ~~ you can't ~ hit me
64. B: do you believe that?
65. S: partly
66. B what do you mean, 'partly' *[derisive tone]*
67. S: a bit
68. B: what do you mean, 'a bit' *[argumentative]* [4:40] It's logical. Isn't it?'
69. S: . . . I dare say ~ I don't want to see him

70. B: *[insistently]* I beg your pardon?
71. S: ~ maybe . . . I don't want to see him
72. B: Aah. Aah. 'I don't want to see him'. What effect does that have?
73. S: it makes me mad.
74. B: no it doesn't, *[lightly]* it makes you impotent. It paralyses you. 'I'm not looking at the person who's hitting me. And he continues to hit me because I don't look at him.' [5:08] Hey, how about saying that? I like that. Off you go.
75. S: I don't look at the person that's hitting me . . .
76. B: yes
77. S: . . (because I don't want to)
78. B: right. 'I've trained myself to . . . '
79. S: and umm . . . .
80. B: 'he continues to hit me'
81. S: that makes me small and impotent, that's like keeping me . . .[at 2]
82. B: so my advice is to look at him – OK?
83. F: I had a little thing to say there which is . . . . [5:42]

Continues. This is an excerpt from over 3 hours of group work. The above is my best rendering of the audio – check it out yourself on www.DrBob Johnson.org/audio.

Table 2.

dialogue	My comment on what's happening
1. B: [to Freda] So how does your experience agree with Sam's?	Moving from Sam to include Freda, and bounce Sam's ideas/insights off her.
2. F: um ~~ very much ~ the same	A bit broken, but she agrees
3. B: Go on – in what way?	My task is to highlight her 'thought' problem, so she can acknowledge it in safe surroundings, and so correct it.
4. F: I'm finding it SO difficult to think . . . and not just th~. . I find it ~ to think about what's being said, so difficult	This is the pathology – thinking is blocked, which she doesn't want it to be
5. B: [softly] Wow. That's interesting, isn't it. Why is it so difficult to think?	Please explain why/how it's blocked. No hectoring, or mocking here on my part – she knows it's wrong, and is seeking ways to correct it.
6. F: In this context . . .	
7. B: yes	
8. F: . . we're talking about thinking about what we're thinking about . .	The meaning here is perfectly clear – it's the very process of thinking that is failing her.
9. B: yes	
10. F: how to ~ stop our parents stop us thinking. What I'm doing ~. It happens ~ that I can't think about it. But I can't think ~ about the supermarket shopping when my mum's in my head either. It goes on everywhere. But here, I can't ~ I tried to get on the point of what Sam's saying, 'cos it's relevant. . .	Here, the thinking itself is letting her down – coherence is hampered, but she sees what she cannot describe. Cognition suffers. This reference to supermarket shopping – when she's stressed, she looks for her mother in the distance – pure 2-year-old survival patterns, well out of date, and ineffective, here.

dialogue	My comment on what's happening
11. B: It is relevant, yes.	
12. F: . . . and I can't think [sighs exasperatedly]. I can't think properly [sighs again].	Her exasperation is plain, and also her confidence that I can help.
13. B: [gently] It's training, right. You've trained yourself not to think	This is the 'defence' the child has – don't think – it's not really happening to me. . . .
14. F: mmm	
15. B: say that	Again, I want her to own it, to see that thinking and saying it is not calamitous, but can mend things.
16. F: ~~ I've trained ~. I have ~ trained, I've trained myself not to think.	Practice in the painful area. This sentence is heavily 'blocked', the contrast with line 18 is astonishing.
17. B: yes, 'and now I have to train myself TO think.'	Here I'm providing gentle 'thought' coaching, which she readily accepts.
18. F: [smoothly] and now I have to train myself to think.	This phrase suffers none of the pathology of the earlier one – the neurological pathways, the brain enzymes, the genetics are all intact – it's the emotions and the 'choice' that have floundered.
19. B: what do you have to think?	
20. F: I have to ~ think ~ what I want to think, individually	Struggling, but she's very clear that she has her own thoughts, and needs to deploy them – reality.
21. B: yes? And what with respect to your mum?	Focus on the locus – it's thoughts about mum which were blocked aged 2, and if they still are, they shouldn't be.
22. F: ummm. I want ~ if I want. I want her to go. I want to think her gone. I really have to believe that, that I want to think her gone, so that I can think. I get myself little rhythms, and tongue tied things that I . . .	Freda sees that memories of mum are the problem – but getting rid requires thought, which is blocked, so far. *"I want to see her gone"* – why doesn't she go? Who is in charge of her mental furniture? She is.
23. B: you also have to look her in the eye, I'm afraid. And beat *her. Not in a physical sense, but in a victorious sense. 'I'm stronger than you mum' – off you go.*	Aged 2, she had no defence against mum – now she does, if only she will allow herself to. Verbalising this simple truth works wonders.
24. S: [coughs]	Sam has been listening acutely, and makes a non-verbal here, to show that we are hitting one of his sore spots too.
25. F: er ~ I ~~~ I'm stronger than ~ you-mum. [rapidly]	Freda knows what she needs to say, but still can't quite manage it. What I like about all this, is that it is the simple truth, not a common feature in discussions of psychotic symptoms.
26. B: well, that wasn't very convincing was it?	Gently chiding her to do better, my confidence that she can, helps.
27. F: [brightly] I actually believe it.	Here she hits gold.
28. B: what do you believe?	
29. F: that I'm stronger than my mum	She copes with my challenge.

Table 2. (Continued)

dialogue	My comment on what's happening
30. B: well say so then, not with burble, it's called muttering. Come on. Off the top, come on . . .	
31. F: I'm stronger than you mum.	
32. B: it's a bit feeble still, isn't it? [2mins 18]. I mean you know, it wasn't, you know, 100%. Sit her down there [loudly] 'HELLO MUM' . . and tell her, go on.	I want her to say it as clearly as I would – I'm not being rude, just expecting more, which she appreciates. Again, the truth of the situation is my, and their, strong point.
33. F: umm. Hello mum, I'm stronger than you	Sounds good, but is it?
34B: do you believe that?	
35. F: I~ um~~. I can't say it.	Here the trouble strikes again – this pivotal thought is again explicitly blocked
36. B: [loudly, lots of emphasis] WHY NOT?	
37. F: [giggles nervously] ~ for thinking and speaking ~ for myself	Practice in this area, with rock-solid emotional support, and her mum will 'go'.
38. B: a very good idea, try again	
39. F:~~ I'm stronger than you mum	More blocking, but progress. I judge she has had enough for the time being, and needs to rest back on support from Sam
40. B: [to Sam] what do you think of that diction? It's not good, is it?	I draw Sam back into the dialogue, with the emphasis on the stumblings.
41. S: mmm	He is a slow starter.
42. B: what do you think? What's your comment on that diction? [2:54]	I emphasise the diction, but we both know it's really the 'blocking'.
43. S: . . . ummm. [softly] Doesn't quite believe it.	Sam is being honest, though finding it a little painful.
44. B: she doesn't, does she?	
45. S: no	
46. B: go on, tell her.	
47. S: ugh.	Sam declines my invitation.
48. B: [brightly] what about you? Are you stronger than your dad?	I therefore move onto where I know he sticks. Again, the reality, the truth of the situation TODAY, is my guide.
49. S: . . . . I don't, I don't think so, no.	Here is a complete illogicality – we all know he is stronger, but he can't say so, yet.
50. B: well I want you to say 'HELLO DAD, I'M STRONGER THAN YOU, you're 70, heh, heh, heh'.	A bit of humour, helps.
51. S: all right, OK. Hello dad, I'm stronger than you, you're 74. [3:28]	Sam accepts the challenge, and does a reasonable job in voicing it.
52. B: 74? It's gone up since I last asked. And what happens to you when you say that?	When I first asked this, his dad was 70.

dialogue	My comment on what's happening
53. S: . . . a little tiny bit of relief	Chary with success. No confidence in it, or at least not enough, yet.
54. B: Ha! So if you said it and believed it you'd have lots of relief. Is that correct?	Relief is what we are aiming for, so I challenge him on the point, and he half-concedes.
55. S: probably, yeah	
56. B: what do you mean 'probably'. The whole object of the exercise is to get	I joke.
you some relief. 'Tiny bit of relief!' Do it again.	
57. S: hello dad, I'm stronger than you, you're 74 [chuckles briefly]	He is surprised at his own courage. We all know he is stronger than his dad, but he struggles to say so – to think so – hence the key pathology in psychotic symptoms.
58. B: Hey ! See the giggle. So what happened then?	I encourage healthy responses – more please.
59. S: . . . . ummm . . . . like he dies or something?	He genuinely doesn't know – I need to steer heavily away from ghosts and fantasy nightmares, into today.
60. B: it's just real. If you're stronger than him, he's not going to hit you. Say that please.	We move to the phantom 'hitting', which shows why he is still terrified – the hitting has never actually stopped in his mind.
61. S: if I'm stronger than you, you can't hit me [hurried] . . ~ can't hit me	He knows it's true, but struggles to say so coherently.
62. B: what happened to that sentence? Say it again [insistently].	
63. S: if I'm stronger than you, ~~ you can't ~ hit me	
64. B: do you believe that?	Again, testing how secure is the obvious truth in his mind.
65. S: partly	
66. B what do you mean, 'partly' [derisive tone]	Here again, I'm jousting with him, judging how far I can challenge/push him without going too far, and re-traumatising him so that he slips back into fantasy land.
67. S: a bit	
68. B: what do you mean, 'a bit' [argumentative] [4:40] It's logical. Isn't it?'	
69. S: . . . I dare say ~ I don't want to see him	Again he is being beautifully honest – he says *"I don't want to see him"*. The only possible explanation for this nonsense is that it paid him not to look when he was small – not now.
70. B: [insistently] I beg your pardon?	I don't let this 'slip' go.
71. S: ~ maybe I don't want to see him	
72. B: Aah. Aah. 'I don't want to see him'. What effect does that have?	
73. S: it makes me mad.	

Table 2. (Continued)

dialogue	My comment on what's happening
74. B: no it doesn't, [lightly] it makes you impotent. It paralyses you. 'I'm not looking at the person who's hitting me. And he continues to hit me because I don't look at him.' [5:08] Hey, how about saying that? I like that. Off you go.	Again, a down-to-earth explanation. It's obvious that if someone is hitting you and you refuse, *"don't want to"* see it, then it continues unabated. This perpetuates the psychosis, and is devilish hard either to penetrate to, or to evaporate.
75. S: I don't look at the person that's hitting me . . .	I try to assert today's logic.
76. B: yes	
77. S: . . (because I don't want to)	
78. B: right. 'I've trained myself to'	
79. S: and umm	
80. B: 'he continues to him me'	
81. S: that makes me small and impotent, that's like keeping me . . .[at 2]	He volunteers this – I no longer need to prompt him to do so.
82. B: so my advice is to look at him – OK?	I would say this to anyone who thought they were being hit.
83. F: I had a little thing to say there which is . . . . [5:42]	Freda presses on, but our space has run out.

My objective in printing this extensive excerpt is to bring to the attention of readers, not all of whom will have had direct experience of, or been able to explore first hand, what psychotic symptoms are, and how 'blocking' actually happens. My hope is that this brief excerpt, despite the difficulties of transcription will demonstrate how critical is normal straightforward thinking, and how debilitating it is when distorted as it is in all such psychotic conditions, and how this ensures it's self-perpetuating. This is also the evidence which convinces me that all such symptoms are 100% curable, if only support and access can be brought to bear on where the lesion actually is – hence the desperate need to re-evaluate consciousness.

Conclusion

Consciousness boils down to two words, 'plan ahead'; while its twin perils, violence and psychosis, slim to one, 'unreal' – the rest is sophistry. Reliable forward planning is impossible without realistic data. Dinosaurs were unable to predict the asteroid strike so, being land animals needing regular food and drink, they became extinct, extinguished by that dust cloud which then deprived the earth of vital solar energy. Their contemporary cousins the crocodiles being aquatic, and enjoying carrion, survived. We are too much like the former, to survive anything similar. Our forward planning might explode impending asteroids, except we plan a different use for our thermonuclear energies. Global dust clouds, whether unplanned or not, home-made or otherwise, deflect, even terminate, evolution – as dinosaurs demonstrated, succinctly, even 'scientifically'.

Freud, like all of us, wanted to know how the mind worked. He assumed, like most do, that we lived in a reasonable world, for which sensible explanations would eventually be known. He knew little of Uncertainty, and nothing of the Dark Matter and Dark Energy which now constitute 95% of the cosmos, leaving us with less than 5% 'knowable' – Bin C, the Unknowable, is huge, indeed infinite. His wish was for a clockwork universe for which he'd found the coiled 'spring'. If minds can change on a whim, with no regard for any Law, scientific or otherwise, then his idealised wishful thinking collapses. Choice, 'intent' or will-power was anathema to him, and still is to too many. In our real world, there is only limitless, inanimate chaos, through which our consciousness might steer us, generally, on a reliable path. Never 100%, but if we are *responsible* in an evolutionary, technical sense, we can choose to survive rather than wait to perish, if we apply ourselves hard enough, clearly enough and soon enough.

Violence breaks the one Law which does survive Hume's Scepticism, that is the Iron Law of Evolution – adapt or perish. Planned violence, with the overt intent that other humans should perish, is unreal. It is based on a version of reality that existed in infancy, but flails in adulthood. The Blair-Bush wars more resemble tantrums than statesmanship, and if Hitler had launched H-Bombs from his bunker, Europe would still be radioactive. Could it be that our prolonged adolescence is our evolutionary Achilles' heel, which omits to give us enough time to discard our childhood reality, where might was right, and the strongest did win, whatever the merits of their case, or their grasp of reality. Psychoses are also based firmly in an earlier unreality – again one learnt too deeply in infancy to be easily rescinded. You could say violence is psychotic, and psychosis is violence turned inwards – both profoundly unreal. Either way, the real punishment for unreality is not divine retribution, nor human legislation, just perishing more swiftly than otherwise, in our hostile inanimate world.

In the Merchant of Venice, our hero doesn't choose the golden casket. It sounds like the best, and most economists will predict he would do so. But the 'Best' can be the enemy of the 'Good' – and so it is with 'choice'. Because we cannot choose everything we wish, too many plump for no choice at all. This emasculates evolution. It also saps our innate capacity for creativity, imagination, aesthetics, generosity and art – creating acts and works that were never there before. At heart, consciousness is the most ineffable entity ever – why not celebrate it, glorify it, share it – and become even more alive, while we can.

IN SUM, My 5-Rules-of-Thumb:

1. Consciousness equips us to plan ahead.
2. All violence and psychosis vanish 100%, when fed enough real, non-childhood data.
3. We poison the biosphere as if we weren't part of it – thereby ensuring we won't be.
4. Unaccustomed thinking frightens the children, so we scorch heretics.
5. Cross-fertilising minds yields our richest, most beautiful harvest, empowering all to blossom.

REFERENCES

Freud, S. (1896). The Aetiology of Hysteria (*Über die Ätiologie der Hysterie*).
Rovelli, C. (2011). The First Scientist: Anaximander and His Legacy. Westholme Publishing, U.S.
Zulueta, Felicity de, (2006). From Pain to Violence: The Traumatic Roots of Destructiveness. Whurr.

In: Consciousness
Editor: Lloyd Alvarado

ISBN: 978-1-63485-023-0

Chapter 7

WHERE IS THE OS OF THE BRAIN?: PHYSICAL CONSCIOUSNESS OUTSIDE THE BRAIN

*Takashi Taneichi**
Institute of Theoretical Physics attached to International Research Institute
Sonno-cho, Inage-ku, Chiba-city, Chiba, Japan

ABSTRACT

Consider the rehabilitation. Local functions of the brain can be complemented by other parts by training, even if they were lost by an accident such as external injury and internal bleeding. This is the dynamical redistribution of functions inside the brain. It can be regarded as a result of the Operating System (OS) function of the brain, on the analogy of computers. On the other hand, the passive consciousness hypothesis is known to be a powerful hypothesis in the sense that it figures out the difficult problems concerning consciousness such as the frame problem, binding problem, etc. Intrinsic problem of the hypothesis, however, lies in the dubious mechanism by which collective opinions are decided by "majority vote" in the unconscious system and are collected to the local conscious system in a bottom-up manner. No one has elucidated, so far, how the unconscious system and the conscious one are connected in the neural network. The Parasite Fermion Model is a physical model that solves those problems. The Model asserts that, only by assuming the multi-dimensional universe that is nowadays commonly discussed in the modern physics and two types of fermions (material particles), there exists the materialistic subject, called Parasite Fermion Object (PFO), in the extra-dimensional space. One can avoid above-mentioned difficulties, by assuming that the PFO plays a significant role in the OS function and decision process of the unconscious system. It is shown that the Model gives us an insight into the possibility of "life after death."

* sanshiro201@yahoo.co.jp.

Introduction

Monism and Dualism

Take, for example, a political discussion. Those who are convinced try to justify their statements through discussions. It is a collision between the "reasoning of one's arguments" or "justifiable grounds." The world of natural science, however, is a bit different. In general, it is possible to argue that, "Although it is not clear yet at this point if it is justifiable, we could say blah blah blah as a possibility." This is a "presentation of a hypothesis." Everyone has the right to present their own hypothesis, so long as it remains to be a hypothesis. The hypotheses will be theoretically and experimentally examined afterwards, resulting in some of them fading away at an early stage with their lies quickly being exposed, and others gaining publicity and going through a relatively long period of examination. Just a small portion of them will be considered valid and gain a status as an accepted notion, and may appear in the textbooks. Even in that case, however, experiments for the purpose of review will be continued to examine the limit of application of the theory. No matter how reasonably the theoretical observation is made on the hypothesis at the time of its presentation, its corollary still remains at a hypothesis level. A hypothesis in the area of the natural science must be examined by "nature" through experiments and observations. An argument without the proven grounds shall be taken as one merely implying a possibility. This is the very reason that differentiates the quality of the science from that of the religion where "the truth" is conveyed in a top-down manner.

There are generally two points of view that you could take when you think about the mind-body problem; namely, the monism and the dualism. In short, the monism argues that the "mind" and the "body" relevant to the mind-body problem are consisted of a single substance, whereas the dualism argues that each of them are consisted of something which cannot be the source of the other. In the world of modern physics, the predominant study policy is based on the materialism, that is, a perception that the materials are the source of everything in this world, and the mind, consciousness, and personalities of the human beings are a phenomenon that accompanies the functions of the brain comprised of the materials. It is not just predominant; rather, it is the only study policy publicly accepted. According to the religious interpretation of the world, on the other hand, the existence of the inner world which is not based on the materials is generally presumed. In this sense, the materialism and the religions are inconsistent in their interpretation of the world. Needless to say, there are some individual scientists who are publicly based on the materialism but have different thoughts in their mind. Dr. Hideki Yukawa, who is the Nobel Prize laureate in physics, who later believed in the Buddhism, is a good example. Mind-body problem are rare in that, a perception which has reached a consensus to a significant extent in the academic community has only reached a consensus so low as this in the world. In reality, there are many other categories, and it is not just an either-or between the monism and the dualism. Various arguments are being made based on each of such standpoints. This being said, setting aside how the individual researchers perceive inside their mind, the fact is that, the materialism is indeed firmly maintained by the modern physics studies. What, then, are we able to argue within this scope about the mind-body problem? For instance, are we able to presume "a mind which is independent from the brain" within the meaning of the materialism?

Re-Examine the Basis—What Else Do We Need?

Which functions of the brain bring us about our mind? No established theory is available by the modern science as an answer to the question that has been posed through the ages. The improvements in the measurement technology, including the functional magnetic resonance imaging (fMRI), have allowed the hemodynamics in the brain to be visualized. As a result, a relationship between the state of consciousness, such as emotions, feelings and thoughts, and the state of the brain activities are beginning to be revealed. However, this will not be of any evidence to indicate that the brain activities generate the mental states. Although it implies the linkage or the relationship between the brain activities and the mental states, it does not indicate in any sense the causal association between them, that is, a linkage between the cause and effect, such as "This activity of the brain generates that psychological state." On the other hand, the reports are made on some cases where people remembered the happenings that had occurred around them and the flush of emotions that had arisen while their brain activities stopped, and reported about such experiences after they restored consciousness. Some scientists even argue the possibility of the perpetuity of the afterworld mind, consciousness and personalities. A study on the "reincarnation" is one of such examples. In the study of Dr. Ian Stevenson and Dr. Jim Tucker, the University of Virginia, more than 2,500 cases were collected all over the world (Tucker 2008, XIV). A tendency is shown that they start talking about what they call their previous lives around the age of three and stop talking about them closer to six or seven. While some researchers try to explain this phenomenon through a memory mechanism particular to the childhood, such as the childhood amnesia, Tucker conducted a detailed investigation on the cases where he could identify who those people were in their previous lives based on their evidence on the memories of their previous lives, and argues that the "reincarnation" is a phenomenon that truly exists. If this is true, the next required step would be to explore a scientific theory that accepts the reincarnation phenomenon. As a matter of course, the relevant modification in the relevant academic area, including the modern brain science and the physics, would be required. On the contrary, if one denies the existence of the "reincarnation," one would have to be able to explain the background of a number of cases suggesting the memories of previous lives without using the "reincarnation" as a reason. In this sense, the direction of the abovementioned research attributing the causes of the evidence on the memories of previous lives to the childhood amnesia is naturally acceptable. On the other hand, if you argue that the reincarnation does not exist by denying the very existence of over 2,500 cases evidencing the memories of the previous lives, saying that "it is inexplicable by the modern science," such attitude is inappropriate as a scientist.

I would like to hereby cite the words of the two other people who accept the perpetuity into the afterworld. Dr. Eben Alexander, a neurosurgeon, states as follows: "Without knowledge of the larger geography of where we came from and where we are going again when our physical bodies die, we are lost." (Alexander 2014, XXXIII) Dr. Naoki Yahagi, the head of the Emergency Department and the Intensive Care Department of the University of Tokyo Hospital, states as follows: "Death is not the end. Our soul is perpetual. The essence of our being, in the first place, is not the body but the soul. Therefore, there is actually no reason for us to fear the disease and aging." (Yahagi 2014, 162) Given these statements, is it not unjust to exclude from the start the potential existence of the mental activities independent from the brain activities? As a matter of course, however, it is difficult to think that, given the fMRI example as mentioned earlier, the brain activities and the mind are totally independent and irrelevant. Inside our brain, there may be the phenomena, be it the source of our mind or not, that are yet unknown but are related to the mental states. If any physical grounds could exist independently from our brain as a subject that engages in the mental activities called consciousness and personalities, and if, further, they are the causes of the brain activities observed by the abovementioned visualizing technology, the next question to come would be in what form do such materials exist, and how do they interact with the brain. Moreover, a question must also be posed as to how they could escape the medical and biological observation until now. In the latter half of this discussion, I would like stick to the materialist perspective to look into the pattern that the soul dwells in the body, based on the latest outcome of the research concerning the new patterns of existence of the material particles. It is a hypothesis to challenge the statement that says "A materialist must explain the consciousness as part of the brain functions dwelling in this cranium. If you accept a consciousness independent from the brain, the monism would not work."

To date, the entire outcome of the experiments of the elementary particle physics can be explained by what is called the "Standard Model." Now that the Higgs boson, the lastly discovered particle among the particles anticipated in the Standard Model, was discovered, the firm footing of the Standard Model has been made furthermore solid. Could we then totally leave all physical phenomena in the world to the Standard Model? The answer is no. The Standard Model has been successful in describing three out of the four physically known interactions—that is, all except the gravity. However, it has not been able to quantize the gravity, leaving the gravity outside of its theoretical scope. In short, it is a "defective" theory. It is the general theory of relativity that describes the gravity. The two theories are concomitant but play in the different fields—should we call only one of them "standard"? Would there not be the true "standard" model in charge of all forces that we have not yet discovered? There are a number of physicists who are feeling ashamed. However, except for those limited number of theorists who make living by exploring the "true standard model," the reality is that we can live without being distracted by this issue—which is not surprising, as all experimental outcomes and observations that we see these days can be explained by either of the two theories.

Should there be a pitfall, it may be somewhere around here. When we try to deal with the mind-body problem physically, some theoretical defect may be deceiving our eyes to lead us to a conclusion different from the truth. In the modern physics, two unintegrable—that is, two incompatible theories, namely, the Standard Model and the relativity co-exist, which means that the fundamental theories of the physics are not being integrated without inconsistency. As such, the modern physics is blatantly defective, and it is obvious what actually the defect is. It implies the future development of the physics, where the two theories are integrated without inconsistency and the next-generation standard model will be completed. Generally speaking, no person would agree to a statement such as to say, for example, that "The science has now reached its highest point of development, thus leaving no room for a further progress." However, on a more specific basis, rarely do we encounter a case where the current situation is understood that the two incompatible theories co-exist and its meaning and the direction of the future development are examined particularly in relation to the mind-body problem. We may be in a situation where, with an incomplete interpretation of the world drawn from the incomplete physics, we are unable to get out of the circumstance of being forced to perceive things in a narrow scope even with respect to the matter of our current interest, which is the mind-body problem, and we do not even have the slightest chance of recognizing the situation. At least, it may be worthwhile examining the possibility. I would like to take time to look into this issue in the following discussion.

The two principal pillars of the modern physics, the quantum theory, which is the basis of the Standard Model, and the relativity, have both presented in their respective initial periods an outlook on nature which is drastically challenging to the people's common sense. The substantial changes to the outlook on nature occurred intensely at the beginning of the 20th century which significantly undermined the traditional outlook on nature, including the perceptions that the position and the momentum cannot be precisely determined at the same time, that the "existence probability" is the only measure to properly formulate the variation corresponding to the lapse of time using the equations, and not the positions of the particles or the velocity, that the wave-particle duality exists, that the time can be regarded in the same light as the space (the concept of the "space-time") and it gets distorted due to the existence of the mass (= energy), and that such distortion is the gravity itself, etc. Tremendous efforts were made by the forerunners who established the new theories based on the observational consequences that are inexplicable by the traditional theories and the crackbrained ideas beyond the common sense that had existed. Undoubtedly, a similar theoretical breakthrough can be achieved any time in the future. It is more natural to think that, although it is hard to anticipate the timing, the next breakthrough will surely be made before too long. A highly probable expectation is that the upcoming breakthrough would be something that would be "unconventional," defying our existing knowledge, as the substantial changes had been at the beginning of the 20th century.

With respect to the mind-body problem, the current mainstream from the scientific perspective is that the mind is generated as a result of biological and chemical action of the brain. Our inner experiences, such as emotions, memories and senses, are said to be the manifestation of the functions of the brain as a material. However, nothing has been revealed in relation to the cause and effect between the specific individual functions and the experiences. Given this circumstance, it may be reasonable to some extent to assume that the source of the mind may not be the brain. The upcoming next breakthrough in the physics may be decisive in bringing an end to this disarrayed mind-body problem. If this is not absolutely impossible, it would be worthwhile to hope for it, and your life would be more blessed with that thought. Before we go on to examine the matters related to the mind-body problem, I would like to talk a little bit about some related issues in the following Section, namely, the theoretical study beyond the Standard Model of the physics.

Section 1. Multidimensional Universe – Our Universe Is Not the Only Universe!

Dissatisfaction with Status Quo Is the "Steppingstone to the Development"

"An artificial black hole can be made possible." In the early 2000's, such a controversial news was reported. This was about an experiment performed at an experimental facility for the high-energy physics, "Large Hadron Collider" (LHC), located near the national border of

Switzerland and France in Europe. "Hadron" is a collective term given to the particles comprised of 2 to 3 quarks that are a kind of the elementary particle. The constituent particles of the atomic nucleus, the neutron and the proton that you learn at school, are among the hadron. The meson, the existence of which was predicted by Dr. Yukawa, and the existence of which was later confirmed, is also included. In the experiment using the LHC, the protons are accelerated inside the giant circular vacuum tube the total circumference of which reaches about 27 km, the protons that are rotating in nearly the speed of light are collided with each other, and the broken pieces that are generated (the new particles) are observed and analyzed to sort out the physical phenomena that have happened. The collider is in a circular shape to allow the protons to continue to accelerate until they collide, and the facility is huge so that a high energy can be obtained with a higher efficiency. As for the black hole, everyone seems to have some kind of an image. It is something in the cosmic space that absorbs everything. If it could be made artificially and on the ground, it might not only be "fantastic and interesting," but also eerie to some people. In fact, a certain researcher who is engaged in the physical experiments of the atomic nucleus bothered to explain in his press conference that there would be no such effect whatsoever of "the entire globe being swallowed" as generally concerned. This mere fact suggests that the public opinion was concerned to a considerable extent, and that at the same time, people were relatively interested. A black hole, if in fact generated by this LHC, would be minimum. In addition, it would cease to exist after releasing the energy in an extremely short period of time in accordance with a mechanism called the Hawking radiation. As such, there is no risk of damage at a macroscopic level. In any event, it is good if a lot of people were driven to pay attention to the science through a high-profile topic.

Meanwhile, what is the purpose of colliding the protons, and with the energy as high as possible? Think about when you boil water with a kettle. As the temperature rises, the water vapor jets out. By heating, the water molecules that had been intertwined with each other to constitute the liquid water get energy, and cut off the connection among themselves to independently move and evaporate. What will happen if we raise the temperature of this water vapor? This time, the individual molecules will be further decomposed, and the atoms of the oxygen and the hydrogen will be separated. If we further raise the temperature, the decomposition will be further advanced, and the atoms are decomposed into the electrons and the positive ions that comprise the atoms to enter an ionized stage called plasma. The higher the temperature of the materials are, the more fragmented they become and turn into the more minuscule constituent particles. The physicists try to decompose the materials into as smaller parts as possible to see their interior in order to find out the basic particles that comprise the materials and clarify the forces acting amongst them. How then, do we "decompose" the materials? "To heat" means to give energy. By putting the materials in a higher energy state, we are able to observe the physics of a more microscopic world. A colliding accelerator is, in short, a device that decomposes the particles by placing energy from the exterior through acceleration of the particles (by giving a kinetic energy) and their collision. When you have a proton collide with another proton, various kinds of particles will be generated depending on the quantity of the energy. The larger amount of energy you put in, the more particles you will see that could not be seen before and you would be able to expect an interaction that you have never observed or the physics that you have never seen. For this purpose, we construct a giant accelerator that could create as large amount of energy as possible with a huge budget.

A black hole can be made through an experiment—this, in itself, is extremely interesting as well as impressing in a sense that it is somewhat SFish. Putting that aside, let us reconsider what it implies. The Standard Model is a tentatively "complete" physics theory which is able to thoroughly describe the experiments and the observational consequences of the modern physics. I say "complete" because currently, we have in fact no problem interpreting the experimental outcomes and observational consequences using this model. I also say "tentatively," because the observations are beginning to be made on the phenomena deviating from the traditional frame of the Standard Model, as can be seen in the observation of the neutrino oscillations (the phenomenon where the neutrinos coming to the earth transform into different types; it suggests that the neutrinos have mass, whereas the mass of the neutrinos is considered to be zero in the Standard Model). It is expected that the progress in such observations, with the accumulated new discoveries, will lead to an establishment of a new theory beyond the Standard Model. There are reasons to why, despite the current Standard Model being able to consistently describe the observational experiments, people are making such expectation. The types of the particles that comprise the materials are one of such reasons. The quarks that comprise the protons, mesons and the like inside the atomic nucleus are classified into generations called the first, second and third generations. The Standard Model predicted the existence of two types of particles in each generation, with a total of six types of particles, and all of them have in fact been discovered. It is unknown as to why the number of the generations is three—the fourth and the fifth generations could potentially exist as well. However, no experimental outcome to date indicates such possibility. The most significant issue is that, among what is called the quarks, only the particles in the first generation, namely, the up quarks and down quarks, exist spontaneously in this universe. What, then, are the raisons d'etre of the second and thereafter generations? This is yet to be known to date. In addition, with respect to the interactions that exist in this universe (the forces that act among the particles), 4 of them are known today. They are the electromagnetic force and gravity (that are familiar to us), as well as the "strong force" and the "weak force." What makes it difficult for us to understand is that only the gravity from among the 4 forces is extremely small. It is so small that it is only approximately $1/10^{34}$ (that is, 1/10 billionth of 1/trillionth of 1/trillionth) of the smallest of the remaining 3 forces, which is the "weak force." The ratio of power of the 3 remaining forces stay within the range of $1 : 10^{6}$. That is, only the gravity is extremely small in strength compared to the other forces. The Standard Model does not provide us with any persuasive explanation on this apparent unnaturalness. This issue is particularly called the "hierarchy problem." I will talk about this in the Sections that follow. Another issue of the current Standard Model is that there are too many parameters that have to be given manually by human, such as the strength of the forces. However, the fundamental theory that we are looking for has to start from a guiding principle which is as simple as possible, and has to be something that allows us to obtain various physical constants as a natural consequence.

Does Superstring Theory Save Physics?

Given the abovementioned circumstance, the physicists have an expectation for an updating of the Standard Model. Above all, the more significant issue of the modern physics is the fact that the quantum mechanics and the theory of relativity, each of which are extremely successful, have not been integrated into one unified theory without inconsistency. This is a huge problem. The two main pillars of the modern physics are incompatible with each other. A circumstance where each of them is successful is where, in an aspect where you can disregard the effect of either of the quantum mechanics and the theory of relativity, you can rely on the other theory to well describe and predict the relevant phenomenon. This means that in an aspect where the effects of both theories are prominent and cannot be disregarded, it cannot be appropriately described by the language of the current physics. Such aspects include, for instance, the initial period of the universe when the level of the energy was extremely high and the curvature of the universe' space-time was extremely high, or, the dynamics of a black hole. The theory in relation to which a research is under progress with an expectation to resolve this issue is the string theory. Under the existing Standard Model, the elementary particle, which is much smaller than the atomic nuclei and are the basis comprising the materials, and the gauge particle, such as the photon, which mediates forces, is considered to be one very point which does not have a spatial extent. The string theory considers this to be a one-dimensional string-like object, and attributes the diversity of the types of particles to the difference in the vibrational state of this string. The string theory is currently considered to be the prime candidate for the theory that integrates the quantum mechanics and the theory of relativity.

There is a by-product to the string theory, which is the dimension number. Both the quantum mechanics and the theory of relativity view the world as being comprised of a total of 4 dimensions, 3 of which are for a space and one for the time, while the string theory delineates the world as being comprised of multiple dimensions larger than four. Rather, in order for the theory to keep consistency, the world cannot be four-dimensional. The reason that the Standard Model and the theory of relativity have not been integrated may be because the number of their dimensions had been wrong. The string theory which is able to describe not only the particles that mediates the forces but also the material particles is called, in particular, the superstring theory, the number of dimensions of which is ten. It is difficult to imagine the dimensions so many as this, as it is far from our common sense. However, on top of the surprisingly large number of dimensions proposed thereunder, the impression given by the superstring theory as an ultimate candidate theory which will be the standard model of the next-generation is quite strong. On the other hand, there are still some issues that need to be solved with respect to this superstring theory that has captivated a lot of physicists. First of all, if the world is in fact comprised of multiple dimensions, why are we only able to see 4 dimensions, namely, the space and the time? The Standard Theory that we currently have at hand is a 4-dimension theory, and we are able to explain all experiments on elementary particles based on this theory. If we are unable to detect the extra-dimension space, that is, the dimensions other than the 4 dimensions, due to the reason that the energy level of the experiment is too low, we need to explain the reason why it is invisible in the low energy region. The dimensions that exist but that are invisible. What is it that is hiding the extra dimensions?

A mechanism that has been worked out as one of the answers to this issue is the "compactification." This is a relatively simple concept where it is perceived that, although the extra dimensions exist, their extent is too small to be visible or observable. The high-energy experiments to date have succeeded to observe a space in the scale of 10^{-16} cm (1/10,000 of 1 trillionth). This means that, if the concept of the compactification is accurate, the size of the extra dimensions are smaller than this size. If the extra dimensions exist in the compactified size so small as to be unobservable, it is effectively the same as living in the 4-dimension world from the beginning.

Brane Model

Apart from the compactification, there is another mechanism called the brane model, which makes the extra dimensions invisible. The "brane" is a term which has derived from a word "membrane." Although originally, it means the "membrane," in the string theory, it refers to the low-dimensional space-time integrated into the high-dimensional universe (Figure 1).

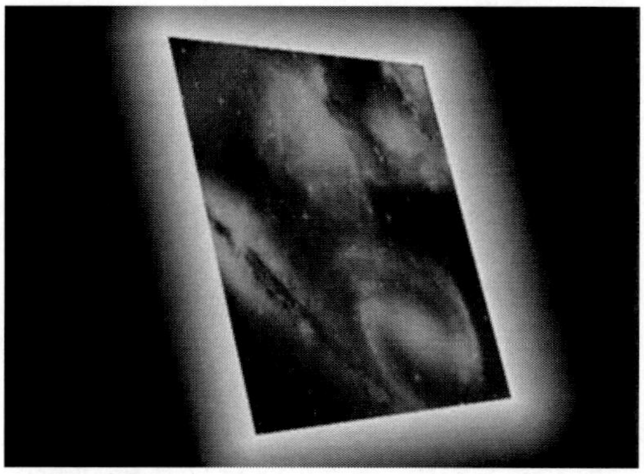

Figure 1. Brane universe.

A term which forms a counterpart is "bulk," which refers to the entire high-dimensional universe that includes the brane. The brane is an object which is integrated into this bulk or which forms the boundary with the bulk. Very conveniently, in fact, a cosmic view which suggests that the (3+1) brane is integrated into the high-dimensional bulk space-time sheds a light on the various issues in the modern physics. Such issues include the hierarchy problem, unravelling of the dark matter, and the exploration on the cause of the cosmic expansion. Now then, why is it called the "brane"? When we say brane, we imagine something that is thin. Why is this expansive universe called the "brane"? Normally, when we call something a "brane," it is indeed something thin, be it the bubble brane in the wire hoop, the oil membrane in the puddle, or whatever. Precisely speaking, even a bubble brane has a definite thickness as thick as several microns, and in this sense, it is 3-dimensional. However, I would like to glamourize and disregard the thickness of these branes here. As a result, a brane can be considered as a 2-dimensional object when we observe it from the 3-dimensional space where we live. Normally, we call a 2-dimensional object a brane. In a more general sense, an object with a certain number of dimensions can be described to be a brane when observed from the world with a larger number of dimensions. The 4-dimensional space-time where we live is a brane when observed from the 10-dimensional space-time. Interestingly, the brane on which the universe where we live exists is not necessarily the only brane that exists in the bulk. There may be multiple other branes. They may be intersecting, colliding, or located or interacting in various ways. Its depth is immeasurable, such that a theory has been submitted arguing that the famous Big Bang can be explained based on the dynamics of the brane. Further, the number of the dimensions of the brane itself may not necessarily be four; various numbers of the dimensions can be perceived.

Path to Solution for "Hierarchy Problem" – ADD Model

One of the effects of an extra dimension expected of the LHC is the aforementioned generation of a black hole. Before I look into how it is structured, I would like to get off the point for a while (it is however a still important point). In establishing a model using a brane, a challenging point is the hierarchy problem, which is too unnatural in its difference in strength of the interactions that I mentioned earlier. Something that paved the way to resolving this issue is the "large extra dimensions model." I would like to call this the ADD Model after the three persons who devised the model, namely, Arkani-Hamed, Dimopoulos, and Dvali (Arkani-Hamed, Dimopoulos, and Dvali 1998). In this model, the abnormal weakness of the gravity is resolved by the magnitude of the extra-dimensional space. In the superstring theory, the material particles and the particles which mediate interactions between them are described as a "string". There are two types of strings—an open string which is a one-dimensional object with two end points and a closed string which is an elastic band-like loop with no end points. The gravitons which mediate the gravity can be described by a closed string, whereas all the rest of the particles are described by an open string (Figure 2). Although the two ends of an open string can move around on the brane, they do not deviate from the brane. As such, an open string is bound down on the brane. On the other hand, solely the gravitons, which are described by the closed string, can break loose from the brane. When you look at the physical four "forces," while the three forces, namely, the electromagnetic force, the "strong force," and the "weak force" can only exist inside the brane where we live, only the gravity is able to act on outside of the brane. Looking it from our side which is trapped inside the brane, the gravity appears to have been "thinned down," as it were, and have weakened, compared to the former three forces that are similarly trapped inside the brane. More particularly, it would be that in the multi-dimensional picture such as this, the gravitational constant that we feel is in fact a deceptive figure, and the true gravitational constant is indeed much larger. The true gravity is not particularly weak; it is merely that it is structured so that we feel that it is extremely weak. Accordingly, the ADD Model has paved a path to the resolution of the hierarchy problem.

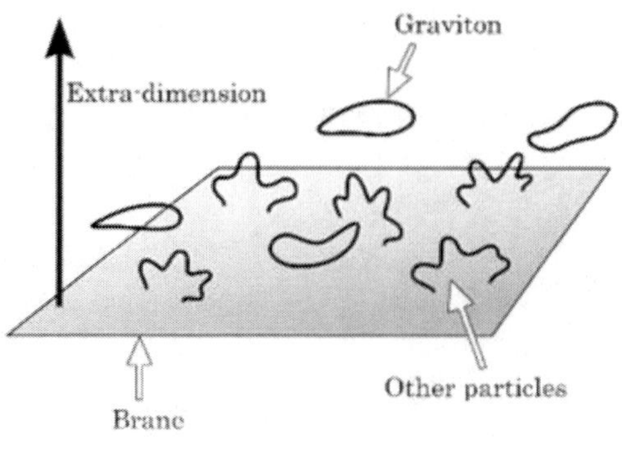

Figure 2. Various types of strings.

The photons are the particles that mediates the electromagnetic force. It is an open string trapped in the brane. More particularly, it is in principle impossible to capture the extra dimensions through an observation by light no matter how. What measures can we think of then, to capture the extra dimensions experimentally? In this respect, the sole particles that are not trapped in the brane are the gravitons. The gravity could be a keyword. One of such efforts is the generation of a black hole through a high-energy experiment. Why then, is a black hole generated when the high-energy particles are collided in the LHC? The quantity which is proportional to the inverse of the square root of the gravitational constant (G) is called the Planck mass (M_P).

$$\frac{1}{\sqrt{G}} \propto M_P$$

When the particles are accelerated and collide, if the energy amounts to approximately this Planck mass, a black hole is generated. Based on the perception to date that the gravity is extremely small compared to the other three forces, that is, G is very small, the Planck mass is on the contrary extremely large as you can see from the formula above, and it has been believed that it is virtually impossible to reach that area through an experiment. However, the different circumstances apply when you use the ADD Model. It is a misperception to feel that the gravitational constant is small. It is actually larger than what you actually feel. The true Planck mass may not be as large as it had been perceived, making it possible for the LHC to achieve the Planck mass and generate a black hole. If a generation of a black hole is confirmed in the LHC, it could be a piece of evidence which suggests the multidimensionality of this universe!

The study on the multi-dimensional universe per se was inspired by the study at the beginning of the previous century at the latest, where the integration of the theory of relativity and the electromagnetics had been sought. Although it has been over a century since then, it is only very recently that the possibility of the observation has come under close scrutiny. As a matter of course, it is totally different to point out that there is a theoretical possibility of existence and to prove the existence. For instance, at the beginning of the 20th century, the general theory of relativity suggested the theoretical existence of a black hole. However, for half a century since then until a black hole was actually observed in the universe, many of the physicists thought that it was purely a theoretical product, and few thought that it actually existed. Nowadays, a lot of observational results have been obtained that indicate the existence of a black hole, and very few people doubt its existence (although it is not completely zero). Although as a corollary of the string theory, it is considered that our universe is multi-dimensional, the string theory per se is far from being accepted as a standard theory at the moment. Indeed, there are numerous issues that need to be resolved, including a necessity to verify a mechanism which allows the extra dimensions to be invisible for having low energy (such as the abovementioned compactification), a theoretical resolution on a huge gap extending to 16 digits between the energy scale of the string theory and the energy scale of the current Standard Model which takes care of the phenomena of the low-energy elementary particles, the explanations on the initial inflation and the accelerating expansion of the universe. On top of that lies the fact as a more fundamental issue that the guiding principle for the string theory is yet to be unraveled. On the other hand, it is also true that the string theory is positioned on the far right wing with a potential of being a standard theory of the next generation which integrates the theory of relativity and the current Standard Model. If multidimensionality is indicated as a result of an experiment, it would certainly be a material breakthrough out of the paradigm. It is difficult even just to imagine what theoretical predictions we are able to get as a corollary of the new multi-dimensional physics theory. I am sure that the nature will reveal an amazing fact that we would never be able to imagine no matter how much we struggle to conjecture this and that now. Those phenomena that are said to be psychic and are currently ineligible for a scientific examination—even they could be a subject of science. Dr. Randall, who is a researcher of a brane world model, when she revealed to her co-worker that she was considering installing a new space dimension and was asked that "It is about the world where you will have a spiritual experience or the afterworld, no?" is said to have responded, "No way." Although I do fully understand why she would want to swear, as one researcher who has dipped into the modern physics world, I would like to bother to point out that it may not be the case.

Warped Universe – RS Model

In the ADD Model which has large extra dimensions, there are extra dimensions as large as several millimeters. From the view of energy, this is about 10^{-4} eV, and conversely, is 15 digits far to the smaller side compared to the energy scale of the Standard Model. With this size of the scale, it could be said that the hierarchy problem has not yet been resolved but has rather been rehashed. Is it possible then, to establish a model where the energy scales do not vary as much as this? Dr. Randall and Dr. Sundrum (RS) have overcome this problem by devising a model where the extra dimensions are warped (Randall and Sundrum 1999).

In this RS Model, two branes of the 4-dimensional space-time are placed in the 5-dimensional space-time across each other with the fifth space dimension in the middle (the Initial RS Model) (Figure 3). That is, there will be just one extra dimension. The Standard Model particles are trapped in one of the branes. This is the brane where we live in and is called the weak brane. As a matter of course, the Standard Model particles include not only the fermions that constitute the materials but also the bosons that mediate the electromagnetic forces, strong forces, and the weak forces. Similarly with the ADD Model, only the gravity is not trapped in this brane and is able to propagate through the bulk. On the weak brane, the fermions interact with each other through the bosons, and only the bosons called the gravitons that mediate the gravity are able to exist anywhere in the 5-dimensional space-time. The important consequence of the RS Model is that the gravitons are not distributed evenly in the bulk. In the general theory of relativity, a gravitational field is literally a distortion of the space-time. Any object that has mass distorts the surrounding space-time. It is famous that, in 1919, as an embodiment of this prediction provided by the general theory of relativity, the space-time near the sun was distorted due to the gravity of the sun, and as a result, the distorted light path coming from the fixed star at the back of the sun was observed (the gravitational lens effect). The distortion of the space-time propagates to the surroundings as an object which has mass moves, forming a gravitational wave. On 2016, this wave was firstly observed.

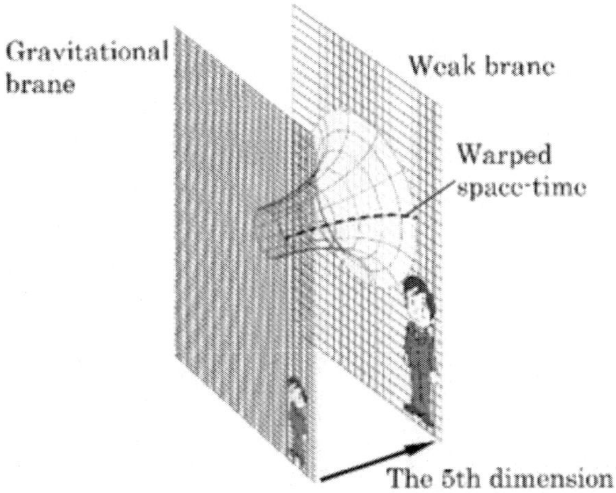

Figure 3. RS model.

RS paid attention to the fact that the brane itself has mass, and solved the Einstein' equation, which links the distribution of the energy (=mass) in the space-time and the distortion of the space-time with respect to the 5-dimensional space-time where the two branes with different mass exist. They then clarified the warp of the extra-dimensional space. According to them, when you set (x^0,x^1,x^2,x^3) as the coordinates in the space-time inside the brane (with x^0 being the time axis and the rest being the space axes) and x^5 as the extra-dimensional coordinate, the gravitational field in the 5-dimensional space-time varies as a function of x^5 only. The gravitational field in the brane is multiplied by the constant in correspondence with the position x^5 of the brane in the extra-dimensional space, and the constant is expressed by the exponential function of x^5. It is presumed that the brane itself is flat and there is no gravitational field inside it. However, the gravitational field in the brane varies in correspondence with its position within the extra dimension, and, as shown in the figure, the pitches of the time and the space of the space-time inside the brane vary. The fact that the space is warped in the direction of the fifth dimension means that, as a matter of course, the gravity works differently depending on the location within the space. From the perspective of the gravitons, which propagates the gravity, it means that it shows a distribution in accordance with the distribution function which is solely dependent on x^5, rather than (x^0,x^1,x^2,x^3). Naturally, this distribution function reflects the features of the warped space-time, and exponentially varies between the maximum on one brane and the minimum on the other brane. The brane where the distribution function is minimum is the weak brane, which is where we live, and the distribution function will be the maximum on the other brane. This brane is called the gravitational brane. On the gravitational brane, the gravitons exist densely. As you leave this brane to enter the extra dimensions and approach the weak brane, the density of the gravitons which exist in the surroundings becomes exponentially lower in a rapid pace, reaching the minimum on the weak brane. Naturally, the higher the density of the gravitons is, the stronger the gravity is, and the lower the density of the gravitons is, the weaker the gravity will be. The reason why we feel that the gravity is particularly weak is that the density of the gravitons on the weak brane is extremely low. On the contrary, the gravity is extremely strong on the gravitational brane due to the distribution density of the gravitons. If you perceive this as the true strength of the gravity, the hierarchy problem is solved. The point in this model is that the strength of the gravitational field is expressed by the exponential function on the coordinate of the extra dimensions. By virtue of this, we do not have to attribute the extreme smallness of the gravity on the weak brane to the hugeness of the extra-dimensional space. The moment we leave the gravitational brane, the distribution density of the gravitons become lower in accordance with the distance therefrom and the exponential function, which is a rapidly changing function. For this reason, it is not necessary to have so large extra-dimensional space as is required under the ADD Model, regardless of how small we feel the gravity is. The distribution function of the gravitons become sufficiently small, keeping the extra-dimensional space as small as it is, thereby requiring no large extra-dimensional space such as is required under the ADD Model. The difference in the gravity strengths on the gravitational brane and the weak brane can be described with a distance which is not so much different from the length of Planck, if you take a look at the distance between the branes.

Section 2. Advance Model of "Consciousness Independent from Brain"

What Is Non-Computability of Intellect?

Our consideration aims at pursuing the horizon to see to what extent we are able to press hard on the mind-body problem taking advantage of the modern physics, particularly, to what extent it is physically possible to examine the substance of the consciousness which exists independently from the brain. From this point, I would like to consider the specific possibility of the existence of the consciousness which is independent from the brain. It could be called our personalities, or our mind. Let me say that such thing exists separately from our body, and independently. I would, however, like to stick here to the point that it is something that has material grounds, as does our body, rather than something ideological. That is, this has to be something which could be a subject of research of the modern physics—I will ensure this. Based on this, I would like to say that it is comprised of a material particle, which is fermion. Where do we seek the whereabouts of the consciousness? A physicalistic aspect based on the monism which seeks the whereabouts in the brain functions, and the aspect of dualism which assumes the existence separate from the materials, accepting the existence of consciousness as a substance apart from the brain. It is not simple, as each aspect has their various details as a matter of course. I would like to ask myself if, as the third alternative, something like a "monism where the consciousness exists separately from the brain." First of all, I will look into the current status of the researches on "the consciousness which is independent from the brain." A consciousness as a substance which exists not as a result of the brain activities but independently from the brain—is such a thing possible? How much have the researches progressed?

Dr. Stuart Hameroff, an American anesthesiologist, advocates in his unique study something ultramicro called "Proto-conscious," which is independent from the brain. According to him, the Proto-conscious continues to be even after the perishing of the brain, and gains an opportunity to dwell in another brain to "be born" again in this world. Underlying in his study of the mind-body problem is the "Orch – OR Model" which he proposed with Dr. Roger Penrose, a theoretical physicist. "Orch" is an abbreviation for "Orchestrated," and "OR" is that of an "Objective Reduction." What is this model? What is going to be orchestrated and what is going to reduce?

One thesis that constitutes a foundation of Penrose' study on the consciousness is an argument that the "Thoughts of the human beings are non-computational." Artificial intelligence, which is a popular topic among the researchers, is an example. It is an effort to imitate human's intelligence using a computer. Some researchers consider as follows: With the progress in the study on the artificial intelligence, it will eventually evolve into something which can be called an artificial consciousness. It will have a desire and appetite, and will be able to apply the information obtained through perception to the actions in line with its own desire based on the "cognizance." It will be able to predict the future events to some extent (it does not have to be able to predict everything, as it is not possible even for the human beings), and it will have the thought patterns and emotions unique to itself as the human beings do, eventually possessing "personality." However, those who believe that the thoughts are non-computational argue that there is no possibility that the artificial intelligence will make such a development. They say this is because the current artificial intelligence is as computational as one can be. Being "computational" means that each individual problem can be reduced to a computation which will be made in line with a program that gives an algorithm to solve that problem. An algorithm is a set of rules utilized for the computation to solve the problems, and is a computational process. Penrose and Hameroff believe that the thinking ability of the human beings cannot be reduced to something like this, and that it is non-computational. To be non-computational means that there is no algorithm for the computing. More particularly, a certain status of consciousness cannot be derived from a status at a preceding point in terms of time through a process of algorithm. They first reached this conclusion, and then set up a mechanism that supports such process.

Which of the materials and the mind is primordial? This is a question that the mankind has pursued since several thousands of years ago. It is the materialism that requires materialistic support for the mental activities, and it is also called the reductionism and the physicalism. An opposing concept is the idealism, which considers that the spiritual existence constitutes those things that are considered material. Regardless of which concept you will have your basis on, an important theme will be how you consider the qualia. The qualia is a subjective experience that appear in the image. Such experience includes, for example, the "redness" or the "rose-likeness" that you feel when you look at a red rose, or the hurt you feel when you touch the thorns. "What is the source of such qualia?" This is an enormous challenge. The modern brain science and neuroscience reveal the association between the parts in the brains and the perceptions and emotions, such as a phenomenon where a specific part of the brain makes some kind of reaction when a person obtains some visual information. It is already evident that the qualia and the brain activities are not irrelevant. However, what causes the qualia to occur is totally unknown at the moment. It is sufficiently presumed that the brain functions are involved. However, how they get involved and which certain function of the brain causes the qualia to occur under what mechanism is in an area which is intact, rather than just remaining unsolved. Reflecting the status quo of the scientific research as mentioned above, there is an argument which can be viewed as an escape way on the side of the philosophical conception of nature, which is the neutral monism (I am not saying that the neutral monists are aiming at evading the abovementioned difficult problem). They do not believe that the fundamental entity of the world should be chosen from either of the material or the spirit; rather, their argument is that a certain kind of neutral existence, which is neither of the material nor the spirit, is the very entity which is the source of the materials and the spirits. Based on this argument, it is possible to say that a qualia itself is the source. If this is the case, there is no need to think about the source of the qualia.

A similar argument is the panpsychism, which argues that all materials have the attribution to constitute the consciousness. Even the elementary particles such as the electrons have a primary consciousness, if not on the same level as that of the human beings. This concept belongs to the neutral monism, and similarly, does not require an exploration into how a qualia is generated based on what material grounds. This is because they consider that a qualia also exists based on the consciousness as a fundamental entity on an elementary particle level. The views of Penrose and Hameroff are largely a part of the panpsychism. Having said this, their argument is characterized by the point that the consciousness is affected by the quantum effect within the material. If it is revealed that the human intelligence contains the non-computable factors, the inconsistency of the neural network model to date will be brought to light, as it is considered that the neural network works purely classically. If it is classical, it should be computable. If it is non-computable, there should be a quantum mechanics involved—which is the only area among the natural laws known today that contains (that could contain) the non-computability. The non-computability of the thought is the manifestation of the quantum effect. In the quantum mechanics, the state of the materials is described by the wave function. Unlike the image of the particles in the classical mechanics, in the quantum mechanics, we are only able to express the certain positions or a particular momentum of the particles stochastically. This is an attribute of the quantum mechanics inherent in the natural world, rather than the lack of our measuring ability or the cognitive ability. The wave function quantifies the distribution of this probability. The probability means that a certain physical quantity does not necessarily have a specific value but forms a ranging probability distribution. When you specifically observe, however, the observer discovers a specific measured value. You do not obtain the scattering measured values with a certain range through an observation of just one time. A measured value is just one. The wave function is originally devised to describe the non-classical movements of the particles (the wave nature). Although you can only obtain one measured value through an observation of just one time, a group of measured values will be distributed relatively sparsely if you measure multiple times, showing as a result the nature as a wave (including the interference or diffraction). Then, does the wave function, which has been introduced to theoretically take care of the nature of the wave, exist in the natural world? Alternatively, is it only meaningful for the purpose of computation and not an entity, with the cause of the coexisting relationship between the nature of the particle and the nature of the wave arising from another mechanism which is yet to be known? No common grounds have been reached definitively in this relation. The interpretations thereof include various theories including, among others, the parallel universe theory as well as those which doubt the existence of the wave function itself. A historically main stream among such theories is what is called the "Copenhagen Interpretation." Needless to say, "Copenhagen" is the capital city of Denmark. The interpretation is called as such, as it was devised at the famous Niels Bohr Institute in Copenhagen. According to this Interpretation, the wave function indeed exists. Under the Copenhagen Interpretation, the process where something which existed with a range prior to the observation indicates a specific value at the time of measurement is described as the "collapse of the wave function." More particularly, the particles the measured values of which range (such as a wave) and which also have the nature of the wave actually collapse through the process of observation to form one state that indicates their measured values. If the wave function exists, so does the process of this collapse, which occurs in the natural world. As a matter of course, this process of collapse, as well as the states preceding the observation, are not directly observed (although it is fundamentally impossible to "observe the states preceding the observation," because if you observe the states preceding the observation, it would already be "observed"). The wave function within the meaning of the quantum mechanics is a concept obtained in an effort to establish a theory which can predict the measured outcome to the maximum extent possible and give an "interpretation" to the natural phenomena that show both the nature of the particles and the nature of the wave. To date, however, as mentioned earlier, it is not at all evident as to if the wave function itself exists, or if it is something that is not perceivable and is quite different from the real world but is only convenient for the purpose of the computation. Based on the Copenhagen Interpretation, which is one of the various possible interpretations, the wave function itself and the collapse thereof indeed actually exist in the natural world.

Penrose and Hameroff seek the factor of the non-computability, which is the intrinsic attribute of the human thoughts, exactly within this collapse of the wave function. A system which can be described by the classical physical laws is computable, that is, an algorithm exists for it and physically it can be reconstructed by a computer. However, if an intelligence is featured by the non-computability, it is impossible to think that the intelligence will emerge from such system. They have understood that the true value of the quantum mechanics is that it includes the non-computability, and that its source is nothing other than the collapse of the wave function. At the moment, there is no other way than to depend on the quantum mechanics, if you want to seek the non-computability within the source of the consciousness. Meanwhile, for the quantum system, an observational act from the exterior which causes the collapse of the wave function and a disturbance from the surrounding environment (such as a thermal energy) are equivalent. The two are indistinguishable in that both of them disturb the quantum-theoretical coherence by the exterior disturbance and cause the collapse. It is possible to distinguish them through the difference in the appellations, by referring to the collapse caused by an observation by an observer who has a consciousness as the "Subjective Reduction." In any event, the collapse occurs randomly under the circumstance where there are random effects of the environment. If, however, a system is isolated, the coherent state thereof (the quantum-superposition state) is maintained under the circumstance where it is sufficiently insulated from the environment (and the observational act of the observer), and the coherence is broken to cause the collapse to occur not randomly but autonomously (objectively), that is when the "consciousness" will be born (this collapse is called the "Objective Reduction"). That is, the autonomous collapse of the wave function is the very process which brings about the non-computable factor. Then, what does it mean that the collapse occurs autonomously rather than randomly? What causes the collapse, if it is not due to the disturbance from the environment? The answer to this problem given by Penrose and Hameroff was extraordinary. They said that it was a structural change in the space-time geometry related to the general theory of relativity.

Theoretical Effect of General Relativity Generates the "Consciousness"!?

Under the Orch-OR Theory, it is the cell architecture in the brain that constitutes the very wave function that collapses. More specifically, it is the structure in the neuron cells which constitute the neural circuits in the brain and mediate the information processing and transmitting. Largely divided, the neuron cells are comprised of three parts, namely, the cell body which includes the cell nuclei, the multiple dendrites of the signal input parts, and one nerve fiber which is in charge of the signal output, the so-called axon. At the end of the axon, the neurotransmitters are exchanged with the other cells through the synapse. The axon transmits the information electrically toward a certain direction, from the cell body side to the end of the axon. This axon has another role. In the axon, a microtubule exists, which maintains its long form as a cell skeleton. The microtubule plays a role of a transport pipe which supports the transportation inside the cell. Instead of a signal, a protein which is necessary for the maintaining and the activity of the cells is transported. The molecules that constitute this microtubule are called the tubulins. The α - tubulin and β - tubulin, the macromolecules each of which has a molecular weight exceeding 50,000, form a heterodimer. Those heterodimers lining up in the long axis direction form a protofilament. 13 of these protofilaments are bundled in a loop to form a microtubule with a cylindrical structure of about 25 nanometers in diameter (1 nanometer is equal to 1 over 10 million centimeters). Each of these protofilaments are used as a rail to allow a transport vesicle loaded with the protein molecules to move from a cell body to the end of the axon like a cargo vehicle with the help of the motivity of a molecular motor, carrying out an axonal transport.

The collapse of the wave function devised by Penrose and Hameroff as a source of the emergence of the consciousness. This collapsing wave function is the wave function of a tubulin dimer that constitutes this microtubule. Hameroff, who is an anesthesiologist, found out that an anesthesia gas molecule affects the molecular structure of this tubulin dimer. As is well known, anesthesia, particularly the general anesthesia causes the loss of consciousness without interfering the other brain functions necessary for the maintenance of life. Based on this fact, Hameroff got an idea that the movement of the molecular structure of the tubulin dimer directly acts on the occurrence of the consciousness. Physically, each of the dimers is in an "open" state or a "closed" state (Figure 4).

Classically, only one of the two states are possible. However, it is not the case with the quantum mechanics. A state called the quantum superposition can be perceived, where both states are stochastically possible at the same time. When the anesthesia gas molecules get through the interspace of the dimers, the quantum-superposition state will be released due to the interaction with the anesthesia gas molecules which came near (the collapse of the wave function), fixing the dimers that had been in a quantum-superposition state to either of the open or the closed state concerning their system. At this point, the consciousness is lost. Based on this fact, Hameroff gained an insight that this superposition state of the dimers in their open or closed states is deeply involved in the generation of the consciousness.

The fact that something is non-computational per se does not directly link to the issue of the whereabouts of, for instance, a qualia. However, it could be a key factor to understanding the physical activities in the background. In order for a system to be maintained in a coherent state to allow the autonomous collapse of the wave function to occur, the state has to be sufficiently remote so that there will be no disturbance from the environment. Through an autonomous collapse, which is not random, a system will show a non-computational phenomenon. A coherent and super-positional state preceding the occurrence of OR is called a preconscious process, and a non-computational OR which occurs instantaneously is called a conscious event. Under the preconscious process, a quantum-mechanical computation will take place. Each individual OR is an irreversible process in terms of time, and thus it determines the direction of time. With the occurrence of the ORs that are discrete in terms of time, a "flow" of time and consciousness will occur. In this relation, a bridge molecule called a microtubule-related protein is connected to the microtubule, and the microtubules are physically bound together. According to Penrose and Hameroff, this binding "adjusts" the quantum oscillation of the preconscious process in the quantum states, and realizes the orchestration toward a possible result of the collapse.

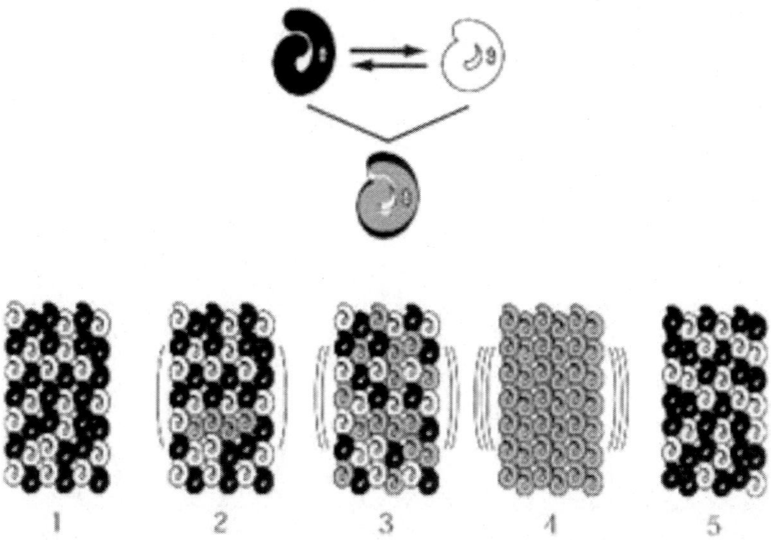

Figure 4. Time propagation of quantum mechanical tubulin.

How does an OR actually occur autonomously, as described by them? They argue that a quantum gravity effect contributes. An OR is not something that came from a micro-viewpoint based on the wave function of the individual tubulin. Under the preconscious process, a coherent state spreads from one tubulin to another. The flow spreads within the tubulin dimers that constitute a microtubule, from a classical "open" or "closed" state to a quantum-coherent state which is super-positional. Eventually, a considerable number—a non-negligible number of dimers in a microtubule participate in this superposition state. It is considered that each of the two extremes, namely, the state where the total count is open and the state where the total count is closed, possesses a particular geometric structure within the space-time. The more dimers there are that participate in the superposition state, the larger the discrepancy of the mass distribution in the space-time will be between these structures. The larger the level of this discrepancy will be, the more unstable the superposition state will be, eventually collapsing to become a simple state. The level of this unstableness is determined by the quantum gravity theory. It takes longer than a cosmic age for a simple system such as one electron to collapse its superposition state with the OR, whereas the larger the system is, the shorter it will require for the OR to take place. A macro-system such as this microtubule would require a much shorter time to become destabilized. The two factors required for the generation of the consciousness are that a system is secluded from an environmental noise until the OR occurs, and that the time required for the OR to reach the threshold value for it to occur is short enough to be of advantage in the thought process. The process of selection where certain state is chosen at the time of each OR event is non-computational, and it is a process where the geometry of the space-time selects on their own. As such, the non-computational process gets involved in the process inside the brain through a microtubule. In the course of expansion of a superposition state of a tubulin where it expands from a micro-scale to a macro-scale, the superposition state transforms through the OR into a classical macro-structure released from the superposition state. A quantum wave which expressed multiple possibilities prior to the OR falls into one macro-reality. That is, one of the eigenstates that exist will be selected. The selection of an eigenstate caused by the collapse of the wave function follows an unknown and non-computational theory which cannot be deduced algorithmically. Although it is unknown, its non-computability has a substantial significance for the consciousness which includes the activity styles that cannot be reduced to the algorithm.

Issue on "Non-Computability = Collapse of Wave Function"

The problem of this model is apparent. It is hard to imagine a quantum effect which actualizes in a macro-scale. In this model, a coherent state actualizes in the axon of the neuron cells inside the brain, on the rail called the microtubule which is used for the transportation of the molecules. Although the rail is only about 25 mm in diameter, some of them are as long as several dozens of cm—a sufficiently macroscopic system. According to the Orch-OR Theory, the coherent state lasts stably for as long as several hundreds of milliseconds. The greatest wall standing there in the way is the temperature. Generally, a quantum effect is an effect which appears in the micro world. As such, in order for the quantum effect to actualize on a macro-scale, be it superconductive or superfluid, an extremely low temperature, which cannot be experienced in our daily life, has to be prepared in the laboratory. Although the phenomena such as "a high-temperature" superconductivity has already been actualized in cuprate and the like, it is something like minus 170 degrees Celsius, which is far from the room temperature or the body temperature. The "high temperature" means that it is only higher than the temperature of the previously known superconductors (around minus 270^{0}C) or that of the liquid nitrogen frequently used in a low-temperature experiment (minus 196^{0}C). The superfluidity is also a phenomenon which occurs in a super-low temperature as low as around minus 270^{0}C. In addition, these materials, be it cuprate or liquid helium, are of a system with extremely simple compositions. Not only are there too much disturbance inside the brain due to a too-high-temperature as high as a body temperature, but they are the extremely complicated systems where the protein molecules with an extremely large molecular weight and a lot of living cells are mixed. Thus, the significant issue is if it is possible at all to stabilize a macro quantum effect. In fact, because of this reason, the Theory is not much supported, which is understandable.

Proto-Conscious – Consciousness Which Stays Alive After Death

As you can see in this video site (https://youtu.be/jjpEc98o_Oo), Hameroff further talks about the "proto-conscious." He says that the consciousness which is born in the brain is extremely small—as small as the elementary particles—and that it goes in and out of the human brain. Formerly, he has sought the cause of the generation of the consciousness in the quantum effect inside the axon of the neuron cells. He may have felt that it is difficult to explain the mechanism solely based on the phenomena inside the brain, or has come to more proactively accept the continuance of the consciousness after death taking into consideration the cases of the "reincarnation"—we are unable to presume what he had in mind. In any event, he started to advocate this proto-conscious, which is a consciousness independent from the brain. He states that the micro consciousness diffuses across the universe as a person dies. When it once again returns to the brain, it is the resuscitation, and a so-called "near-death experience" is actualized. If no resuscitation occurs, the consciousness floats around in the universe, and "reincarnates" as it gets connected to another living matter. However, such super-micro consciousness theory contains another issue. First of all, we need to pay attention to the mechanism of conjunction between the brain and the proto-conscious. It is directly linked to the association between the OR, which Hameroff himself described as being the source of generation of the consciousness, and the proto-conscious. Inside our brain, which is in the size of 10 cm, there are several dozens of billions of neuron cells. How does a "super-micro" consciousness as small as an elementary particle communicate with the phenomena within the microtubule inside these huge number of neuron cells in the macroscopic area? Hameroff takes out the "quantum entanglement" to describe this, saying that the information is exchanged among the neuron cells inside the brain, and between the neuron cells and the proto-conscious. However, this is also difficult. In principle, an exchange of information based solely on the "quantum entanglement" is not possible. What the quantum information theory tells us is that the transmission of the quantum state (quantum teleportation) and the communication of the classical information (quantum dense coding) are only made possible when accompanied by another communication route. On top of that, as a matter of course, it is impossible to instantly transmit the information beyond the light speed. As such difficulty being evident as a physicist, even his ally, Penrose, seems to be skeptical about this proto-conscious theory.

There is still another extremely significant problem. When you look at the cases of a "near-death experience," it is reported that the patients go through various experiences prior to the resuscitation stage. A tunnel, a bright light beyond the tunnel, an encounter there and conversation with the families who preceded in death, ownself lying in a hospital room and the surrounding healthcare professionals and their conversation. They suggest that the five senses (at least the sense of vision and the sense of hearing, based solely on the examples I cited here) are working. If you want to interpret the reincarnation and the "near-death experiences" with a "super-micro consciousness," you need to be able to reconstruct the sensory tissues such as the retina and the cochlea as well as the functions of the sensory nerves with the super-micro particles as small as an elementary particle. Naturally, the sophisticated mental activities and the intelligence such as memories and thoughts also have to be reconstructed. It is doubtful if such a thing is possible. If the super-micro particles collectively function, how do they transmit the information among themselves? I would like to reiterate that the mere sharing of the quantum entanglement does not allow the information transmission to happen. It is presumed that the reason that he sought the substance of the consciousness independent from the brain in these super-micro materials is to keep consistency with the fact that it has not been observed to date. He had no choice other than to describe that it was extremely small—so small that it could not have been observed in any of the experiments to date, including the high-energy physics experiments. Indeed, no substance of the consciousness which exists outside of the brain has been found in the 4-dimensional space-time where we live in. It is therefore understandable to think that such substance is "super-micro" to keep consistency with this fact. This very presumption, however, has brought about further difficulties such as mentioned above.

Capturing of "Consciousness Independent from Brain" through Brane World – John Smythies Theory

Assuming that a substance of the consciousness independent from the brain exists, in what form could it exist? If it is comprised of the materials similarly with the brain, why is it invisible to us? A concept that immediately comes to us is that "it is too small to be visible." If this is the case, to what extent of the size could it be perceived as reasonable as being "sufficiently small"? Obviously, given that it has not been found to date, it is absolutely not in a level as that it is invisible with the unaided eyes. It should be smaller than 10^{-16} cm, which is approximately the scale of the space which can be decomposed through today's high-energy experiments. However, even if there were an instrument in charge of the consciousness so extremely small as such, we cannot avoid the inconsistencies arising from the very fact that it is small, as explained above. If the "smallness" is the cause of the difficulty, we should establish a model which allows the substance of the consciousness to have a macroscopic scale to avoid such difficulty. However, is such a thing possible? The substance of the consciousness exists with a macroscopic scale—several millimeters or several dozens of centimeters large—and it is still invisible to us—is such a theory model ever possible?

The development of the modern physics gives us a picture of a multi-dimensional universe. This is a theory which argues that there are more than four dimensions that are visible in the universe where we live. What kind of a model can be perceived based on this picture? If the universe is 4-dimensional, it is impossible to assume the existence of a material which is of a macroscopic size but is still invisible. It may not be the case, if there are a larger number of dimensions—the fifth dimension, the sixth dimension, and so on. The problem that we need to address from now on is to consider if we can assume such existence in the picture of a multi-dimensional universe.

In the previous Section, I have explained the outline of the brane models. Based on these models, naively, we come up with a brane model comprised of the two brane worlds. For example, supposing that we live on a brane, are we able to presume that there is another brane that exists, and the so-called "consciousness" is the existence on such brane (Figure 5)? What would be the relationship between the consciousness and the brain in that case?

Figure 5. Soul on another brane?

This is how I describe it. On one brane, this universe where we live in exists, and our Earth and the bodies of ourselves who live there exist thereon. On this brane, the world which we feel daily exists. The profoundness of the universe as well as the microscopic world which can be captured by all kinds of equipment exist there. Let us call this a visible brane. We know that our body, naturally including the brain, exists on this brane. Now, we are trying to think that the consciousness is an existence which is separate from the brain. We consider that the substance of the consciousness exists on another brane. This is why we need to have two brane worlds. We call the brane where the consciousness exists the "consciousness brane." It is possible to consider that the substance of this consciousness is invisible from us even if it is in a macroscopic size, as it exists on another brane. It seems that it is possible, at least tentatively, to set a circumstance such as this in a multi-dimensional universe model using the brane. I would like to examine the appropriateness of this setting later. This independent brane model resolves the existence of a consciousness independent from the brain in a form which could most naively be perceived in the brane world model. The brain and the consciousness exist separately in the two branes—the visible brane and the consciousness brane. The consciousness has a will, emotion and memory, obtains the information from the body such as the sense of vision, sense of hearing and sense of pain, and conveys the will as an order to the brain to cause an action to occur. The brain plays a role of a receiver, and somehow exchanges the information with the consciousness. The model of John Smythies is an example of such model (Smythies 2003).

Smythies tried to apply the latest topics in the modern physics, such as the superstring theory and the brane universe, to the mind-body problem. He named the space-times existing in the abovementioned two independent branes—the visible brane and the consciousness brane—the physical space-time and the phenomenal space-time, respectively (Figure 6).

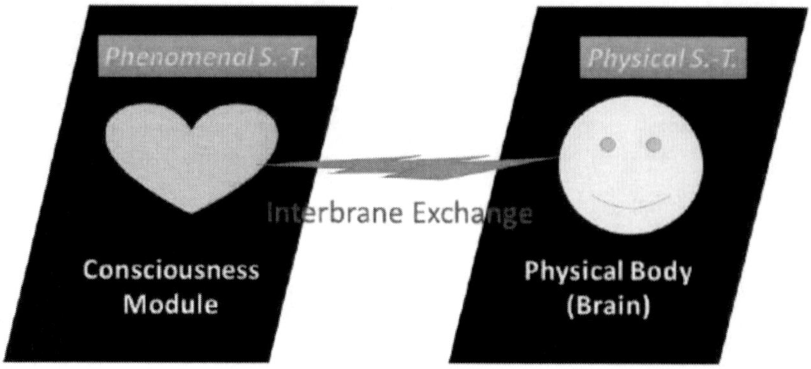

Figure 6. Schematic view of Smythies model.

Our body exists in the former, whereas the phenomenal consciousness is a separate and independent substance which belongs to the latter. Based on his unique psychophysical experiment, he believes in the representational theory, driving out the direct realism which argues that the world exists just as perceived by the human beings through the sense of vision. Under this theory, the information obtained through the sense of vision is computed by our brain as something that should be, and it is not capturing the world as is. When we capture a chair with our sense of vision, the chair as a phenomenal object which we recognized through our sense of vision exists in the "phenomenal space-time," independently from the external object which exists in this physical world. Under the representational theory, it is argued that the direct appearance of the chair as an exterior object which exists in the physical space-time and the phenomenal object which exists in the phenomenal space-time do not have to be the same, and may be totally different. For instance, a chair that we recognize when we are looking at the chair is a final product obtained through a process in the bodily physical organization such as the eyes, skin, and nerve which is separate from the chair as an exterior object. The phenomenal space-time is allocated as a unique real space against our consciousness. Through his consideration on the sensory abnormalities such as visual agnosia, vision disorder and phantom limb, Smythies argues the existence of a phenomenal space-time. More particularly, he says that it is not that one of the phenomenal space-time and the physical space-time is the real world and the other is ideological. Rather, he says that both are equally positioned in the real world. It is a parallel world, if you will. Smythies displays his unique cosmic view, applying here the brane world picture which is the leading concept of the modern physics. They exist on the independent branes, and a physical body exists and acts in the physical space-time, whereas a bodily image exists and acts in the phenomenal space-time. The physical events and the psychological events occur in the different space-times which do not share the same dimension. He points out that the reason that we are only able to see the physical space-time and are not able to see the phenomenal space-time is because the light cannot be exchanged between the parallel worlds. He considers that there is a sense that can be experienced directly without the light mediating, believing that the counterpart of the object in the physical space-time is generated in the phenomenal space-time through the senses. He took the sense of vision as an example to marshal the process of perception as "object – photon – retina – brain – intersection with different branes – field of vision sense," thereby naming this process the causal chain. He also stated that a hallucination is caused in the latter half of this chain, that is, "brain – intersection – field of vision sense." The point in this model is the existence of intersection of information between the branes that bridge the physical space-time and the phenomenal one. Smythies argues that the concept arguing that the consciousness lies in a unique brane in a separate dimension outside of the physical world is extremely in line with the trend of the modern physics. However, precisely speaking from a physical perspective, it is not an issue so simple as such to actualize an intersection of information between the branes in the chain of cause and effect. I would like to talk about this later. Smythies calls the combination of these various senses, image fields and subjective self, which exist in the phenomenal space-time beyond the physical body, a "consciousness module."

As mentioned earlier, there was a significant problem in the super-micro consciousness theory. That is, it is not possible for a particle so small as an elementary particle to equip the sensory tissues and sensory nerves. On the contrary, the Smythies Theory, which has in mind the brane model, still has a potential in this sense. In this model, it is argued that our body including our brain exists on one brane, and a "consciousness module" as a substance of the consciousness exists on another brane. The difficulty of the super-micro consciousness theory lies where it considers the substance of the consciousness super micro. In the background of this difficulty, there is a fact that we have not been able to find the substance of the consciousness existing independently from the brain. For the purpose of rationalizing this fact, it had to be "super-micro." In this relation, the Smythies Theory argues that this substance of the consciousness exists in another brane universe, and thus it is "invisible" from the beginning. Because it is invisible, it does not have to be "super-micro." It can be large. This is a huge advantage over the super-micro consciousness theory.

What we need to pay attention to is the point that, as a fundamental position, Smythies fundamentally adheres to the position of Dr. Andrei Linde, who is a theoretical physicist who argues that there are three independent basic configuration bodies in this world, namely, the space-time, materials, and consciousness. This is qualitatively different from the monism in that it considers that each of the consciousness and the materials is an elementary entity which does not consider the other as its own source (in this sense, Andrei Linde himself is somewhat peculiar as a physicist). He bothers to propose a hypothesis which presumes an existence of the consciousness independent from the brain based on the picture of a brane universe, which is the latest concept in the modern physics. Given this situation, it is worth examining if there are any problems hiding somewhere in the path through an achievement of the modern physics. Smythies is not an expert in the area of physics. It is an interesting idea to assume an existence of the parallel world in a multi-dimensional universe as a concept, to assume some kind of interactions with that and our universe, to assume something called a consciousness module, thereby commenting on the existence of our consciousness independent from the brain. However, if we want to treat this as part of the scientific topics, the steps are definitely required to examine what kind of difficulties lie ahead at this stage and if there are any problems. The physical challenges hiding in the Smythies Theory are, simply put, what can be described as a "hierarchy problem." Let us take a look at this hierarchy problem, which appeared again at this point.

Trap in Simple Application of Brane Model

I would like to examine the appropriateness of the Smythies Theory based on the ADD Model and the RS Model. Is it possible to apply the concept of the information communication between the branes to a mind-body problem, that is, the idea of "the consciousness as a substance independent from the brain," as Smythies says? Is it reasonable to think that the "mind" and the "body" exist on the different branes and implement a communication between themselves—that is, exchange information through information intersection between the branes as described in the Smythies Theory? On what mechanism is the intersection between the branes based on, if it exists at all? How much credible in terms of physics is the idea that the "consciousness module" which is the subject of the consciousness and our body (particularly the brain which lies in our skeleton) exist on the separate branes, and that they are somehow communicating the information?

First of all, under the ADD Model, the gravitons are the only thing that are considered to move back and forth between the branes. In this Model, even if the parallel world existed, it is possible for only the gravity among the four interactions to walk back and forth among two worlds, and interaction using, for example, the light is impossible. The information intersection between the branes, if it ever exists, has to rely on the gravitons within the meaning of this Model. What happens if, for instance, the photons can also jump out of the brane into the extra-dimensional space? In this Model, the energy of these photons have to be proportionately small because the extra-dimensional space is large in this model. In that case, we have to have already found through the experiments the dimensions in the number larger than four. If we say something extreme, if the level of the energy of the photons that can move to and from the extra-dimensional space is in the area same as the energy of the electromagnetic force that we handle regularly, our understanding and the skills that are dependent on the formulation at the 4-dimensional space-time would not be valid. More particularly, if the number of the extra-dimensions is two and the millimeter-order extra-dimensions truly existed, something such as the Coulomb's law would already be invalid in such space scale. This would rock the foundation of the architecture of the semiconductor device based on the electronic engineering to date—which, however, has not yet occurred. Given this situation, we can say that, even if the model that proposes a large extra-dimensions such as the ADD Model were true, the light cannot move to and from the extra-dimensional space based on this Model. Is the information intersection between the branes possible, then, if the gravity is used? The general theory of relativity describes the gravity as a distortion of the space-time. As such, when some disturbance is caused in the gravitational field in the cases of, for instance, a binary star system where the two fixed stars go around each other, or a supernova explosion, this distortion is propagated. An effort to detect this "gravitational wave" has been made for a long time. On February 2016, a successful detection was eventually reported by the gravitational wave observatory LIGO (Laser Interferometer Gravitational-wave Observatory) in USA. A detection range required for the detection of a distortion in the space-time is so sensitive that it has to be able to detect, for example, the change in the size of a hydrogen molecule against the distance between the sun and the Earth. For example, in Japan, an experimental facility for the detection called the LCGT (which goes by KAGRA) is under construction, aiming at a full-fledged operation in 2017. This is a huge Michelson interferometer with the length of the base line as long as 3,000 m. The reason that such a huge experimental facility as this is required is that, as a matter of course, the gravitational wave is extremely weak. In order secure the required accuracy, the length of the base line of the interferometer has to be enormous, because the gravitational wave is too weak. Even after the completion of this facility, the expected observational events will be only several times a year. That is, the gravitational wave is so weak that, even with such an enormous observational equipment as this, it can only be observed in rare occasions. Should the consciousness module and the brain be exchanging the information via this gravitational wave, it would be that the brain as large as 10 square centimeters large at the most has a sensitivity that supersedes the observational facility with the length of the base line as long as 3 km in detecting the gravitational wave. This is plainly impossible. It cannot be considered that the information intersection between the branes is carried out through the exchanges of the graviton signals so extremely subtle as this. There is another point. When we say the information intersection between the branes, it should not only include the brain's receiving of the gravitational wave but also the transmitting. For the purpose of simulating the brain "generating the gravitational wave," the equipment has to be made that generates the gravitational wave in the scale the same as the brain. This is also desperately impossible. As it is difficult to detect the gravitational wave coming from the universe, which was caused by a supernova explosion or the like, it is even more difficult and impossible to artificially create a gravitational wave on the ground which is detectable.

If we need to depend on such an unreliable technique for a gravitational wave to communicate with the other brane, it is effectively impossible to do such a communication, even if there was another brane world and there were the residents who have a consciousness module or an intelligence. Although the existence of the brane per se can be indirectly presumed from the string theory required to keep consistency in the physical theories, at this point where it is impossible for the branes to interact, it makes no difference on our perception basis whether there were another brane or not. However, we do not need to jump to the conclusion. At this stage when the brane world model itself has not yet become an accepted view and there are a variety of opinions relating thereto, we do not have to despair and give up, thinking that "there is no other communication tool than the gravitational wave." There is a possibility that in the future, other forms of brane interaction is discovered. In fact, a model which enables the propagation of the photons within the extra-dimensional space already exists at this point—the RS Model.

Second Hierarchy Problem

The RS Model has brought about a new insight relating to the hierarchy problem. While the ADD Model seeks the cause of the tremendous weakness of the gravity in the gravitational diffusion into the huge extra-dimensional space, the RS Model seeks it in the warp of the extra-dimensional space. Separately from the brane where we live in, there is a gravitational brane which generates the gravity, and the gravitational brane exists across the bulk from our brane. Similarly with the extraordinary distortion of the space-time around the black hole which has an enormous mass, the fifth-dimensional space between the gravitational brane and our brane is warped in accordance with the general theory of relativity, and the gravitons are distributed disproportionately closer to the side of the gravitational brane which has a larger energy. The mechanism was that because the fewer gravitons are distributed near our brane, we feel the gravity extremely weakly. In this Model, the extra-dimensional space need not be enormous, as it does not consider the gravitational diffusion into the large extra-dimensional space as a solution to the hierarchy problem. The ADD Model drew a high attention, arguing that in some cases, the invisible extra-dimensional space may have the size as large as several millimeters. However, in this Model, it can be extremely small, as small as the Planck scale. The large extra-dimension in the ADD Model increased the impact of the model itself, but was at the same time the weak point. It shows a certain solution to the hierarchy problem arising from the weakness of the gravity, but contains an issue in that the millimeter-order extra-dimension is too small in energy scale. In this respect, the RS Model is able to explain the weakness of the gravity without invoking a new unnatural energy gap, because the extra-dimensions are small. Further, because the extra-dimensional space is small, even if the photons, in addition to the gravitons, propagate through the extra-dimensional space and move to and from the other brane, it is consistent with the observed facts. It opens the possibility of the communication with the other brane using the photons.

Is the information intersection between the branes possible, then, under the RS Model? In this Model, the exchanges of the light between the branes are indeed permitted, which is plainly different from the circumstance under the ADD Model where it is only permitted to the gravitons. Is this a good news? Actually, not necessarily. In this Model, if you want to exchange the light with the other brane, the light has to have an ultra-high energy. The high-energy light (electromagnetic wave) is the gamma ray. Although there is a considerable range in the energy value of the gamma ray, typically, it is around 10^6 eV. However, the light energy which traverses the extra-dimensional space in this Model has to be, in theory, at least 6 digits higher than that in energy. If not, we should already have found the trace of the extra-dimensions through the high-energy physics experiments. What makes it worse is that we do not yet have the skill of freely generating and detecting such ultra-high energy beams with an experimental equipment in a size as small as about a laboratory, much less a function in our brain which is able to receive and transmit such ultra-high energy electromagnetic wave. Therefore, it cannot be that an information intersection between the branes is conducted through an exchange of such ultra-high energy photons. When we try to explain the "mind independent from the brain" by the RS Model, we cannot avoid running into this wall of huge energy gap. This significant issue can be addressed as the second hierarchy problem. If we want to perceive our mind-body problem as a physical phenomenon and interpret it through the brane world model, it is inevitable that we solve this second hierarchy problem.

SECTION 3. PARASITE FERMION MODEL

Formulation by Quantum Field Theory

One challenge in the brane world picture is to find a probable scenario by which the movement of the particles are restricted within the brane. We live in the 4-dimensional world (at least, it appears that we do). For this purpose, the fermions (the matter particles) and the bosons (the particles which mediate interactions such as the electromagnetic forces, and the Higgs boson) inside the high-dimensional bulk have to be bound down on the brane with dimensions as low as just four. Otherwise, even the Newton's law would not be valid. The low-dimensional standard model particles are trapped on the brane. Then, what would be the probable scenario by which the movement of the particles are bound on the brane, that is, on the membrane of the low-dimensional space-time? The physicists have provided some insights. Under the D brane Model in the string theory, the standard model particles are described by the open-end string (open string), and describe that the both ends move only on the D brane. For this reason, the binding of this particle movement is just natural. The D brane was rather devised in the beginning as an object on which the both ends of an open string are fixed. On the other hand, in the quantum field theory, the mechanisms which localize each of the low-energy 4-dimensional vector (gauge) field, scalar, and fermion field has been proposed individually. Based on the quantum field theory, I would like to talk about the "Parasite Fermion Model," which is a new type of the fermion restricting mechanism (Taneichi 2013). We refer to the 4-dimensional brane where we live in and the fermions trapped in the brane. To this point, it is the same as the theories that have already existed. Now, I would like to newly consider another type of fermion which actualizes the localization into the brane via this existing fermion field. The former fermion is called the host fermion and the latter is called the parasite fermion. The parasite fermion gets connected with the host fermion by a fermion interaction, an interaction between those two types of fermion, feels the potential energy created by the host fermion, and localizes around the brane. It is literally "parasitic" on the host fermion and is indirectly bound down on the brane through the fermion interaction.

I would like to mention here the 5-dimensional bulk and one brane therein. Let us assume that both the bulk and the brane are flat; that is, its space-time is not distorted, and it is a Minkowski space. In reality, a brane has stars and black holes as you can see in our universe, and because of their mass, it is naturally not flat but is a space-time with a structure. In this model, however, I would like to disregard such structure inside the brane and assume the flatness inclusive of the extra-dimensions. The scalar field here is a type of 1-dimensional soliton which is called a kink solution. A soliton is a form of wave where an energy is localized. In the case at hand, if we take a look at the coordinate axis in the fifth dimension, the potential energy of the scalar field is localized on the position where there is a brane. A brane is described by something called the scalar field in the quantum field theory. On the other hand, the matter particles are a "matter field" but are described by something called the fermion field (or the Dirac field). Among the fermion fields, there are two types—namely, the abovementioned host fermion field and the parasite fermion field. The host fermion is a previously known matter field. Any and all materials in our environment including our body itself, as well as all materials confirmed through the experiments are included here. This couples to the abovementioned scalar field, namely the brane, through the Yukawa Interaction. This means that it is directly coupled to the brane. This is what is meant by the explanation that "the materials are trapped on the brane" (Figure 7). A host fermion field coupled to a scalar field is expressed in a formula as follows:

$$\lambda\overline{\Psi}_1\Phi\Psi_1 \quad (1)$$

Ψ_1 is the host fermion field, and Φ is the scalar field. λ is the coupling coefficient, indicating the degree of coupling of the two fields. This is an extraction of the relevant part from the quantity called the "lagrangian." In the physics, there is a quantity called the action integral. All movements of an object in the world stay in an orbit where this quantity will be minimized. This is called the least-action principle. Although lagrangian is indeed relatively unfamiliar compared to the energy and the momentum, it is extremely important in terms of the physics, as it is a component of the action integral which appear in this principle. Such is the image of binding of the host fermion field and the scalar field.

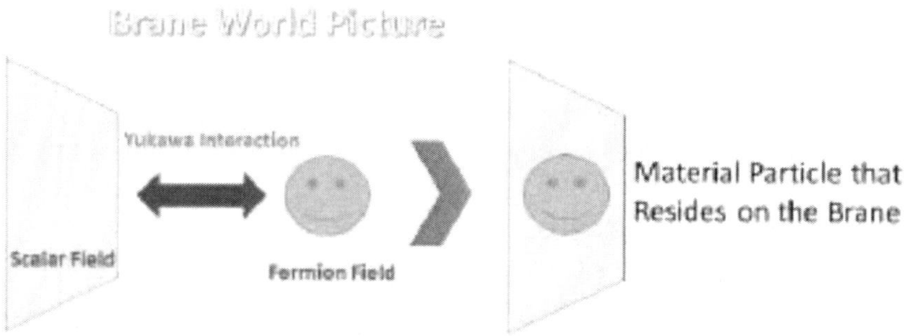

Figure 7. Particle on a brane expressed by the quantum field theory.

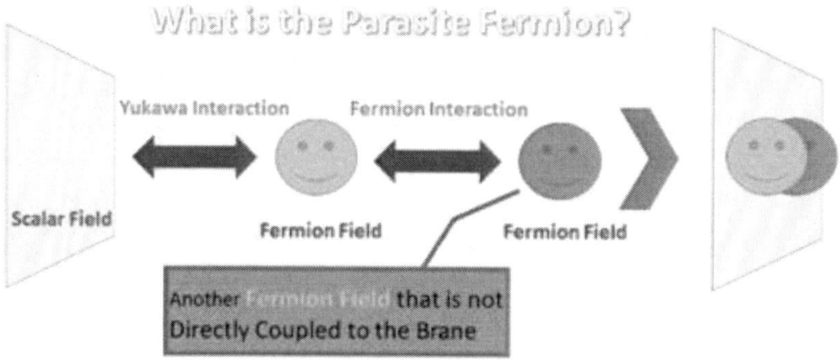

Figure 8. Parasite fermion indirectly trapped on the brane.

On the other hand, the parasite fermion couples to the host fermion field through the fermion interaction. An expression of "parasite" would fit this image (Figure 8). This fermion does not have a channel to directly couple to the scalar field. A formula to express this would be as follows:

$$\kappa\overline{\Psi}_2\overline{\Psi}_1\Phi\Psi_1\Psi_2 \tag{2}$$

Ψ_2 is the parasite fermion field, κ is a coupling constant. It is not a pure fermion interaction as there is a scalar field in it. However, it is natural to think that the scalar field has an effect somehow since the host fermion is involved. In addition, when calculated without a scalar field, only unstable tachyon solutions have been obtained. As such, a scalar field is necessary in this term also for the purpose of obtaining a stable solution. Accordingly, a localization of a parasite fermion field on the brane will be carried out indirectly through a coupling to the host fermion. Secondly, let us divide the parasite fermion field into a coordinate component within the brane (4 dimensions) and the coordinate component within the extra-dimensions (1 dimension), and assume that the field is indicated by their product.

$$\Psi_2(x,z) = f_{2L}(z)\psi_{2L}(x) + f_{2R}(z)\psi_{2R}(x) \tag{3}$$

x is the coordinate component within the brane, z is the coordinate component within the extra-dimensions, and ψ and f are the components in the parasite fermion field corresponding to each of these coordinates. The two added letters L and R are the signs related to a property called "chirality" of the particles, meaning the left and the right (their details shall be omitted here). Anyway, by doing this, an equation of motion relating to the bulk coordinate component

$$-\partial_{zz}f_{2L} + W_L f_{2L} = m_2^2 f_{2L} \tag{4a}$$

and

$$-\partial_{zz}f_{2R} + W_R f_{2R} = m_2^2 f_{2R} \tag{4b}$$

can be obtained. m_2 is a pseudo-mass of a parasite fermion on the brane (4D mass). In this equation of motion, a kinetic energy term, potential energy term ($W_{L/R}$), and eigenvalue (the square of m_2) are included, and the solution is an energy conservation solution, that is, eigenstates. The potential is expressed by a term which contains the product of a scalar field and the host fermion field.

$$W_L = \kappa[\kappa(\overline{\Psi}_1\Phi\Psi_1)^2 - \partial_z(\overline{\Psi}_1\Phi\Psi_1)] \tag{5}$$

The steady solution in the bulk coordinate component $f_{2L/R}$ indicates the localized probability distribution of the parasite fermion in this potential. Setting the position of the brane as an origin of the extra-dimensional coordinate, the potential energy curve is illustrated.

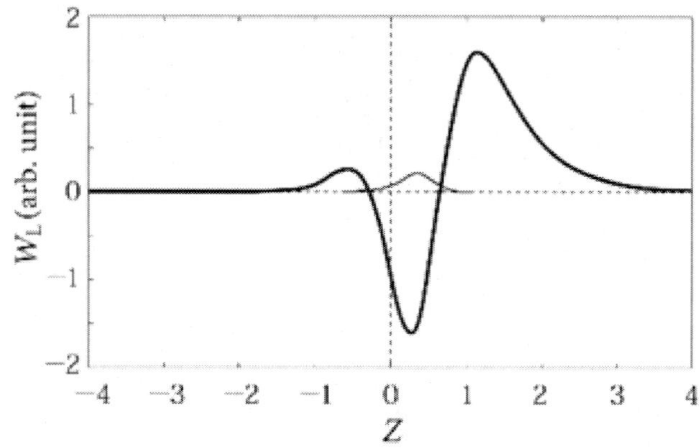

Figure 9. Potential curve that parasite fermion feels (thick solid line) and its presumable existence probability (thin solid line).

As mentioned earlier, the eigenvalue of the parasite fermion is a square of the 4D mass. If this is negative, it means that the mass is a pure imaginary number, meaning that it is a superluminal particle tachyon which is hypothetical. Therefore, I would like to exclude this for now. The potential well where the parasite fermion stabilizes is located in a position about a brane thickness off the position of the brane (Figure 9). This indicates that the parasite fermion stabilizes not on the brane but in a position off to the direction of the extra-dimensions. A stable parasite fermion solution is a solution where the energy eigenvalue is 0, that is, where the mass is 0, which is indicated with a thin solid line in the illustration. In order to allow the solution to have a mass, other mechanism such as the Higgs mechanism may be needed to be considered. The fermion interaction with the host fermion may function as another type of 4D mass. Further consideration is needed for this issue.

In any event, a parasite fermion exists in a totally different form from a host fermion which localizes on the brane. If we are comprised of the host fermions bound on the brane, the difference of the form of existence between the host fermion and the parasite fermion should certainly be reflected in the difference of how they are viewed from and captured by us who are on the brane. The two fermions interact with each other through the fermion interaction. The strength of such interaction depends on how much distant each of them are in the direction of the extra-dimensions, that is, how much distant the potential dent and the brane are, how much localized the host fermions are on the brane, how much localized the parasite fermions are in the potential dent, and the coupling constant of the fermion interaction.

Outlook on Parasite Fermion Model

The possible solution to the second hierarchy problem is the parasite fermion model which is introduced here. The center of the existence of the parasite fermion is outside of the 4-dimension world where we live in, in the extra-dimension. However, as it is coupled to the host fermion through the fermion interaction, it is able to have an influence over our world. Although it is not evident as to how much the influence would be, it could be partially visible, or could interact with the particles in this world. The interaction is not something too weak to be controlled or detected like a gravity; rather, it can be possible through an electromagnetic force. It is neither required to be a super-high energy. This is because the parasite fermions "partially" exists, as it were, in the brane universe where we are. It could either be that they interact but are not visible, or they are visible but their interaction is of a degree that can be disregarded. It could be that the force of the interaction varies timewise and spacewise.

In this model, I have formulated the combination of a substance inside the extra-dimensions as a material (parasite fermion) with a substance inside the brane as a material (host fermion) based on the quantum field theory. If we assume the former as being the grounds of the "consciousness" which has a material basis, the latter as being our brain, we are able to express the binding between the brain and the consciousness existing independently from the brain. To put it simply, it is a "wired method," rather than a "wireless method" as is in the Smythies Model. That is, it is not a Wi-Fi but an Ethernet method. In this way, we are able to avoid the second hierarchy problem. This is because the communication between the brain which is comprised of the host fermions and the "consciousness" which is comprised of the parasite fermions is carried out through a communication media which is similarly comprised of the parasite fermion, and it is consistent with our daily sense and the experimental outcome, even without assuming that they are carried out by the gravitons or a super-high energy photons.

"Passive Consciousness Model" is an example of totally materialistic cognitive model in which our mind is assumed to be comprised of material particles (Maeno 2005). This is a hypothesis that assumes that there are a conscious part and an unconscious part inside our brain, and that the unconscious part plays a main role in the activity of mind. Mind activities such as perception, representation of knowledge, emotion, willpower, and memory (learning) are not what the conscious part independently performs, but they are established via unconscious autonomous distributed and parallel recursive processing. The conscious part plays only a small role, accepts outcomes of the unconscious part, misunderstands that it is independently responsible for them, and pass them to the "episode memory" part. According to Maeno's metaphor, there are lots of dwarfs (they are actually neurons or collection of neurons), and they show various function such as, for instance, being struck by the beauty, feel a bit sad, have a will to prepare for dinner, as seeing the sunset. They decide one outcome by majority. If the collective opinion is to feel beauty, the conscious part accept the outcome passively, it asserts that it was independently moved by the beauty, and pass the outcome to the episode memory. In this way, one wrongly recognizes that his/her consciousness was moved by the beauty of the sunset on its own initiative. Maeno asserts that many difficult problems concerning cognitive models, such as how to establish qualia sensitivity in the neural network, the binding problem, and frame problem, are solved by his model.

In this model, however, a problem can be found as to how the majority decision of the unconscious can be achieved in the neural network in which each signal transmitted through synapse has no record on which neuron it had passed up to that point. To establish the majority decision, we may need to assume that some object plays a role as supervisor that cannot be in neural network. An object comprised of the parasite fermion (PFO: Parasite Fermion Object) is a strong candidate for that, because it exists outside the brain although it is surely connected to the brain and exchanges information. This supervisor manages the "meeting" of dwarfs and extracts one result of majority. The supervisor also can perform a maintenance and even medical treatment, in a sense, to the network, which are realized in the rehabilitation. This is actually the "Operating System" of the neural network!

Assuming that the parasite fermion particles exist, it is totally unknown as to how they are organized and compose a "consciousness" that has five senses and intelligence. For now, there is no other way than to put off the issue, but such a cognitive model serves as a very useful reference. The difficulty seems to be much smaller than when it has to be reduced to a super-micro particle such as an elementary particle. I would like to reiterate that, because the "consciousness" existing in the extra-dimensional space and which is comprised of the parasite fermions may be in a macro-scale size, it is able to avoid the difficulty that the super-micro consciousness theory has. In addition, it is possible to take in the Orch-OR Theory which focuses on the non-computability of the consciousness. The original Orch-OR Theory has been criticized of its difficulty to keep the quantum coherence in a macroscopic scale at room temperature for a long period of time. However, we do not necessarily think that the PFO, which resides in the extra-dimensional space, is at room temperature. Rather, it is difficult to imagine that it is in an environment where the temperature is about the same level as our body temperature. If this is the case, we need to assume some kind of heat source inside the extra-dimensional space. It is natural to think that it is in an extremely low temperature as close as the absolute zero. In such environment, a non-computational process may be actualized by a macro quantum coherence and its collapse inside the "consciousness" comprised of these parasite fermions as perceived by Hameroff. Although it is difficult to prove it as it has been to prove the parasite fermion itself, at least, it looks more hopeful than assuming a quantum coherence with the neuron cells inside the brain.

Historically, we have tended to sense something unscientific, religious, or of an occult in a phrase such as an "inhabitance of a soul." However, we can say that such a thing has been formulated now. The consciousness is perceived as a substance comprised of the materials, existing in the extra-dimensions—the dimensions that we normally do not recognize—based on the perspective of a multi-dimensional universe. The inhabitance of mind in the brain is, so to say, modeled by a fermion interaction between the matter particles. This idea may somehow contribute to the future studies which seek to find the forms of existence of mind as a substance interacting with but existing independently from the brain. The circumstances where a parasite fermion couples to a host fermion through a fermion interaction matches with an image where the "soul" inhabits in the "body," at least in so far as the appearance goes. Naturally, it is not sufficient just to say that it matches the image. Although it is certain that the host fermions comprise our body, it is essential as a next step that we obtain solid evidence that the "mind" existing separately from the brain is comprised of the parasite fermions, and clarify the mechanism where such mind inhabits in the body (brain) through the fermion interaction as the fetus grows and releases itself from the coupled body along with an event called death. Through what kind of an experiment, are we able to prove the existence of a parasite fermion and that it comprises the consciousness separately existing from the brain? Even if the Parasite Fermion Model were expressing the truth, it would require quite a lot of time and effort for the human beings today, who have no experience of having observed any phenomenon clearly involving the extra-dimensions, to obtain and fully understand these new forms of existence of the materials. This being said, the science progresses without doubt. It is understandable that we helter-skelter searching for the whereabouts of the mind, as we have not yet sensed the extra-dimensions. However, it is egoistic, indiscreet, and arrogant to write off all studies going around concerning the continuance after death as being unrelated to the science, trivial and a sheer nonsense even to dispute about. The models have been proposed that solve, respectively, the first hierarchy problem which has haunted the physicists for long, and the issues arising from the ADD Model which has been devised to solve the first hierarchy problem. On top of these is the Parasite Fermion Model, which is a model that solves the second hierarchy problem which surfaces when handling the consciousness outside of the brain from a scientific perspective. Some other different solutions may be further proposed, and the experimental examinations will certainly proceed. We are neither able to make a hasty prediction on the future development nor allowed any unfounded prejudgement. A scientific optimism would be what is required of us now. It is wrong to think that there is nothing there just because it cannot be justified at this point. Such an attitude would make the scientific researches too boring.

CONCLUSION

Rationality Judgment and Trap

We often see the words perceiving that it is rational (or irrational) not to believe (or to believe) in spirits. Those who believe in the existence of a spirit, continuance after death, after-world, and spiritual phenomena are determined to be irrational. How do we perceive this rationality, then? A rational theory is not equivalent to a theory to which the entire world agrees. Otherwise, there will be almost no rationality in the world. Perhaps, we can list two methods of judgment—an aided judgment on rationality and a self-judgment on rationality. The former is a judgment based on the thoughts supported by the theories and the knowledge systems established and examined based on the objectively existing natural phenomena or the reproducible experimental outcome. On the other hand, the latter is an examination of the appropriateness through a judgment criterion based on the subject or instinct of the individuals. If the objective of the physics is to clarify the mechanism of the universe, and if the so-called spiritual phenomena are an emergence of an unrevealed structure of the universe that accompanies the reproducible natural phenomena, they all have to undergo an examination through the physical studies. If, after excluding the mental actions, misconceptions and fakes, there is still a possibility of the phenomena objectively being generated, this is a scientific agenda. If we call an attitude unscientific that unnecessarily attributes something to a spiritual thing that has no material basis, the waver of an effort to clarify would also be considered unscientific. When you make a judgment based on the aided judgment on rationality, it is important that you refrain from absolutizing the existing knowledge. A true scientific attitude would be to understand that the scientific knowledge shall always be updated, and recognize that it is yourself who update the knowledge.

What makes it confusing is that people tend to be influenced by a self-judgment on rationality which is strongly dependent on the instinct. A succeeding outcome of the aided rationality judgment which took more time and is based on a hardheaded insight is easily changed by an outcome of a self-judgment on rationality previously conducted, although the situation may vary depending on the insight of the former. Judging someone from an appearance is a good example. Although the appearance shows the personality of a person to some extent, we cannot fully evaluate the person's inner surface merely based on the appearance. The cases are not rare where we are surprised by the unpredicted quality of a person. However, the first impression has a strong influence on the evaluation of the person. In the training of a sales person or a seminar on communication, a significant emphasis is put on the importance of the first impression. This first impression directly acts on the self-judgment on rationality, that is, a rationality judgment after your style which is strongly based on your instinct. The TV shows and solicits to a religious group exactly make use of the feature of this rationality judgment of the people. In a TV show, an audience is easily transported to the terminal station on the rail through the performance effects such as an impression from the appearance, acts of the entertainers making a fuss, and intentional cheers of the studio viewers. These are all a result of a self-judgment on rationality.

Why do the spirits that were witnessed or taken by a photo have clothes on (though, of course, I would not want them to come out naked)? Where did they procure their clothes? Do changes similar to those which occur to the appearance of us living in this world caused by aging also occur after death? How do they occur and proceed? If they do not occur, what is the reason therefor? What is the mechanism by which the "death," that is, the transition of a spirit from this world to the after-world is invoked by the damage to the body? How much lower forms of animals have their own spirit? It is intuitively possible for anyone to raise any number of questions. It is easy to cut off the possibility of the continuance after death with these questions. However, this is the very opportunity where an aided rationality judgment, that is, a lucid judgment based on the modern science and the investigational activities toward the development of science will be required.

In reality, there are extremely few fields where the spirits and the continuance after death are considered as a scientific agenda. A predominant number of cases are just being ignored, the reason being that it is considered unscientific, rather than not attracting any interest. What does "unscientific" mean? Should it mean that "it is not yet explained by the modern science," the whole world would be full of unscientific stuff. An important factor which makes them being considered unscientific is the lack of reproducibility of the observational cases which indicate their existence (i.e., the spiritual experiences). Although a spirit photo or a movie can never be the pieces of evidence or a subject of study and thus should be excluded, a so-called spiritual experience cannot be any more than an unexpected and transient experience for the very person who had the experience. It is nothing other than an experience to be talked about in a past tense. In the process of examining and generalizing the hypothesis or a theory that have been made based on the natural phenomena, it is imperative that the observations and the experimental outcomes are accumulated in a reproducible manner. Under the same conditions, any person is able to obtain the same result through an experiment within the margin of error. That is what the natural phenomena should be. Needless to say, the difficulty of procuring these "same conditions" varies depending on the experiments, and there are indeed cases where it is extremely difficult to examine or to do a replication study. Having said this, the "difficulty" and the "impossibility" are evidently different. Even if it is indeed impossible, it is not a fair approach to the science to exclude it from the scope of scientific studies for such reason. The possibility of an "orthodox" observation is a different issue from whether something is true or not.

The scientists whom I raised in the outset who argue that the mind continues to exist after death have, among good company, reached their respective conclusions through their past actual and personal experiences such as their own near-death experiences or experiences of being present at some other persons' deaths. Although these conclusions have been reached based on their own rationality through a number of their individual experiences, they are not reproducible, and the experiments for examination are impossible. It is far from being recognized as a scientific truth if it cannot be examined, no matter how certain they are about their conclusion spun out through their separate and individual experiences. If a deductive method does not work, what about the opposite? Historically, there has been extremely few theories in the field of physics which support the continuance after death. There are cases where a would-be spiritual master uses a jargon, wearing a clothes of rationality, commentates on the phenomena through the mass media. They may refer to the terms such as an out-of-body experience, transition to an astral world, or "the evil spirits have been gathered through an accumulation of the negative energy." Such statements are vague in the definition of the used terms, and nobody talks about how they are related to the interpretations in terms of the natural science. If we are unable to understand them without standing on an equal footing with them, such "interpretation" would mean nothing. Even if the issue of the definition of the terms are cleared, if it cannot be examined by public, it is merely a straw man argument in that it would only be that the spiritual master's statement would be questioned.

Having said this, now we have with us a theory which indicates the forms of existence of a matter particle which is different from those in the existing theory based on the Parasite Fermion Model. In this circumstance, our future step would be the examination process of the theory, including the examination of the appropriateness of the theory and the scope of application thereof, and running of the predicted outcome against the observed facts. Particularly with respect to the theory of continuance after death, it means that we are going to step into a new stage of examination of a general theory, which is essentially different from an accumulation of the individual experiences that are unverifiable. This is a part of the studies of the theoretical physics, and thus, it is a new aspect which had never occurred in terms of the studies on the continuance after death. The significant point is that a new study on the continuance after death based on an inductive method has been made possible due to this Model.

The new forms of existence of the fermions, if revealed that it is true, will lead to a modification of the traditional viewpoints in various fields of science. One of such fields is the mind-body problem. Historically, from a materialistic perspective, efforts have been made to deduce the forms of existence of mind to a group of chemical or biological reactions inside the brain. The modern scientists who try to explain the mechanism under which the mind is generated seek the source of mind in the phenomena inside the brain such as the firing of the neurons. The best evidence of this theory would be to make an artificial device equipped with the firing of neurons, and display how they perform the movements of the mind including the thoughts, senses and emotions. This is because generally, a reproducibility must be guaranteed in the field of the natural science. However, as a matter of course, no such device exist at the moment. The very scientists who engage in the neuroscience honestly admit that the mechanism under which an image is generated and extinguishes inside the brain which is purely comprised of the materials and the mechanism by which the mind is generated as a result of the brain functions remain unknown. On one hand, they say that it is undoubtedly true that our mind arises from the firing of the neurons, but on the other hand, they admit that the studies have just begun to reveal the association between the factor and the mind generated as a result thereof. Some researchers seek the factors in something other than the firing of the neurons. All of these circumstances put together, we are not in a stage where we can determine that we have obtained some kind of conclusion regardless of the form thereof, based on the studies on the source of mind to date. Under the circumstance where we are still unable to identify the relationship between the neural activities and the generation of the mind, although it is the essence of the problem, and further where we have not even obtained any circumstantial evidence, it is too early to determine that the mind is generated through the neural network activities.

As such, the concept of the parasite fermion may release us from our search of the source of mind in the neural network right in front of us or in the brain. If we are in the first stage of the studies of mind from a natural scientific approach, we should not exclude any possibility from our study on this mind-body problem. The non-traditional and multi-dimensional forms of existence of the matter particles may be among such possibilities.

References

Alexander, Eben. 2014. *The Map of Heaven*. New York: Simon and Schuster.

Arkani-Hamed, Nima, Savas Dimopoulos, and Gia Dvali. 1998. "The Hierarchy Problem and New Dimensions at a Millimeter." *Physics Letters B* 429: 263-272.

Maeno, Takashi 2005. "How to Make a Conscious Robot –Fundamental Idea based on Passive Consciousness Model-." *Journal of the Robotics Society of Japan* 23: 51-62 (Japanese).

Randall, Lisa, and Raman Sundrum. 1999. "Large Mass Hierarchy from a Small Extra Dimension." *Physical Review Letters* 83: 3370-3373.

Smythies, John. 2003. "Space, Time and Consciousness." *Journal of Consciousness Studies* 10: 47-56.

Taneichi, Takashi. 2013. "Fermion Field in the Vicinity of a Brane." *Natural Science* 5: 1127-1131.

Tucker, Jim. 2008. *Life Before Life*. New York: St. Martin's Griffin.

Yahagi, Naoki. 2014. *Okagesama de Ikiru*. Tokyo: Gentosha.

Biographical Sketch

Name: Takashi Taneichi

Affiliation:
Institute of Theoretical Physics attached to International Research Institute

Education:
Tohoku University
Graduate School of University of Tokyo

Address:
1108-2, Sonno-cho, Inage-ku, Chiba-city, Chiba 263-0051, Japan

Research and Professional Experience:

Taneichi's career as a scientist started in the area of theoretical chemistry, mainly in the field of computer experiments on elementary processes of the photochemical reaction. Afterward, his research field has shifted to theoretical quantum optics. Concerning experimental outcomes of ultrafast transient phenomena in various molecular or solid state systems, theoretical interpretation for them had been given based on nonlinear optical theory. Prediction of experimental results and proposals for future experiments were also given based on theoretical consideration. He also trained graduate students as experimental researchers, relating to theoretical aspect of nonlinear optics. On 2009, he started a theoretical research on physical aspects of the brain science with respect to the quantum field theory. He got an insight concerning the relation between brain science and space science. Today, while teaching physics and mathematics at colleges, he is studying on the interdisciplinary field.

Professional Appointments: Researcher and Lecturer

Publications Last 3 Years:

Taneichi, T. (2013) Fermion fields in the vicinity of a brane. Natural Science, **5**, 1127-1131.

Takashi TANEICHI, "Does the Mind Really Reside in the Brain? - from the Viewpoint of the Modern Physics, Especially of the Hierarchy Problem -," J. Intl. Soc. Life Info. Sci. Vol.33, No.1, p.62-69.

Taneichi T. Physical Consciousness Outside the Brain: Parasite Fermion Model for Substance of Consciousness. NeuroQuantology 2015; 13: 134-140.

Takashi TANEICHI, ""New Horizon" of Physics with respect to the PF model," J. Intl. Soc. Life Info. Sci. Vol.33, No.2, p.145-149.

Takashi TANEICHI, "Fusion of the Space Science and the Brain Science – A New Possibility of the Materialism -," J. Intl. Soc. Life Info. Sci. Vol.33, No.2, p.153-162.

Reviewed by: Hideyuki Kokubo (International Research Institute).

In: Consciousness
Editor: Lloyd Alvarado

ISBN: 978-1-63485-023-0

Chapter 8

NEUROMODULATION: WHAT CAN IT TELL US ABOUT DISORDER OF CONSCIOUSNESS?

Rocco Salvatore Calabrò*[*] *and Antonino Naro
IRCCS Centro Neurolesi "Bonino-Pulejo", Messina, Italy

ABSTRACT

Neuromodulation consists in the alteration of neural activity through the delivery of electrical stimuli or chemical agents to targeted sites, as defined by the International Neuromodulation Society. It is possible to modify neurons' activity by shaping their synaptic plasticity properties through the application of electromagnetic stimuli, weak currents, or neurochemical agents. Electric currents may modify neurons' membrane polarity, thus affecting their synaptic and non-synaptic plasticity (which is the ability of synapses to strengthen or weaken over time in response to increases or decreases in their activity) according to, e.g., long-term potentiation or depression-like plasticity or spike-time dependent plasticity phenomena, depending in turn on possible several mechanisms, including depolarizing blockade, stochastic normalization of neural firing, axonal blockade, reduction of neural firing, and modulation of neural network oscillations. Electric current can be delivered by either electric stimulators, using constant or alternating currents (for transcranial electric stimulation), or magnetic stimulators (for transcranial magnetic stimulation), or implanted pulse generators wired to intra-cranial electrodes (for deep brain stimulation). In addition, technical advances have allowed other neuromodulation approaches, including auditory brainstem implant, functional electrical stimulation, peripheral nerve stimulation (vagus, hypoglossal, and occipital nerve), sacral neuromodulation, and spinal cord stimulation. Moreover, a newly emerging therapeutic approach, namely electroceutical, aims to find the electro-neural signature of disease at a cellular and neuronal network level, in order to restore the normal electro-signature patterns, potentially involving new neuromodulation therapy families, including optogenetics and nanotechnologies. Existing and emerging neuromodulation treatments have been employed in several diseases, including drug-resistant epilepsy, chronic pain

[*] Corresponding author: Rocco Salvatore Calabrò, IRCCS Centro Neurolesi "Bonino-Pulejo," S.S. 113, Contrada Casazza, 98124, Messina, Italy, phone: +3909060128954; fax: +3909060128950; e-mail: salbro77@tiscali.it.

conditions, Alzheimer's disease, stroke, spinal cord injury, sensory deficits, bladder or bowel or respiratory control, and chronic disorders of consciousness. Aim of this article is to review the current range of electric neuromodulation approaches in chronic disorders of consciousness, and their rationale of employment.

INTRODUCTION

Normal consciousness is the condition of the normal person when awake. In this state, the individual is fully responsive to a thought or perception and indicates by his behavior and speech the same awareness of self and environment as that of the examiner (Zeman 2008). Consciousness has two main clinical components: i) wakefulness, which is mediated by the ascending reticular activating system of the brainstem and its thalamic and hemispheric projections; and ii) awareness of one's self and the environment, which is mediated by the cerebral cortex, its intrinsic connections, and the networks with thalamus and other subcortical structures (Zeman 2006).

A disorder of consciousness (DOC) results when one or both of these components are compromised (Laureys et al. 2007). DOC represents a broad category encompassing a spectrum of cognitive dysfunction, ranging from mild confusional states, such as delirium, to dementia, coma, locked-in syndrome, vegetative state (VS), minimally conscious state (MCS), and brain death. Chronic DOC is a tragic and ironic failure of high-technology treatment to preserve or restore brain function, which is the primary aim of therapeutics. Management of DOC patients requires carefully reaching the correct diagnosis, pronouncing an evidence-based prognosis, and thoughtfully considering the medical, ethical, and legal elements of optimum treatment (Bernat 2006).

Development of interventions for treatment and rehabilitation of DOC patients is a crucial challenge for current and future generations of neuroscientists. Pharmacologic interventions, sensory stimulation, physical management procedures, hyperbaric oxygen therapy, and deep brain stimulation (DBS) have all been utilized for rehabilitative purposes. To date, there is no effective standardized treatment for DOC patients, even though many potential pharmacological, as well as non-pharmacological interventions, have been employed in the last decade. However, no treatment has been empirically shown to be clinically effective in restoring consciousness, cognition, or functional capacity. Nonetheless, there is growing evidence that some interventions may promote recovery, particularly in MCS patients. To this end, several drugs have been tested (including Zolpidem, Amantadine, Levodopa, Bromocriptine, Apomorphine, and Baclofen) (Clauss et al. 2000; Clauss et al. 2004; Whyte and Myers, 2009; Whyte et al. 2005; Zafonte et al. 2000; Giacino et al. 2012; Passler and Riggs, 2001; Fridman et al. 2010; Taira and Hori, 2007). Furthermore, invasive (IBS) and non-invasive brain stimulation electrophysiological tecniques (NIBS) have been developed to the end of either improving the differential diagnosis or ameliorating the level of consciousness. A promising and progressively growing field of non-pharmacological therapeutic trials for DOC patients is represented by the application of IBS and NIBS electrophysiological techniques.

RATIONALE OF BS TECHNIQUES IN DOC

As general rule, “a certain degree of cortical activation” is necessary in order to be aware, independently from arousal (Zeman 2001). Nonetheless, DOC implies the potential deterioration of an extremely great number of neuropsychological variables, neuronal structures, and neural circuits supporting consciousness generation and maintenance (Rosanova et al. 2012). Thus, the choice of the best potentially therapeutic interventions remains extremely challenging.

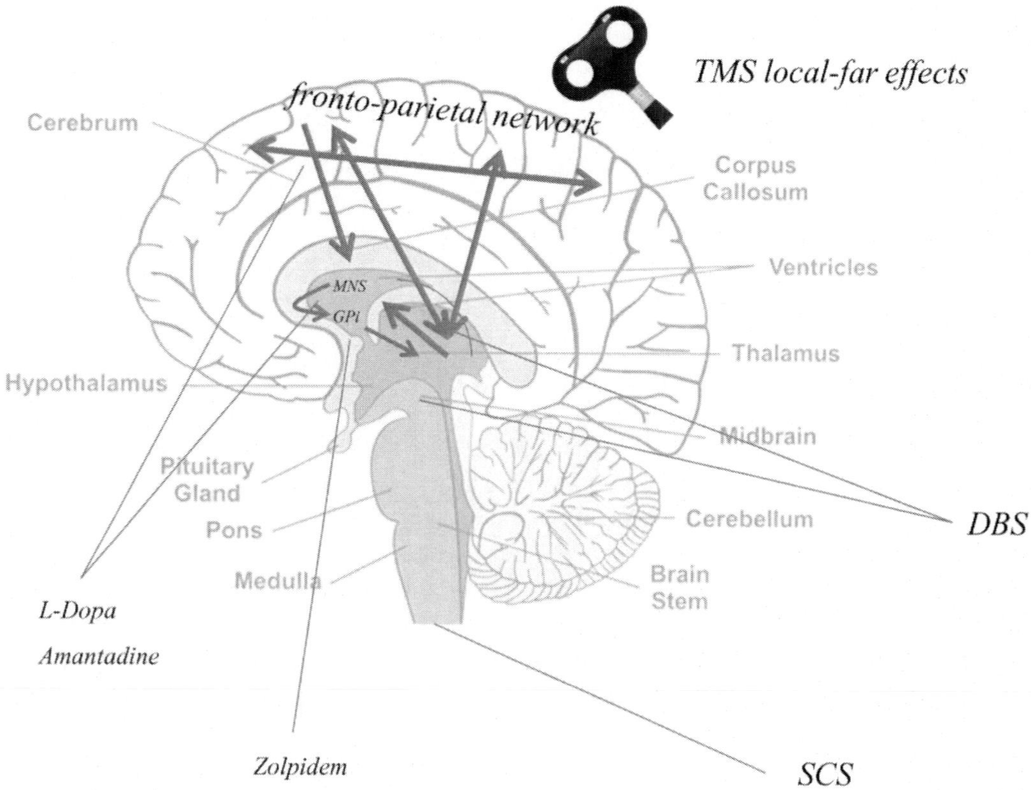

Figure 1. The figure summarizes the main sites of NM. rTMS can trigger locally and, indirectly, far targes within a wide fronto-parietal network (FPN) (including supplementary motor, DLPFC, M1, occipital and parietal cortices) sustaining arousal, vigilance, movement organization, and cognition. Such networks activate the medium spiny neurons (MSN) of the striatum and the thalamus. DBS targets central thalamus, the centro-median parafascicular complex in the non-specifc nucleus, and the nucleus cuneiformis of the mesencephalic reticular formation, through glutamatergic afferents activation. The thalamus excites the FPN and the MSN (blue arrows) that in turn inhibits globus pallidum internum (GPi) and therefore the thalamus (red arrows). SCS acts on spinal cord at cervical level. For completition, the targets activated by L-Dopa, amantadine, and zolpidem are also included.

It is possible by means of IBS to directly engage the diffusely-projecting and unspecific thalamo-cortical radiations, and the anatomical connections between mesencephalic and diencephalic structures, which are involved in the arousal system, as described in neuroanatomical studies. The link between arousal and awareness was demonstrated by Morison and Dempsey (1942), Moruzzi and Magoun (1949), and Dieckmann (1968), who showed a "cortical recruiting response" to the low-frequency stimulation of unspecific thalamic nuclei characterized by an incremental high-voltage synchronization waves and a desynchronization of the EEG pattern to the high-frequency stimulation. Therefore, the rationale of stimulating arousal system is to indirectly obtain a global cortical activation, taking advantage of the diffuse-patterned modality of synapsing of these thalamo-cortical projections, which are the common final pathway of the arousal system.

On the other hand, there are several attempts to ameliorate awareness by means of transcranial magnetic stimulation (TMS) and transcranial electric stimulation, which entrain descending cortico-subcortical pathways through triggering either directly cerebral cortex or indirectly subcortical structures. Indeed, such approaches can also modulate the synaptic activity of the mesolimbic and mesostriatal dopaminergic systems, increasing the release of dopamine in subcortical structure -such as the dorsal hippocampus and nucleus accumbens- (Keck et al. 2002), being thus potentially able to modulate also the subcortical arousal system, if the correct target is individuated. The main approaches and their targets are summarized in Figure 1.

Invasive Brain Stimulation

Deep Brain Stimulation (DBS)

DBS consists in implanting a kind of pacemaker that delivers electrical stimuli into specific brain targets. The structure that was targeted for the first time ever in patients with post-traumatic chronic MCS was the centrolateral thalamic nucleus (Sturm et al. 1979).

DBS targets the central thalamus (including anterior and posterior intralaminar nuclei and the paralaminar portions of related thalamic association nuclei- median dorsalis, ventral anterior, ventral lateral, and inferior pulvinar), since its primary role in arousal regulation (mesocircuit model) rather than in background arousal state control (Schiff 2010). In particular, the central lateral intralaminar nucleus and adjacent paralaminar components of the central thalamus (rich in calbindin staining neurons that strongly project to the supragranular cortical regions) are of actual interest. In addition, its neurons are selectively vulnerable to a severe BI.

The criteria for accessing DBS should include a desynchronization on continuous EEG frequency analysis, and a preservation of the V wave of the auditory evoked potentials and N20 of somatosensory evoked potentials (Tsubokawa et al. 1990; Yamamoto et al. 2003). Biphasic stimuli with square-wave pulses (90ms per phase), delivered in 100ms trains, with a rate of 130 pulses/sec, intertrain interval of 1.25s, with an intensity of 2-3mA are usually employed for anterior intralaminar thalamic DBS (Cohadon et al. 1984; Cohadon et al. 1985; Tsubokawa et al. 1990).

The rationale for central thalamic DBS is to enhance the arousal in an attempt to improve the level of awareness, since arousal regulation adjusts brain activation in order to allow effective behaviors during tasks requiring adjustments in sustained attention, working memory, and motor preparation (Yamamoto et al. 2010; Schiff et al. 2007) (Tables 1 and 2).

Table 1. Main DBS studies in DOC patients

N. Patients	Study type	Results	Reference
8 VS	PC	4: VS >> MCS	Tsubokawa 1990
21 VS 5 MCS	PC	8: VS >>MCS 4: MCS >> eMCS	Yamamoto 2003
25	PC	13 recovered some degree of consciousness	Cohadon 1993
1	double-blind alternating cross-over	behavioural improvements	Schiff 2007

Legend: VS, vegetative state; MCS, minimally conscious state; eMCS emergence from MCS; PC prospective cohort.

Table 2. Rationale for Anterior Intralaminar Thalamic Nuclei DBS in Severe Brain Injury (BI)

BI usually impairs central thalamus	Thalamic dysfunctions are due to an anatomical connectivity breakdown between cortex and forebrain.
	Cortico-thalamic neurons within the cortico–striato-pallidal–thalamo-cortical system are negatively affected by the reduced background activity in the cortico-thalamic system.
Central thalamus DBS may facilitate a normal central thalamus outflow, which regulates a broad network including cortical, basal ganglia, and thalamic loops, sustaining behavioral and cognitive processing.	
Specific parts of intralaminar nuclei oversee the integration of long-range cortico–cortical and cortico–striato-pallidal–thalamo-cortical networks.	
Maintaining the activation of central thalamus may produce long-lasting changes in behavioral responsiveness	

Typically, central thalamus receives inputs from the neuromodulatory “arousal systems” coupled with strong cortico-thalamic and mesencephalic excitatory neurotransmission, thus setting at higher level the overall cerebral background activity (Nieuwenhuys et al. 1979; Morel et al. 1997). To this end, DBS should elicit action potentials along the axons of central thalamic neurons, consequently depolarizing target neurons within the cerebral cortex (particularly regions of medial frontal and prefrontal cortex) and striatum, by fostering the release of excitatory neurotransmitter at the thalamocortical and thalamostriatal synapse (Bruno et al. 2011) (Figure 2).

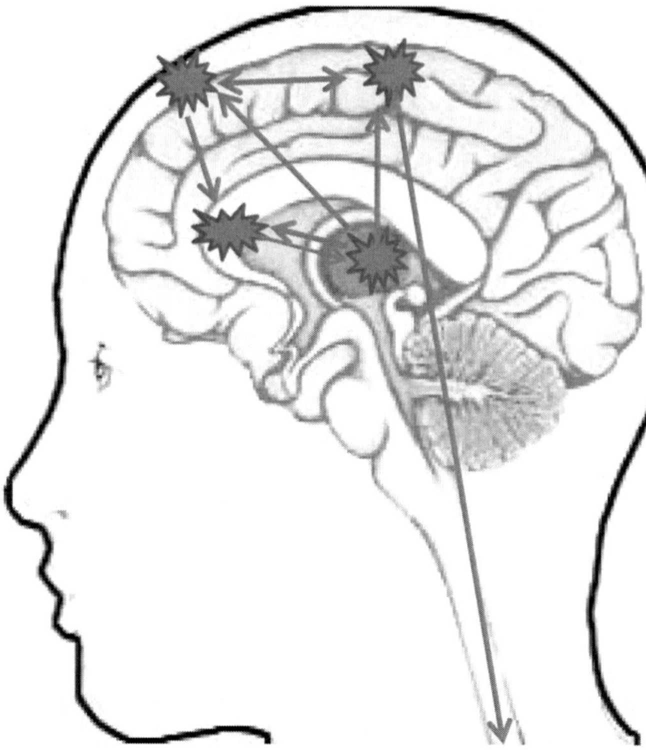

Figure 2. Effects of DBS. It may induce: i) depolarization of cortical and striatal neurons (blue and red cells); ii) inhibition of the pallido-thalamic projections and release of thalamo-cortical transmission (red and thalamic cells –blue one inside the green area); iii) facilitation of cortico-cortical connections (cortical blue cells); and iv) facilitation of synaptic plasticity (everywhere).

The medium spiny striatal neurons (MSNs) may have a striking role. In fact, the background high levels of cortico-striatal and thalamo-striatal firing (Behrens et al. 2003) may be significantly weakened in presence of an impaired MSN output, strengthened inhibitory pallido-thalamic outputs, and broad passive inhibition of thalamic neurons (following a depletion of excitatory synaptic contacts due to cerebral damage) (Sadikot and Rymar, 2009). Activation of the MSNs may thus have a particularly strong impact in releasing both thalamo-cortical and thalamo-striatal outflow in a chronically underactive brain. Facilitation of long-range cortico-cortical interactions by central thalamic outflow is proposed as one of the functional roles for central thalamic neurons, thus representing the main target of DBS (Schiff 2008; Pinault 2004).

Spinal Cord Stimulation (SCS)

Another approach indirectly perturbing the arousal structure consists in the cervical SCS (Kanno et al. 1987, 1989) by means of epidural electrodes. Many patients showed clinical, electrophysiological and blood perfusion changes, with a more widespread alpha waves, and some neurological improvements within 2 weeks from the beginning of the treatment, according to age and structural cerebral integrity (Morita et al. 2007; Kanno et al. 2009; Matsui et al. 1989). SCS usually triggers the dorsal/posterior column at C2-C4 level. Pulses with 120ms width of and 2-3V amplitude are delivered at 70Hz, using a cyclic mode of 15min-on/15min-off. Diencephalic damage or cerebral atrophy are the exclusion criteria for SCS implementation.

SCS could trigger spino-thalamo-cortical projections in a manner similar to DBS, although with less target specificity and strength on thalamus. In addition, the twitches-related feedback inputs could indirectly stimulate the frontal neocortex that is part of the awareness and attention network (Yamamoto et al. 2010, 2012). A prospective cohort study documented a clinical improvement in about 40% of the enrolled VS individuals (Kanno et al. 1989).

NON-INVASIVE BRAIN STIMULATION

Transcranial Magnetic Stimulation

TMS delivers rapidly alternating magnetic fields that non-invasively induces neural activity by means of long-term changes in neural plasticity[1] (Butler and Wolf, 2007; Duffau 2006; Purves 2008; Cooke and Bliss 2006; Massey and Bashir 2007; Figiel et al. 1998; O'Reardon et al. 2007; George et al. 2010).

TMS is a relative safety method, since it may induce only transient side effects. Although, the major concern with TMS is the risk of seizure-induction (Rossi et al. 2009; Wassermann et al. 1996).

Despite the potential risks, TMS has been employed in DOC (Demirtas-Tatlidede et al. 2012; Castel-Lacanal et al. 2014; Knoch et al. 2006). Louise-Bender Pape et al. (2009) examined the safety and restorative effects of rTMS by attempting to restore consciousness following a severe traumatic brain injury (TBI). They applied a repetitive TMS (rTMS) to the right dorsolateral prefrontal cortex (DLPFC) in a chronic DOC 26-year-old male after a severe TBI. The authors reported shift from VS to MCS, characterized by an evident improvement in motor skills, visual ability, vocalizations, and basic communication up to one year, without any significant side-effect.

Manganotti and colleagues (2013) administered high-frequency rTMS to primary motor cortex (M1) in three patients (two MCS and one VS) suffering from severe TBI. There were neither clinical responses nor adverse effects. Indeed, the ineffectiveness of rTMS to M1 in DOC individuals has been recently confirmed (Cincotta et al. 2015).

Instead, a single session of rTMS to DLPFC in DOC patients has furnished promising results (Naro et al. 2015). Ten post-anoxic VS subjects underwent a single/paired pulse TMS paradigm evaluating the inhibitory and facilitatory intra-M1 circuits. In addition, several inter-regional interactions between M1, dorsal and ventral premotor, supplementary motor, and posterior parietal cortex areas were investigated by means of dual-coil TMS technique.

---

[1] Cerebral plasticity is the ability of the brain to reorganize itself, enabling short- and long-term remodeling of neural communication that outlasts an experimental manipulation or period of training. It can occur at various levels of brain organization (from the ultrastructural to synaptic level) and the goal of these processes is the improvement of the functioning of brain networks.

Long Term Potentiation (LTP) An *increase* in synaptic strength that could last for days or even weeks and months, which could be induced in experimental conditions as a result of brief high-frequency stimulation.

Long Term Depression (LTD) An activity-dependent *reduction* in the efficacy of neuronal synapses lasting hours or longer following a long patterned stimulus, that occurs in many areas of the CNS with varying mechanisms depending upon brain region and developmental progress.

Therefore, the patients received a 10Hz rTMS to the right DLPFC. There were not adverse events and three patients showed a transient, but significant, awareness improvement, associated with a reshape of brain connectivity. Therefore, a single session of 10Hz rTMS over the right DLPFC may transiently improve consciousness and partially restore the connectivity within several cortical areas in some VS patients. It should be further evaluated whiter such approach could be employed in either treating DOC or identifying DBS candidate.

Transcranial Direct Current Stimulation (tDCS)

tDCS delivers low amplitude currents by means of anodal or cathodal stimulation, which can alter the neuronal firing (Demirtas-Tatlidede et al. 2012), and induce focal and far shifts of cortical excitability (Nitsche and Paulus, 2000, 2001). Adverse effects of tDCS treatment include moderate fatigue (35%), mild headache (12%), nausea (3%), and a transient itching sensation in area of stimulation (Nitsche and Paulus, 2009; Poreisz et al. 2007). Interestingly, no cases of seizure have been reported in relation to the use of tDCS as a clinical intervention (Nitsche et al. 2003).

Angelakis et al. (2014) treated TBI VS patients by means of a weekly left DLPFC tDCS. The efficacy of tDCS intervention depended on the severity of DOC (with MCS patients responding better than VS), and the time since injury (with more recent injuries showing better responses).

Thibaut et al. (2014) performed a large-sample sham-controlled randomized double-blind study to determine the effect of left DLPFC tDCS in DOC patients. A subset of patients showed a transient improvement in coma recovery scale-revised (CRS-R) score following a single session of tDCS. A group effect was seen for the MCS group, but not for the VS one. No adverse tDCS-related side effects were detected.

Recently, the usefulness of tDCS has been re-assessed by using anodal tDCS over the orbitofrontal cortex (Naro et al. 2015b). Although such approach did not ameliorate consciousness level assessed through CRS-R, it identified electrophysiological parameters that might potentially express the presence of residual networks sustaining fragmentary behavioral patterns, even when no conscious behavior can be observed. Orbitofrontal tDCS seems therefore useful by a diagnostic point of view.

On the other hand, Sharova and colleagues (2007) induced a clinical improvement in 5 out of 6 DOC patients (concerning emotional reactions and fixation of gaze) by means of a repetitive transcranial electric current stimulation.

Median Nerve Stimulation (MNS)

MNS has been employed since the median nerve is a sort of "peripheral portal to the central nervous system" (Cooper et al. 2005), thanks to synaptic connections between the reticular component of the median nerve ascending pathway and the brainstem component of the arousal regulation system (Parent 1996). Modest effects of MNS are although reported in literature in DOC individuals (Liu et al. 2003; Yokoyama et al. 1996) (Table 3).

Table 3. Studies on median merve stimulation (MNS) in DOC patients

N. Patients	Study type	Results	Ref
6	PC, double-blind	Earlier arousal, better functional and cognitive outcome	Cooper 1999
10	Double-blind randomized controlled trial	No significant differences in outcomes	Peri 2001
Review of MNS versus standard rehabilitation		Earlier arousal, better functional and cognitive outcome	Cooper 2003
6	PC	4 patients recovered from coma within 35 days	Liu 2003

Legend: see Table 1.

Notably, there are some specific exclusion criteria: severe cardiac arrhythmias, implanted defibrillators, pacemakers, uncontrolled seizures, cervical spinal cord or brachial plexus injury, large intracranial hematomas, gunshot wound to the head, right median nerve injury, and positive pregnancy (Peri et al. 2001). However, further studies should be fostered, considering the low cost and the security of this procedure, although the neurophysiological mechanism of action is still poorly understood and the real efficacy is doubtful.

Last Advances

Paired Associative Stimulation (PAS) has come to prominence as a potential therapeutic intervention for the treatment of brain injury/disease, and as an experimental method by which to investigate Hebbian plasticity principles in humans (Wolters et al. 2003; McKay et al. 2002; Stefan et al. 2002). Prototypically, a single electrical stimulus is directed to a peripheral nerve before a TMS pulse delivered to the contralateral M1. Repeated pairing of the stimuli (i.e., association) over an extended period may increase or decrease the excitability of corticospinal projections from M1, in a manner that depends on the interstimulus interval (ISI). It has been suggested that these effects represent forms of associative long-term potentiation (LTP) and depression (LTD) processes that bear resemblance to spike-timing dependent plasticity (STDP) (Nitsche et al. 2007; Stefan et al. 2004; Quartarone et al. 2003; Müller-Dahlhaus et al. 2010). Taking into account the large body of empirical evidence that has emerged since the cardinal features of PAS were described, and the succeeding variations from the original protocol, it is opportune to consider whether the phenomenology of PAS remains consistent although changing the characteristic features. This obviously affects the interpretation of PAS after-effects in relation to the specific cellular pathways that are putatively engaged (including those that adhere to the rules of STDP). Indeed, the mechanisms that contribute to LTP and LTD phenomena induced by PAS differ according to the precise nature of the induction protocol that has been used.

Recently, different type of sensory stimulation have been employed in PAS protocols in DOC patients. Such studied were primarily aimed to differentiate clinical entities, including VS, MCS, and functional locked-in syndrome. However, these approaches also propose themselves as promising treatment strategies in DOC patients, since they were able to strength wide fronto-parietal network connectivity, and transiently improve the level of consciousness in MCS and even in some VS patients.

A first approach is represented by the audio-motor PAS (Naro et al. 2015c), which consisted in the application of rTMS over the left M1 paired to transauricular alternating current stimulation. This protocol induced a potentiating of either the audio-motor integration or M1 excitability, paired to a CRS-R improvement in all of the MCS patients. Similarly, a visuo-motor PAS (consisting of a double tDCS on the DLPFCs and the parieto-occipital areas, paired to a transorbital alterning current stimulation) consistently shaped the visuomotor and premotor-motor connectivity, paired to a CRS-R improvement, in all of the MCS patients and even in one VS (Naro et al. 2015d).

A particularly important issue in DOC patients is represented by conscious pain perception. Since it has been affirmed that a potential pain experience should be considered even in VS individuals, independently from their communication skills (De Salvo et al. 2015; de Tommaso et al. 2013, 2015), a PAS employing pain pathways has been applied in DOC. A first protocol attempted to entrain the γ-band oscillatory activity (γBO) in centroparietal areas, considered as a marker of either subjective pain perception processes or pain-related motor behavior preparation, by means of rTMS to anterior cingulate cortex (Naro et al. 2015e). Some DOC patients were responsive to this treatment, thus suggesting that these ones may not be able to respond to pain stimuli, although awarely feeling them. The possibility of detecting residual pain perceptions by means of a noninvasive neuromodulation paradigm, studying the correlation between the anterior cingulate cortex and centroparietal γBO, may help clinicians to better assess pain in such individuals.

In another PAS protocol, pairs of nociceptive laser stimuli were paired to rTMS pulses to M1 (namely, laser-PAS) in an attempt to shape pain-motor integration (Naro et al. 2015f). This was achieved in some post-anoxic VS individuals, who showed a restored pain-motor integration with a partial M1 excitability modification. Laser-PAS seems therefore a feasible and suitable technique in order to induce plastic changes within pain matrix in some VS individuals, allowing the production of "cortical" responses to painful stimuli, which are signs of at least partially ("focal") preserved consciousness.

Hypotheses of New Neuromodulation Approaches

New NIBS paradigms employs periodical electric currents (i.e., alternating current stimulation -tACS) (Herrmann et al., 2013), or random time-varying waveforms (transcranial random noise stimulation -tRNS) (Terney et al., 2008). Even if still unemployed, they may contribute in the future to more effective NIBS efforts in DOC patients.

In fact, tACS up- and down-regulates the neuronal firing rate affecting neuronal spike timing at a specific frequency, with the potential to synchronize or desynchronize activity between targeted brain regions (Reato et al., 2010; Fries, 2005). This could allow modulating brain oscillations and inter-area communication in a very-specific manner. Such a paradigm may be used for tailoring highly individualized interventions aimed at coupling or decoupling activities between specific brain regions within fronto-parietal networks sustaining awareness. On the other hand, tRNS deliver alternating currents at random frequencies, thus conjugating alternating and direct currents (neither anodal nor cathodal) (Miniussi et al., 2013). tRNS has been shown to elicit powerful cortical excitability modulations with longer after-effects than tDCS (Chaieb et al., 2011). This approach may provide a new way to modulate excitability in damaged brains, either locally or along fronto-parietal networks sustaining awareness.

MOVING TOWARDS A STRATEGY

As shown so far, a relatively small arsenal of therapeutic options is available concerning the amelioration of awareness level in DOC patients. Although, there are no clear evidences that can support the best BS choice for a patient.

It has been proposed that pharmacological treatments should work better in the acute phase, promoting the arousal (Saniova et al. 2004). After 4-6 weeks of unsuccessful pharmacological treatment (including L-Dopa, methylphenidate, bromocriptine, or amantadine) it would be necessary to adopt BS strategies. The MNS (paired to multi-channel sensory stimulation) is a suitable and of easy application rehabilitative option (Cooper et al. 1999). In treated patients, a positive trend towards recovery of consciousness was observed and the treatment could be considered a helpful tool if a definite therapeutic protocol would be established.

As a second step, it could be necessary to introduce tDCS and/or rTMS. Although, the potential implications of this technique are not fully understood. Nonetheless, the lack of response to rTMS/tDCS could be considered as a negative prognostic factor for awareness recovery. In addition, the identification of suitable targets remains a major problem.

Before employing more invasive BS techniques, it could be useful to try with a minimally invasive BS approach, i.e., the SCS. Nonetheless, this seems to improve vegetative and biological parameters, but poorly the clinical picture.

Thereafter, more aggressive techniques should be attempted in the non responsive patients, above all when dealing with young individuals (<40 years) and a short disease duration (<3 months). In fact, the probability of spontaneous arousal is low after these temporal ranges. The most promising technique in such situations is the DBS. Even if the great part of DBS trials included patients in a 3-6 months of disease duration, positive responses might be observed also after 6 months, above all in MCS cases with a consistent preservation of cerebral integrative networks (Schiff et al. 2007).

It is well known that a first important step in rehabilitation setting is the correct assessment of patients' clinical status. In the neurostimulation field, this issue becomes striking, since DBS can be effective in helping patients to emerge from reduced consciousness conditions according to their baseline clinical status. In fact, the patients showing relatively preserved cortical networks (above all within the anterior forebrain) and primary damages in arousal centers, better recover consciousness. The problem of the correct identification of preserved connectivity could be solved by means of TMS-EEG approaches (e.g., Sarasso et al. 2014; Napolitani et al. 2014; Massimini et al. 2012), beyond functional neuroimaging. To date, clinical application of DBS in MCS is strongly promising to ameliorate functional executive skills and to emerge from MCS (Schiff et al. 2007; Yamamoto and Katayama, 2003). Unfortunately, there are not sufficient evidences for VS patients. In analogy to NIBS, the non-responsiveness to DBS should be considered as a negative prognostic factor.

Conclusion

BS approaches could represent an efficacious way to treat DOC patients. Further large-sample studies should validate the aforementioned successful stimulation procedures. Even though there is a dealt of still unsolved problems (including targets, procedures, time of application, and candidate selection), there are anyway sufficient elements to affirm that BS can improve the level of consciousness.

More efforts should be made in order to define a standardized procedure, although disorders of consciousness represent a complex and wide spectrum of disorders that make hard a rigorous and standardized approach for treatment. Therefore, each patient should be considered as a single particular case, according to the specific underlying pathophysiological conditions.

Hence, in parallel to pharmacological procedures (Beis et al. 2009), future studies should be fostered to the end of combining different electrophysiological techniques, also targeting different components of the nervous systems.

The Authors state neither financial support nor conflict of interest.

References

Angelakis, E; Liouta, E; Andreadis, N; Korfias, S; Ktonas, P; Stranjalis, G; Sakas, DE. Transcranial direct current stimulation effects in disorders of consciousness. *Arch Phys Med Rehabil*. 2014;95:283–9.

Behrens, TEJ; Johansen-Berg, H; Woolrich, MW; Smith, SM; Wheeler-Kingshott, CA; Boulby, PA; Barker, GJ; Sillery, EL; Sheehan, K; Ciccarelli, O; Thompson, AJ; Brady, JM; Matthews, PM. Non-invasive mapping of connections between human thalamus and cortex using diffusion imaging. *Nat Neurosci* 2003;6(7):750–7.

Beis, JM; Seyer, JL; Brugerolle, B; Le Chapelain, L; Thisse, MO; Mainard, D; Paysant, J; André, JM. Care protocol for persistent vegetative states (PVS) and minimally conscious state (MSC) in Lorraine: retrospective study over an 18-year period. *Ann Phys Rehabil Med*. 2009;52:374-81.

Bernat, JL. Chronic disorders of consciousness. *Lancet*. 2006;367:1181-92.

Bruno, MA; Vanhaudenhuyse, A; Thibaut, A; Moonen, G; Laureys, S. From unresponsive wakefulness to minimally conscious PLUS and functional locked-in syndromes: recent advances in our understanding of disorders of consciousness. *J Neurol* 2011;258:1373–84.

Butler, AJ; Wolf, SL. Putting the brain on the map: use of transcranial magnetic stimulation to assess and induce cortical plasticity of upper extremity movement. *PhysTher* 2007.

Castel-Lacanal, E; Tarri, M; Loubinoux, I; Gasq, D; de Boissezon, X; Marque, P; Simonetta-Moreau, M. Transcranial magnetic stimulation in brain injury. *Ann Fr Anesth Reanim*. 2014;33:83–7.

Chaieb, L; Paulus, W; Antal, A. Evaluating aftereffects of short-duration transcranial random noise stimulation on cortical excitability. *Neural Plast*. 2011; 2011: 105927.

Cincotta, M; Giovannelli, F; Chiaramonti, R; Bianco, G; Godone, M; Battista, D; Cardinali, C; Borgheresi, A; Sighinolfi, A; D'Avanzo, AM; Breschi, M; Dine, Y; Lino, M; Zaccara, G; Viggiano, MP; Rossi, S. No effects of 20 Hz-rTMS of the primary motor cortex in vegetative state: A randomised, sham-controlled study. *Cortex.* 2015;71:368-76.

Clauss, R; Sathekge, M; Nel, W. Transient improvement of spinocerebellar ataxia with zolpidem. *N Engl J Med* 2004; 351:511-2.

Clauss, RP; Guldenpfennig, WM; Nel, HW; Sathekge, MM; Venkannagari, RR. Extraordinary arousal from semi-comatose state on zolpidem. A case report. *S Afr Med J* 2000; 90: 68-72.

Cohadon, F; Richer, E. Deep cerebral stimulation in patients with post-traumatic vegetative state, 25 cases. *Neurochirurgie 1*993;39:281-92.

Cohadon, F; Richer, E; Rougier, A; Deliac, P; Loiseau, H. Deep brain stimulations in cases of prolonged post-traumatic unconsciousness. In: Gybels J, Hitchcock ER, Ostertag C, Rossi GF, Siegfried J, Szikla G, editors. Advances in Stereotactic and Functional Neurosurgery. Vienna: Springer-Verlag;1984; 535–7.

Cohadon, F; Richer, E; Rougier, A; Deliac, P; Loiseau, H. Deep brain stimulation in cases of prolonged post-traumatic unconsciousness. In: Lazorthes Y, Upton ARM, editors. Neurostimulation: an overview. Mt. Kisco, New York: Futura Publishing Company; 1985; 247–50.

Cooke, SF; Bliss, TV. Plasticity in the human central nervous system. Brain 2006.

Cooper, EB; Cooper, JB. Electrical treatment of coma via the median nerve. *Acta Neurochir Suppl* 2003;87:7-10.

Cooper, EB; Scherder, EJ; Cooper, JB. Electrical treatment of reduced consciousness: experience with coma and Alzheimer's disease. *Neuropsychol Rehabil* 2005; 15: 389-405.

Cooper, JB; Jane, J; Alves, W; Cooper, E. Right median nerve electrical stimulation to hasten awakening from coma. *Brain Inj* 1999;13:261-7.

De Salvo, S; Naro, A; Bonanno, L; Russo, M; Muscarà, N; Bramanti, P; Marino, S. Assessment of nociceptive system in vegetative and minimally conscious state by using laser evoked potentials. *Brain Inj.* 2015;29:1467-74.

de Tommaso, M; Navarro, J; Lanzillotti, C; Ricci, K; Buonocunto, F; Livrea, P; Lancioni, GE. Cortical responses to salient nociceptive and not nociceptive stimuli in vegetative and minimal conscious state. *Front Hum Neurosci.* 2015;9:17.

de Tommaso, M; Navarro, J; Ricci, K; Lorenzo, M; Lanzillotti, C; Colonna, F; Resta, M; Lancioni, G; Livrea, P. Pain in prolonged disorders of consciousness: laser evoked potentials findings in patients with vegetative and minimally conscious states. *Brain Inj.* 2013;27:962-72.

Demirtas-Tatlidede, A; Vahabzadeh-Hagh, AM; Bernabeu, M; Tormos, JM; Pascual-Leone, A. Noninvasive brain stimulation in traumatic brain injury. *J Head Trauma Rehabil.* 2012;27:274–92.

Demirtas-Tatlidede, A; Vahabzadeh-Hagh, AM; Bernabeu, M; Tormos, JM; Pascual-Leone, A. Noninvasive brain stimulation in traumatic brain injury. *J Head Trauma Rehabil.* 2012;27:274–92.

Dieckmann, G. Cortical synchronized and desynchronized responses evoked by stimulation of the putamen and pallidum in cats. *J Neurol Sci* 1968; 7: 385-91.

Duffau, H. Brain plasticity: from pathophysiological mechanisms to therapeutic applications. *J Clin Neurosci* 2006.

Figiel, GS; Epstein, C; McDonald, WM; Amazon-Leece, J; Figiel, L; Saldivia, A; Glover, S. The use of rapid-rate transcranial magnetic stimulation (rTMS) in refractory depressed patients. *J Neuropsychiatry Clin Neurosci.* 1998;10:20–5.

Fridman, EA; Krimchansky, BZ; Bonetto, M; Galperin, T; Gamzu, ER; Leiguarda, RC; Zafonte, R. Continuous subcutaneous apomorphine for severe disorders of consciousness after traumatic brain injury. *Brain Inj* 2010; 24: 636-41.

Fries, P. A mechanism for cognitive dynamics: neuronal communication through neuronal coherence. *Trends Cogn. Sci.* 2005; 9:474–480.

George, MS; Lisanby, SH; Avery, D; McDonald, WM; Durkalski, V; Pavlicova, M; Anderson, B; Nahas, Z; Bulow, P; Zarkowski, P; Holtzheimer, PE 3rd; Schwartz, T; Sackeim, HA. Daily left prefrontal transcranial magnetic stimulation therapy for major depressive disorder: a sham-controlled randomized trial. *Arch Gen Psychiatry*; 2010;67:507–16.

Giacino, JT; Whyte, J; Bagiella, E; Kalmar, K; Childs, N; Khademi, A; Eifert, B; Long, D; Katz, DI; Cho, S; Yablon, SA; Luther, M; Hammond, FM; Nordenbo, A; Novak, P; Mercer, W; Maurer-Karattup, P; Sherer, M. Placebo-controlled trial of amantadine for severe traumatic brain injury. *N Engl J Med* 2012;366:819-26.

Herrmann, CS; Rach, S; Neuling, T; Strüber, D. Transcranial alternating current stimulation: a review of the underlying mechanisms and modulation of cognitive processes. *Front. Hum. Neurosci.* 2013;7:279.

Kanno, T; Kamei, Y; Yokoyama, T; Jain, VK. Neurostimulation for patients in vegetative status. *Pacing Clin Electrophysiol* 1987; 10:207-8.

Kanno, T; Kamel, Y; Yokoyama, T; Shoda, M; Tanji, H; Nomura, M. Effects of dorsal column spinal cord stimulation (DCS) on reversibility of neuronal function--experience of treatment for vegetative states. *Pacing Clin Electrophysiol* 1989; 12: 733-8.

Kanno, T; Morita, I; Yamaguchi, S; Yokoyama, T; Kamei, Y; Anil, SM; Karagiozov, KL. Dorsal column stimulation in persistent vegetative state. *Neuromodulation* 2009; 12: 33-8.

Keck, ME; Welt, T; Muller, MB; Erhardt, A; Ohl, F; Toschi, N; Holsboer, F; Sillaber, I. Repetitive transcranial magnetic stimulation increases the release of dopamine in the mesolimbic and mesostriatal system. *Neuropharmacology* 2002;43: 101-9.

Knoch, D; Gianotti, LR; Pascual-Leone, A; Treyer, V; Regard, M; Hohmann, M; Brugger, P. Disruption of right prefrontal cortex by low-frequency repetitive transcranial magnetic stimulation induces risk-taking behavior. *J Neurosci.* 2006;26:6469–72.

Laureys, S; Perrin, F; Brédart, S. Self-consciousness in non-communicative patients. *Conscious Cogn.* 2007;16:722-41.

Liu, JT; Wang, CH; Chou, IC; Sun, SS; Koa, CH; Cooper, E. Regaining consciousness for prolonged comatose patients with right median nerve stimulation. *Acta Neurochir Suppl* 2003; 87: 11-4.

Louise-Bender Pape, T; Rosenow, J; Lewis, G; Ahmed, G; Walker, M; Guernon, A; Roth, H; Patil, V. Repetitive transcranial magnetic stimulation-associated neurobehavioral gains during coma recovery. *Brain Stimul.* 2009;2:22–35.

Manganotti, P; Formaggio, E; Storti, SF; Fiaschi, A; Battistin, L; Tonin, P; Piccione, F; Cavinato, M. Effect of high-frequency repetitive transcranial magnetic stimulation on brain excitability in severely brain-injured patients in minimally conscious or vegetative state. *Brain Stimul.* 2013;6:913–21.

Massey, PV; Bashir, ZI. Long-term depression: multiple forms and implications for brain function. *Trends Neurosci* 2007.

Massimini, M; Ferrarelli, F; Sarasso, S; Tononi, G. Cortical mechanisms of loss of consciousness: insight from TMS/EEG studies. *Arch Ital Biol.* 2012;150:44-55.

Matsui, T; Asano, T; Takakura, K; Yamada, R; Hosobuchi, Y. Beneficial effects of cervical spinal cord stimulation (cSCS) on patients with impaired consciousness: a preliminary report. *Pacing Clin Electrophysiol* 1989; 12: 718-25.

McKay, DR; Ridding, MC; Thompson, PD; Miles, TS. Induction of persistent changes in the organisation of the human motor cortex. *Exp Brain Res.* 2002; 143:342-9.

Miniussi, C; Harris, JA; Ruzzoli, M. Modelling non-invasive brain stimulation in cognitive neuroscience. *Neurosci. Biobehav. Rev.* 2013;37:1702–1712.

Morel, A; Magnin, M; Jeanmonod, D. Multi-architectonic and stereotactic atlas of the human thalamus. *J Comp Neurol* 1997;387:588–630.

Morita, I; Keith, MW; Kanno, T. Dorsal column stimulation for persistent vegetative state. *Acta Neurochir Suppl* 2007; 97: 455-9.

Moruzzi, G; Magoun, HW. Brain stem reticular formation and activation of the EEG. *Electroencephalogr Clin Neurophysiol* 1949;1: 455-73.

Müller-Dahlhaus, F; Ziemann, U; Classen, J. Plasticity resembling spike-timing dependent synaptic plasticity: the evidence in human cortex. *Front Synaptic Neurosci.* 2010; 2:34.

Napolitani, M; Bodart, O; Canali, P; Seregni, F; Casali, A; Laureys, S; Rosanova, M; Massimini, M; Gosseries, O. Transcranial magnetic stimulation combined with high-density EEG in altered states of consciousness. *Brain Inj.* 2014;28:1180-9.

Naro, A; Calabrò, RS; Russo, M; Leo, A; Pollicino, P; Quartarone, A; Bramanti, P. Can transcranial direct current stimulation be useful in differentiating unresponsive wakefulness syndrome from minimally conscious state patients? *Restor Neurol Neurosci.* 2015b;33:159-76.

Naro, A; Leo, A; Bramanti, P; Calabrò, RS. Moving Toward Conscious Pain Processing Detection in Chronic Disorders of Consciousness: Anterior Cingulate Cortex Neuromodulation. *J Pain.* 2015e; 16:1022-31.

Naro, A; Leo, A; Cannavò, A; Buda, A; Bruno, R; Salviera, C; Bramanti, P; Calabrò, RS. Audiomotor Integration in Minimally Conscious State: Proof of Concept! *Neural Plast.* 2015c;2015:391349.

Naro, A; Leo, A; Filoni, S; Bramanti, P; Calabrò RS. Visuo-motor integration in unresponsive wakefulness syndrome: A piece of the puzzle towards consciousness detection? *Restor Neurol Neurosci.* 2015d;33:447-60.

Naro, A; Leo, A; Russo, M; Quartarone, A; Bramanti, P; Calabrò, RS. Shaping thalamo-cortical plasticity: a marker of cortical pain integration in patients with post-anoxic unresponsive wakefulness syndrome? *Brain Stimul.* 2015f;8:97-104.

Naro, A; Russo, M; Leo, A; Bramanti, P; Quartarone, A; Calabrò, RS. A Single Session of Repetitive Transcranial Magnetic Stimulation Over the Dorsolateral Prefrontal Cortex in Patients With Unresponsive Wakefulness Syndrome: Preliminary Results. *Neurorehabil Neural Repair.* 2015a;29:603-13.

Nieuwenhuys R, Voogd J, Huijzen C. The human central nervous system: a synopsis and atlas. Berlin: Springer-Verlag; 1979.

Nitsche, MA; Liebetanz, D; Antal, A; Lang, N; Tergau, F; Paulus, W. Modulation of cortical excitability by weak direct current stimulation – technical, safety and functional aspects. *Suppl Clin Neurophysiol*. 2003;56:255–76.

Nitsche, MA; Paulus, W. Excitability changes induced in the human motor cortex by weak transcranial direct current stimulation. *J Physiol.* 2000;527:633–9.

Nitsche, MA; Paulus, W. Noninvasive brain stimulation protocols in the treatment of epilepsy: current state and perspectives. *Neurotherapeutics.* 2009;6:244–50.

Nitsche, MA; Paulus, W. Sustained excitability elevations induced by transcranial DC motor cortex stimulation in humans. *Neurology.* 2001;57:1899–901.

Nitsche, MA; Roth, A; Kuo, MF; Fischer, AK; Liebetanz, D; Lang, N; Tergau, F; Paulus, W. Timing-dependent modulation of associative plasticity by general network excitability in the human motor cortex. *J Neurosci.* 2007; 27:3807-12.

O'Reardon, JP; Solvason, HB; Janicak, PG; Sampson, S; Isenberg, KE; Nahas, Z; McDonald, WM; Avery, D; Fitzgerald, PB; Loo, C; Demitrack, MA; George, MS; Sackeim, HA. Efficacy and safety of transcranial magnetic stimulation in the acute treatment of major depression: a multisite randomized controlled trial. *Biol Psychiatry.* 2007;62:1208–16.

Parent, A. Spinal cords: Fiber tracts; Medulla. In: Parent A, Carpenter MB, editor; Carpenter's human neuroanatomy. Williams and Wilkins; 1996.

Passler, MA; Riggs, RV. Positive outcomes in traumatic brain injury-vegetative state: patients treated with bromocriptine. *Arch Phys Med Rehabil* 2001; 82: 311-5.

Peri, CV; Shaffrey, ME; Farace, E; Cooper, E; Alves, WM; Cooper, JB; Young JS; Jane, JA. Pilot study of electrical stimulation on median nerve in comatose severe brain injured patients: 3-month outcome. *Brain Inj.* 2001;15:903-10.

Pinault, D. The thalamic reticular nucleus: structure, function and concept. *Brain Res Brain Res Rev* 2004;46:1–31.

Poreisz, C; Boros, K; Antal, A; Paulus, W. Safety aspects of transcranial direct current stimulation concerning healthy subjects and patients. *Brain Res Bull.* 2007;72:208–14.

Purves, D. Synaptic plasticity. In: Purves D, Augustine GJ, Fitzpatrick D, Hall WC, LaMantia AS, McNamara JO, White LE, editors. Neuroscience. Sunderland, MA: Sinauer Associates Inc; 2008.

Quartarone, A; Bagnato, S; Rizzo, V; Siebner, HR; Dattola, V; Scalfari, A; Morgante, F; Battaglia, F; Romano, M; Girlanda, P. Abnormal associative plasticity of the human motor cortex in writer's cramp. *Brain.* 2003; 126:2586-96.

Reato, D; Rahman, A; Bikson, M; Parra, LC. Low-intensity electrical stimulation affects network dynamics by modulating population rate and spike timing. *J. Neurosci.* 2010; 30:15067–15079.

Rosanova, M; Gosseries, O; Casarotto, S; Boly, M; Casali, AG; Bruno, MA; Mariotti, M; Boveroux, P; Tononi, G; Laureys, S; Massimini, M. Recovery of cortical effective connectivity and recovery of consciousness in vegetative patients. *Brain.* 2012;135:1308-20.

Rossi, S; Hallett, M; Rossini, PM; Pascual-Leone, A. Safety, ethical considerations, and application guidelines for the use of transcranial magnetic stimulation in clinical practice and research. *Clin Neurophysiol.* 2009;120:2008–39.

Sadikot, AF; Rymar, VV. The primate centromedian parafascicular complex: anatomical organization with a note on neuromodulation. *Brain Res Bull* 2009;78:122–30.

Saniova, B; Drobny, M; Kneslova, L; Minarik M. Outcome of patients with severe head injuries treated with amantadine sulphate. *J Neural Transm* 2004; 111: 511-4.

Sarasso, S; Rosanova, M; Casali, AG; Casarotto, S; Fecchio, M; Boly, M; Gosseries, O; Tononi, G; Laureys, S; Massimini, M. Quantifying cortical EEG responses to TMS in (un)consciousness. *Clin EEG Neurosci.* 2014;45:40-9.

Schiff, ND. Central thalamic contributions to arousal regulation and neurological disorders of consciousness. *Ann N Y Acad Sci* 2008;1129:105–18.

Schiff, ND. Recovery of consciousness after brain injury: a mesocircuit hypothesis. *Trends Neurosci.* 2010 Jan;33(1):1-9.

Schiff, ND; Giacino, JT; Kalmar, K; Victor, JD; Baker, K; Gerber, M; Fritz, B; Eisenberg, B; Biondi, T; O'Connor, J; Kobylarz, EJ; Farris, S; Machado, A; McCagg, C; Plum, F; Fins, JJ; Rezai, AR. Behavioral improvements with thalamic stimulation after severe traumatic brain injury. *Nature* 2007;448:600–3.

Sharova EV; Mel'nikov, AV; Novikova, MR; Kulikov, MA; Grechenko, TN; Shekhter, ED; Zaslavskii, AY. Changes in spontaneous brain bioelectrical activity during transcranial electrical and electromagnetic stimulation. *Neurosci Behav Physiol* 2007; 37:451-7.

Stefan, K; Kunesch, E; Benecke, R; Cohen, LG; Classen, J. Mechanisms of enhancement of human motor cortex excitability induced by interventional paired associative stimulation. *J Physiol.* 2002; 543:699-708.

Stefan, K; Wycislo, M; Classen, J. Modulation of associative human motor cortical plasticity by attention. *J Neurophysiol.* 2004; 92:66-72.

Sturm, V; Kühner, A; Schmitt, HP; Assmus, H; Stock, G. Chronic electrical stimu-lation of the thalamic unspecific activating system in a patient with coma due to midbrain and upper brain stem infarction. *Acta Neurochir* (Wien) 1979;47:235–44.

Taira, T; Hori, T. Intrathecal baclofen in the treatment of post-stroke central pain, dystonia, and persistent vegetative state. *Acta Neurochir Suppl* 2007;97:227-9.

Terney, D; Chaieb, L; Moliadze, V; Antal, A; Paulus, W. Increasing human brain excitability by transcranial high-frequency random noise stimulation. *J. Neurosci.* 2008; 28;14147–14155.

Thibaut, A; Bruno, MA; Ledoux, D; Demertzi, A; Laureys, S. tDCS in patients with disorders of consciousness: sham-controlled randomized double-blind study. *Neurology.* 2014;82:1112–8.

Tsubokawa, T; Yamamoto, T; Katayama, Y; Hirayama, T; Maejima, S; Moriya, T. Deep brain stimulation in a persistent vegetative state: follow up results and selection of candidates. *Brain Inj* 1990;4:315-27.

Tsubokawa, T; Yamamoto, T; Katayama, Y; Hirayama, T; Maejima, S; Moriya, T. Deep brain stimulation in a persistent vegetative state: follow-up results and criteria for selection of candidates. *Brain Inj* 1990;4:315–27.

Wassermann, EM; Grafman, J; Berry, C; Hollnagel, C; Wild, K; Clark, K; Hallet, M. Use and safety of a new repetitive transcranial magnetic stimulator. *Electroencephalogr Clin Neurophysiol.* 1996;101:412–7.

Whyte, J; Katz, D; Long, D; DiPasquale, MC; Polansky, M; Kalmar, K; Giacino, J; Childs, N; Mercer, W; Novak, P; Maurer, P; Eifert, B. Predictors of outcome in prolonged posttraumatic disorders of consciousness and assessment of medication effects: A multicenter study. *Arch Phys Med Rehabil* 2005;86:453-62.

Whyte, J; Myers, R. Incidence of clinically significant responses to zolpidem among patients with disorders of consciousness: a preliminary placebo controlled trial. *Am J Phys Med Rehabil* 2009;88:410-8.

Wolters, A; Sandbrink, F; Schlottmann, A; Kunesch, E; Stefan, K; Cohen, LG; Benecke, R; Classen J. A temporally asymmetric Hebbian rule governing plasticity in the human motor cortex. *J Neurophysiol.* 2003; 89:2339-45.

Yamamoto, T; Katayama, Y. DBS therapy for a persistent vegetative state: ten years follow-up results. *Acta Neurochir Suppl* 2003;87:15–8.

Yamamoto, T; Katayama, Y; Kobayashi, K; Oshima, H; Fukaya, C; Tsubokawa, T. Deep brain stimulation for the treatment of vegetative state. *Eur J Neurosci* 2010;32:1145–51.

Yamamoto, T; Katayama, Y; Obuchi, T; Kobayashi, K; Oshima, H; Fukaya, C. Spinal cord stimulation for treatment of patients in the minimally conscious state. *Neurol Med Chir (Tokyo)* 2012;52:475-81.

Yokoyama T, Kamei T, Kanno T. Right median nerve stimulation for comatose patients. *Soc Treat Coma* 1996;5:117–25.

Zafonte, RD; Lexell, J; Cullen, N. Possible applications for dopaminergic agents following traumatic brain injury: part 1. *J Head Trauma Rehabil* 2000;15:1179-82.

Zeman, A. Consciousness: concepts, neurobiology, terminology of impairments, theoretical models and philosophical background. *Handb Clin Neurol.* 2008;90:3-31.

Zeman, A. What do we mean by "conscious" and "aware"? *Neuropsychol Rehabil.* 2006;16:356-76.

In: Consciousness
Editor: Lloyd Alvarado

ISBN: 978-1-63485-023-0

Chapter 9

CONSCIOUSNESS AND MEDITATION: TWO PARTIALLY OVERLAPPING NETWORKS

Jordi Manuello[1], Andrea Nani[1,2,3,*] and Franco Cauda[1,2,3,4]
[1] GCS fMRI, Koelliker Hospital and University of Turin, Turin, Italy
[2] Department of Psychology, University of Turin, Turin, Italy
[3]Functional Neuroimaging and Complex Systems Group,
Department of Psychology, University of Turin, Turin, Italy
[4]Neuroscience Institute of Turin, University of Turin, Turin, Italy

ABSTRACT

Consciousness is a phenomenon that puzzled many thinkers of the past in disparate fields, including theology, literature, art and philosophy, and continues to be a hot topic of debate at present. However, in the last few decades, the change of paradigm brought by cognitive psychology and the emergence of new techniques, which allowed the *in vivo* study of the human brain, have made the investigation of consciousness a respectable field of scientific research. In particular, the neuroscience of consciousness aims to find the biological roots of conscious states by identifying the brain mechanisms capable of supporting them. On the other hand, a complete different approach has been taken by the Eastern wisdom, which has always looked at the conscious mind as something essential for the human well-being, following the precept that having a healthy mind is necessary for having a healthy body. This tenet lies at the basis of all the different techniques aiming to train the mind, of which the most relevant is probably meditation. Although meditation has been practiced in the East for more than two millennia, Western scientific research and healthcare programs have only recently drawn their attention to it, especially to what is called "mindfulness meditation". To date there is increasing evidence that meditative practices can influence cognitive and emotional processes with benefit to physical and mental health. In this chapter we consider both consciousness and mindfulness meditation within a neuroscientific framework, reviewing some of the most interesting theoretical models as well as scientific findings about the brain areas that are thought to underlie conscious and meditative states. In particular, the anterior cingulate cortex, posterior cingulate cortex, prefrontal cortex, insula and thalamus are supposed to

[*]Corresponding author: Andrea Nani, PhD andrea.nani@unito.it.

be crucially involved in both processes. This suggests that these brain areas may be part of two partially overlapping networks, which, notably, appear to play an important role in social cognition as well.

Keywords: mindfulness meditation, consciousness, brain networks, anterior cingulate cortex, posterior cingulate cortex, prefrontal cortex, insula, thalamus

THE QUEST FOR THE NEURAL CORRELATES OF CONSCIOUSNESS

Consciousness is such a pervasive aspect of our lives that intuitively everyone knows what it means to be conscious. However, contrary to this common intuition, scientists and philosophers are far from an agreement about a shared definition of this phenomenon. This is not surprising, as consciousness puzzled many thinkers of the past in disparate fields, including philosophy, theology, and literature. Quite recently, however, consciousness has become a respectable subject of scientific inquiry, especially thanks to the technological advances that have made possible the *in vivo* investigation of the human brain (e.g., PET, MRI, and fMRI). This has opened the quest for the neural correlates of consciousness – i.e., the brain processes that are supposed to be associated with conscious phenomena – and at the same time has allowed a new level of analysis for ancient questions. Rapidly, a set of interconnected disciplines (ranging from neuroscience and psychology to medical and computational sciences) are now aiming to study the human brain under different and converging aspects (structural, functional, developmental, cellular, molecular, clinical, and computational) (Seth 2010).

From a neurobiological perspective, neurophysiological and neuroimaging studies provide evidence that the neural correlates of consciousness can be better addressed with the help of a bidimensional model, based on the two parameters of the objective level and subjective content of consciousness (Cavanna et al. 2011; Laureys 2005; Laureys et al. 2004; Nani et al. 2013). The level is a parameter addressing the degree of arousal, ranging from full alertness to coma; whereas the content is a parameter addressing the qualitative features of consciousness, referring thereby to the vividness and intensity of sensations, emotions, thoughts, memories, intentions, etc. (Baars et al. 2003; Blumenfeld 2009; Laureys and Boly 2008; Plum and Posner 1980; Zeman 2001). Both the ascending pontomesodiencephalic reticular pathways and the thalamocortical projections are essential for the emergence and maintenance of the level of consciousness (Steriade 1996a, b). The contents of consciousness are all the feelings that characterize our inner world (which are called "qualia" in the neurophilosophical jargon). The contents can be elicited by both exogenous factors, which come from the external environment, and by endogenous factors, which come from the internal bodily milieu (e.g., proprioception, interoception, focal attention, etc.). Furthermore, these subjective experiences are often related to viscemotor reactions and a degree of emotional salience, which is associated to the activity of temporolimbic regions (Critchley 2005; Johanson et al. 2003).

On the grounds of the distinction between exogenous and endogenous factors, we can identify an *external awareness*, whose contents depend on what we perceive through the senses, and an *internal awareness*, whose contents depend on what we perceive within the body, independently of the surrounding world (Demertzi et al. 2013). Importantly, the distinction between internal and external awareness is not just conceptual, as it involves the activity of two different brain networks, one that can be referred to as *the internal awareness network*, which includes the posterior cingulate cortex (PCC), the anterior cingulate cortex (ACC), the precuneus and the medial prefrontal cortex (mPFC); and another that can be referred to as the *external awareness network*, which includes the dorsolateral prefrontal cortex (dlPFC) and the posterior parietal cortex (PPC).

Finally, on the basis of the bidimensional model, we can also distinguish an intransitive or a transitive use of the terms "conscious" and "consciousness". The intransitive use is linked to the level parameter and refers to the state of awareness or vigilance – as it is shown by the sentence "The patient never regained consciousness". In contrast, the transitive use is linked to the content parameter and refers to the conscious elaboration of a specific piece of information – as it is shown by the sentence "She was suddenly conscious of the alarm clock".

The Self and Its Embodied Agent

The *sense of self* remains a crucial and as yet unresolved issue of the neuroscience of consciousness. Some theories (e.g., Damasio's approach and the models that consider consciousness a sort of social construction) consider the sense of self, or at least a kind of proto-realization of it, to be fundamental for any conscious experience. On the other hand, other theories, which are characterized by a neurobiological or computational stance, consider consciousness (especially in its phenomenal dimension) as being largely independent of the self. An understanding of the nature of self, therefore, could provide valuable insight into this debate.

Currently, two main neuroscientific approaches aim to address the problem. The former is based on the concept of *agency*, while the latter is based on the concept of *embodiment* (Metzinger and Gallese 2003; Pacherie 2008; Roessler and Eilan 2003). According to the *agency approach*, the self is defined as "the sense that a person's action is the consequence of his or her intention" (Seth et al. 2012). In contrast, according to the *embodiment approach*, the self is defined as "the sense of being localized within one's physical body" (Arzy et al. 2006). Since both the approaches can be supported by clinical data, they are likely to be complementary. In fact, disruption of both the sense of agency and the feeling of being embodied is frequently manifested by patients with brain injuries. Symptoms often appear in form of autoscopic phenomena – i.e., illusory visual experiences during which the subject has the impression of seeing a second own body in extrapersonal space (Blanke 2004; Blanke and Mohr 2005; Brugger 2006; Devinsky 1989). These phenomena suggest a more general impairment of the so-called "minimal phenomenal selfhood" (MPS), that is, "the experience of being a distinct, holistic entity capable of global self-control and attention, possessing a body and a location in space and time" (Blanke and Metzinger 2009). Thus, the MPS might provide the basis on which the sense of being *an embodied agent* (an entity that results from the combination of agency and embodiment) can be constructed.

The Predicting Brain

An embodied agent is able to link both the internal and external awareness in a coherent and unitary conscious representation. The sense of agency in conjunction with interoception – which includes not only visceral signals but also information coming from the skin, the internal organs, muscles and articulations (Cauda et al. 2012; Craig 2002) – would play a fundamental role in this process. In particular, the model proposed by Seth et al. (2012) suggests that a sense of conscious presence emerges when interoceptive prediction signals match real input signals, so that no error signals are produced (Seth et al. 2012). The orbitofrontal cortex, ACC and insula are thought to be the brain areas mainly involved in this process (Critchley et al. 2004); especially the insula is supposed to be important, as it is associated with the integration of interoceptive and exteroceptive information (Cauda et al. 2011; Seth et al. 2012).

In this picture, the brain is regarded as an organ that fundamentally makes predictions; it generates expectations of future states of a given parameter and subsequently verifies whether or not these expectations match reality. Friston's computational theory of the *free energy principle* follows this line of thought (Friston et al. 2006). This theory holds that "any self-organizing system that is at equilibrium with its environment must minimize its free energy" (Friston 2010). According to this idea, every biological system has to maintain a high level of internal stability if it hopes to face the ever-changing environment. In order to do so, the system must maintain entropy at low levels. However, unexpected encounters can perturb its internal balance, increasing thereby entropy. Thus, to avoid perturbations every biological system needs a stable and updated model of the surrounding world, which can be used to make pertinent predictions that, in turn, help minimize the system's free energy. The feature of consciousness of being at the intersection of the inner and the external worlds makes it the best candidate to provide such an interactive model.

A similar line of reasoning considers the brain a sort of Bayesian machine. This hypothesis sustains that we are always trying to infer the causes of our sensations and perceptions on the basis of a generative model of the world (Dayan et al. 1995; Knill and Pouget 2004; Lee and Mumford 2003). So, in order to be able to make predictions, the brain must take into account what happened in the past (i.e., events, sensory stimuli, etc.). This idea is at the heart of Moshe Bar's (2007) model of the *proactive brain*. According to Bar's model, the brain is incessantly occupied in making predictions on the basis of sensory and cognitive inputs. Recent resting state fMRI evidence supports this hypothesis; it has in fact been demonstrated that most of the brain areas constituting the default mode network (DMN) – which is the network that appears to be active when the brain does not focus on a specific task – are also recruited during associative processes (Bar et al. 2007; Tang et al. 2012). In the light of that, it seems plausible to hypothesize that the spontaneous baseline activity of the brain might be a sort of prediction making process.

The Network Approach

One of the most exciting results of neuroimaging techniques is the high-resolution visualization of the normal brain's functional anatomy. This led to the findings that the performance of even simple tasks is associated with activation of more distributed brain networks than it was previously thought on the grounds of postmortem data of patients with cerebral lesions. It is now well understood that brain regions that appear to be active together can form specific functional networks. These networks show a high level of spontaneous baseline cerebral activity. Thus far, neuroimaging investigations have identified at least ten different functional networks (Beckmann et al. 2005; Fransson 2005; Salvador et al. 2005; van de Ven et al. 2004; van den Heuvel et al. 2008). These webs of connections include the visual network, the motor network, two lateralized networks formed by superior parietal and superior frontal areas, the dorsal attention network, a network composed of bilateral temporal insular and anterior cingulate cortex regions, and the so-called DMN. The DMN, in particular, is a widespread network including PCC, precuneus, temporoparietal junction, medial prefrontal cortex, parahippocampal gyrus, superior frontal sulcus, and the nonspecific nuclei of the thalamus (Buckner and Vincent 2007; Fox and Raichle 2007; Fox et al. 2005; Raichle and Snyder 2007).

Neuroscientific studies have therefore revealed that, in addition to functional differentiation (which depends on localized cerebral modules), cognitive processes also result from the integration of brain areas able to constitute widespread functional networks (Buchel and Friston 2001; Bullmore and Sporns 2009; Friston 1994; McIntosh and Gonzalez-Lima 1994). Consequently, new interesting questions arose about the interplay of these networks. For instance, how do widespread brain regions functionally interact while performing a cognitive task? And how can we determine the causal influence of a brain area over the others? Answers in these exciting research topics are going to open new perspectives on the functional organization of the brain.

With regard to the study of consciousness, the network approach has revived interest in global workspace (GW) theories. These models hold that conscious access to information can be made possible only within a workspace where conscious contents are constructed and represented (Baars 1988). In other words, conscious experience would depend on the distributed availability of information, which is obtained by two different computational neural systems (Dehaene et al. 1998). First, activation of the ascending reticular formation of the brainstem and midbrain, as well as the outer shell of the thalamus and the groups of neurons projecting from the thalamus to the neocortex, would be central for sustaining the global workspace. Second, bidirectional and horizontal long-range projections between cortical regions would be responsible for the distribution and availability of information within the GW. The important property of reportability, which is thought to be a crucial feature of consciousness, could depend on this type of connections (Weiskrantz 1997).

A recently improved version of GW is the *global neuronal workspace* (GNW) (Changeux and Dehaene 2008; Dehaene and Changeux 2005, 2011; Dehaene et al. 2006; Dehaene and Naccache 2001). According to the GNW, groups of cortical pyramidal neurons with long-range projections (which are mainly present in prefrontal, cingulate, and parietal areas), along with thalamocortical loops, could sustain a mental workspace capable of connecting many specialized, automatic and nonconscious brain modules. In virtue of their long and abundant projections, GNW groups may maintain a global broadcast of specific conscious contents, ranging from phenomenal experiences to verbal reports, memories, plans, and intentions (Dehaene and Naccache 2001). As a consequence, the difference between conscious and nonconscious processes would depend on the degree of distribution of information: an encapsulation of informative content in discrete modules would result in nonconscious activity, whereas a global availability of this information would lead to a full-fledged conscious state (Dehaene and Changeux 2011).

Within the GNW architecture, von Economo neurons (VENs) might play an important role (Cauda et al. 2014; Cauda et al. 2013; Critchley and Seth 2012; Medford and Critchley 2010; Menon and Uddin 2010). VENs, which are large spindle-shaped neurons of the frontoinsular cortex and the anterior cingulate cortex characterized by long-range projections (Cauda et al. 2014), appear to be involved in the processes of proprioception, interoception, and salience evaluation (Allman et al. 2005; Medford and Critchley 2010; Palaniyappan and Liddle 2012; Seeley et al. 2007). In virtue of their long connections, VENs could provide a fast integration of emotional and interoceptive signals, supporting the process of discrimination between the self and the external environment, as well as the global maintenance and availability of this information within the mental workspace.

Mindfulness Meditation and the Eastern Wisdom

A radically different approach to the mind and its functions can be found in the Eastern world, where spirituality has always profoundly influenced the cultural and social background. In this milieu the primary way of keeping the mind healthy as well as enhancing awareness is the practice of meditation (Siegel et al. 2008). Although meditation cannot be univocally defined, it is nevertheless possible to grasp intuitively its meaning by saying what it is not. Meditation is neither a way of dulling the mind nor a way of feeling emotionally uninvolved. It is also neither the road to a state of bliss, nor the recipe for avoiding sorrow and pain. Conversely, a basic feature of meditation is *sati*, a Pali term usually translated into *mindfulness*, which is "the awareness that emerges through paying attention on purpose, in the present moment, and nonjudgmentally to the unfolding of experience moment to moment" (Kabat-Zinn 2003). Therefore, the practice of mindfulness meditation is far from being confined to an esoteric or religious activity, as the state of being mindful "is not at all a 'mystical' state, beyond the ken and reach of the average person. (…) [On the contrary,] in its elementary manifestation, known under the term 'attention', [mindfulness] is one of the cardinal functions of consciousness without which there cannot be perception of any object at all" (Thera 1962).

However, only recently the Western scientific community has become interested in this fascinating meditative practice. In fact, particularly in the last two decades a number of scientific studies have investigated mindfulness meditation and, on the grounds of intriguing findings, favored its introduction in healthcare treatment programs within psychotherapeutic contexts. As a result, many different therapeutic approaches based on meditation, known as mindfulness-based interventions (MBIs), are now available. Among those the most significant are mindfulness-based stress reduction (MBSR), mindfulness-based cognitive therapy (MBCT), and integrative body-mind training (IBMT). An increasing amount of scientific findings is proving the benefits of these treatments, even though the brain mechanisms underlying their efficacy remain to be understood (Tang et al. 2015).

MEDITATION AND ITS NEURAL CORRELATES

Interoceptive attention (IA) is likely to be involved in mindfulness meditation. This process deals with different sensations coming from the body, including those related to breathing, blood circulation, digestion and proprioception (Farb et al. 2013). The insular cortex and the anterior cingulate cortex (ACC) are supposed to be the brain areas primarily involved in interoception (Craig 2009; Flynn 1999). A recent study showed that, after 8 weeks of MBSR treatment, participants had significant increase in the functional connectivity of the posterior insula and anterior insular gyrus (Farb et al. 2013). These brain areas are thought to be related to the awareness of the present moment (Craig 2009; Farb et al. 2007), which is a fundamental feature of mindfulness meditation (Kabat-Zinn 2003). What is more, the aforementioned study by Farb et al. (2013) reported a decrease of activity in the dorsomedial prefrontal cortex (dmPFC). Intriguingly, dmPFC deactivation has been associated with exogenous stimulation of interoceptive signaling pathways, for instance during gastric distension (Van Oudenhove et al. 2009).

Mindfulness meditation appears to promote the functional integration of different brain networks relating to cognitive and internal bodily signals evaluation. This could explain why MBSR is more effective than aerobic exercise in regulating negative emotions in people with social anxiety (Goldin et al. 2013). Furthermore, there is evidence suggesting an association between long-term meditators and cortical thickening, particularly in the prefrontal and right anterior insular cortices (Lazar et al. 2005). Following this line of research, the use of a multivariate pattern recognition method (called "support vector machine") allowed to distinguish meditators from non-meditators by analyzing subtle differences in participants' brains (Sato et al. 2012). Of note, the thalamus appeared to be one of the most revealing cerebral areas.

A PARTIAL OVERLAP

In this chapter we considered the study of the conscious mind under different approaches. We also considered relevant contributions coming from the Eastern culture, especially with regard to the practice of mindfulness meditation. Recent studies provide evidence that this kind of meditation can improve both cognitive flexibility and attention in terms of control, maintenance, and orientation (Aftanas and Golosheykin 2005; Goldin et al. 2013).

Thus, if mindfulness meditation has an influence on consciousness by altering attentive and interoceptive states, it can be argued that there should be a certain degree of overlap between the cerebral areas involved in both processes. Neuroscientific investigations have in fact found that the activation of important brain areas is related to both meditation and consciousness. It has therefore been proposed that the brain networks supporting both consciousness and mindfulness meditation could partially share some areas and pathways (Manuello et al. 2016). In particular, four cortical regions and one subcortical site (i.e., the insula, ACC, PCC, PFC, and thalamus) are thought to be substantial in underlying both meditative and conscious states (**see Figure**).

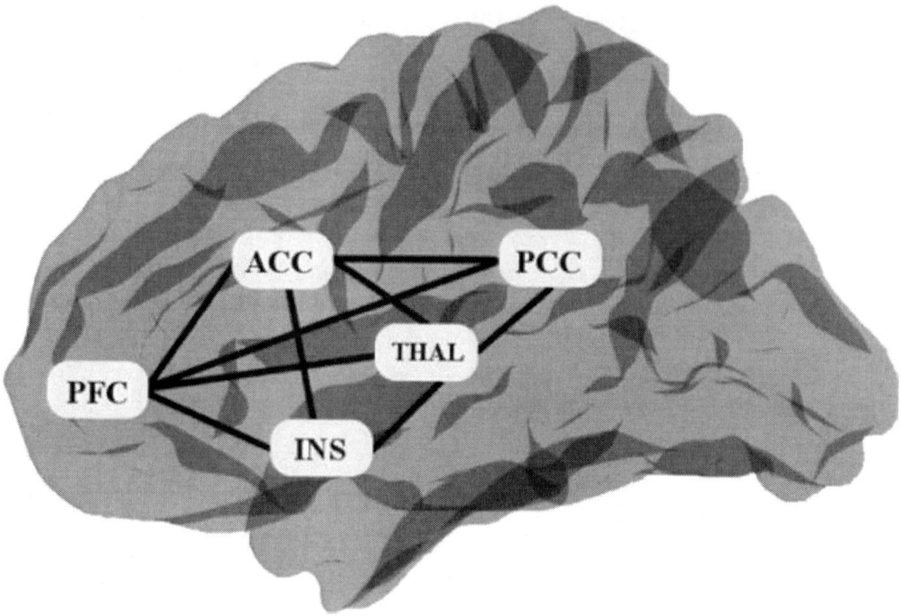

Schematic illustration of the five brain areas that partially overlap in both the processes of consciousness and mindfulness meditation. ACC = anterior cingulate cortex; INS = insula; PCC = posterior cingulate cortex; PFC = prefrontal cortex; THAL = thalamus.

This overlap may explain why the practice of meditation can lead to both structural and functional alterations of the brain networks that are able to promote and maintain consciousness. These alterations are more likely to occur within the brains of long-term meditators (Goleman 1988; Shapiro 2008) and might be responsible for what is described by meditators as a sort of "altered experience of time and space" (Berkovich-Ohana et al. 2013). A decreased activation of the PCC might be associated with this peculiar experience (Brewer et al. 2013).

This hypothesis is supported by a number of studies providing evidence that during states of deep meditation both the left insula and the ACC are functionally activated, while the lateral PFC and parietal cortex decrease their activity (Craigmyle 2013; Hasenkamp et al. 2012; Hölzel et al. 2011; Posner et al. 2010; Tang et al. 2009; Tang and Posner 2009). As we have previously said, the ACC is supposed to play an important role in sustaining an *internal awareness network* (Demertzi et al. 2013) and, along with the insular cortex, appears to be an essential element of Seth's interoceptive prediction model (Seth et al. 2012).

The insular and anterior cingulate cortices appear to be structurally altered in long-term meditators (Craigmyle 2013; Lazar et al. 2005). What is more, they are also abundant in VENs (Cauda et al. 2014) and their degeneration has been linked to the loss of emotional evaluation and self-consciousness in patients suffering from frontotemporal dementia (Seeley et al. 2006, 2007; Sturm et al. 2006). Within the theoretical model of the predicting brain, ACC seems to be involved in the process of error prediction (Brown and Braver 2005), as well as in the monitoring of explorative behavior (Aston-Jones and Cohen 2005). Together with the mPFC, the ACC is supposed to sustain the process of evaluation of possible future outcomes (Ridderinkhof et al. 2004). This is consistent with the *proactive brain* theory.

Furthermore, ACC is reckoned to be an important hub of the GNW model (Dehaene et al. 1998).

There is evidence that the lateral PFC and parietal cortex are less activated when meditators focus their attention on a specific object – e.g., breath (Hölzel et al., 2011; Posner et al. 2010; Tang et al. 2009; Tang and Posner 2009). This finding is in line with the idea of considering these cerebral areas as parts of the *external awareness network* (Demertzi et al. 2013). In turn, PCC, which is thought to be part of Demertzi's *internal awareness network*, is functionally active during normal conscious experiences and, on the other hand, frequently impaired during coma or vegetative state (Cauda et al., 2009, 2010; Demertzi et al., 2013). Finally, changes in the activity of the thalamus, which is part of the *internal awareness network* as well, appear to be one of the most telltale signs in order to distinguish between meditators and non-meditators (Sato et al., 2012).

From the sociobehavioral standpoint, it has been suggested that mindfulness meditation may positively influence the regulation of emotions and emotional reactivity, by reducing symptoms' severity in people with social anxiety disorders (Goldin et al., 2013). A growing number of studies report that the practice of meditation is a way of reducing stress as well as of improving the quality of life of people doing stressful jobs (Dos Santos et al., 2015). Similar positive results have been showed for people suffering from chronic diseases and for their caregivers (Danucalov et al., 2015; Marconi et al., 2015). But the benefits of mindfulness meditation extend well beyond the clinical context. For instance, meditators' ability to regulate emotions has been found to improve quality of interpersonal relationships (Grecucci et al., 2015). Furthermore, a study provided evidence that, even in the short term, mindfulness meditation can enhance empathy and the understanding of mental states (Tan et al., 2014).

These findings are not surprising, as the four cortical areas (i.e., insula, ACC, PCC, and PFC), which appear to be principally involved in both conscious and meditative states, are also found to be frequently involved in processes related to social cognition. In fact, the insular cortex has been found to be involved in empathy (Kanske et al., 2015). Moreover, a study reported that activation of prefrontal areas and their functional connectivity with PCC were positively associated with obtaining more precise performances when trying to estimate preferences of other people (Kang et al., 2013). With regard to social interaction, ACC has been suggested to be involved in the evaluation of cost-benefits in reward tasks (Apps and Ramnani 2014). Finally, these findings suggest the intriguing perspective that the same brain areas playing an important role in underlying conscious and meditative states might play an important role as well in underlying social cognitive functions. Future investigations on this issue are worth pursuing for both mindfulness and consciousness research.

REFERENCES

Aftanas, L. and Golosheykin, S. (2005). Impact of regular meditation practice on EEG activity at rest and during evoked negative emotions. *Int J Neurosci*, *115*(6), 893-909. doi: 10.1080/00207450590897969.

Allman, J. M., Watson, K. K., Tetreault, N. A. and Hakeem, A. Y. (2005). Intuition and autism: a possible role for Von Economo neurons. *Trends Cogn Sci*, *9*(8), 367-373. doi: 10.1016/j.tics.2005.06.008.

Apps, M. A. and Ramnani, N. (2014). The anterior cingulate gyrus signals the net value of others' rewards. *J Neurosci*, *34*(18), 6190-6200. doi: 10.1523/jneurosci.2701-13.2014.

Arzy, S., Thut, G., Mohr, C., Michel, C. M. and Blanke, O. (2006). Neural basis of embodiment: distinct contributions of temporoparietal junction and extrastriate body area. *J Neurosci*, *26*(31), 8074-8081. doi: 10.1523/jneurosci.0745-06.2006.

Aston-Jones, G. and Cohen, J. D. (2005). An integrative theory of locus coeruleus-norepinephrine function: adaptive gain and optimal performance. *Annu Rev Neurosci*, *28*, 403-450. doi: 10.1146/annurev. neuro.28.061604.135709.

Baars, B. J. (1988). *A Cognitive Theory of Consciousness*: Cambridge University Press.

Baars, B. J., Ramsoy, T. Z. and Laureys, S. (2003). Brain, conscious experience and the observing self. *Trends Neurosci*, *26*(12), 671-675. doi: 10.1016/j.tins.2003.09.015.

Bar, M. (2007). The proactive brain: using analogies and associations to generate predictions. *Trends Cogn Sci*, *11*(7), 280-289. doi: 10.1016/j.tics.2007.05.005.

Bar, M., Aminoff, E., Mason, M. and Fenske, M. (2007). The units of thought. *Hippocampus*, *17*(6), 420-428. doi: 10.1002/hipo.20287.

Beckmann, C. F., DeLuca, M., Devlin, J. T. and Smith, S. M. (2005). Investigations into resting-state connectivity using independent component analysis. *Philos Trans R Soc Lond B Biol Sci*, *360*(1457), 1001-1013. doi: 10.1098/rstb.2005.1634.

Berkovich-Ohana, A., Dor-Ziderman, Y., Glicksohn, J. and Goldstein, A. (2013). Alterations in the sense of time, space, and body in the mindfulness-trained brain: a neurophenomenologically-guided MEG study. *Front Psychol*, *4*, 912. doi: 10.3389/fpsyg.2013.00912.

Blanke, O., Landis, T., Spinelli, L. and Seeck, M. (2004). Out-of-body experience and autoscopy of neurological origin. *Brain*, *127*(2), 243-258. doi: 10.1093/brain/awh040.

Blanke, O. and Metzinger, T. (2009). Full-body illusions and minimal phenomenal selfhood. *Trends Cogn Sci*, *13*(1), 7-13. doi: 10.1016/j.tics.2008.10.003.

Blanke, O. and Mohr, C. (2005). Out-of-body experience, heautoscopy, and autoscopic hallucination of neurological origin Implications for neurocognitive mechanisms of corporeal awareness and self-consciousness. *Brain Res Brain Res Rev*, *50*(1), 184-199. doi: 10.1016/j.brainresrev.2005.05.008.

Blumenfeld, H. (2009). Epilepsy and consciousness. In S. Laureys and G. Tononi (Eds.), *The Neurology of consciousness*, (pp. 247-260). Amsterdam: Elsevier.

Brewer, J. A., Garrison, K. A. and Whitfield-Gabrieli, S. (2013). What about the "Self" is Processed in the Posterior Cingulate Cortex? *Front Hum Neurosci*, *7*, 647. doi: 10.3389/fnhum.2013.00647.

Brown, J. W. and Braver, T. S. (2005). Learned predictions of error likelihood in the anterior cingulate cortex. *Science*, *307*(5712), 1118-1121. doi: 10.1126/science.1105783.

Brugger, P. (2006). From phantom limb to phantom body: Varieties of extracorporeal awareness. In G. Knoblich, I. M. Thornton, M. Grosjean and M. Shiffrar (Eds.), *Human Body Perception From the Inside Out*, (pp. 171-209): Oxford University Press.

Buchel, C. and Friston, K. (2001). Interactions among neuronal systems assessed with functional neuroimaging. *Rev Neurol (Paris)*, *157*(8-9 Pt 1), 807-815.

Buckner, R. L. and Vincent, J. L. (2007). Unrest at rest: default activity and spontaneous network correlations. *NeuroImage*, *37*(4), 1091-1096; discussion 1097-1099. doi: 10.1016/j.neuroimage.2007.01.010.

Bullmore, E. and Sporns, O. (2009). Complex brain networks: graph theoretical analysis of structural and functional systems. *Nat Rev Neurosci*, *10*(3), 186-198. doi: 10.1038/nrn2575.

Cauda, F., D'Agata, F., Sacco, K., Duca, S., Geminiani, G. and Vercelli, A. (2011). Functional connectivity of the insula in the resting brain. *NeuroImage*, *55*(1), 8-23. doi: http://dx.doi.org/10.1016/j.neuroimage. 2010.11.049.

Cauda, F., Geminiani, G., D'Agata, F., Sacco, K., Duca, S., Bagshaw, A. P. and Cavanna, A. E. (2010). Functional Connectivity of the Posteromedial Cortex. *PLoS One*, *5*(9), e13107. doi: 10.1371/journal.pone.0013107.

Cauda, F., Geminiani, G. C. and Vercelli, A. (2014). Evolutionary appearance of von Economo's neurons in the mammalian cerebral cortex. *Front Hum Neurosci*, *8*, 104. doi: 10.3389/fnhum.2014.00104.

Cauda, F., Micon, B. M., Sacco, K., Duca, S., D'Agata, F., Geminiani, G. and Canavero, S. (2009). Disrupted intrinsic functional connectivity in the vegetative state. *Journal of Neurology, Neurosurgery and Psychiatry*, *80*(4), 429-431. doi: 10.1136/ jnnp.2007.142349.

Cauda, F., Torta, D. E., Sacco, K., D'Agata, F., Geda, E., Duca, S. and Vercelli, A. (2013). Functional anatomy of cortical areas characterized by Von Economo neurons. *Brain Structure and Function*, *218*(1), 1-20. doi: 10.1007/s00429-012-0382-9.

Cauda, F., Torta, D. M. E., Sacco, K., Geda, E., D'Agata, F., Costa, T. and Amanzio, M. (2012). Shared "Core" Areas between the Pain and Other Task-Related Networks. *PLoS ONE*, *7*(8), e41929. doi: 10.1371/journal.pone.0041929.

Cavanna, A. E., Shah, S., Eddy, C. M., Williams, A. and Rickards, H. (2011). Consciousness: a neurological perspective. *Behav Neurol*, *24*(1), 107-116. doi: 10.3233/ben-2011-0322.

Changeux, J. P. and Dehaene, S. (2008). The neuronal workspace model: conscious processing and learning. In J. Byrne and R. Menzel (Eds.), *Learning Theory and Behavior,* (Vol. *1*, of Learning and Memory: a comprehensive reference, pp. 729-758). Oxford: Elsevier.

Craig, A. D. (2002). How do you feel? Interoception: the sense of the physiological condition of the body. *Nat Rev Neurosci*, *3*(8), 655-666.

Craig, A. D. (2009). Emotional moments across time: a possible neural basis for time perception in the anterior insula. *Philos Trans R Soc Lond B Biol Sci*, *364*(1525), 1933-1942. doi: 10.1098/rstb.2009.0008.

Craigmyle, N. A. (2013). The beneficial effects of meditation: contribution of the anterior cingulate and locus coeruleus. *Front Psychol*, *4*, 731. doi: 10.3389/fpsyg.2013.00731.

Critchley, H. and Seth, A. (2012). Will studies of macaque insula reveal the neural mechanisms of self-awareness? *Neuron*, *74*(3), 423-426. doi: 10.1016/ j.neuron.2012.04.012.

Critchley, H. D. (2005). Neural mechanisms of autonomic, affective, and cognitive integration. *J Comp Neurol*, *493*(1), 154-166. doi: 10.1002/cne.20749.

Critchley, H. D., Wiens, S., Rotshtein, P., Ohman, A. and Dolan, R. J. (2004). Neural systems supporting interoceptive awareness. *Nat Neurosci*, *7*(2), 189-195.

Danucalov, M. A., Kozasa, E. H., Afonso, R. F., Galduroz, J. C. and Leite, J. R. (2015). Yoga and compassion meditation program improve quality of life and self-compassion in family caregivers of Alzheimer's disease patients: A randomized controlled trial. *Geriatr Gerontol Int*. doi: 10.1111/ggi.12675.

Dayan, P., Hinton, G. E., Neal, R. M. and Zemel, R. S. (1995). The Helmholtz machine. *Neural Comput*, *7*(5), 889-904.

Dehaene, S. and Changeux, J. P. (2005). Ongoing spontaneous activity controls access to consciousness: a neuronal model for inattentional blindness. *PLoS Biol*, *3*(5), e141. doi: 10.1371/journal.pbio.0030141.

Dehaene, S. and Changeux, J. P. (2011). Experimental and theoretical approaches to conscious processing. *Neuron*, *70*(2), 200-227. doi: 10.1016/j.neuron.2011.03.018.

Dehaene, S., Changeux, J. P., Naccache, L., Sackur, J. and Sergent, C. (2006). Conscious, preconscious, and subliminal processing: a testable taxonomy. *Trends Cogn Sci*, *10*(5), 204-211. doi: 10.1016/j.tics.2006.03.007.

Dehaene, S., Kerszberg, M. and Changeux, J. P. (1998). A neuronal model of a global workspace in effortful cognitive tasks. *Proc. Natl. Acad. Sci. USA*, *95*.

Dehaene, S. and Naccache, L. (2001). Towards a cognitive neuroscience of consciousness: basic evidence and a workspace framework. *Cognition*, *79*(1-2), 1-37.

Demertzi, A., Soddu, A. and Laureys, S. (2013). Consciousness supporting networks. *Curr Opin Neurobiol*, *23*(2), 239-244. doi:10.1016/j.conb. 2012.12.003.

Devinsky, O., Feldmann, E., Burrowes, K. and Bromfield, E. (1989). AUtoscopic phenomena with seizures. *Archives of Neurology*, *46*(10), 1080-1088. doi: 10.1001/archneur.1989.00520460060015.

Dos Santos, T. M., Kozasa, E. H., Carmagnani, I. S., Tanaka, L. H., Lacerda, S. S. and Nogueira-Martins, L. A. (2015). Positive Effects of a Stress Reduction Program Based on Mindfulness Meditation in Brazilian Nursing Professionals: Qualitative and Quantitative Evaluation. *Explore (NY)*., doi: 10.1016/j.explore.2015.12.005.

Farb, N. A. S., Segal, Z. V. and Anderson, A. K. (2013). Mindfulness meditation training alters cortical representations of interoceptive attention. *Soc Cogn Affect Neurosci*, *8*(1), 15-26. doi:10.1093/scan/nss 066.

Farb, N. A. S., Segal, Z. V., Mayberg, H., Bean, J., McKeon, D., Fatima, Z. and Anderson, A. K. (2007). Attending to the present: mindfulness meditation reveals distinct neural modes of self-reference. *Soc Cogn Affect Neurosci*, *2*(4), 313-322. doi: 10.1093/scan/nsm030.

Flynn, F. G. (1999). Anatomy of the insula functional and clinical correlates. *Aphasiology*, *13*(1), 55-78. doi: 10.1080/026870399402325.

Fox, M. D. and Raichle, M. E. (2007). Spontaneous fluctuations in brain activity observed with functional magnetic resonance imaging. *Nat Rev Neurosci*, *8*(9), 700-711. doi: 10.1038/nrn2201.

Fox, M. D., Snyder, A. Z., Vincent, J. L., Corbetta, M., Van Essen, D. C. and Raichle, M. E. (2005). The human brain is intrinsically organized into dynamic, anticorrelated functional networks. *Proc Natl Acad Sci U S A*, *102*(27), 9673-9678. doi: 10.1073/pnas.0504136102.

Fransson, P. (2005). Spontaneous low-frequency BOLD signal fluctuations: an fMRI investigation of the resting-state default mode of brain function hypothesis. *Hum Brain Mapp*, *26*(1), 15-29. doi: 10.1002/hbm.20113.

Friston, K. (1994). Functional and effective connectivity in neuroimaging: a synthesis *Hum Brain Mapp*, *2*, 56-78.

Friston, K. (2010). The free-energy principle: a unified brain theory? *Nat Rev Neurosci*, *11*(2), 127-138. doi: 10.1038/nrn2787.

Friston, K., Kilner, J. and Harrison, L. (2006). A free energy principle for the brain. *J Physiol Paris*, *100*(1-3), 70-87. doi:10.1016/j.jphysparis.2006. 10.001.

Goldin, P., Ziv, M., Jazaieri, H., Hahn, K. and Gross, J. J. (2013). MBSR vs aerobic exercise in social anxiety: fMRI of emotion regulation of negative self-beliefs. *Soc Cogn Affect Neurosci*, *8*(1), 65-72. doi: 10.1093/scan/nss054.

Goleman, D. (1988). *The Meditative Mind: The Varieties of Meditative Experience*: Tarcher.

Grecucci, A., De Pisapia, N., Kusalagnana Thero, D., Paladino, M. P., Venuti, P. and Job, R. (2015). Baseline and strategic effects behind mindful emotion regulation: behavioral and physiological investigation. *PLoS One*, *10*(1), e0116541. doi: 10.1371/journal.pone.0116541.

Hasenkamp, W., Wilson-Mendenhall, C. D., Duncan, E. and Barsalou, L. W. (2012). Mind wandering and attention during focused meditation: A fine-grained temporal analysis of fluctuating cognitive states. *Neuroimage*, *59*(1), 750-760. doi: http://dx.doi.org/10.1016/j.neuroimage.2011.07.008.

Hölzel, B. K., Lazar, S. W., Gard, T., Schuman-Olivier, Z., Vago, D. R. and Ott, U. (2011). How Does Mindfulness Meditation Work? Proposing Mechanisms of Action From a Conceptual and Neural Perspective. *Perspect. Psychol. Sci.*, *6*, 22. doi: doi: 10.1177/1745691611419671.

Johanson, M., Revonsuo, A., Chaplin, J. and Wedlund, J. E. (2003). Level and contents of consciousness in connection with partial epileptic seizures. *Epilepsy Behav*, *4*(3), 279-285.

Kabat-Zinn, J. (2003). Mindfulness-Based Interventions in Context: Past, Present, and Future. *Clinical Psychology: Science and Practice*, *10*(2), 144-156. doi: 10.1093/clipsy.bpg016.

Kang, P., Lee, J., Sul, S. and Kim, H. (2013). Dorsomedial prefrontal cortex activity predicts the accuracy in estimating others' preferences. *Front Hum Neurosci*, *7*, 686. doi: 10.3389/fnhum.2013.00686.

Kanske, P., Bockler, A. and Singer, T. (2015). Models, Mechanisms and Moderators Dissociating Empathy and Theory of Mind. *Curr Top Behav Neurosci*. doi: 10.1007/7854_2015_412.

Knill, D. C. and Pouget, A. (2004). The Bayesian brain: the role of uncertainty in neural coding and computation. *Trends Neurosci*, *27*(12), 712-719. doi: 10.1016/j.tins.2004.10.007.

Laureys, S. (2005). Death, unconsciousness and the brain. *Nat Rev Neurosci*, *6*(11), 899-909.

Laureys, S. and Boly, M. (2008). The changing spectrum of coma. *Nat Clin Pract Neurol*, *4*(10), 544-546. doi: 10.1038/ncpneuro0887.

Laureys, S., Owen, A. M. and Schiff, N. D. (2004). Brain function in coma, vegetative state, and related disorders. *Lancet Neurol*, *3*(9), 537-546. doi: 10.1016/s1474-4422(04)00852-x.

Lazar, S. W., Kerr, C. E., Wasserman, R. H., Gray, J. R., Greve, D. N., Treadway, M. T. and Fischl, B. (2005). Meditation experience is associated with increased cortical thickness. *Neuroreport*, *16*(17), 1893-1897.

Lee, T. S. and Mumford, D. (2003). Hierarchical Bayesian inference in the visual cortex. *J Opt Soc Am A Opt Image Sci Vis*, *20*(7), 1434-1448.

Manuello, J., Vercelli, U., Nani, A., Costa, T. and Cauda, F. (2016). Mindfulness meditation and consciousness: An integrative neuroscientific perspective. *Conscious Cogn*, *40*, 67-78. doi: 10.1016/j.concog.2015. 12.005.

Marconi, A., Gragnano, G., Lunetta, C., Gatto, R., Fabiani, V., Tagliaferri, A. and Pagnini, F. (2015). The experience of meditation for people with amyotrophic lateral sclerosis and their caregivers - a qualitative analysis. *Psychol Health Med*, 1-7. doi: 10.1080/13548506.2015.1115110.

McIntosh, A. R. and Gonzalez-Lima, F. (1994). Structural equation modeling and its application to network analysis in functional brain imaging. *Hum Brain Mapp*, *2*, 2-22.

Medford, N. and Critchley, H. D. (2010). Conjoint activity of anterior insular and anterior cingulate cortex: awareness and response. *Brain Structure and Function*, *214*(5-6), 535-549. doi: 10.1007/s00429-010-0265-x.

Menon, V. and Uddin, L. (2010). Saliency, switching, attention and control: a network model of insula function. *Brain Structure and Function*, *214*(5-6), 655-667. doi: 10.1007/s00429-010-0262-0.

Metzinger, T. and Gallese, V. (2003). The emergence of a shared action ontology: building blocks for a theory. *Conscious Cogn*, *12*(4), 549-571.

Nani, A., Seri, A. and Cavanna, A. E. (2013). Consciousness and Neuroscience. In A. E. Cavanna, A. Nani, H. Blumenfeld and S. Laureys (Eds.), *Neuroimaging of Consciousness* (pp. 3-21). Berlin: Springer Verlag.

Pacherie, E. (2008). The phenomenology of action: A conceptual framework. *Cognition*, *107*(1), 179-217. doi: http://dx.doi.org/10.1016/j.cognition. 2007.09.003.

Palaniyappan, L. and Liddle, P. F. (2012). Does the salience network play a cardinal role in psychosis? An emerging hypothesis of insular dysfunction. *J Psychiatry Neurosci*, *37*(1), 17-27. doi: 10.1503/jpn.100176.

Plum, F. and Posner, J. B. (1980). *The diagnosis of stupor and coma* (3rd ed.). Philadelphia: Davis.

Posner, M. I., Rothbart, M. K., Rueda, M. R. and Tang, Y. (2010). Training effortless attention. In B. Bruya (Ed.), *Effortless Attention: A New Perspective in the Cognitive Science of Attention and Action*: Mit Press.

Raichle, M. E. and Snyder, A. Z. (2007). A default mode of brain function: a brief history of an evolving idea. *NeuroImage*, *37*(4), 1083-1090; discussion 1097-1089. doi: 10.1016/j.neuroimage.2007.02.041.

Ridderinkhof, K. R., van den Wildenberg, W. P., Segalowitz, S. J. and Carter, C. S. (2004). Neurocognitive mechanisms of cognitive control: the role of prefrontal cortex in action selection, response inhibition, performance monitoring, and reward-based learning. *Brain Cogn*, *56*(2), 129-140. doi: 10.1016/j.bandc.2004.09.016.

Roessler, J. and Eilan, N. (2003). *Agency and Self-Awareness: Issues in Philosophy and Psychology*: Oxford University Press.

Salvador, R., Suckling, J., Coleman, M. R., Pickard, J. D., Menon, D. and Bullmore, E. (2005). Neurophysiological architecture of functional magnetic resonance images of human brain. *Cereb Cortex*, *15*(9), 1332-1342. doi: 10.1093/cercor/bhi016.

Sato, J. R., Kozasa, E. H., Russell, T. A., Radvany, J., Mello, L. E., Lacerda, S. S. and Amaro, E. Jr. (2012). Brain imaging analysis can identify participants under regular mental training. *PLoS One*, *7*(7), e39832. doi: 10.1371/journal.pone.0039832.

Seeley, W. W., Allman, J. M., Carlin, D. A., Crawford, R. K., Macedo, M. N., Greicius, M. D. and Miller, B. L. (2007). Divergent social functioning in behavioral variant frontotemporal dementia and Alzheimer disease: reciprocal networks and neuronal evolution. *Alzheimer Dis Assoc Disord*, *21*(4), S50-57. doi: 10.1097/WAD.0b013e31815c0f14.

Seeley, W. W., Carlin, D. A., Allman, J. M., Macedo, M. N., Bush, C., Miller, B. L. and DeArmond, S. J. (2006). Early frontotemporal dementia targets neurons unique to apes and humans. *Annals of Neurology*, *60*(6), 660-667. doi: 10.1002/ana.21055.

Seeley, W. W., Menon, V., Schatzberg, A. F., Keller, J., Glover, G. H., Kenna, H. and Greicius, M. D. (2007). Dissociable intrinsic connectivity networks for salience processing and executive control. *J Neurosci*, *27*(9), 2349-2356. doi: 10.1523/jneurosci.5587-06.2007.

Seth, A. K. (2010). The grand challenge of consciousness. *Front Psychol*, *1*, 5. doi: 10.3389/fpsyg.2010.00005.

Seth, A. K., Suzuki, K. and Critchley, H. D. (2012). An interoceptive predictive coding model of conscious presence. *Front Psychol*, *2*. doi: 10.3389/fpsyg.2011.00395.

Shapiro, D. H. (2008). *Meditation: Self-Regulation Strategy and Altered State of Consciousness*. NY: Aldine De Gruyter.

Siegel, R. D., Germer, C. K. and Olendzki, A. (2008). Mindfulness: What Is It? Where Did It Come From? In F. Didonna (Ed.), *Clinical Handbook of Mindfulness*. New York: Springer.

Steriade, M. (1996a). Arousal: revisiting the reticular activating system. *Science*, *272*(5259), 225-226.

Steriade, M. (1996b). Awakening the brain. *Nature*, *383*(6595), 24-25. doi: 10.1038/383024a0.

Sturm, V. E., Rosen, H. J., Allison, S., Miller, B. L. and Levenson, R. W. (2006). Self-conscious emotion deficits in frontotemporal lobar degeneration. *Brain*, *129*(9), 2508-2516. doi: 10.1093/brain/awl145.

Tan, L. B., Lo, B. C. and Macrae, C. N. (2014). Brief mindfulness meditation improves mental state attribution and empathizing. *PLoS One*, *9*(10), e110510. doi: 10.1371/journal.pone.0110510.

Tang Y. Y., Holzel, B. K. and Posner, M. I. (2015). The neuroscience of mindfulness meditation. *Nat Rev Neurosci*, *16*(4), 213-225. doi: 10.1038/nrn3916.

Tang, Y. Y., Ma, Y., Fan, Y., Feng, H., Wang, J., Feng, S. and Fan, M. (2009). Central and autonomic nervous system interaction is altered by short-term meditation. *Proc Natl Acad Sci U S A*, *106*(22), 8865-8870. doi: 10.1073/pnas.0904031106.

Tang, Y. Y. and Posner, M. I. (2009). Attention training and attention state training. *Trends Cogn Sci*, *13*(5), 222-227. doi: 10.1016/j.tics. 2009.01. 009.

Tang, Y. Y., Rothbart, M. K. and Posner, M. I. (2012). Neural correlates of establishing, maintaining, and switching brain states. *Trends Cogn Sci*, *16*(6), 330-337. doi: 10.1016/j.tics.2012.05.001.

Thera, N. (1962). *Heart of Buddhist Meditation* Kandy, Sri Lanka: Buddhist Publication Society.

van de Ven, V. G., Formisano, E., Prvulovic, D., Roeder, C. H. and Linden, D. E. (2004). Functional connectivity as revealed by spatial independent component analysis of fMRI measurements during rest. *Hum Brain Mapp*, *22*(3), 165-178. doi: 10.1002/hbm.20022.

van den Heuvel, M., Mandl, R. and Hulshoff Pol, H. (2008). Normalized cut group clustering of resting-state FMRI data. *PLoS ONE*, *3*(4), e2001. doi: 10.1371/journal.pone.0002001.

Van Oudenhove, L., Vandenberghe, J., Dupont, P., Geeraerts, B., Vos, R., Bormans, G. and Tack, J. (2009). Cortical deactivations during gastric fundus distension in health: visceral pain-specific response or attenuation of 'default mode' brain function? A H215O-PET study. *Neurogastroenterology and Motility*, *21*(3), 259-271. doi: 10.1111/j.1365-2982.2008.01196.x.

Weiskrantz, L. (1997). *Consciousness Lost and Found: A Neuropsychological Exploration.* New York: Oxford University Press.

Zeman, A. (2001). Consciousness. *Brain*, *124*(Pt 7), 1263-1289.

In: Consciousness
Editor: Lloyd Alvarado
ISBN: 978-1-63485-023-0

Chapter 10

Consciousness as Emergent Property of the Interaction Between Cognitive Levels

Rita Pizzi[*]
Department of Computer Science
University of Milan, Milan, Italy

Abstract

The search for possible neural correlates of consciousness is a particularly complex issue. Nonetheless it appears ascertained that consciousness is the result of the simultaneous interaction between several brain areas. At a cognitive level, consciousness can be represented as an emergent structure typical of superior animal species that manages and coordinates different cognitive levels. However, the subjective characteristic of the conscious experience does not seem to be fully explained either by neural correlates or by a cognitive interpretation. The paper presents a formal solution of the so-called "hard problem" that takes as its starting point the important works of D. Hofstadter, G. Spencer-Brown and F. Varela.

Introduction

By "emergent property" we can mean a discontinuous step towards a greater acquisition of the system autonomy with respect to the environment. However, it must be said that there is a lack of clearness about the degree of irreducibility of such a discontinuous step: in fact the notion of "emergent property" has been adopted both by the reductionism and by the vitalism.

According to S. Alexander (Space, Time and Deity, 1920) and C.L. Morgan (Emergent Evolution, and The Emergence of Novelty, 1923) more and more complex levels of evolution produce new qualities which are not predictable on the basis of the lower-level laws [1].This position originated in the frame of the controversy between reductionism and vitalism, and it

[*] via Bramante 65, 26013 Crema, e-mail: rita.pizzi@unimi.it.

is debatable if it means that every emergent quality will remain absolutely irreducible even after the development of further theories.

But it is an open problem to find out if there exist absolutely irreducible laws in principle.

According to C.D. Broad (The Mind and its Place in Nature, 1918), it can be shown that, for instance, in chemistry it is in principle impossible to deduct the property R starting from the interactive components $C_1, C_2, \ldots, C_n$, if R is a secondary quality, i.e., a disposition to some specific sensations, for example a pungent smell: whereas it would be possible to deduct R if it were a physical disposition of the components.

Broad asserts that "neither the archangel of Mathematics could predict the smell of NH3 if no one before had smelt it".

Thus the law "if $(C_1, C_2, \ldots, C_n)$ then Q" is emergent if it must be directly confirmed by perception of examples of Q before deducing it from a general composition law.

It can be drawn that such a quality Q can include predicates defined ostensively, which must indicate already tested qualities. But it is not possible to figure out non experite qualities, because a law which puts in relationship variations of physical quantities with variations of experienced qualities (e.g., "more resonant"), is absolutely emergent due to the limits of the semantic analysis [1]. Besides, it is clear that the transition from an organizational level to the next involves a change of the description language, which includes - differently expressed - the previous elements, but whose new elements result to be formally inconsistent with the previous language. However, this fact does not have any vitalistic meaning.

V. Weisskopf suggests (cited in [2]) that when a discontinuity is not quantitatively explainable, it should be treated as a qualitatively different whole, due to a significant relationship among its parts.

According to Weisskopf the quantum indeterminism could be avoided if an effective quality theory existed. However, as we mentioned before, the methodological problem of quality is its lack of a complete relation of order: Lasswell has proposed a configuration method, which can be treated with a matrix calculus or graph theory.

THE ROLE OF THE SUBJECT

The Weisskopfs interpretation of emergence is meant in a holistic way: we can define an emergent quality as what makes the whole different from the sum of its parts, emerging from their interrelations.

A clear example are the Gestalt perceptions, which can be different even in the presence of the same components (see the renown picture in Figure 1).

This presupposes the presence of a percipient subject able to distinguish and integrate a set of factors not determinable through the usual analitic method.

A matrix model for the qualitative analysis could fit with the Eccles-Popper preception model [3], where different Gestalts could be distinguished due to a different opening of emotional modules linked to the limbic system of the brain.

Figure 1. Gestalt theory: classical picture.

In other words, it can be said following Hofstadter [4] that the complexity of the brain structure originates the emergent quality "consciousness", which determinates our ability of perception of qualities as well as our ability of managing self-reference forms.

According to Hofstadter, in fact, consciousness is an epiphenomenon of the "tangled" complexity of the brain.

Thanks to the "foldback" (or "strange loop") the brain is able to self-observe itself "from the outside" and to overcome in this way those self-referent situations which cause an infinite loop in a computer. Following Hofstadter, computers don't have the emergent property "consciousness" because they did not yet reach an analogous degree of tangled complexity.

A Formal Model

In order to formalize such ideas it can be useful to apply the theory of F. Varela and H. Maturana [5]. The authors define an autopoietic system as a homeostatic system characterized by the interconnection and the self-organization of its own internal processes. The autopoietic systems turn out to have emergent features of autonomy and individuality.

Living systems are autopoietic machines. J. Goguen and F. Varela developed these ideas by using a formalism [6] which goes back to the G. Spencer-Brown's calculus of indications [7].

The main feature of the Spencer-Brown's algebra is the use of the two operators

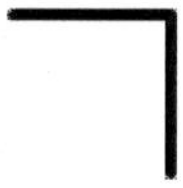 (indication)

and

(non-indication)

and of the two axioms

Condensation

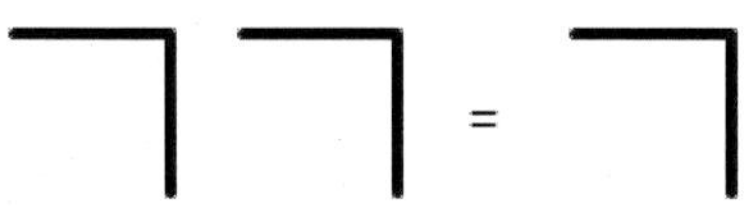

Cancellation

According to Spencer-Brown, the original act of the subject's perception is the distinction of the “id” from the background.

As any distinction is indication of a value, we can speak of a calculus of indications. An important feature of this calculus is its particular way of handling self-reference and making it consistent, by expressing forms like

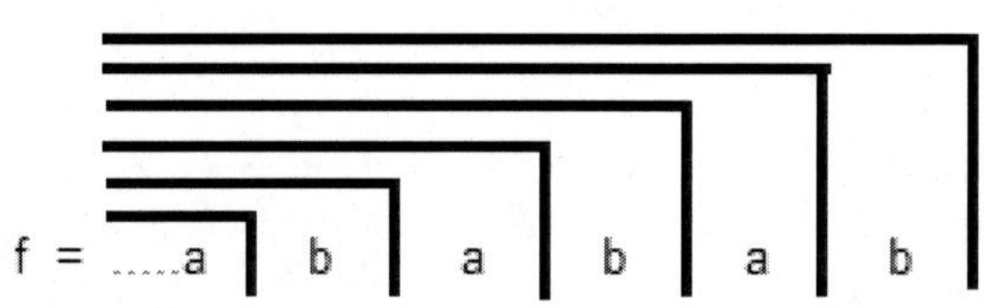

as

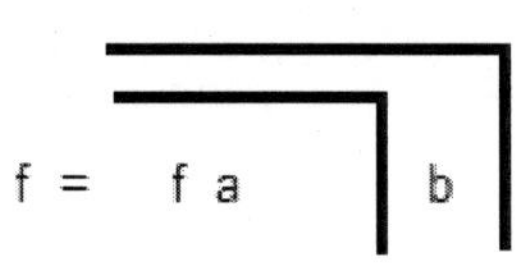

This is to say that the expression f *re-enters* into itself, *in-forms* itself, as a Klein's bottle or a Moebius' ring.

Maturana and Varela carry forward the Spencer-Brown's formalism by indicating the re-entering form with

and expand the calculus by including a third state, called the *autonomous state* indicated by

The axioms of the extended calculus of indications are now

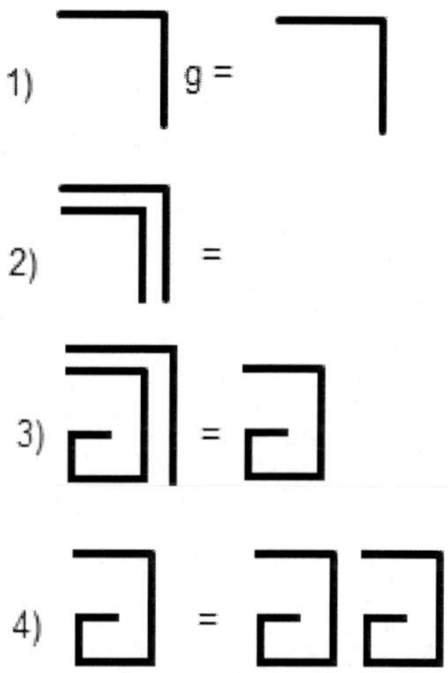

The basic idea is that self-reference is now included in the calculus, by introducing a third state which forms itself in an autonomous way by self-indication. The third state is *not reducible* to the laws of the two early states, but comes out from the co-operation of the elements of a two-valued systems.

An example can be the autopoietic organization of cells, given by a set of chemical species interacting each others.

In the molecular self-organization the interaction among the component variables leads to the emergence of an autonomous unity.

Douglas Hofstader confirmed his theory in [10]. The formalism presented above has been enhanced in [8], [9] by developing a fixed-point equation which represents the emergence of an autonomous state (in this case the consciousness) from the act of the subject's self-observation.

Conclusion

All the theories above mentioned have developed a conceptual model of the interaction between cognitive levels where the role of the perceiving subject is inseparable from the phenomenology of the environment.

The cognitive levels present a strict interaction where circular connections are not vicious thanks to the presence of the subject in a double role: of physical being and of self-conscious mind which can look *from the outside* at the system which the subject is set in.

The circular connection between cognitive levels allows - once a threshold of complexity has been overcome - the emergence of properties whose features are non reducible to lower levels.

A formalism due to H. Maturana and F. Varela has been chosen to represent this model, and new developments have been carried on to justify consciousness as an autonomous state coming from the complex interconnection of the mind's processes.

References

[1] Pap, Arthur. 1962. *An Introduction to the Philosophy of Science*. New York: Free Press of Glancoe.

[2] Lerner, Daniel., ed. 1961. *Quantity and Quality*. New York: Free Press.

[3] Popper, Karl, and Eccles, John C. 1977. *The Self and its Brain - an argument for interactionism*. Berlin: Springer Verlag 1977.

[4] Hofstadter, Douglas. 1980. *Goedel, Escher, Bach: An Eternal Golden Braid.* Brighton: Harvester Press.

[5] Maturana, Humberto, and Varela, Francisco. 1973. *De Máquinas y Seres Vivos: Una teoría sobre la organización biológica.* Santiago: Editorial Universitaria.

[6] Spencer-Brown, George. 1969. *The laws of Form*. London: Allen and Unwin.

[7] Varela, Francisco. 1979. *Principles of Biological Autonomy*. New York: Elsevier.

[8] Pizzi, Rita, Degli Antoni, Giovanni. 1990. "An Introductory Model of Artficial Reality: Relationship with Spencer Brown's Calculus of indications." *Proc. First Conference on Cyberspace,* Austin, May 1990: 79-81.

[9] Degli Antoni, Giovanni and Pizzi, Rita. 1991. "Virtuality as a Basis for Problem Solving ?" *AI* and *Society* 5: 239—254.

[10] Hofstadter, Douglas. 2007. *I am in a strange loop.* New York: Basic Books.

In: Consciousness
Editor: Lloyd Alvarado

ISBN: 978-1-63485-023-0

Chapter 11

ELEMENTARY SENSATION PRIMACY CREATING A FIRST TO THIRD PERSON GAP OF CONSCIOUSNESS

Franz K. Jansen*
F-126 chemin Fesquets, 34820 ASSAS, France

ABSTRACT

Three main mental functions are global perception, memory imagery and abstract reflection, which are distinguished by the activity, passivity or neutrality of sense organs. Global perception is composed of elementary sensation and stimulated reminiscence. Elementary sensation is an uninterrupted physical chain of bottom-up information from extra-mental reality to active sense organs and specialized brain regions. Stimulated reminiscence and memory imagery without sense organ activity represent top-down information from different brain regions. Abstract reflection without sense organs allows abstraction by categorization, structuring and establishment of relations. Elementary sensation with direct physical interactions between the extra-mental environment, sense organs and specific brain regions reflects the present and is primary, self-evident, intense, unchangeable and incommunicable. Memory imagery retrieving anterior perceptions represents the past and is secondary, faint, modifiable, reproducible and communicable. Abstract reflection allows the abstraction of memory imagery to objective concepts allowing general consensus. Neurobiological investigations showed that elementary sensation with active sense organs activates the same brain regions as memory imagery without sense organ activity, whereas abstract reflection takes place in different prefrontal brain regions. The different brain locations may explain the hard problem. A first to third person gap does not allow an identical content of consciousness in two persons, since elementary sensation of the first person cannot be directly transmitted to a third person, but has to be recreated with the same environment and the sense organs of that person. Nevertheless, differences in sense organ constitution or information processing will not allow reconstitution of an identical content of consciousness. Especially experience from inside sense organs, like pain, cannot be transmitted to third persons. Elementary sensation is the starting point of a continuous process leading from sense organ transmitted bottom-up information to the two other mental functions, which build up human knowledge. By initiating the global perception function, elementary

* Corresponding author: jansen.franz@orange.fr; www.jansen-fk.com.

sensation acquires epistemic primacy, which induces complex subjective experiences representing the present and are encoded in the memory as fixed episodes of the past. They can be retrieved by the function of memory imagery. Finally the function of abstract reflection objectifies this information by abstraction into concepts. Epistemic primacy of elementary sensation has to be distinguished from ontological primacy of consciousness concerning the non-material existence of experienced consciousness different from the material world. However, epistemic primacy remains indecisive with respect to ontological primacy concerning the philosophical theories of materialism, dualism or panpsychism.

Keywords: elementary sensation, global perception, memory imagery, abstract reflection, neurobiological correspondence, hard problem, consciousness primacy, subjective experience, objectification

1. INTRODUCTION

Consciousness leads to the unsolved "hard problem" on the origin of conscious experience (Chalmers 1995). On the one hand, it is considered as an absolute, for everybody self-evident entity which *"can by no means be reduced to structure"*; so that "*consciousness is and remains methodologically primary*" (Bitbol, 2008 p.69). On the other hand, it has to be brought into relation with bio-physical matter, since its evolution and functions depend on a healthy brain. Consciousness as the starting point for the objectification process has primacy; therefore Varela suggested a new stance by *"embedding phenomenological reports and objective findings within a unique structure"* (Bitbol 2008, p.70).

Chalmers (1995) described two different kinds of the brain-consciousness problems, the soft problem and the hard problem. The soft problem could be solved more easily and concerns functions like discrimination, categorization, information integration, access to one's internal states and distinction between wakefulness and sleep. The hard problem is linked to states of conscious experience dependent on perception with different perception organs, which lead to qualia in conscious, such as the experience of redness or of hearing the sound of an instrument or of smelling a rose (Jackson 1982). As Levine (1983) explained, there is an explanatory gap between subjective experience and brain functions, when explained by neurobiological processes. The physicist Zeh (1998) confirmed such a gap, since perceived color is not a property of physical light. Therefore, it remains incomprehensible how and why physical wavelengths induce the subjective experience of the color red.

Consciousness can be explored from an introspective first person view and from a neurobiological third person view. Philosophically Chalmers (1995) discriminated two states in consciousness, a more cognitive state with general awareness corresponding to the soft problems and a phenomenal state represented by the experience of perception, defined as the hard problem.

In this article a special type of "elementary sensation" is proposed, which induces the same properties as the subjective experience of phenomenological consciousness (Jansen 2014, p 4/11). Elementary sensation corresponds to the interaction of the physical environment with the corresponding sense organs transmitted to specialized brain regions and appears to be primary, intense, unchangeable and incommunicable. Memory imagery derived from elementary sensation is secondary, faint, modifiable, and communicable. Abstract reflection allows objectification to concepts and structural relations. Since elementary sensation is incommunicable to third persons, it creates a first to third person gap in consciousness. For each mental function, the different phenomenological qualia correlate with a different location of the involved brain regions. Thus the phenomenal gap between global perception and memory imagery on the one side and abstract reflection on the other side might explain the hard problem by different interconnections of the corresponding brain regions (Jansen, submitted).

2. THREE MAIN MENTAL FUNCTIONS

Mental activity allows the acquisition of human knowledge on extra-mental reality by a continuous process following three main mental functions from: **global perception** (I) **to memory imagery** (II) and finally **abstract reflection** (III). The function of global perception can be subdivided into two subunits, **elementary sensation** (Jansen 2014 p 4/11) complemented by **stimulated reminiscence** (Figure 1). Elementary sensation is physical bottom up information from the sense organs to the brain. It is characterized by a chain of uninterrupted physical interactions, such as photons reflected from outside objects entering the eye and depolarizing nerve cells in the retina. The neural activation is further transported through the nerve system to brain regions in the occipital cortex specialized for optical signals.

The mental representation of extra-mental reality in the brain simultaneously needs bottom-up elementary sensation complemented with top-down stimulated reminiscence by retrieving encoded information from the memory, which contains episodic memory of the past. Recognizing a friend requires bottom-up elementary sensation by photons reflected from a distant body, but also top-down information from the memory imagery of the past characterizing the body as a person and a friend. Elementary sensation and stimulated reminiscence together form the function of **global perception**, induced by sense organ activity.

In contrast, if the eyes are closed, the chain of physical interactions between the outside and the brain is interrupted, the extra-mental object can still be mentally represented, but now only by top-down information retrieved from the episodic memory. Memory imagery corresponds in neuroscience to mental imagery and concerns already fixed episodes encoded in the memory but only representing past events no longer depending on sense organ activity in the present.

Global perception with sense organs allows a mental representation of the extra-mental reality evaluating the near or distant environment of the body. A distant stimulus can be represented by photons of electromagnetic waves or sounds of mechanical waves, which enter their corresponding reception organ and are transmitted to the brain. In a similar way, perception organs for the inside of the body depend on an uninterrupted chain of physical interactions from their specific environment to the brain. Elementary sensations are necessarily conscious for the representation of extra-mental reality and depend on physiological brain functions, which are rapidly lost after injury of the brain such as insufficient blood oxygenation.

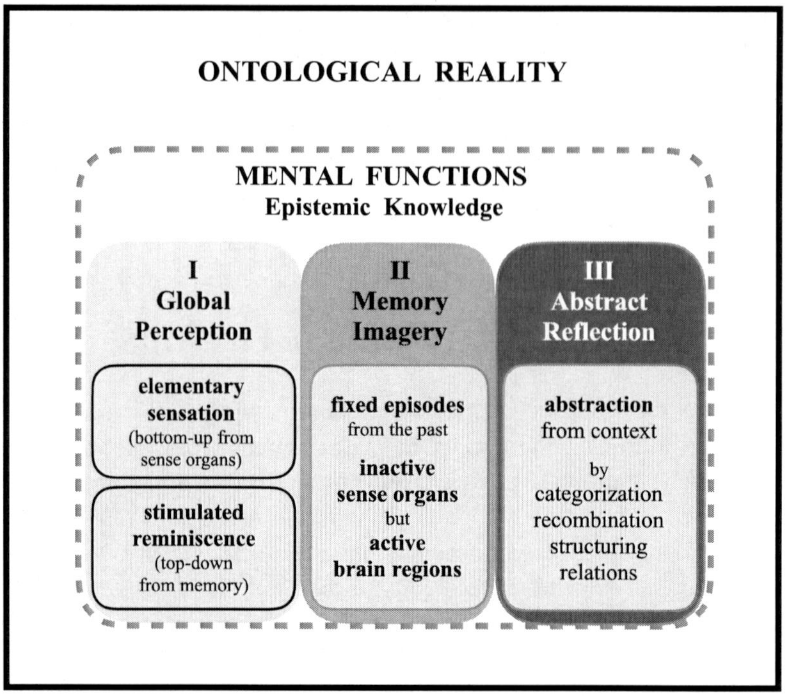

Figure 1. Mental Functions Providing Epistemic Knowledge.
There are three main mental functions: global perception, memory imagery and abstract reflection. Only global perception is divided into two subunits, elementary sensation and stimulated reminiscence, which are complementary for the constitution of global perception.

3. Mental Function I: Global Perception

Global perception combines elementary sensation as bottom-up information coming from all sense organs and stimulated reminiscence as top-down information from already encoded information in the memory, which represents prior experiences. Both sub-functions are intimately linked and form global perception with no apparent distinction. But after closing the eyes or ears, the prior perception can still be imagined, showing a clear distinction between global perception with active sense organs and memory imagery devoid of sense organ activity. In global perception, elementary sensation retrieves only directly linked episodes from the memory, whereas memory imagery contains all encoded prior episodes. The main distinction between the three mental functions depends on sense organ activity, which is active for elementary sensation and thereby for global perception, passive for memory imagery, but absent in abstract reflection (Figure 1).

3.1. Sense Organs

Sense organ activity allows a mental representation of extra-mental reality through perception in humans as well as animals. However, sense organs should be taken in a much larger sense according to Bayne (2011), not only limited to the classical five senses of Aristotle (350 BC) comprising sight, audition, smell, taste and touch. Sense organs have the task of orienting living beings in their environment and avoiding survival dangers. Sense organs are situated at different sites in the body and could be classified according to three vital functions for survival. They can alert with outside-directed sense organs for dangers at distance, with surface sensory organs for dangers in direct contact with the body and with inside sense organs for disturbed organ functions in the body.

Perception at the outside of the body necessitates highly specialized outside sense organs, such as vision, audition and smell. Perception at the surface of the body is effected by receptors in the skin for contact, pressure, vibration, thermoception as well as for taste in the mucosa membranes of the oral cavity. Inside perception within the body and its organs is supervised by sense organs for alerting abnormal functions of inner organs of the body. Specialized receptors are localized in many organs, for instance for pulmonary stretch regulation of breathing, gastrointestinal tract functions, bladder fullness, and others. As long as inner organs function normally, the sense organ perception remains unconscious, but becomes conscious for intense organ functions, such as forced respiration, violent heartbeats, abundant transpiration and for all organ dysfunctions. Any disturbance of sense organs is indicated by nociception with pain, thus outside organs like eyes can be blinded, surface organs can be burned and inner organs disturbed such as by bad digestion. Unlocalizable permanently active inside sense organs indicate general feelings, such as tonicity associated with muscular tension or weakness with lowered muscular tension. The concert of all activated sense organs for outside and inside perception might constitute an important part of conscious awareness.

The activity of sense organs is variable. Some sense organs can be voluntarily inactivated, whereas others remain continuously active (Table 1). Closing the eyes, closing the ears with fingers or holding the nose closed can inactivate outside sense organs. However, disturbed surface senses of the skin cannot be discarded from awareness, such as the feeling of pressure, heat or other surface injuries. A permanent activity of these surface organs is necessary for indicating life-threatening dangers and could be regarded as security guards indicating problems for essential survival functions of the body. Under normal functions they remain unconscious, but with disturbed organ functions they become perceptible and induce pain. Inside sense organs cannot be inactivated either, some of them indicate organ functions, but others general feelings such as tonicity or weakness as well as illness or well being of the body.

Awareness can comprise multiple sense organs simultaneously, but can also become extremely restricted to only one sense such as breathing, which was experienced during incomplete anesthesia. Muscle inhibitors are necessary to relax muscular tensions during operations of the abdomen, but also inhibit breathing. When injected too early before profound anesthesia is reached, the respiratory inhibition can become conscious again and is felt as an extreme urge of breathing, but without any other sense organ perception. With increasing anesthesia the isolated awareness of one isolated disturbed sense organ disappears again.

Table 1. Voluntary and Involuntary Interruption of Sense Organ Activities

	distant outside sense organs	Proximate outside sense organs	inside sense organs	conscious awareness
voluntary interruption	+	–	–	–
spontaneous disappearance	+	+	+	–

Depending on the kind of sense organ, (distant, proximate or inside) it can be voluntarily interrupted or has to wait for the spontaneous disappearance of the stimulating agent. Only consciousness cannot disappear unless profound sleep is reached.

3.2. Elementary Sensation

All sense organs, such as seeing, hearing, tasting and others, lead to global perception with sense organ activity including elementary sensation and stimulated reminiscence. Elementary sensation is limited to the contact of sense organs with their special environment by an uninterrupted chain of physical interactions. In normal life elementary sensation and stimulated reminiscence are indistinguishable from each other, so that pure elementary sensation, like seeing redness or just hearing a sound, is more difficult to encounter. In general elementary bottom-up sensation is associated to stimulated top-down reminiscence. Therefore elementary sensation is a theoretical concept, defined as pure bottom-up perception devoid of any top down perception associated with prior episodes, concepts or emotions, which easily come in mind when perceiving an object. Thermoception is a better indicator of elementary sensation, since it is less associated to objects. The pure form of elementary sensation is more an exception, only rarely found in normal adults, for instance when they encounter completely new situations, but more present in the evolving young child, when it has not yet acquired prior experiences.

Elementary sensation has five characteristic properties (Table 2). When taking a bath, one might be cautious to feel the water temperature with the hand first. If there is an immediate ***intense*** pain by too hot water, the hand is instantaneously retired from the bath. The intense feeling of heat corresponds to the direct physical contact of the thermoception receptors in the skin with too hot water. The intensity of the heat feeling remains ***unchangeable*** during the whole contact period with the water. But the intense pain induces the reflex of a rapid withdrawal of the hand. Elementary sensation during environmental contact of all sense organs, such as seeing blinding light, hearing disturbing sounds or feeling burning pain, can only be passively endured without any possibility to diminish its intensity, unless by escaping the unfavorable environment. Elementary sensation is limited to the direct contact of sense organs with the environment, such as thermoception receptors with too hot water. Without the direct physical contact, its intensity becomes ***irreproducible*** from the memory by voluntary actions a day later. For the same reason, it remains ***incommunicable*** to third persons, until they undergo the same direct environmental contact with their own sense organs, in order to obtain the same elementary sensation. Thus elementary sensation is a true mental representation of the ongoing extra-mental reality, since it is only ***reflecting the present*** (Jansen 2014 b).

Table 2. Properties of Elementary Sensation and Memory Imagery

	ELEMENTARY SENSATION	MEMORY IMAGERY
	unbroken physical chain	**broken** physical chain
1.	intense	faint
2.	unchangeable	changeable
3.	irreproducible	reproducible
4.	incommunicable	communicable
5.	reflecting the present	reflecting the past
	UNIQUENESS	**REPRODUCTION**

Elementary sensation and memory imagery have opposite properties. Stimulated reminiscence, a subunit of global perception, is part of memory imagery, but represents only that part, which is linked to elementary sensations in the past and directly stimulated by it.

The fact that elementary sensation is unchangeable could have a biological sense. If it were modifiable, consciousness could overlook the importance of a dangerous situation. Thus a voluntary diminution of sense organ sensitivity could delay dangerous situations, whereas intense pain will force to escape a threatening situation immediately. In this respect, intense, unchangeable elementary sensation represents the environment in the present and increases survival chances, like security guards.

3.3. Stimulated Reminiscence

Global perception (I) requires besides the sense organ dependent elementary sensation complementary information from past experiences, necessary for the identification of the perceived extra-mental objects. Elementary sensation as a bottom-up stimulus induces the reminiscence of directly linked past experiences by retrieval of top-down information encoded in the episodic memory (Figure 1).

Stimulated reminiscence presents past experiences directly stimulated by the elementary sensation, such as the identification of the perceived object by its name and special properties as well as the associated feelings, like gladness or anger. Together elementary sensation and its stimulated reminiscence form the function of global perception in the present. Stimulated reminiscence is only a selected part of the total memory imagery, retrieved by the specialized stimulus of elementary sensation (see next chapter).

4. Mental Function II: Memory Imagery

Sense organs remain passive during memory imagery, but their corresponding brain regions represent them. Thereby memory imagery without active sense organs acquired five new properties, different from elementary sensation, which now allow quite different actions. First, in contrast to the intensity of elementary sensation, memory imagery remains ***faint***, for instance when the perception of the contact of the hand with the too hot water is retrieved a day later (Table 2). Second, although elementary sensation is unchangeable by voluntary actions, memory imagery has become ***changeable***, since it can be forgotten or recalled in consciousness again. Third, epistemic memory is based on encoded information and becomes ***reproducible*** by retrieval from the episodic memory. Fourth, it becomes ***communicable*** by signs or language to a third person, which can retrieve similar episodic events from her-own memory. Fifth, since memory imagery without sense organ activity was fixed during encoding, it is ***reflecting the past***, which may be different from the evolving actual present (Jansen 2014 b). In contrast to elementary sensation, which is unique, memory imagery is a reproduction of the past, but with more liberties than the strong dependence of elementary sensation on sense organs for the representation of extra-mental reality in the present.

All global perceptions are automatically encoded in the unconscious memory, from which they can be retrieved. The fact that memory imagery is changeable, presents an enormous advantage, since it can now be modified by abstract reflection for categorization, recombination, comparison and the establishment of relations. With the raw material of memory imagery, abstract reflection can invent a new, objective world based on physical, biological and psychological structures. Thus, if the subjective memory imagery of pain after too hot water is compared to a thermometer in the bath, the correlation of subjective feeling to objective features would allow avoiding another bath with too hot water in the future again.

Global perception with sense organs represents the present of extra-mental reality and memory imagery the past. Due to their opposite properties, both functions can be considered as independent, but complementary entities.

5. Mental Function III: Abstract Reflection

Memory imagery representing a fixed past allows with abstract reflection the decomposition into its elements by abstraction for further analysis of the past or for the recombination of different elements probably predicting the future. Reflection can be considered as neutral, since it is in general no longer associated to emotions and tries to consider dispassionate reasoning through abstraction and recombination of memory imagery. Global perception and memory imagery are considered as subjective experiences, representing high complexity of personal experiences. Abstract reflection continues the process of acquiring knowledge and decomposes memory imagery into more abstract elements, which can more easily obtain consensus shared by third persons and is then considered as objective. This seems to be concordant with some interpretations in philosophy "*… scientific knowledge shows us that objective domains of knowledge are elaborated in two steps, with conscious experience as an implicit departure point…*" (Bitbol 2008, p.54-55)

Abstraction by abstract reflection allows **categorization**, which eliminates individual properties for only considering general properties of a group. **Relations** of different groups to each other could show common **structures** and reveal causal interactions between structural elements. **Recombination** of adequate structural elements might then allow the constitution of new causal structures, which could represent a potential future behavior of nature or a human invention not realized by nature.

Abstract reflection allows the extrapolation into the past and the future of general concepts extracted from global perception. Whereas elementary sensation is limited to the present and memory imagery to the past of a person, abstract reflection can extrapolate general concepts into the past far beyond a person's birth, by going back to the father, grandfather or even Homo Sapiens, about hundred thousand years ago. Now the self-evidence of elementary sensation is lacking and replaced by logical evidence. For certain relations, general consensus can be obtained, whereas others in a too distant past remain potential hypothesis. Extrapolation into the future follows similar rules. Regular happening events in the present and the recent past like the earth revolution can be extrapolated into the future with relative confidence, whereas others based on irregular behavior in the present and past like weather conditions can only be extrapolated as probability or potentiality into the future. Thus the certainty of conviction decreases from self-evidence for elementary sensation in the present to logic evidence for memory imagery and finally to probabilities for abstract reflection concerning the far past and future. Nevertheless, even probabilities could give a hunch on the constitution of the universe.

6. Concordance with Neuroscience

Elementary sensation and memory imagery seem to utilize almost the same brain circuits. Neurobiological methods with fRMI proved that mental imagery of a movement requires almost the same brain circuits as the execution of the movement itself. Roth et al. (1996) found that brain regions activated by the contraction of muscles during a movement are also activated when the movement is only imagined. Thereby the mental simulation of movements involves the primary cortex in a similar way as the execution of the imagined movement. This important finding was confirmed by Jeannerod (1997), Nyberg et al. (2006), Olsson et al. (2008) and others.

The same principle was found for visual perception by Kosslyn et al. (2001) and Ganis et al. (2004). Direct perception is found to activate almost the same brain regions in a bottom-up process as mental imagery in a top-down process for the same vision (Ganis and Schendan 2008; Schendan and Ganis 2012). This is well illustrated by a spectacular case with complete loss of color vision after brain damage. A painter became color blind after a car accident and could no longer see colors with open eyes, but even with closed eyes he was unable to imagine colors, since all remained grey (Sacks and Wassermann, 1987). This directly showed that the same brain circuits were required as well for direct perception of color as for mental imagery of color.

According to the findings on vision, direct audio perception and memory audio perception also need the same brain circuits. Perceiving and imagining songs are associated with bilateral neuronal activity in the secondary auditory cortices as explored with functional magnetic resonance imaging (fMRI) and cerebral blood flow (CBF) (Zatorre et al., 1996, Halpern et al. 2004). The practice of mental imagining can even improve performances, although not to the same level as real practice (Zatorre and Halpern, 2005).

During mental imagery of the motor cortex, the activation of the brain circuit is reduced to about 30% (Jeannerod 2001) showing a considerable difference between imagery and execution of motor actions. A similar reduction of brain circuit activity may be expected for visual and audio perception, but is not yet mentioned in the literature. Neurobiological findings are in agreement with the fact that during elementary sensation the sense organs and their corresponding brain regions are fully active and that memory imagery with lacking sense organ activity needs almost the same brain regions.

The different brain location of mental imagery in sense organ associated brain regions and abstract reflection in prefrontal regions might allow explaining the hard problem of consciousness by the inhibition of sense organ linked brain regions for experience, when prefrontal regions are stimulated for reflection.

7. First to Third Person Gap for Consciousness

Elementary sensation always requires activity of sense organs; therefore it cannot be reproduced in a first person from memory imagery without sense organ activity, since the continuous physical chain of elementary sensation is interrupted. As a consequence, it can also in no way be communicated from a first to a third person by signs or language. In order to acquire the same experience of elementary sensation in a third person, it has to be re-created in that person by establishing the same sense organ circuit with the same environment, but now with the proper sense organs of the third person. The experience of a particular wine can be approximately described with words, but words are unable to induce an identical wine experience in a third person, if she never had tasted this wine before. Thus elementary sensation is incommunicable to a third person by words or gestures.

On the contrary, stimulated reminiscences can be retrieved from the episodic memory of a third person through language or special signs, if it already existed before. If the third person already tasted the same wine, she can retrieve it from her memory imagery, but if she never tasted any wine in her life, which could be the case at the age of a child, she would be unable to imagine the taste of a wine. Thus, experience from memory imagery of a third person can only be retrieved, if she already had the same experience before.

A first person might expect that her-own elementary sensation re-created under the same conditions in a third person, should be identical. However, no elementary sensation can directly connect the consciousness of a first and a third person by physical interactions, therefore the identity of experience can never be perceived nor proven. Nevertheless, it is easily projected from a first person on a third person by imagining that she might have identical experience. Although this might perhaps be possible in identical twins, there are many reasons against identical experiences, instead suggesting a profound first to third person gap.

7.1. Sense Organ and Behavioral Differences

Differences can be caused by the biological constitution of the sense organs or by the treatment of the perceived signal in the third person's consciousness. A color-blind person from birth will never have the same visual perception of a colored object, as a normal person. Human sense organs in different persons are rarely identical. Thus vision varies for its degree of acuity due to myopia or cataract, audition diminishes with increasing age for the sensitivity to certain wave frequencies and sensitivity to cold temperature increases with age. Therefore even recreation of elementary sensation with the sense organs of a third person does not warrant identity between a first and third person, at most a certain degree of approximation, which confirms the first to third person gap.

Elementary sensation is entirely depending on its corresponding sense organ, so that other perception organs are of no help. A person blind from birth never experiencing color sensations has an intact audition, which is completely different from visual experience. A second sense like audition can become more activated than in normal persons and be helpful by paying more attention to the sound, but the help by other sense organs is only indirect.

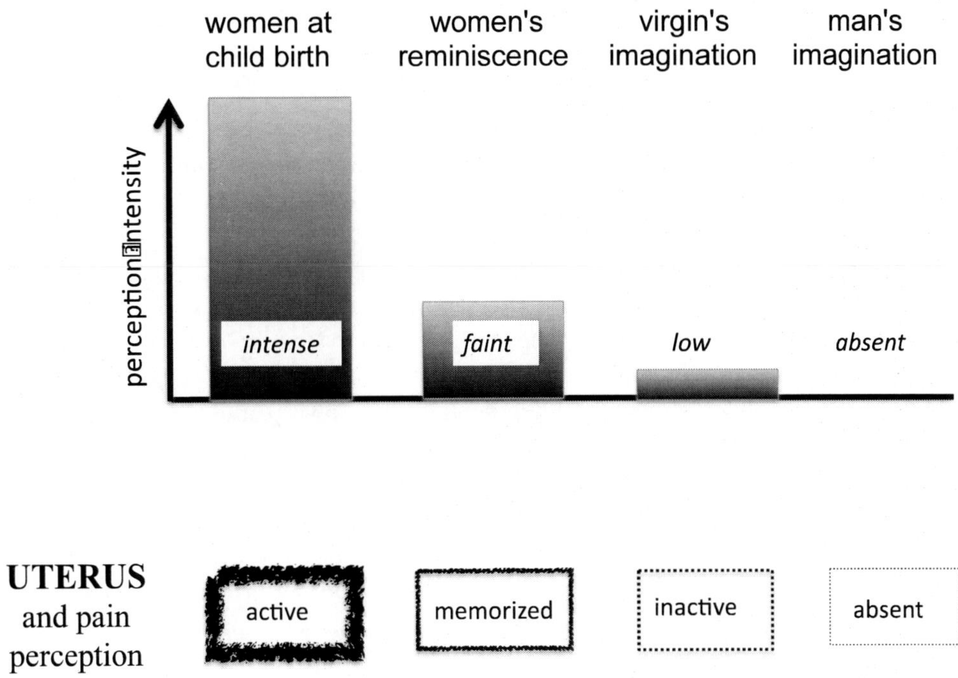

Figure 2. Pain Perception at Childbirth Compared to Imagined Pain by Others.
Direct perception of pain in a first person can only be imagined in a third person, if the specialized sense organ allowing pain perception (uterus) is present and if it already had the corresponding activity in the past.

Under some conditions, memory imagery of a first person cannot be expected in the third person, since it requires first the same sense organ and second the same prior activity in the third person. A man is unable to have memory imagery of the pain of a woman during childbirth, since he is lacking the same organ, the uterus. Therefore he can only remind pain of other organs by supposing that it could be an approximate correlate to the pain felt during childbirth. A virgin with an intact uterus will also be unable to experience the pain of childbirth, but menstruation pain could give her a slight hunch. Therefore even memory imagery needs the presence and full activity of the corresponding sense organs, for becoming similar in a third person (Figure 2).

The behavior of a first person after elementary sensation can also be very different from the one of a third person. A person extremely fearful of spiders will show exaggerated emotions compared to normal persons, when seeing a spider.

Although there are certainly differences in the content of experience, only some general structures of experience might be considered identical in first and third persons, such as awareness contrasting with deep sleep, responsiveness to verbal or other stimuli and context induced behavior, such as empathy. However, this view of third person consciousness is extremely reduced to general concepts, which no longer include all the complex content of the first person consciousness, only its main structures.

7.2. First Person Consciousness

Elementary sensation in the first person is limited to a certain range of distances, which changes with the kind of perception organ. Outside directed sense organs, for distant perception, like eyes and ears, perceive in the range of kilometers, outside directed sense organs for proximate perception like touching or temperature sensation, are active within about a meter, but inside directed sense organs like pain feeling or illness are strictly limited to the inside of the body.

A medical doctor knows pain feelings from his own elementary sensation, but when he is confronted to a patient with pain feelings, he has no sense organ for perceiving neither the special character nor the intensity of the patient's pain. He can only imagine his own experienced pain feelings and project a vague concept of potential pain feelings on the patient in the sense that she should have something similar to his own pain experiences. This is an objectification of pain in general, which is devoid of the precise subjective pain experience based on elementary sensation at the first person level and replaced by a vague thought concept derived from multiple kinds of pain feelings. The objectification process reduced the unique, self-evident primary perception to a group of potential pain feelings already known in memory imagery from prior elementary sensations. Thus any projected pain experience on third persons remains doubtful and uncertain with respect to its special properties and its intensity.

The interruption of sense organ activity and thereby of elementary sensation can have two causes. Distant outside sense organs, like seeing and hearing, can be voluntarily interrupted or the extra-mental objects interfering with sense organs can spontaneously disappear from perception. Proximate outside organs, like temperature feelings and all inside sense organs like pain feelings cannot be voluntarily interrupted; only their cause can disappear, like an illness causing pain. Nevertheless, proximate and inside senses have memory imagery with one exception concerning consciousness itself. The elementary inside perception of consciousness remains permanently present until it is interrupted by deep sleep. Even memory imagery of consciousness, as it was in the past, is impossible. Thus consciousness evoked by language in a third person can only induce her existing actual conscious experience.

7.3. Third Person Consciousness

Although first person experience is considered as complete and self-evident knowledge, a first person can only obtain incomplete knowledge on the third person's consciousness. Thus a first person is limited to a projection of her-own content of consciousness on a third person. Since a mental projection is no longer an uninterrupted chain of physical interactions between the first and the third person, it is subjected to major errors, which render the estimation of third person consciousness uncertain and create the first-to-third person gap (Table 3).

The importance of this gap must be considered for the concept of consciousness by distinguishing two different definitions, one for experienced consciousness at the first person level and another for projected consciousness on the third person level. Since both concepts are completely different, any confusion would necessarily lead to misunderstandings.

7.4. Uncertainty Concerning Third Person Consciousness

The content of third person's consciousness can only be estimated with the help of independent outside sense organs, like seeing and hearing, if the third person gives specific signs on her inner feelings by language or gestures, such as by lamentations or painful attitudes (Table 3). The interpretation of these signs is in general based on correlations made by the first person between her-own conscious experience and the corresponding context. Although there might be some correlation, there is no certainty. If a medical doctor is faced with the pain feelings of patients, their intensity is difficult to evaluate, since identical gestures like a sting with a syringe produce very different reactions, suggesting different pain feelings by patients in an identical context. There are also medical sufferings, which can be rapidly eliminated by placebos, showing the uncertainty of interpretation of signs from third persons. Thus the main characteristic of projected consciousness on third persons is a high degree of uncertainty.

The uncertainty of projected consciousness becomes much more pronounced, when projecting human consciousness on animals. There are certain signs such as the response to rewards or punishments or observation of behavior reminding human behavior, like empathy, which seem to allow the projection of human consciousness on animals. Nevertheless, animal consciousness must be different from the experience of human consciousness, since animals are unable to produce the same mental performances. The degree of difference in character and intensity is extremely difficult to evaluate. In higher animals, like dogs and cats, there could be a general agreement for consciousness, although of a lower level than experiential human consciousness at the first person level. However, it becomes more doubtful, if such kinds of consciousness could also be projected on lower animals, like worms or ants, whereas it is very difficult to imagine that experienced consciousness could be projected on unicellular amoeba or on plants.

Table 3. Differences in Global Perception for a First and Third Person

Global Perception		Outside sense organs	Inside sense organs
experienced by **first person**	through elementary sensation	primary, self-evident	primary, self-evident
GAP			
projected on **third person**	after re-creation	non-identical	no re-creation possible
	by language / signs	incomplete	incomplete
	only by context	doubtful	doubtful
	on animals	uncertain	uncertain

The content of consciousness in the first person as the reference is compared to the probable content of consciousness in a third person under different circumstances.

Nevertheless, panpsychism extrapolates consciousness to every kind of animals, plants and even molecules, but here the definition of consciousness is quite different and corresponds more to proto-consciousness, i.e., a precursor form of consciousness, which still needs complementation to become experienced first person consciousness.

8. Primacy of Elementary Sensation

Acquisition of knowledge is a continuous process requiring the three main mental functions of actual global perception (I), fixed memory imagery (II) and abstract reflection (III). Elementary sensation as the starting element of global perception introduces a character of uniqueness only depending on the actual present (Table 2). It is linked to an uninterrupted chain of physical interactions from the object through sense organs to the brain and undergoes in the present the slightest changes of extra-mental objects and their environment (Jansen 2014). In addition it is intense, unchangeable, irreproducible and incommunicable, which reinforces the character of uniqueness and requires its primacy.

Since elementary sensation directly depends on sensory organs, it is the only entry path for the connection of extra-mental reality to mental representation. This is the reason why it acquired primacy with respect to the other mental functions, which means that it is the starting point, not reducible to other prior conscious elements. Human knowledge is a further derivative of elementary sensation, since it depends on the information provided by all sense organs.

The other mental functions II and III further transform the initial subjective information by memory imagery and abstract reflection into abstract concepts. Memory imagination reflects a fixed encoded copy of prior global perception, thereafter abstract reflection further reduces memory imagery by abstraction with categorization, structuring, recombination and establishment of relations to concepts, which can lead to general consensus (Figure 3).

Primary global perception resembles the primacy claimed by philosophers for the phenomenology of consciousness. *" ...we tend to mean by "consciousness", taken as* ***immediate experience*** *rather than self-awareness"* (Bibol 2008, p. 53). *"It is not something that can be known or described by us in the third person as if we were separated from it; but it is what we dwell in and what we live through in the first person. I would recapitulate this by saying that* ***consciousness is existentially primary****"* (Bitbol 2008, p 54).

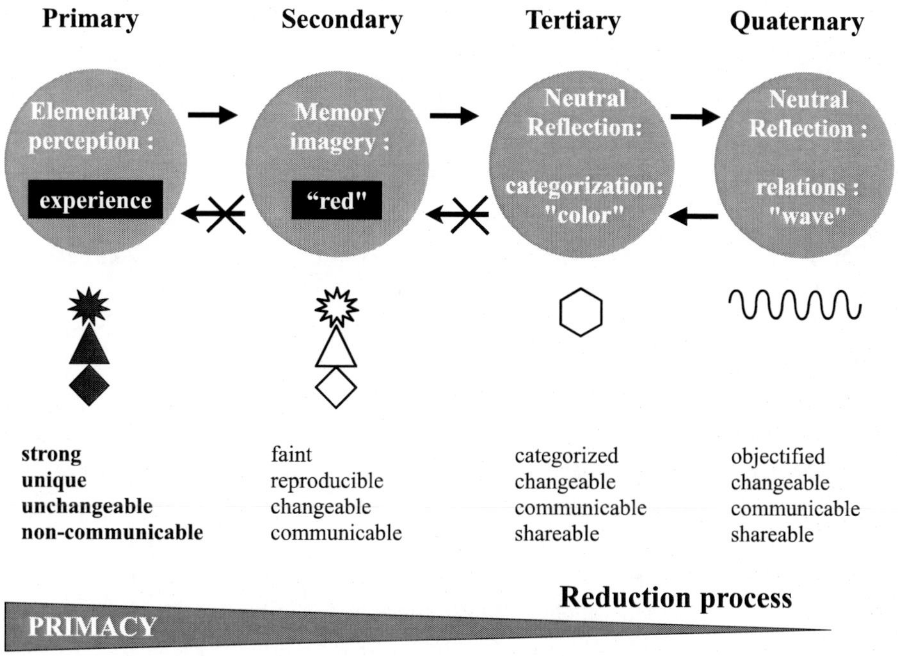

Figure 3. Process of Knowledge Acquisition by Successive Mental Functions.
Elementary sensation with subjective experience is automatically encoded in memory imagery, which allows abstract reflection to categorize and to further objectify the initial subjective experience by reduction with increasing abstraction to general concepts.

CONCLUSION

Consciousness allows the acquisition of knowledge by a process employing three successive mental functions, starting with subjective global perception, followed by subjective memory imagery and leading to objective abstract reflection. The three functions are distinguishable by the activity, passivity or absence of sense organs. All sense organs of the body in the widest sense are intimately linked to consciousness and simultaneously explore the outside, the surface and the inside of the body. Nevertheless, they can under special circumstances of anesthesia be extremely limited to only one special sense. Outside sense organs can be voluntarily turned off, whereas surface and inside sense organs are permanently turned on, as if they were security guards for the body. Activity or passivity of sense organs distinguishes between two mental functions: global perception and memory imagery. Global perception is based on elementary sensation plus stimulated reminiscence of past experiences. Elementary sensation is limited to the period of direct contact of sense organs with their special environment through an uninterrupted chain of physical interactions. When the chain of physical interaction through sense organs is broken, memory imagery can retrieve all global perceptions of the past. In normal life, elementary sensation and stimulated reminiscence are intimately interlinked, so that pure elementary sensation is rarely found in adults, but should be more frequent in the young child, still lacking sufficient prior experience encoded in the memory. Since elementary sensation is the only instant of direct contact between extra-mental reality, sense organs and the brain, it reflects the present. Memory imagery is a fixed and faint reminiscence of prior global perception and represents the past. Elementary sensation seems to correspond to the philosophical concept of sensation. *"... any sense modality... can function either perceptually or non-perceptually. In the latter case, what the sense gives rise to are mere sensations, not perceptions."* (Smith, 2011, loc. 5186)

According to neuroscience, global perception and memory imagery activate about the same brain regions (Ganis et al. 2004), whereas abstract reflection is essentially found in different prefrontal brain regions (Kandel et al. 2013). According to the hard problem of Chalmers (1995) there is a phenomenological gap, when global perception and memory imagery are compared to abstract reflection, this might correspond in neuroscience to their localization in different brain regions with probably different stimulations.

A considerable gap exists for the communication between a first and a third person consciousness. Elementary sensation is in general incommunicable by language or behavior from a first person to a third person, for instance for the taste of wine. The psychoanalyst Lebrun (2008) described that the symbolism of language represents discontinuity, which does not reflect the continuity of sensitivity in a singular person. For outside directed sense organs, the global perception of a first person experience can only be induced in a third person through re-creation with the same outside environment by utilizing the own sense organs and brain circuits of that person, which correspond to the first person experience. But re-created elementary sensation in a third person does not warrant an experience identical to the first person, since the sense organs or the treatment of information can be very different in a third person. Thus elementary sensation as intense, unchangeable, non-reproducible, incommunicable and part of global perception can be very different in a first and third person consciousness, reflecting a first to third person gap.

With outside sense organs, an approximate re-creation of elementary sensation in a third person can be more appropriate than with inside directed sense organs. Here the first-to-third person gap becomes much more pronounced, since there is no way of re-creating inside events for elementary sensation in the third person, for instance for inducing pain. The only possibility is a correlation of the inside experience of the first person to her environmental context by imagining that the same context should yield the same elementary sensation in the third person. However, such correlations are highly uncertain, not allowing conclusions on an identical content of global perception in a first and third person. Only indirect signs by language or gestures from the third person can be interpreted by the first person and suggest the content of her global perception.

Abstract reflection continuous the objectification process from the complexity of subjective global perception and memory imagery to more simplified objective concepts, which can obtain general consensus. Thereby subjective experience becomes reduced to invariant structural relations, as described by Bitbol : *"Firstly, one progressively pushes aside any feature of experience on which conscious subjects cannot agree, such as individual tastes, community values, or the emotional tinge ..."* and *" Secondly, one only retains a sort of structural residue of conscious experience that can be the object of a consensus ..."* (Bitbol 2008, p. 54-55).

Elementary sensation with its character of uniqueness is the starting point for the other mental function, memory imagery and abstract reflection, which continue the treatment of the initial, unique subjective information. Thereby elementary sensation acquires absolute primacy over the other mental functions. Varela described global perception as lived experience where one starts from (Varela 1998). In agreement with the certain and self-evident character of the first person experience, Bitbol claimed its primacy. "*There are good reasons to think that pure experience, or elementary consciousness, or phenomenal consciousness, is no secondary feature of an objective item but plainly here, **primary** in the strongest sense of the word.*" (Bitbol 2014, 266).

Primacy of elementary sensation is a consequence of its consideration as the entry door for information allowing the acquisition of knowledge, which corresponds to epistemic primacy. Ontological primacy, in the sense of an independent, non-material consciousness, requires a judgment at the abstract reflection level (Jansen 2014 c). When comparing the evolution of consciousness in different biological entities, a human sperm cell can become a child and a spore a plant, but only the child acquires consciousness, whereas the plant is generally not considered to possess consciousness. Therefore, the material difference between a plant spore and a human sperm cell must have some influence on the appearance of first person consciousness in the child; at least it must be responsible for a minimal material disposition, necessary for allowing the expression of non-material first person consciousness. Thus, epistemic primacy of elementary sensation alone is not a sufficient argument in favor or against philosophical theories concerning materialism, panpsychism or dualism. In any case, epistemic primacy allowing the constitution of knowledge has to be distinguished from ontological primacy claiming the existence of an independent non-material first person consciousness.

REFERENCES

Aristotle, 350 BC. On the Soul (De Anima) In *The complete works of Aristotle: The Revised Oxford Translation (1984)*. Barnes. J. (ed) Princeton University Press.

Bayne, T. (2011). The sense of agency. In *The Senses. Classical and Contemporary Philosophical Perspectives*. Macpherson F. (ed). Oxford University Press.

Bitbol, M. (2008). Is consciousness primary? *NeuroQuantology*, *6*, 53-71.

Bitbol, M. (2014). On the primary nature of consciousness. In *The Systems View of Life*, F. Capra and P.L. Luisi (eds), Cambridge University Press, 266-268.

Chalmers, D. J. (1995). Facing up to the problem of consciousness. *Journal of Consciousness Studies.*, *2*, 3, 200-219.

Ganis, G., Thompson W. L. and Kosslyn S. M. (2004). Brain areas underlying visual mental imagery and visual perception: an fMRI study. *Cognitive Brain Research*, *20*, 226–241.

Ganis, G. and Schendan, H. E. (2008). Visual mental imagery and perception produce opposite adaptation effect on early brain potentials. *NeuroImage*, *42*, 1714-1727.

Halpern, A. R., Zatorre, R. J., Bouffard, M. and Johnson, J. A. (2004). *Neuropsychologia*, *42*, 1281–1292.

Jackson, F. (1982). Epiphenomenal Qualia. *The Philosophical Quarterly*, *32*, 127-136.

Jeannerod, M. (1997). *The Cognitive Neuroscience of Action*. Blackwell, Oxford.

Jeannerod, M. (2001). Neural stimulation of action: A unifying mechanism for motor cognition. *NeuroImage*, *14*, S103- S109.

Jansen, F. K. (2014 a). The Observer's Now, Past and Future in Physics from a Psycho-Biological Perspective. *Cosmology*, *18*, 376-401 (Cosmology. com).

Jansen, F.K. (2014 b) Elementary and memory sensation versus cognition with implications for the brain-consciousness problem. *Towards a Science of Consciousness Conference*, Tucson, abstr.

Jansen, F.K. (2014 c) Timelessness and Time Dependence of Human Consciousness From a Scientific Western Viewpoint. *Philosophy Study,* 4.8, 525-536. doi: 10.17265/2159-5313/2014.08.001

Kandel, E. R., Schwartz J. H., Jessel T. M., Siegelbaum S. A. and Hudspeth A. J. (2013). *Principles of Neural Science*, Fifth Edition, Mc Graw Hill, New York.

Kosslyn, S. M, Ganis, G. and Thompson, W. L. (2001). Neural foundations of imagery. *Nat Rev Neurosci.*, *2*, 635–42.

Lebrun, J. P. (2008). Colloque "A tout Psy, quelles limites?" http://www.freud-acan.com/articles/article.php?url_article=jlebrun130208.

Levine, J. (1983). Materialism and qualia: The explanatory gap. *Pacific Philosophical Quaterly*, *64*, 354 - 361.

Nyberg, L., Eriksson J., Larsson, A. and Marklund, (2006). Learning by doing versus learning by thinking: an fMRI study of motor and mental training. *Neuropsychologia*, *44*, 711-717.

Olsson, C. J., Jonsson, B. and Nyberg, L. (2008). Learning by doing and learning by thinking: an fMRI study combining motor and mental training. *Front. Hum. Neurosci.*, *1*. doi: 10.3389/neuro.09. 005.2008.

Roth, M., Decety, J., Raybaudi, M., Massarelli, R., Delon-Martin, C., Segebarth, C., Morand, S., Gemignani, A., Décorps, M. and Jeannerod, M. (1996). Possible involvement of primary motor cortex in mentally simulated movement. A functional magnetic resonance imaging study. *NeuroReport*, *7*, 1280–1284.

Sacks, O. and Wasserman, R. (1987). The Case of the Colorblind Painter. *The New York Review of Books*.

Schendan, H. E. and Ganis, G. (2012). Electrophysiological potentials reveal cortical mechanisms for mental imagery, mental simulation, and grounded (embodied) cognition. *Front. Psychol*. doi:10.3389/fpsyg.2012.00329.

Smith, A. D. (2011). Tastes, Temperatures and Pains. In: *The Senses. Classical and Contemporary Philosophical Perspectives*. Macpherson F. (ed). Oxford University Press.

Varela, F. (1998). Neurophenomenology: a methodological remedy for the hard problem. in: *Explaining consciousness, the hard problem*, Shear J (ed.) MIT Press.

Zatorre, R. J., Halpern, A. R., Perry, D. W., Meyer, E. and Evans, A. C. (1996).

Hearing in the Mind's Ear: A PET Investigation of Musical Imagery and Perception. *Journal of Cognitive Neuroscience*, *8*, 29-46.

Zatorre, R. J. and Halpern, A. R. (2005). Mental Concerts: Musical imagery and auditory cortex. Minireview. *Neuron*, *47*, 9–12.

Zeh, H. D. (1998). Über die Zeit in der Nature. in *Evolution and Irreversibilität*, eds. H.J. Krug and L. Pohlmann (Dunker and Humblot, Berlin).

In: Consciousness
Editor: Lloyd Alvarado

ISBN: 978-1-63485-023-0

Chapter 12

ROSENTHAL ON ESSENTIALLY INDEXICAL SELF-REFERENCE

Javier Vidal*
Department of Philosophy, University of Concepción,
Concepción, Chile

ABSTRACT

In this paper I argue against the conception of first-person thoughts defended by D. Rosenthal. According to this conception, the essentially indexical self-reference of a first-person thought only consists in one's being disposed to describe the individual that thought is about as the thinker of that thought. First, I try to show that such a disposition does not make a difference between an essential reference to oneself and an accidental reference to oneself. Second, I establish that in Rosenthal's approach there is no guarantee that one dispositionally takes the individual a first-person thought is about to be the thinker of that thought.

Keywords: essentially indexical self-reference, first-person thought, higher-order thought, immunity to error through misidentification, Rosenthal

1

According to a certain conception of the first-person thoughts (Rosenthal, 2004, 2005a, 2012) the mental analogue of 'I' in a thought 'I am *F*' does not explicitly refer to oneself, the thinker, *as the thinker of that thought*. The idea therefore is that a first-person thought does

* Email: fravidal@udec.cl.
This chapter was written with the financial support granted by the Chilean Government (CONICYT) through the Regular Fondecyt 2014 N° 1140395. I would like to thank Sebastián Briceño (University of Concepción) for his valuable review.

not have such an explicit reflexive content.[1] However, Rosenthal proposes an essentially indexical self-reference that should be distinguished from any other way of referring accidentally to oneself as, for instance, when Oedipus, who does not know he is the son of Laius, unwittingly refers to himself by having a thought 'the son of Laius is *F*'. Rosenthal's idea is that besides referring to oneself, the essentially indexical self-reference of a first-person thought consists in one's being *disposed* to describe to oneself as the thinker of that thought. One is not required to describe explicitly to oneself in the first-person thought as the thinker of that thought, but does need to have the disposition to describe to oneself in another thought about the first-person thought as the thinker of that thought. In the words of Rosenthal:

> But whenever I do have a first-person thought that I am *F*, my having that thought disposes me to have another thought that identifies[2] the individual that thought is about as the thinker of that thought. In that way, every first-person thought thus tacitly or dispositionally characterizes the self it is about as the thinker of that thought. Nothing more is needed for essentially indexical self-reference. (Rosenthal, 2004, p. 167; 2005a, pp. 348–353; 2012, pp. 28–34)

Obviously, the thought one is disposed to have when one has a first-person thought 'I am *F*', the thought by which the individual the first-person thought is about would be explicitly described as the thinker of that thought, is a higher-order thought (henceforth, a HOT) 'I think that I am *F*'.[3] It certainly seems that when Oedipus has a first-person thought 'I am *F*', he is disposed to have a HOT 'I think that I am *F*'.[4] Assuming that both the token of 'I' in the first-person thought and the first token of 'I' in the HOT refer to Oedipus, the HOT effectively describes the individual the first-person thought is about as the thinker of that thought. It is not only that the first token of 'I' in the HOT refers to Oedipus, and thus the HOT describes Oedipus as the thinker of that thought. Given that the token of 'I' in that thought also refers to Oedipus, the HOT describes *the individual the thought 'I am F' is about* as the thinker of that thought.

---

[1] Rosenthal is the leading exponent of a higher-order thought theory of the consciousness. According to this theory, a mental state is conscious when it is accompanied by a higher-order thought (henceforth, a HOT) about that state. It is a HOT simply because it corresponds to an intentional mental state about another mental state. In fact, the HOT is a first-person thought. But Rosenthal argues that if a first-person thought, and therefore a HOT, had an explicit reflexive content that consisted in describing the thinker as the thinker of *that* thought, that thought would necessarily be conscious. By means of the HOT one would be conscious of having *that* HOT (Rosenthal, 2004, pp. 167; 2005a, pp. 343; 2010, p. 271 note 1; 2012, p. 30). However, this consequence is unsatisfactory among other things, because it does not allow distinguishing between conscious mental states and mental states that, in addition, occur under introspection (Rosenthal, 1997, pp. 745–746; 2002, pp. 207–208; 2005c, pp. 107–113).

[2] Rosenthal speaks indistinctly of one's being disposed to be described or to be identified as the thinker of that thought.

[3] Or, equivalently, "I am the thinker that I am *F*". As with any other HOT, a thought of that form is a higher-order thought because it corresponds to an intentional mental state about another mental state, in this case a first-person thought which is a lower-order thought.

[4] Although it is a higher-order first-person thought with respect to a lower-order first-person thought, for simplicity henceforth I will speak only of HOT and first-person thought, respectively.

2

Now, I will argue that it is not possible to distinguish between an essential reference to oneself and an accidental reference to oneself in terms of the disposition to have such a HOT. It seems that if one has any thought, whether or not it is a first-person thought then one is disposed to have a HOT about that thought. In fact, Rosenthal addresses this idea in the context of arguing that there is a performative equivalence, or equivalence in the conditions of use, between an utterance of '*p*' and an utterance of 'I think that *p*', in the sense that if one performs an utterance of the first form one is disposed to perform an utterance of the second form. A creature with language which not only possesses the capacity of having thoughts but also the concept of thought (and the first-person concept), possesses the ability to describe itself as the thinker of its thoughts, i.e., it possesses the capacity to have HOTs about its thoughts. Now, let us suppose that, in addition, the creature also has a folk conception of its thoughts according to which a thought can be expressed verbally by means of an utterance of '*p*'. Then, given that the creature has a conception of its thoughts as verbally expressible intentional states, this will be automatic for such a creature, a kind of second nature, to be disposed to perform an utterance of 'I think that *p*' every time it performs an utterance of '*p*'. Moreover, given that it has a conception of its thoughts as verbally express*ible* intentional states, it will be disposed to perform an utterance of 'I think that *p*' when it has a thought which is verbally expressible by means of an utterance of '*p*', although no utterance of '*p*' is performed. But obviously an utterance of 'I think that *p*' verbally expresses a HOT 'I think that *p*'. Then, every time the creature has a thought it will be disposed to have a HOT about that thought, because its being disposed to say that it thinks that *p* when it has a thought reflects an underlying disposition to think that it thinks that *p* when it has that thought. Indeed, according to this approach not every creature which has a thought is disposed to have a HOT about that thought. The disposition, inclination or tendency to have a HOT requires, among other things, having a folk conception of thoughts as intentional states that can be verbally expressed (Rosenthal, 2005b, pp. 301–305).

Let us suppose for instance that Oedipus, who is a creature that satisfies the requirements considered above, has a thought 'Ulysses is *F*'. Then, Oedipus is disposed to have a HOT 'I think that Ulysses is *F*'. This HOT describes Oedipus as the thinker of the thought 'Ulysses is *F*'. However, the HOT does not describe *the individual the thought 'Ulysses is F' is about* as the thinker of that thought. Obviously, the token of 'Ulysses' in that thought refers to Ulysses, not Oedipus. But let us now examine the case in which Oedipus refers accidentally to himself, i.e., he unwittingly refers to himself when he has a thought 'the son of Laius is *F*'. If Rosenthal's linguistic argument -according to which any thought disposes a creature such as Oedipus to have a HOT about that thought- is correct, then Oedipus will be disposed to have a HOT 'I think that the son of Laius is *F*'. Assuming that both the token of 'the son of Laius' in the thought 'the son of Laius is *F*' and the first token of 'I' in the HOT refer to Oedipus, it follows that the HOT describes the individual the thought 'the son of Laius is *F*' is about as the thinker of that thought. It is not only that the first token of 'I' in the HOT refers to Oedipus, and thus the HOT describes Oedipus as the thinker of that thought. Given that the token of 'the son of Laius' in that thought also refers to Oedipus, the HOT describes *the individual the thought 'the son of Laius is F' is about* as the thinker of that thought. However, Rosenthal's idea was that the disposition to have a HOT that describes the individual a thought 'I am *F*' is about as the thinker of that thought would make the difference between the essential reference to oneself which is typical of a first-person thought and any other accidental reference to oneself.

It is possible to challenge this line of argument from the idea that the essential reference to oneself involves a separate disposition. When Oedipus has a first-person thought 'I am *F*', he is specifically disposed to have a HOT 'I think that I am *F*'. In Rosenthal's approach, this disposition is not a case of a generic disposition to have a HOT 'I think that *p*' from a thought '*p*'. Taking Rosenthal's linguistic argument into account, an objector would instead say that when Oedipus has a thought 'the son of Laius is *F*', the disposition to have a HOT 'I think that the son of Laius is *F*' is a case of the generic disposition to have a HOT 'I think that *p*', where in this particular instance '*p*' is 'the son of Laius is *F*'.[5] However, I fail to see in what sense this dispositional difference can invalidate the previous line of argument against the conception Rosenthal has about first-person thoughts. Suppose that Rosenthal likes cheese so he has a generic disposition to eat cheese, but I only like French cheese so I only have a specific disposition to eat French cheese. However, if Rosenthal is travelling across France it does make perfect sense to say that he is now specifically disposed to eat French cheese. Likewise, although it corresponds to different dispositional bases, the fact is that by having a thought 'the son of Laius is *F*', as with having a thought 'I am *F*', Oedipus is disposed to have a HOT that describes the individual that thought is about as the thinker of that thought.

The significance consisting in certain current efficiency to the action, which is supposed to have the first-person thoughts (Rosenthal, 2005a, pp. 351–352; 2012, pp. 32–33), should be taken into account at this point. The difference between having the thought that he himself is in danger and having the thought that the son of Laius is in danger is that in the first case, but not in the second, Oedipus will try to avoid the danger (if, in addition, he has the desire to avoid the danger). In Rosenthal's approach, the current efficacy for the action in which the significance of a first-person thought consists, must be explained in terms of the disposition to have a HOT that describes the individual the first-person thought is about as the thinker of that thought. The essentially indexical self-reference of a first-person thought is explained in terms of such a disposition and is thus explained that the thought has the significance it has, as a first-person thought. However, from the previous argument it can immediately be observed that the significance of the first-person thoughts cannot be explained in such way. Indeed, when Oedipus has the thought that the son of Laius is in danger, he is also disposed to have a HOT that describes the individual that thought is about as the thinker of that thought. Therefore, if the current efficacy for the action was dependent on the disposition to have such a HOT, Oedipus will try to avoid the danger when he has the thought that the son of Laius is in danger. But this should only occur when Oedipus has the thought that he himself is in danger.[6]

---

[5] Nevertheless, regarding the disposition to have a HOT 'I think that I am *F*', the problem of a dispositional over-determination would be posed. Although there is a specific disposition to have such a HOT from a thought 'I am *F*', it is also true that according to the linguistic argument by Rosenthal this would at the same time be a case of the generic disposition to have a HOT 'I think that *p*' from a thought '*p*', where in this particular instance '*p*' is 'I am *F*'.

[6] Moreover, I fail to see in what sense can be relevant to the effectiveness a first-person thought has *now* a disposition to have a HOT which has not been fulfilled.

3

I also want to point out another line of argument against Rosenthal's approach. The previous argument was based on Rosenthal's idea that when one has a first-person thought 'I am *F*', one is disposed to have a HOT 'I think that I am *F*' which describes *the individual the first-person thought is about* as the thinker of that thought. The problem is that according to Rosenthal's theory of HOTs there is no guarantee of this being so. A HOT, as with any other first-person thought, refers to oneself, the thinker of that HOT. In such a case, a HOT 'I think that I am *F*' describes *the individual the HOT is about* as the thinker of a first-person thought 'I am *F*'. Therefore, the essentially indexical self-reference of a first-person thought actually consists in one's being disposed to have a HOT that describes the individual that HOT is about as the thinker of the first-person thought. Certainly, in normal conditions both the first-person thought and the HOT about that thought refer to the same individual and, for that reason, describing the individual that HOT is about as the thinker of the first-person thought *is* describing the individual that first-person thought is about as such.

However, Rosenthal points out that a HOT about a mental state is not immune to error *through misidentification*:

> So, however unlikely it may be that one is ever right in thinking that somebody is in a particular state but wrong that the individual in that state is oneself, such error is not impossible. (Rosenthal, 2004, p. 170; 2005a, pp. 355–356; 2010, p. 274)

Therefore, the first token of the mental analogue of 'I' in a HOT 'I think that I am *F*' is not immune to error through misidentification. It is possible that a HOT about a first-person thought which describes to oneself, i.e., the individual the HOT is about, as the thinker of that first-person thought is false in this regard. It is not impossible that one is right in higher-order thinking that somebody is the thinker of a first-person thought but wrong that the thinker of that thought is oneself, the individual the HOT is about. The individual the first token 'I' in the HOT is about may not be identical to the individual the token 'I' is about in the first-person thought. This means that having a HOT which describes the individual the HOT is about (i.e., the thinker of that HOT) as the thinker of a first-person thought does not effectively guarantee that the individual that first-person thought is about (i.e., the thinker of that first-person thought) is who is described as such.

It is important to note that Rosenthal denies that there is immunity to error through misidentification, not only when the HOT about a mental state is based on a conscious inference, for instance from the observation of the behaviour, but also when it is a non-inferential thought. A HOT about a mental state is non-inferential when the consciousness of that state thus obtained seems direct or immediate in the phenomenological sense. The HOT by means of which a mental state becomes conscious cannot be based on a *conscious* inference, given that we are not aware of any inference in the thought when we are aware of a mental state. However, Rosenthal only rejects that from a phenomenological perspective there is some inference when we are aware of a mental state. This does not exclude that the HOT by means of which a mental state becomes conscious actually *is* the conclusion of an inference which certainly would be an unconscious inference (Rosenthal, 1997, pp. 737–738; 2002, pp. 207; 2005a, p. 340). Undoubtedly, a HOT which is the fulfillment of a prior disposition to have it from a first-person thought is also a non-inferential thought. It involves a non-inferential process in the phenomenological sense, whether or not it is the conclusion of an unconscious inference. The consciousness of the first-person thought thus obtained will seem direct and immediate.[7] In consequence, a disposition to have a HOT that describes the individual that HOT is about as the thinker of a first-person thought can be fulfilled without that, effectively the thinker of that first-person thought is who is described as such.

Now, Rosenthal also points out that a first-person thought is immune to error *relative to the intended referent*:

> I see somebody's reflection in a mirror and mistakenly think that I am that person (…). If I take the person in the mirror to be me, I can be wrong about whether the reflection is actually of me. But even here I cannot be wrong about who it is that I take the reflection to be of; I take the reflection to be of the very individual who is doing the taking. (Rosenthal 2004, p. 173; 2005a, p. 356; 2010, p. 274)

That is, although a first-person thought 'I am *F*' is not immune to error through misidentification, it is not possible that one is wrong about who one is thinking about. It is impossible that one does not take the individual that thought is about to be the thinker of that thought. Now, such an immunity relative to the intended referent is undoubtedly constitutive of the essentially indexical self-reference of a first-person thought. And the latter, according to Rosenthal's approach, depends on the disposition to have a HOT 'I think that I am *F*' which thus should describe the individual the first-person thought is about as the thinker of that thought. Equivalently, it should be impossible that one does not tacitly or dispositionally take the individual that thought is about to be the thinker of that thought. But the HOT is not immune to error through misidentification, which means that there is no guarantee that the HOT will describe the individual the first-person is about as the thinker of that thought. Then, the first-person thought would be not immune to error relative to the intended referent, contrary to the nature of essentially indexical self-reference.[8] Thus, it does not make any sense that the essentially indexical self-reference of a first-person thought is based on a disposition whose fulfillment can fail like that.[9]

---

[7] As an example, cases of multiple or dissociative personalities are taken into account (Rosenthal, 2012, pp. 42–44). These are precisely the cases where a personality or *alter ego* has a non-inferential HOT (in the phenomenological sense) about a mental state that actually belongs to another personality. Thus, it is possible that one personality fulfills the disposition to have a HOT which erroneously describes itself as the thinker of a first-person thought, which actually is the thought of another personality.

[8] Moreover, a HOT is a first-person thought so it also is not immune to error relative to the intended referent, given that its essentially indexical self-reference depends on the disposition to have another HOT, 'I think that I think that I am *F*', which also is not immune to error through misidentification, and so on.

[9] It could be argued that Rosenthal has an easy way out by restoring the immunity to an error through misidentification. In fact, most authors consider that a non-inferential HOT (in the phenomenological sense) about a mental state has to be immune to error through misidentification due to the lack of basis for the error. However, Rosenthal cannot solve the problem like that: his higher-order thought theory of the consciousness whereby a mental state is conscious when it is accompanied by a HOT about that state establishes that the relation between a mental state and the HOT about that state is *contingent*, given that they are numerically different mental states. Therefore, the HOT is not infallible (Rosenthal, 2005a, pp. 353–354; 2012, pp. 35–36). Thus, it is contingently possible that the subject of the HOT, the individual that HOT is about, is not the subject of the mental state.

REFERENCES

Rosenthal, D. (1997). A theory of consciousness. In N. Block, O. Flanagan and G. Güzeldere (Eds.), *The Nature of Consciousness*. Cambridge, Mass: The MIT Press, pp. 729-753.

_______ (2002). Persons, minds, and consciousness. In R. Auxier y L. Hahn (Eds.), *The Philosophy of Marjorie Grene*. La Salle: Open Court, pp. 199-220.

_______ (2004). Being conscious of ourselves, *The Monist*, 87/2, 159–181.

_______ (2005a). Unity of consciousness and the self. In D. Rosenthal, *Consciousness and Mind*. Oxford: Oxford University Press, pp. 339-363.

_______ (2005b). Why are verbally expressed thoughts conscious? In *Consciousness and Mind*, pp. 282–305.

_______ (2005c). Introspection and self-interpretation. In *Consciousness and Mind*, pp. 103–131.

_______ (2010). Consciousness, the self and bodily location, *Analysis*, 70/2, 270–276.

_______ (2012). Awareness and identification of self. In J. Liu and J. Perry (Eds.), *Consciousness and the Self*. Cambridge: Cambridge University Press, pp. 22-50.

In: Consciousness
Editor: Lloyd Alvarado

ISBN: 978-1-63485-023-0

Chapter 13

General Anesthesia and Consciousness: The Actions of Anesthetics Drugs, and Features, Limits and New Perspectives in Depth of Anesthesia Monitoring

Marco Cascella[*]
Division of Anesthesia, Department of Anesthesia,
Endoscopy and Cardiology, Istituto Nazionale Tumori
"Fondazione G. Pascale" - IRCCS, Naples, Italy

Abstract

Etymologically the term anesthesia derives from the Greek ἀν-, an-, "without"; and αἴσθησις, aisthēsis, "sensation". Thus, general anesthesia is a temporary, medically induced condition that includes loss of consciousness, amnesia, analgesia, relaxation of skeletal muscles, and loss of control of reflexes in the autonomic nervous system.

How the anesthetics cause unconsciousness? Despite substantial advances in our understanding on both neuroscientific and pharmacodynamic aspects of anesthetics, we do not have an overall picture of what happens to the brain during general anesthesia. Recently, several theoretical models have been proposed to describe the mechanisms of general anesthetics. These models, based on electroencephalographic data represent the need to simplify the intricate relationship between anesthesia and consciousness, which still seems particularly difficult to comprehend.

In 1994, Sigl and Chamoun described a novel measure of the level of consciousness during general anesthesia: the bispectral (BIS) analysis. It was the beginning of a revolution in anesthesia monitoring, as during the last 15-20 years a number of EEG-based technologies have become commercially available. Unfortunately, none of these technologies has definitively solved the problem of the anesthesia awareness, thus assessment of depth of anesthesia is still a serious problem.

[*] Corresponding author: Division of Anesthesia, Department of Anesthesia, Endoscopy and Cardiology, Istituto NazionaleTumori "Fondazione G. Pascale" - IRCCS, Naples, Italy, Via Mariano Semmola, Naples, Italy, E-mail: m.cascella@istitutotumori.na.it, Tel: + 39 081 5903586, Fax: + 39 081 5903778.

This work focuses on molecular mechanisms and targets of general anesthetic drugs, as well as features, limits and new perspectives in depth of anesthesia monitoring.

Introduction

Etymologically the term anesthesia derives from the Greek ἀν-, an-, "without"; and αἴσθησις, aisthēsis, "sensation". Thus, general anesthesia is a temporary, medically induced condition that includes loss of consciousness, amnesia, analgesia, relaxation of skeletal muscles, and loss of control of reflexes in the autonomic nervous system. While analgesia and muscle relaxation are respectively obtained with narcotic and neuromuscular-blocking drugs, general anesthetics are used in order to render the patient unconscious. However, how do the anesthetics cause unconsciousness? Despite substantial advances in our understanding on both neuroscientific e and pharmacodynamic aspects of anesthetics [1, 2], we do not have an overall picture of what happens to the brain during general anesthesia. Consequently, the mechanisms of general anesthesia constitute one of the great unsolved problems of classical neuropharmacology. Recently, several theoretical models have been proposed to describe the dynamics of action of anesthetics in causing unconsciousness. These models, based on electroencephalographic data [3-5], represent the need to simplify the intricate relationship between anesthesia and consciousness, which still seems particularly difficult to comprehend.

EEG Pattern, Molecular Mechanisms and Targets of General Anesthetic Drugs

Anesthetics differ significantly in their chemical, physical, and pharmacological properties, greatly varying in size, in chemically active groups and chemical reactions that they may undergo. Pharmacokinetics and pharmacodynamics proprieties, are very complex, with great variability from class to class, and from molecule to molecule. Nevertheless, the action of these drugs converges in the same direction: the loss of consciousness. Thus, the explanation of mechanism(s) of action of anesthetics is a big challenge, since the discovery of anesthesia.

Until a few decades ago researchers assumed that the primary targets of anesthetics were lipid portions of nerve membranes. The so called *lipid theory* was firstly enunciated by Hans Horst Meyer who published, in 1899, the first experimental evidence of the fact that anesthetic potency is related to lipid solubility [6]. Two years later a similar theory was published independently by Charles Ernest Overton [7]. However, recent data show that the effects on lipid bilayers of clinically relevant levels of anesthetics are of limited importance. Although other theories were proposed, in the early 1980s, Franks and Lieb launched a provocation: is it possible that anesthetics act by binding specific receptors rather than work by disturbing the integrity of the nerve cell membrane [8]? The right way was marked and many investigations were carried out in this (molecular) direction.

General anesthesia is obtained with the administration of two types of general anesthetics, the intravenous agents, like etomidate, midazolam, propofol, thiopental and ketamine, and the inhaled agents that include nitrous oxide (the oldest of all anesthetics), various halogenated agents, like halothane, desflurane, isoflurane and sevoflurane, and xenon. Because all general anesthetic agents are relatively apolar, they are able to cross the blood-brain barrier, interacting with their targets - like ion channels that regulate synaptic transmission and membrane potentials - in key regions of the brain and spinal cord. The binding of an anesthetic on one or more targets involves alteration in neuronal activities through neuron hyperpolarization, resulting in an increased neural inhibition or in a decreased synaptic excitation. This is in general the operating mechanism of anesthetics, but as explained below this issue is much more complex.

EEG Patterns during General Anesthesia

The actions of a general anesthetic on the molecular level are reflected on the brain's electrical activity. Indeed, pioneering studies showed that increasing doses of anesthetics, like ether or pentobarbital, caused changes in the electroencephalogram (EEG) [9]. During anesthesia, the administration of anesthetics produces distinct EEG patterns, the most common of which is a progressive increase in low-frequency, high-amplitude activity as the level of general anesthesia deepens. As well shown by Emery Brown, EEG patterns during general anesthesia can be described in relation to the three different periods: induction, maintenance, and emergence [10]. Before induction, the patient has a normal, active EEG, with prominent alpha activity (10 Hz). Starting the induction of the anesthesia the patient may enter in a status referred to as paradoxical excitation (similar to drunkenness), characterized by incoherent speech, euphoria or dysphoria, distorted time perception and depersonalization, with an EEG pattern that shows an increase in beta activity (13-25 Hz) [11]. This phase ends with the loss of consciousness when the patients enters in a right depth of anesthesia status with unconsciousness, depression of brain-stem reflexes, no response to nociceptive stimuli, apnea, and the need of cardiorespiratory and thermoregulatory support. During the phase of anesthesia maintenance, it is possible to observe several EEG patterns, depending on the depth of anesthesia. A light state of narcosis, often defined as light anesthesia, is characterized by a decrease in EEG beta activity (13-30 Hz) and an increase in both EEG alpha activity (8-12 Hz) and delta activity (0-4 Hz), and this pattern is particularly evident with propofol use [12]. As the anesthesia status becomes deeper, beta activity decreases, whereas alpha and delta activity increase, especially in the anterior EEG leads rather than the posterior leads [13]. In this anesthesia status, EEG pattern resembles that seen in non-REM (or slow-wave) sleep. Because this represents our target of unconsciousness, surgery is usually performed during this phase. A further state of deep anesthesia status is characterized by an EEG pattern comprising flat periods interspersed with periods of alpha and beta activity. This pattern of activity, called burst suppression, occurs in pathological states and during deep anesthesia and represents an interesting field of study. As this state of general anesthesia deepens, the time between the periods of alpha activity lengthens, and the amplitudes of the alpha and beta activity decrease, until the most profound state of narcosis in which the EEG becomes isoelectric. As stated in the introduction section, general anesthesia is a reversible loss of consciousness; so, emergence from narcosis is a passive process that depends on the amounts of drugs administered, and in parallel the EEG patterns proceed in approximately reverse order from the several phases of the maintenance period, until an active EEG that is consistent with a fully awake state and consciousness. Although EEG patterns proceed in approximately the reverse order, from different maintenance period phases, it is possible to observe a progressive decrease in alpha power and increased peak alpha frequency before the return of responsiveness. However, emergence is an active process with a distinct neurobiology [14]. Moreover, as recently shown by Hight and colleagues, the classic EEG pattern of emergence is not the only pattern of emergence from deep anesthesia. Indeed, some patients show no obvious progressive EEG change until an abrupt recovery of responsiveness [15].

Not all anesthetics work according to these EEG patterns during induction, maintenance, and emergence from anesthesia. Some drugs, like ketamine, induce a more complex pattern of brain electrical activity with specific EEG features. This represents one of the many limitations of depth of anesthesia monitoring devices.

Molecular Mechanisms of Anesthetics

How do anesthetic drugs induce these EEG patterns and unconsciousness? Over the past decades several ligand channels were studied as molecular targets for general anesthetics. The most investigated is the neurotransmitter-gated ion channel Gamma-aminobutyric acid (GABA) type A receptor (GABAA-R), which is responsible for the majority of inhibitory neurotransmission in the central nervous system. GABAA-Rs are members of the Cys-loop superfamily of ligand-gated ion channels, that includes also receptors for acetylcholine (nAChRs), 5-hydroxytryptamine (5-HT3) and glycine. These receptors are involved in major anesthetic actions. Simplifying, GABAA-Rs are involved in the mechanisms of loss of consciousness, the glycine receptor in immobility, and the nAChRs in memory, autonomous action and neuromuscular relaxation [16]. The extracellular association of an agonist with a Cys-loop receptor is the key point of the action of drugs (such anesthetics) and several endogenous ligands with a prominent role in neuronal signalling. Because the structure of the receptors is associated with the binding of specific ligands, the study of the architecture of Cys-loop receptors could be the right way to develop more-selective drugs to modulate their activity, also in anesthesia.

Cys-loop receptors are pentamers structures: each subunit containing ten beta-strands in the extracellular domain and four alpha-helical transmembrane domains. Also GABAA-R has several subtypes defined by the presence of the $\alpha1$, $\alpha4$, $\alpha5$, $\beta2$, and $\beta3$ subunits and two-pore domain potassium channels, called as TASK-1, TASK-3, and TREK [17]. Two types of inhibitory neurotransmission are mediated via GABAA-Rs, phasic and tonic inhibition. While the first conventional inhibitory mechanism results from the activation of receptors at the synapse by intermittent release of high concentrations of GABA from presynaptic terminals ("synaptic" inhibition), the tonic inhibition is mediated by the continuous activation of receptors located outside the synaptic cleft by low concentrations of ambient GABA ("extrasynaptic" inhibition) [18]. There is a growing amount of experimental research that has revealed the importance of extra-synaptic receptors (ESR) for neural interactions, especially in reference to general anesthesia and anesthetics action [19]. The precise biochemical origin of extrasynaptic inhibition is unknown. According to Bright et al. [20] the tonic current is the consequence of the spillover of excess neurotransmitter from synapses. This is due to incomplete GABA uptake by nearby synaptic GABAA-Rs; thus, the remaining neurotransmitter is able to diffuse to more distant GABAA-Rs via extracellular space.

Another ion inhibitory channel that produces its effects through chloride current is the glycine channel, while Glutamate receptors (N-methyl-D-aspartate NMDA receptors, α-amino-3-hydroxy-5-methyl-4-isoxazole propionate AMPA receptors, and kainate receptors) are responsible for a large portion of excitatory neurotransmission in the mammalian nervous system. More studies have identified GABAA and NMDA receptors in the cortex, thalamus, brain stem, and striatum. While small numbers of inhibitory interneurons control large numbers of excitatory pyramidal neurons, the enhanced GABAA inhibition induced by anesthetics can efficiently inactivate large regions of the brain and contribute to unconsciousness.

Neuronal excitability is also modulated by potassium channels [21], pre- and postsynaptically. There are five subunits known (TREK-1, TREK-2, TASK-1, TASK-3, and TRESK) that can homo- and heterodimerize; nevertheless, they have a different affinity with anesthetics depending by their class, because all five subunits can be modulated by halothane, but they are insensitive to clinically relevant concentrations of intravenous anesthetics. Other receptors are sensitive to anesthetics like Hyperpolarization-activated cyclic nucleotide-gated (HCN), which is a family of channels that increases pacemaker currents with rhythmic or oscillatory activity [22], regulating the dendritic excitability and the neuronal response to synaptic input. Voltage-gated Na^+ and Ca^{2+} channels, critical to excitability and synaptic transmission, also come into play.

Recently, many studies have been carried on the pharmacology of G-protein-coupled receptor (GPCR) signaling, and there is evidence that Metabotropic glutamate receptors carry transmembrane segments similar to other G-protein coupled receptors [23]. These ligand-receptors are possible targets for anesthetics, because some anesthetics inhibit the functions of Gq-coupled receptors, including muscarinic acetylcholine M1, metabotropic type 5 glutamate, 5-hydroxytryptamine 2A, and substance P receptors [24].

This issue is very fascinating though particularly complex, due to the interference of external (i.e., BZDs) and endogenous factors. For example, GABAA-R subunits are subject to the action of different ligands, like kinases, structural proteins, and neurosteroids which are the principal endogenous modulators of GABAA-Rs [25].

Anesthetics Actions on Brain Activity

Different anesthetics induce different patterns of brain activity. Researches on genetically modified worms and mice suggest the hypothesis that intravenous anesthetics act mainly on GABAA-Rs [16, 17]. Indeed, propofol that is administered for induction of general anesthesia, sedation, and for maintenance of general anesthesia, works enhancing inhibition at GABAA-R, prolonging the duration of GABAergic inhibitory post-synaptic currents. Moore et al. demonstrated that the isoflurane acts directly on the sleep-promoting neurons within ventrolateral preoptic nucleus (VLPO), which is a key sleep-promoting region in the hypothalamus [26]. However, volatile anesthetics have multiple molecular targets (GABAA, potassium channels, HCN) [27]. Halogenated have effects on GABAA-Rs, nevertheless these drugs primarily depress excitatory synaptic transmission both presynaptically (reducing the glutamate release) [28] and postsynaptically, by blocking glutamate receptors [29].

The nonhalogenated inhaled anesthetics, such as xenon, nitrous oxide, and cyclopropane, as well as the intravenous anesthetic ketamine, have little or no effect on the GABAA-Rs, but depress excitatory glutamatergic synaptic transmission postsynaptically through NMDA glutamate receptor blockade.

It is fascinating to observe the possible activation of different neuronal circuits by different anesthetics during different phases of narcosis, especially in extreme conditions such as burst suppression. This is a stereotypic pattern of alternating periods of EEG activity and inactivity that occurs in pathological states and in deep anesthesia. While Kenny et al. demonstrated significant differences in the duration, amplitude, and power of burst-suppression patterns induced by sevoflurane and propofol, we can assume this evidence as a further proof that neuronal circuits involved in anesthetics action may differ among different drugs [30].

The intravenous and intramuscular general anesthetic ketamine has a paradoxical mode of action that unhinges many alleged certainties about our knowledge on dynamics of anesthetics. It is also called dissociative anesthetic because low doses cause depersonalization and the so colled out-of-body experiences, while at higher dose the patient falls in a state in which the eyes are open and the faces takes on a disconnected blank stare. Ketamine is a high affinity uncompetitive antagonist of voltage-dependent NMDA receptor. Its action on brain activity is very complex, involving regional metabolic changes and deactivation of executive circuits in occipital, parietal, anterior cingulate cortex and basal glia. It also actives AMPA receptors in the medial prefrontal cortex resulting in a prolonged enhancement of glutamatergic transmission in this area, causing alterations in frontoparietal connectivity patterns [31]. Because the effects of ketamine on the glutamatergic system and the evidence that abnormalities in this neurotransmittor system are present in depression, recent research has seen low-dose ketamine emerge as a novel, rapid-acting antidepressant [32]. This is a significant example of translational research with a linkage between fields of study only apparent far, like anesthesia, neurophysiology, pharmacology, psychiatry and neurology.

Operating Mechanism of the General Anesthetics

While the loss of consciousness and the maintenance of the anesthesia status are realized through the ligand-receptors interacting in different brain areas, however it remains to be analyzed the physical mechanism (or operating mechanism) of the general anesthetics, namely the neural correlates of anesthetic-induced unconsciousness. Indeed, the big question is the exact understanding of the neurofunctional mechanisms by which the anesthetics interfere with cortical and/or subcortical signals.

Research on brain function may provide interesting information. For example, Imas and colleagues investigated in animal models whether general anesthetics may interfere with the exchange of information between frontal and posterior cortices. By assuming the basic role in frontal-posterior interactions through the gamma oscillations (20-60 Hz) they postulated that inhalational anesthetics preferentially impair frontal-posterior information. In other words, there is a lack of information between different cortical areas [33]. Global coherence analysis is a mathematical model used to interpreter EEG recordings. It is explained as the ratio of the largest eigenvalue to the sum of the eigenvalues of the cross-spectral matrix at a given frequency and time. Recent evidence in studies carried out using this model suggest that the point at which propofol induces unconsciousness is well-characterized by the appearance of a highly coherent alpha (9-13 Hz) rhythm in frontal cortices [34, 35].

Thalamus is a structure that is well known to mediate oscillatory activity in the alpha range during sleep, thus there are a lot of thalamocortical models to explain the neural activity during general anesthesia [36]. For example, Ching's model [37] explains the effects of high dose of propofol on the thalamocortical networks: a high increase of GABA conductance due to the transition of the paradoxical beta regime into the alpha frequency and slow oscillation regime. With this observation he claims that thanks to a hyperpolarization activated current (h-current) there is an enhancement in the thalamocortical alpha activity.

"Bottom-Up" and "Top-Down" Mechanisms

The so-called "bottom-up" mechanisms of anesthetic action focusing on subcortical arousal centers and ascending thalamocortical information transfer are contrasted with the more recent cortical "top-down" explanations [38]. Bottom-up explanations of anesthetic-induced unconsciousness focus on subcortical nuclei that mediate the sleep-wake cycle or early cortical areas that mediate sensory processing. However, primary sensory processing (involving thalamus activity) is not sufficient for conscious perception of a stimulus [39] and there is growing evidence that general anesthetics disrupt higher-order cognitive processes and that networks of association cortex may be particularly susceptible to anesthetic effects.

Current evidence from sensory electrophysiology, event-related potentials, and functional brain imaging suggests that the failure of conscious perception at a critical depth of anesthesia may best be interpreted as "information received but not perceived" due to the disintegration of cortical information processing [40]. Thus, the top-down hypothesis focuses on the conscious perception and appears to be the preferential target of anesthetic modulation. In other words, this theory – for instance when applied to the mechanisms of attention - assumes that a central control system (the filter of attention) is in charge of allowing (or not) whether the information produced by the rest of the central nervous system may be able to access at the conscious processing. According to the top-down explanation, such a process could involve the operating mechanism of the general anesthetics. Substantial electrophysiological and neuroimaging evidence from animal and human investigations support these mechanisms as a causally sufficient explanation for anesthetic-induced unconsciousness [41] and, in general, could be useful for understanding the neural basis of consciousness.

However, operating mechanisms of anesthetics and their functional impacts on brain network organization is still an open question. Most probably, bottom-up and top-down processes are not opposites, and studies on visual attention suggest that both a mutual interdependence and a constant interaction between the two processes can be observed [42]. Also regarding the issue of the neural correlates of anesthetic-induced unconsciousness, rather than searching for cases of pure bottom-up or top-down processing, future efforts should address their relative contributions as well as the mechanisms of their interaction in the context of a given task [43].

CONSCIOUSNESS AND ANESTHESIA

Whatever the mechanism, anesthetics interfere with consciousness, but the relationship between consciousness and anesthesia is not so simple to define. Because there are no certainties, only hypotheses can be put forward.

Although many theories on consciousness of interest for the anesthesia have been developed [44, 45], the *Integrated Information Theory* seems to be of paramount relevance because it provides a good explanation of the operating mechanism of anesthetics, and could constitute a good scientific basis to develop more accurate depth of anesthesia monitoring techniques. This theory, formulated by Giulio Tononi is the result of decades of studies initiated by the Nobel Prize Gerald Edelman (1929-2014) [46]. According to Tononi, consciousness could be defined as 'what abandons us every night when we fall into dreamless sleep' [47]. Tononi's theory represents an attempt to characterize the neural basis of consciousness [48, 49]. It is based on two starting-points: firstly, every experience is one among several others and, whether simple or complex, represents a choice among a wide repertoire of alternatives. For this reason, every experience is highly informative. Secondly, every experience is unique and cannot be divided into independent parts; thus, it is integrated. Based on these premises, the theory claims that the level of consciousness of a physical system is tied to the range of several states (information) that can be detected by the system as a whole (integration). In over-simplified terms, a synchronization process would occur with an initial activation of cortical and thalamic triggers with a subsequent centrifuge activation of even more extended brain areas.

Assuming the accuracy of this theory, the action of anesthetic drugs would affect an alteration of the brain communication mechanisms, with functional disconnection between brain areas and subsequent loss of integration, acting mainly on a hypothetical thalamic switch [50]. Nevertheless, the thalamus is not the only protagonist.

The Role of Thalamus and Cortical Effects of Anesthetics

In addition to the studies on the integration theory, neurophysiological studies on the thalamus demonstrated that, in the state of awakeness, this organ perceives the consciousness via a tonic activation. Thus, during this state, the cortical and peripheral sensory inputs are processed by the thalamus and we can experience consciousness. However, during anesthesia the tonically active state is replaced by slower waves (oscillatory rhythm) that represent the functional disconnection of the thalamus.

All these data, and several experimental proofs, could indicate the thalamus as a key target of anesthetic effects on consciousness. For instance, the action of anesthetics is associated with a reduction in thalamic metabolism and blood flow [51], and the injection of the GABA agonists into the central intralaminar nucleus causes asleep and slow EEG patterns in rats [52]. However, recently the central role of thalamus on consciousness is questioned. For instance, ketamine does not decrease thalamic activity, and as well outlined by Alkire and colleagues (including the same Tononi), the effects of anesthetics on thalamus is largely indirect [53]. Significant for this proposal is the reading of old studies. In 1972, Villablanca studied the effects on sleep and EEG patterns in cats without thalamus ("athalamic" cats)

[54], and he carried out the same observations in cats after removal of cerebral cortex and striatum [55]. Through a both simple and effective experimental model, he showed that after thalamic ablation the cortex still produces an activated EEG, suggesting that the thalamus is not the central key in the transition between the state of consciousness and unconsciousness.

More recent studies outline the role of cortical areas, like primary visual cortex [56], primary somatosensory cortex, that is a key area in the processing of nociceptor inputs [57], posterior cingulate cortex, precuneus, and mesial parietal cortex. These mesial cortical areas are functionally specialized regions of the human cerebral cortex, interconnected by a dense network of cortico-cortical axonal pathways. According to a modern neurofunctional approach, based on the so-called cognitive brain architectures [58], all these cortical areas arrange both a structural and functional brain core, which has an important role in functional integration [59]. The action of anesthetic is associated with a specific interaction in these areas [60], while frontal cortex does not seem to play a major role, because different anesthetics have variable effects [61].

Nevertheless, the role of the thalamus is not at all secondary. It plays as a relay in corticocortical communication, because all neocortical areas receive thalamic inputs. Indeed, some thalamocortical pathways relay information from ascending pathways (first order thalamic relays) and others relay information from other cortical areas (higher order thalamic relays). Thus, an efficient communication among cortical areas requires a thalamus integrity and thalamic lesion leads to a functional disarray despite cortical activation [62].

DEPTH OF ANESTHESIA MONITORING

Currently we refer to clinical parameters, for instance, lacrimation, monitoring of ventilator parameters and anesthesia gas delivery (ETAG) in order to have a direct measurement of the depth of anesthesia. Clinical standard monitoring is often combined with depth of anesthesia monitors for the assessment of the level of consciousness during GA. These techniques are incorporated in specific devices, however, depth of anesthesia monitors are not worldwide distributed with the same weight, because while in Unites states in almost every operating theater the clinical assessment is combined with a depth of anesthesia monitor, in United Kingdom these devices are rarely used in anesthetic practice [63]. This could represent an indicator of their effective reliability.

Deep of anesthesia monitors are based on the analysis and quantification of the EEG through standard methods, like the power spectral density (power spectrum EEG) that technically reflects the ‘frequency content’ of the signal, and the distribution of signal power over frequency.

In 1994, Sigl and Chamoun were the first to describe the use of bispectral (BIS) technology for brain monitoring [64]. Their BIS system includes a non-invasive adhesive sensor, a patient interface cable, a digital signal converter, a BIS engine (microprocessor), and a monitor. The technology is also available as a module that can be integrated into other manufacturers' monitoring systems.

Raw EEG signals can be difficult to interpret; thus, the BIS engine processes the EEG data according to an algorithm that combines select EEG features to produce a single dimensionless number, which is the BIS index. This value is a statistically based, empirically derived complex parameter, as well as the weighted sum of several EEG subparameters, including a time domain, frequency domain, and several high order spectral subparameters. It which ranges from 0 (equivalent to EEG silence) to 100. A BIS value between 40 and 60 indicates an appropriate level for general anesthesia with a low probability of consciousness. Based on these criteria, the BIS monitor gives the anesthetist an indication of how "deep" under anesthesia the patient is.

In addition to the BIS index, the device displays other important data, like the BIS trend which is a graphic representation of BIS index values over time. Other data are the signal quality index (SQI) bar and the suppression ratio (SR) number. The first measures the reliability of the signal; thus a higher SQI numbers indicate more reliable BIS values. In addition, the SR number is the percentage of time over the last 63 seconds that the EEG was suppressed (flat-lined). The monitor also displays a single-channel EEG waveform and an electromyography (EMG) bar graph, which like SQI is used to help determine whether the BIS index values are reliable.

BIS monitor was the first EEG-based depth of anesthesia monitor. It is the most widely used system to assess the brain monitoring of general anesthesia, nevertheless during the last 15–20 years a number of EEG-based technologies have been studied [65], some of which have become commercially available, like the E-Entropy and the Narcotrend technologies.

E-Entropy uses a proprietary algorithm to process the entropy of the EEG signal to the behavioral responses of the patients. The degree of disorder of EEG and frontal EMG data are converted in two values that indicate the depth of anesthesia [66]. The first value, response entropy, is based on both EEG and frontal EMG signals and provides an indication of the patient's responses to external stimuli. The rationale is that it may signal early awakening. The second value also based on EEG, called state entropy, is a stable parameter that may be used to assess the hypnotic effect of anesthetic agents on the brain. More ordered signals, with less variation in the wavelength and amplitude, over time, produce high values of entropy and may indicate that the patient is awake. Regular signals, with a constant wavelength and amplitude over time, produce low or zero entropy values, indicating a low probability of anesthesia awareness recall and suppression of brain electrical activity. On the entropy monitors the response entropy scale ranges from 0 (no brain activity) to 100 (fully awake), and the state entropy scale ranges from 0 (no brain activity) to 91 (fully awake). The clinically relevant target range for entropy values is 40–60, as a response entropy and a state entropy values near 40 indicate a low probability of consciousness.

The Narcotrend technology has been developed at the University Medical School of Hannover in Germany. It analyses the raw EEG using spectral analysis to produce a number of parameters. Multivariate statistical methods using proprietary pattern recognition algorithms are then applied to these parameters to provide an automatically classified EEG. The basis for the development of the automatic classification functions were visually classified EEG. On this basis the EEG visual classification scale is from stage A (awake) to stage F (very deep hypnosis), with stage E indicating the appropriate depth of anesthesia for surgery. Also the Narcotrend software includes a dimensionless Narcotrend index from 100 (awake) to 0 (electrical silence) [67].

A field of research in brain monitoring of anesthesia is the study of the auditory evoked potentials (AEP). Evoked potentials measure the EEG responses to repetitive auditory or visual stimuli, and measure the integrity of the neural pathways that bring information from the periphery to the cortex. Thus, the rationale is that while BIS value is an index of hypnosis,

AEP shows response to stimuli. This monitoring technique isolates the neurophysiological signal generated during stimulation of the 8th cranial nerve using a repetitive auditory stimulus, for example with a bilateral click stimulus of 70 dB intensity and 2 ms duration (Alaris AEP Monitor). The repeated sampling allows the signal to be extracted from the background EEG noise. Moreover, the signal is acquired using EEG electrodes located on the mastoid processes, a midline reference electrode and a ground electrode.

Because the raw waveform is difficult to analyze in real time and is subject to inter-observer variability, some authors developed the composite auditory evoked potentials index (cAAI), which uses both cortical EEG and AEP [68]. This composite index was considered a measure of overall balance between noxious stimulation, analgesia, and hypnosis. Unlike the BIS index, the transition from asleep to awake is characterized by a sudden increase in the AEP index. Thus, an index more than 80 is observed in the awake patient and conversely a value less than 50 is detected in anaesthetized one.

The results of the studies on AEP are contradictory. While Horn et al. [69] demonstrated that a combination of EEG and AEP parameters can be used to differentiate degrees of anesthetic effects over a wide range of hypnosis, from the conscious state to deep anesthesia; however, Nishiyama has showed that, in propofol-fentanyl anesthesia, AEP might be better to discriminate anesthetic depth rather than cAAI and BIS [70]. Monitors that process the amplitude and latency changes of the components of AEP, using proprietary algorithms to generate an indexed score between 0-100, are being marketed, like theAlaris AEP Monitor. However, these have not yet gained wide popularity as a depth of anesthesia monitor, partly due to problems relating to signal interference. Thus, new devices based on APE technologies combine several features to strengthen the attractiveness of the products. For instance, the aepEX technology (aepEX Plus) is drawn to dynamically measures the balance between hypnosis, analgesia and surgical stimulation, but the main characteristics are the small size and the battery operation facility, so the unit can move with the patient from induction room, to operating room and on to the intensive care unit, enabling an uninterrupted patient monitoring.

Limitation in Current Depth of Anesthesia Monitors

The BIS monitor could reduce the possibility of unintended intraoperative anesthesia awareness and was initially considered the best tool for monitoring cerebral activity during anesthesia. Because the anesthesia awareness phenomenon has historically been the main fear in anesthesiology, it seemed to have discovered the philosopher's stone of anesthesia monitoring. This signaled the start of a hard-fought battle on the pages of scientific journals, and according to Lang, today the BIS monitor has become the most controversial medical device in anesthesiology [71]. For instance, Avidan and colleagues [72] reported in a popular study the same incidence of unexpected awareness during anesthesia, independently from BIS monitoring. According to the American Society of Anesthesiology (ASA), the sudden recovery of consciousness during anesthesia is prevented by combining preoperative identification of patients at risk for anesthesia awareness with intraoperative combination of clinical and instrumental monitoring of the anesthesia, including brain-function monitoring for this type of patients [73].

The most recent algorithm of the BIS monitor (BIS XP version 4.0) may produce lower BIS scores than those of older models for the same level of hypnosis. This difference is secondary to the inclusion in more recent models of mechanisms that reduce the level of noise, interferences, and EMG activity, resulting therefore in lower BIS values [74]. However, this advance in technology did not solve all the problems related to the reliability of BIS monitoring. Indeed, the manufacturer of BIS recommends that BIS values should be interpreted cautiously in patients with known neurological disorders and in those taking psychoactive medications.

Moreover, limits also affect others depth of anesthesia monitors because of artefacts generated either by the patient (e.g., by eye movements, muscle activity) or from external sources (poor skin contact, mains or power line interference, electrocautery), and clinical situations in which there is a lack of reliability. For instance, E-Entropy is validated only for patients over the age of 2 years; it cannot be used for patients undergoing procedural or conscious sedation, and seizure activity may cause interference. In addition, E-Entropy readings may be inconsistent when monitoring patients with neurological disorders or patients on psychoactive medication. Although Narcotrend is equipped with artefact detection algorithms to exclude segments contaminated with artefact, Narcotrend values should be interpreted cautiously in patients with a history of central nervous system diseases.

According to the National Institute of Health and Clinical Excellence, although these devices allow a modest reduction in general anesthetic consumption and anesthetic recovery times, there is no available evidence on the impact of the technologies on reducing the cases of anesthesia awareness [75] and anesthesists cannot accurately determine the depth of narcosis of their patient. In order to prevent the anesthesia awareness phenomenon, expert opinion suggests that anesthetists must primarily refer to clinical signs, using EEG values only as an additional source of information. If there is a difference between them the priority must be given to the clinical signs [75]. Additionally, the result of the 5th National Audit Project (NAP5) on accidental awareness during general anesthesia showed that 4,3% of all reports judged to be certain, probable or possible episodes of anesthesia awareness without recall, occurred despite use of depth of anesthesia monitors [63]. Overall, only one report of anesthesia awareness in association with depth of anesthesia monitors was followed by adverse psychological sequelae, so the authors concluded that the possibility of a more subtle benefit of depth of anesthesia monitors in protecting against awareness sequelae, like post traumatic stress disorders syndrome, might merit further investigation [63].

New Perspectives in Brain Monitoring

Although several algorithms have been used for patenting brain monitors and many indices are used as references for monitoring the depth of anesthesia at the moment there is no device to assess the exact level of anesthesia.

New perspectives in brain monitoring can be glimpsed from different research areas, engaging many study groups. Among these, Jospin and Jensen have long studied level of consciousness during narcosis. In 2007, they published on the detrended fluctuation analysis of EEG - a scaling analysis method that quantifies a simple parameter to represent the correlation properties of a time series - proposing several indexes in order to characterize the patient state: awake, sedated and anesthetized states [76]. Since then they have carried out their studies, publishing the results of research on two specific EEG-derived indices, called qCON and qNOX. Nevertheless, as stated by them, these indices are able to detect the loss of consciousness [77] but not to assess the exact level of anesthesia.

In the meantime, others have proposed complex algorithms combining EEG analysis and no EEG parameters. Schneider et al. [78] studied a combination of standard monitoring, EEG parameters and patient and drug information demonstrating that it is possible to separate the different anesthetic levels. However, their pattern is a complex analysis with a late construction which is difficult to apply in order to immediately recognize an intraoperative awakening, in particular under neuromuscular blockade. They concluded that "additional studies are required to validate results of the current study". Unfortunately, we have no signals for a rapid identification of an emergence from the state of general anesthesia [79]. Recently, the authors of the Michigan Awareness Control Study [80] concluded that they were not able to find an alert threshold for both anesthetic drugs and BIS values and there is the necessity for an individualized anesthetic strategy.

A significant limit in actual depth of anesthesia indices lies in their neurophysiological basis, because they assume that anesthetics induce slowing in the EEG oscillations with increasing the doses. Thus, slower oscillations should clearly indicate a more profound state of general anesthesia. However, not all anesthetics show this EEG pattern. For instance, ketamine shifts the alpha peaks of bicoherence induced by propofol to higher frequencies, maybe through the modulation of the nonlinear sub-cortical reverberating network [81]. Yet, nitrous oxide suppresses low-frequency power and this action can influence EEG monitoring parameters increasing the value of the indices at clinically accepted doses [82].

This limitation seems to be overcome by the development of devices that incorporate specific algorithms designed in the early years of the new millennium [27]. One of these algorithms is the patient state index (PSI) which is another index of level of hypnosis/awareness. The PSI is calculated by a high-resolution 4-channel EEG monitor that collects information on frequency and phase brain electric activity from anterior-posterior relationships of the brain as well as coherence between bilateral brain regions. It is a continuous numeric value derived from systematic study of the complex of changes in brain state, which were observed to reversibly accompany loss and return of consciousness, independent of anesthetic class. Indeed, the variables selected for incorporation in the PSI displayed very significant heterogeneity of variance at different levels of sedation/hypnosis (sensitivity) but non-significant differences across anesthetic agents at any specified level (specificity) [83]. All these data suggest that technology used PSI (SEDLine monitor) could be superior to other classic EEG monitors, like BIS. However, studies of comparison showed that PSI displayed offered only a better correlation with the end-tidal concentration of desflurane monitor, and PSI values were less affected by electrical interference, in particular, electrocautery. Although PSI showed a better performance during both the induction of and emergence from general anesthesia, however during the maintenance period, the PSI values were comparable to the BIS [84]. Thus, PSI is only a valid alternative to BIS monitors, not completely solving the gaps in brain monitoring during anesthesia.

Another branch of study concerns the amelioration of methods already in use, by improving their constitutive algorithm. As previously mentioned, a recent algorithm of the

BIS monitor allows reducing interferences. In addition, besides to response and state entropy, at least ten entropy algorithms were investigated to assess their capability in depth of anesthesia monitoring and burst suppression detection. Though each entropy index showed advantages and disadvantages the right combination of these indices could help improve current clinical indices for brain anesthesia monitoring [85].

Scientific research has enabled the development of new technologies for cerebral monitoring, also based on the principles of the *Integrated Information Theory*. In this regard, we are witnessing a rapid evolution of the brain monitoring EEG based techniques [86]. The studies of Boly and Tononi [87] on spectral EEG changes after propofol administration are very important and Purdon and the Emory Brown's team [34] published their fascinating research, explaining that EEG pattern and its changing are real time indicators of the transaction of the patient from consciousness to the anesthesia status.

As stated in chapter 17 of this book, transcranial magnetic stimulation (TMS) is a noninvasive method used both to stimulate small regions of the brain, and measure activity and function of specific brain circuits in humans. Indeed, it is used to examine the integrity of the fast-conducting corticomotor pathways in a wide range of diseases associated with motor dysfunction [88]. The principles of this technique can be applied to the study of the relationship between consciousness and anesthesia. Recent studies have investigated the EEG response to TMS in subjects in diverse states of consciousness (e.g., wakeful rest, deep sleep, general anesthesia) [89, 90], also in a propofol induced general anesthesia [91]. Consequently, a technique that was created also to investigate the dynamics of consciousness, could release among the various possible applications, a precise tool for brain monitoring during anesthesia.

The analysis of the tracks has allowed the identification of some characteristic trends; in particular, the loss of consciousness is marked by an increase in the low frequency waves (less than 1 herz) associated with a decrease in the coherence of the oscillations of the alpha occipital area (an index of the synchronization of the neuronal activation in this region of the brain), and to the appearance of oscillations alpha consistent in the frontal area. The changes of cerebral activation were reversed in the phase of recovery of consciousness. All these data suggest that EEG markers represent specific "signatures" to precisely trace the transitions to and from consciousness during general anesthesia.

Others authors have focused on building new algorithms, starting from the analysis of EEG signals. For example, Mirsadeghi et al. [92] proposed a new method for distinguishing between awake and anesthetised states. Their methodology is very interesting: through a specific analysis that uses a dimensionality reduction method (from high-dimensional to low-dimensional data), they processed some linear and non-linear features of raw EEG signals, citing an accuracy of 88.4% for classifying the EEG signal into conscious and unconscious states [92]. More complex algorithms, such as the aforementioned Schneider's algorithm [78], have been proposed to combine EEG features and hemodynamic variables for a better classification of anesthesia status [93].

Is it possible to integrate one of these algorithms into strategies for patient monitoring during anesthesia? We hope that these technologies will be improved and soon distributed on a large scale, in order to permanently solve the anesthesia awareness problem.

CONCLUSION

Anesthesia is one of the most important medical discoveries. Despite the advances in technology we still have limitations in brain monitoring during narcosis and it may be impossible to measure the real depth of the anesthesia status. This limitation leads to a practical consideration: nowadays no specific monitor is yet available to eliminate the risk of anesthesia awareness during narcosis. Indeed, the real problem is driving the anesthesia in a middle-earth, furthest from both the burst suppression (causing postoperative cognitive disorders and others postoperative complications and morbidity) and sudden emergencies with increased risk of anesthesia awareness and its psychological sequelae.

As much is known about brain circuit structure and activity, more and specific mathematical modeling researches can make important contributions to well establish the intricate relationships between anesthetics and brain activities.

REFERENCES

[1] Forman, SA; Chin, VA. General Anesthetics and Molecular Mechanisms of Unconsciousness. *International anesthesiology clinics*, 2008, 46(3), 43-53.

[2] Perouansky, M. The quest for a unified model of anesthetic action: A century in Claude Bernard's shadow. *Anesthesiology*, 2012, 117(3), 465-74.

[3] Hutt, A; Hudetz, AG. Editorial: General anesthesia: from theory to experiments. *Frontiers in Systems Neuroscience*, 2015, 9, 105.

[4] Hutt, A. The anesthetic propofol shifts the frequency of maximum spectral power in EEG during general anesthesia: analytical insights from a linear model. *Front Comput Neurosci*, 2013, 7, 2. doi: 10.3389/fncom.2013.00002. eCollection 2013.

[5] Meyer, HH. Zur Theorie der Alkoholnarkose. *Arch Exp Pathol Pharmacol*, 1889, 42(2-4), 109-18.

[6] Hutt, A; Longtin, A. Effects of the anesthetic agent propofol on neural populations. *Cogn Neurodyn*, 2010, 4(1), 37-59.

[7] Overton, CE. Studien über die Narkose zugleich ein Beitrag zur allgemeinen Pharmakologie. Jena, Switzerland, Gustav Fischer, 1901.

[8] Franks, NP; Lieb, W. Do general anaesthetics act by competitive binding to specific receptors? *Nature*, 1984, 310(16), 599–601.

[9] Gibbs, FA; Gibbs, LE; Lennox, WG. Effects on the electroencephalogram of certain drugs which influence nervous activity. *Arch Intern Med*, 1937, 60, 154–66.

[10] Brown, EN; Lydic, R; Schiff, ND. General Anesthesia, Sleep, and Coma. *The New England journal of medicine*, 2010, 363(27), 2638-50.

[11] McCarthy, MM; Brown, EN; Kopell, N. Potential network mechanisms mediating electroencephalographic beta rhythm changes during propofol-induced paradoxical excitation. *J Neurosci*, 2008, 28, 13488-504.

[12] Feshchenko, VA; Veselis, RA; Reinsel, RA. Propofol-induced alpha rhythm. *Neuropsychobiology*, 2004, 50(3), 257-66.

[13] Tinker, JH; Sharbrough, FW; Michenfelder, JD. Anterior shift of the dominant EEG rhythm during anesthesia in the Java monkey: correlation with anesthetic potency. *Anesthesiology*, 1977, 46, 252–9.

[14] Kushikata, T; Hirota, K. Mechanisms of anesthetic emergence: evidence for active reanimation. *Curr Anesthesiol Rep*, 2014, 4,49-56.

[15] Hight, DF; Dadok, VM; Szeri AJ; García, PS; Voss, L; Sleigh, JW. Emergence from general anesthesia and the sleep-manifold. *Frontiers in Systems Neuroscience*, 2014, 8, 146. doi:10.3389/fnsys.2014.00146.

[16] Grasshoff, C; Drexler, B; Rudolph, U; Antkowiak, B. Anaesthetic drugs: linking molecular actions to clinical effects. *Curr Pharm Des*, 2006, 12(28), 3665-79.

[17] Drexler, B; Antkowiak, B; Engin, E; Rudolph, U. Identification and characterization of anesthetic targets by mouse molecular genetics approaches. *Can J Anaesth*, 2011, 58(2), 178-90.

[18] Farrant, M; Nusser, Z. Variations on an inhibitory theme: phasic and tonic activation of GABA(A) receptors. *Nat Rev Neurosci*, 2005, 6(3), 215-29.

[19] Hutt A. The population firing rate in the presence of GABAergic tonic inhibition in single neurons and application to general anaesthesia. *Cogn Neurodyn*, 2012, 6(3), 227-37.

[20] Bright, DP; Renzi, M; Bartram, J; McGee, TP; MacKenzie, G; Hosie, AM; Farrant, M; Brickley, SG. Profound desensitization by ambient GABA limits activation of delta-containing GABAA receptors during spillover. *J Neurosci*, 2011, 31(2), 753-763.

[21] Patel, R; Singh Patel, K. Simple and specific method for flow injection analysis determination of cationic surfactants in environmental and commodity samples. *Talanta*, 1999, 48(4), 923-31.

[22] Sirois, JE; Lei, Q; Talley, EM; Lynch, C; 3rd, Bayliss, DA. The TASK-1 two-pore domain K+ channel is a molecular substrate for neuronal effects of inhalation anesthetics. *J Neurosci*, 2000, 20(17), 6347-54.

[23] Schrage, R; De Min, A; Hochheiser, K; Kostenis, E; Mohr, K. Superagonism at G protein-coupled receptors and beyond. *Br J Pharmacol*, 2015 Aug 15. doi: 10.1111/bph.13278. [Epub ahead of print].

[24] Minami, K; Uezono, Y. Gq protein-coupled receptors as targets for anesthetics. *Curr Pharm Des*, 2006, 12(15), 1931-7.

[25] Alvarez, LD; Estrin, DA. Exploring the Molecular Basis of Neurosteroid Binding to the β3 Homopentameric GABAA Receptor. *J Steroid Biochem Mol Bio*, 2015, 154, 159-67.

[26] Moore, JT; Chen, J; Han, B; Meng, QC; Veasey, SC; Beck, SG; Kelz, MB. Direct activation of sleep-promoting VLPO neurons by volatile anesthetics contributes to anesthetic hypnosis. *Curr Biol*, 2012, 22, 2008-2016.

[27] Gugino, LD; Chabot, RJ; Prichep, LS; John, ER; Formanek, V; Aglio, LS. Quantitative EEG changes associated with loss and return of consciousness in healthy adult volunteers anaesthetized with propofol or sevoflurane. *Br J Anaesth*, 2001, 87, 421-28.

[28] Dickinson, R; Peterson, BK; Banks, P; Simillis, C; Martin, JC; Valenzuela, CA; Maze, M; Franks, NP. Competitive inhibition at the glycine site of the nmethyl-d-aspartate receptor by the Anesthetics xenon and Isoflurane. *Anesthesiology*, 2007, 107(5), 756-67.

[29] Perouansky, M; Baranov, D; Salman, M; Yaari, Y. Effects of halothane on glutamate receptor-mediated excitatory postsynaptic currents. a patch-clamp study in adult mouse hippocampal slices. *Anesthesiology*, 1995, 83(1), 109-19.

[30] Kenny, JD; Westover, MB; Ching, S; Brown, EN; Solt, K. Propofol and sevoflurane induce distinct burst suppression patterns in rats. *Front Syst Neurosci*, 2014, 8, 237.

[31] Muthukumaraswamy, SD; Shaw, AD; Jackson, LE; Hall, J; Moran, R; Saxena, N. Evidence that Subanesthetic Doses of Ketamine Cause Sustained Disruptions of NMDA and AMPA-Mediated Frontoparietal Connectivity in Humans. *J Neurosci*, 2015, 35(33), 11694-706.

[32] Naughton, M; Clarke, G; O'Leary, OF; Cryan, JF; Dinan, TG. J A review of ketamine in affective disorders: current evidence of clinical efficacy, limitations of use and pre-clinical evidence on proposed mechanisms of action. *Affect Disord*, 2014, 156, 24-35.

[33] Imas, OA; Ropella, KM; Ward, BD; Wood, JD; Hudetz, AG. Volatile anesthetics disrupt frontal-posterior recurrent information transfer at gamma frequencies in rat. *Neurosci Lett*, 2005, 28, 387(3), 145-50.

[34] Purdon, PL; Pierce, ET; Mukamel, EA; Prerau, MJ; Walsh, JL; Wong, KF; Salazar-Gomez, AF; Harrell, PG; Sampson, AL; Cimenser, A; Ching, S; Kopell, NJ; Tavares-Stoeckel, C; Habeeb, K; Merhar, R; Brown, EN. Electroencephalogram signatures of loss and recovery of consciousness from propofol. *Proc Natl Acad Sci U S A*, 2013, 110(12), E1142-51.

[35] Cimenser, A; Purdon, PL; Pierce, ET; Walsh, JL; Salazar-Gomez, AF; Harrell, PG; Tavares-Stoeckel, C; Habeeb, K; Brown, EN. Tracking brain states under general anesthesia by using global coherence analysis. *Proc Natl Acad Sci U S A*, 2011, 108(21), 8832-7.

[36] Hill, S; Tononi, G. Modeling sleep and wakefulness in the thalamocortical system. *J Neurophysiol*, 2005, 93(3), 1671-98.

[37] Ching, S; Cimenser, A; Purdon, PL; Brown, EN; Kopell, NJ. Thalamocortical model for a propofol-induced alpha-rhythm associated with loss of consciousness. *Proc Natl Acad Sci U S A*, 2010, 107(52), 22665-70.

[38] Mashour, GA. Top-down mechanisms of anesthetic-induced unconsciousness. *Front Syst Neurosci*, 2014, 8, 115.

[39] Dehaene, S; Changeux, JP. Experimental and theoretical approaches to conscious processing. *Neuron*, 2011, 70, 200-27.

[40] Hudetz, AG. Suppressing consciousness: Mechanisms of general anesthesia, *Seminars in Anesthesia, Perioperative Medicine and Pain*, 2006, 25(4), 196-204.

[41] Mashour, GA. Cognitive unbinding: a neuroscientific paradigm of general anesthesia and related states of unconsciousness. *Neurosci Biobehav Rev*, 2013, 37, 2751-59.

[42] Theeuwes, J. Top-down and bottom-up control of visual selection. *Acta Psychol (Amst)*, 2010, 135(2), 77-99.

[43] Rauss, K; Pourtois, G. What is Bottom-Up and What is Top-Down in Predictive Coding? *Fron Psychol*, 2013, 4, 276. http://doi.org/10.3389/fpsyg.2013.00276.

[44] Hameroff, S; Penrose, R. Consciousness in the universe: a review of the 'Orch OR' theory. *Phys Life Rev*, 2014, 11(1), 39-78.

[45] Mashour, GA. The Cognitive Binding Problem: From Kant to Quantum Neurodynamics. *Neuro Quantology*, 2004, 1, 29-38.

[46] Edelman, GM; Tononi, G. A Universe Of Consciousness: How Matter Becomes Imagination. New York, Basic Book, 2001.

[47] Block, N; Flanagan, O; Güzeldere, G. editors. The Nature of Consciousness: Philosophical debates. Cambridge, MA, MIT Press. 1997, p. 1-67.

[48] Tononi, G. Consciousness as integrated information: a provisional manifesto. *Biol Bull*, 2008, 215, 216-42.

[49] Tononi, G. An information integration theory of consciousness. *BMC Neurosci*, 2004, 5, 42.

[50] Drexler, B; Antkowiak, B; Engin, E; Rudolph, U. Identification and characterization of anesthetic targets by mouse molecular genetics approaches. *Can J Anaesth*, 2011, 58(2), 178-90.

[51] Alkire, MT; Miller, J. General anesthesia and the neural correlates of consciousness. *Prog Brain Res*, 2005, 150, 229-44.

[52] Miller, JW; Ferrendelli, JA. Characterization of GABAergic seizure regulation in the midline thalamus. *Neuropharmacology*, 1990, 29(7), 649-55.

[53] Alkire, MT; Hudetz, AG; Tononi, G. Consciousness and anesthesia. *Science*, 2008, 322(5903), 876-80.

[54] Villablanca, J; Salinas-Zeballos, ME. Sleep-wakefulness, EEG and behavioral studies of chronic cats without the thalamus: the 'athalamic' cat. *Arch Ital Biol*, 1972, 110(3), 383-411.

[55] Villablanca, J. Permanent reduction in sleep after removal of cerebral cortex and striatum in cats. *Brain Res*, 1972, 36(2), 463-8.

[56] Leopold, DA. Primary visual cortex: awareness and blindsight. *Annu Rev Neurosci*, 2012, 35, 91-109.

[57] Kuo, CC; Lee, JC; Chiou, RJ; Tsai, ML; Yen, CT. Spatiotemporal Changes of Neuronal Responses in the Primary Somatosensory Cortex to Noxious Tail Stimulation in Awake and Pentobarbital-Anesthetized Rats. *Chin J Physiol*, 2015, 58(5), 332-42.

[58] Petersen, SE; Sporns, O. Brain Networks and Cognitive Architectures. *Neuron*, 2015, 88(1), 207-19.

[59] Hagmann, P; Cammoun, L; Gigandet, X; Meuli, R; Honey, CJ; Wedeen, VJ; Sporns, O. Mapping the structural core of human cerebral cortex. *PLoS Biol*, 2008 Jul 1, 6(7), e159. doi: 10.1371/journal.pbio.0060159.

[60] Kaisti, KK; Metsähonkala, L; Teräs, M; Oikonen, V; Aalto, S; Jääskeläinen, S; Hinkka, S; Scheinin, H. Effects of surgical levels of propofol and sevoflurane anesthesia on cerebral blood flow in healthy subjects studied with positron emission tomography. *Anesthesiology*, 2002, 96(6), 1358-70.

[61] Veselis, RA; Feshchenko, VA; Reinsel, RA; Dnistrian, AM; Beattie, B; Akhurst, TJ. Thiopental and propofol affect different regions of the brain at similar pharmacologic effects. *Anesth Analg*, 2004, 99(2), 399-408.

[62] Guillery, RW; Sherman, SM. Thalamic relay functions and their role in corticocortical communication: generalizations from the visual system. *Neuron*, 2002, 33(2), 163-75.

[63] Pandit, JJ; Andrade, J; Bogod, DG; Hitchman, JM; Jonker, WR; Lucas, N. and the Royal College of Anaesthetists; Association of Anaesthetists of Great Britain and Ireland. 5th National Audit Project (NAP5) on accidental awareness during general anaesthesia: summary of main findings and risk factors. *Br J Anaesth*, 2014, 113(4), 549-59.

[64] Sigl, JC; Chamoun, NG. An introduction to bispectral analysis for the electroencephalogram. *J Clin Monit*, 1994, 10(6), 392-404.

[65] Zikov, T; Bibian, S; Dumont, GA; Huzmezan, M; Ries, CR. Quantifying cortical activity during general anesthesia using wavelet analysis. *IEEE Trans Biomed Eng*, 2006, 53(4), 617-32.

[66] Viertio-Oja, H; Maja, V; Sarkela, M; Talja, P; Tenkanen, N; Tolvanen-Laakso, H; Paloheimo, M; Vakkuri, A; Yli-Hankala, A; Merilainen, P. Description of the Entropy algorithm as applied in the Datex-Ohmeda S/5 Entropy Module. *Acta Anaesthesiol Scand*, 2004, 48, 154–61.

[67] Kreuer, S; Wilhelm, W. The Narcotrend monitor. *Best Pract Res Clin Anaesthesiol*, 2006, 20, 111–9.

[68] Weber, F; Zimmermann, M; Bein, T. The impact of acoustic stimulation on the AEP monitor/2 derived composite auditory evoked potential index under awake and anesthetized conditions. *Anesth Analg*, 2005, 01(2), 435-9.

[69] Horn, B; Pilge, S; Kochs, EF; Stockmanns, G; Hock, A; Schneider, G. A combination of electroencephalogram and auditory evoked potentials separates different levels of anesthesia in volunteers. *Anesth Analg*, 2009, 108(5), 1512-21.

[70] Nishiyama, T. Composite auditory evoked potentials index is not a good indicator of depth of anesthesia in propofol-fentanyl anesthesia: Randomized comparative study. *J Anaesthesiol Clin Pharmacol*, 2013, 29(3), 333-6.

[71] Lang, J. Awakening. In: Blum D, Folger T (eds). The Best American Science and Nature Writing 2014. Boston, Houghton Mifflin Harcourt, 2014, p.181.

[72] Avidan, MS; Zhang, L; Burnside, BA; Finkel, KJ; Searleman, AC; Selvidge, JA; Saager, L; Turner, MS; Rao, S; Bottros, M; Hantler, C; Jacobsohn, E; Evers, AS. Anesthesia Awareness and the Bispectral Index. *N Engl J Med*, 2008, 358, 1097-108.

[73] American Society of Anesthesiologists Task Force on Intraoperative Awareness. Practice advisory for intraoperative awareness and brain function monitoring: a report by the american society of anesthesiologists task force on intraoperative awareness. *Anesthesiology*, 2006, 104(4), 847-64.

[74] Duarte, LTD; Saraiva, RÂ. When the bispectral index (Bis) can give false results. *RevistaBrasileira de Anestesiologia*, 2009, 59(1), 99-109.

[75] Shepherd, J; Jones, J; Frampton, G; Bryant, J; Baxter, L; Cooper, K. Clinical effectiveness and cost-effectiveness of depth of anaesthesia monitoring (E-Entropy, Bispectral Index and Narcotrend): a systematic review and economic evaluation. *Health Technol Assess*, 2013, 17(34), 1-264.

[76] Jospin, M; Caminal, P; Jensen, EW; Litvan, H; Vallverdú, M; Struys, MM; Vereecke, HE; Kaplan, DT. Detrended fluctuation analysis of EEG as a measure of depth of anesthesia. *IEEE Trans Biomed Eng*, 2007, 54(5), 840-6.

[77] Jensen, EW; Valencia, JF; López, A; Anglada, T; Agustí, M; Ramos, Y; Serra, R; Jospin, M; Pineda, P; Gambus, P. Monitoring hypnotic effect and nociception with two EEG-derived indices, qCON and qNOX, during general anaesthesia. *Acta Anaesthesiol Scand*, 2014, 58(8), 933-41.

[78] Schneider, G; Jordan, D; Schwarz, G. The European Multicenter EEGAEP Anesthesia Monitoring Study Group and Research Group. European Multicenter EEGAEP Anesthesia Monitoring Study Group and Research Group Knowledge-based Signal

Processing. Monitoring depth of anesthesia utilizing a combination of electroencephalographic and standard measures. *Anesthesiology*, 2014, 120(4), 819-28.

[79] Cascella, M; Bifulco, F; Viscardi, D; Tracey, MC; Carbone, D; Cuomo, A. Limitation in monitoring depth of anesthesia: a case report. *J Anesth*, 2015 Dec 15. [Epub ahead of print]

[80] Shanks, AM; Avidan, MS; Kheterpal, S; Tremper, KK; Vandervest, JC; Cavanaugh, JM; Mashour, GA. Alerting thresholds for the prevention of intraoperative awareness with explicit recall: A secondary analysis of the Michigan Awareness Control Study. *Eur J Anaesthesiol*, 2015, 32(5), 346-53.

[81] Hayashi, K; Tsuda, N; Sawa, T; Hagihira, S. Ketamine increases the frequency of electroencephalographic bicoherence peak on the alpha spindle area induced with propofol. *Br J Anaesth*, 2007, 99(3), 389-95.

[82] Foster, BL; Liley, DT. Nitrous oxide paradoxically modulates slow electroencephalogram oscillations: implications for anesthesia monitoring. *Anesth Analg*, 2011, 113, 758–65.

[83] Prichep, LS; Gugino, LD; John, ER; Chabot, RJ; Howard, B; Merkin, H; Tom, ML; Wolter, S; Rausch, L; Kox, WJ. The Patient State Index as an indicator of the level of hypnosis under general anaesthesia. *Br J Anaesth*, 2004, 92(3), 393-9.

[84] Chen, X; Tang, J; White, PF; Wender, RH; Ma, H; Sloninsky, A; Kariger, R. A comparison of patient state index and bispectral index values during the perioperative period. *Anesth Analg*, 2002, 95(6), 1669-74.

[85] Liang, Z; Wang, Y; Sun, X; Li, D; Voss, LJ; Sleigh, JW; Hagihira, S; Li, X. EEG entropy measures in anesthesia. *Front Comput Neurosc.*, 2015, 9, 16. doi: 10.3389/fncom.2015.00016. eCollection 2015.

[86] Al-Kadi, MI; IbneReaz, MB; Mohd Ali, MA. Evolution of Electroencephalogram Signal Analysis Techniques during Anesthesia. *Sensors (Basel)*, 2013, 13(5), 6605-35.

[87] Boly, M; Moran, R; Murphy, M; Boveroux, P; Bruno, MA; Noirhomme, Q; Ledoux, D; Bonhomme, V; Brichant, JF; Tononi, G; Laureys, S; Friston, KI. Connectivity changes underlying spectral EEG changes during propofol-induced loss of consciousness. *J Neurosci*, 2012, 16, 32(20), 7082-90.

[88] Groppa, S; Oliviero, A; Eisen, A; Quartarone, A; Cohen, LG; Mall, V; Kaelin-Lang, A; Mima, T; Rossi, S; Thickbroom, GW; Rossini, PM; Ziemann, U; Valls-Solé, J; Siebner, HR. A practical guide to diagnostic transcranial magnetic stimulation: report of an IFCN committee. *Clin Neurophysiol*, 2012, 123(5), 858-82.

[89] Ferrarelli, F; Massimini, M; Sarasso, S; Casali, A; Riedner, BA; Angelini, G; Tononi, G; Pearce, RA. Breakdown in cortical effective connectivity during midazolam-induced loss of consciousness. *PNAS*, 2010, 107(6), 2681–86.

[90] Sarasso, S; Rosanova, M; Casali, AG; Casarotto, S; Fecchio, M; Boly, M; Gosseries, O; Tononi, G; Laureys, S; Massimini, M. Quantifying cortical EEG responses to TMS in (un)consciousness. *Clin EEG Neurosci*, 2014, 45(1), 40-9.

[91] Schartner, M; Seth, A; Noirhomme, Q; Boly, M; Bruno, MA; Laureys, S; Barrett, A. Complexity of Multi-Dimensional Spontaneous EEG Decreases during Propofol Induced General Anaesthesia. *PLoS One*, 2015 Aug 7, 10(8), e0133532. doi: 10.1371/journal.pone.0133532. eCollection 2015.

[92] Mirsadeghi, M; Behnam, H; Shalbaf, R; Jelveh Moghadam, H. Characterizing Awake and Anesthetized States Using a Dimensionality Reduction Method. *J Med Syst*, 2016 Jan; 40(1):13. doi: 10.1007/s10916-015-0382-4.

[93] Shalbaf, R; Behnam, H; Jelveh Moghadam, H. Monitoring depth of anesthesia using combination of EEG measure and hemodynamic variables. *Cogn Neurodyn*, 2015, 9(1), 41-51.

INDEX

A

B

C

D

E

F

G

H

N

Q

R

S

T